INFORMATION SYSTEMS:
AN EMERGING DISCIPLINE?

INFORMATION SYSTEMS SERIES

Consulting Editors

D.E. AVISON
BA, Msc, PhD, FBCS
Professor of Information Systems,
Department of Accounting and Management Science,
Southampton University, UK

G. FITZGERALD
BA, Msc, MBCS
Cable & Wireless Professor of
Business Information Systems,
Department of Computer Science,
Birkbeck College, University of London, UK

This series of student and postgraduate texts covers a wide variety of topics relating to information systems. It is designed to fulfil the needs of the growing number of courses on, and interest in, computing and information systems which do not focus on the purely technological aspects, but seek to relate these to business and organisational context.

INFORMATION SYSTEM SERIES

INFORMATION SYSTEMS: AN EMERGING DISCIPLINE?

EDITED BY
DR JOHN MINGERS
Warwick Business School
Warwick University

and

PROFESSOR FRANK STOWELL
Department of Computer Science and Information Systems
De Montfort University

THE McGRAW-HILL COMPANIES

London • New York • St Louis • San Francisco • Auckland
Bogotá • Caracas • Lisbon • Madrid • Mexico • Milan
Montreal • New Delhi • Panama • Paris • San Juan • São Paulo
Singapore • Sydney • Tokyo • Toronto

Published by
McGraw-Hill Publishing Company
Shoppenhangers Road, Maidenhead, Berkshire, SL6 2QL, England
Telephone 01628 502500
Fax 01628 770224

British Library Cataloguing in Publication Data

The CIP data of this title is available from the British Library, UK

Library of Congress Cataloging-in-Publication Data

The CIP data of this title is available from the Library of Congress, Washington DC, USA

McGraw-Hill

A Division of The McGraw·Hill Companies

Typeset by the authors

Printed and bound in Great Britain at the University Press, Cambridge

Printed on permanent paper in compliance with ISO Standard 9706

CONTENTS

CONTENTS

CONTENTS

NOTES ON THE AUTHORS

Ian Angell is Professor of Information Systems at the London School of Economics. His first research interest was in computer graphics. He has published ten books in this area, the latest being *Advanced Graphics on VGA and XGA Cards Using Borland C++* (with D. Tsoubelis). In recent years, his research has concentrated on strategic information systems, computers and risk, and organizational and national IT policies. He has published a book (with S. Smithson) entitled *Information Systems Management: Opportunities and Risks*. On his initiative the LSE has established a Research Centre for the Study of Computer Security. His radical views on the global consequences of IT development have brought him a high-profile reputation as a 'futurologist'.

David Avison is Professor of Information Systems and Head of the Department of Management at Southampton University. He is president of the UK Academy of Information Systems and Vice Chair of the International Federation of Information Processing (IFIP) working group 8.2. David is joint editor of the McGraw-Hill series of texts in information systems and is also joint editor of Blackwell Scientific's *Information Systems Journal* now in its seventh volume. He has published 16 books (plus one translation from the French) as well as a large number of papers in learned journals, edited texts and conference papers. He has given the plenary addresses at recent information systems conferences in Australia, Bahrain, the Netherlands, UK and the USA. His research areas include information systems development, and he is one of the co-authors of the Multiview methodology, as well as the topic of this chapter.

Bob Galliers is Chairman and Professor of Information Management at Warwick Business School, University of Warwick. Prior to his appointment as Chairman he headed Warwick's Doctoral Programme in Information Systems and its Information Systems Research Unit. He was previously Foundation Professor and Head of the School of Information Systems at Curtin University, Australia. He has published widely on IS management and is editor of the *Journal of Strategic Information Systems*. His recent books include *Information Systems Research: Issues,*

Methods and Practical Guidelines, and *Strategic Information Management: Challenges and Strategies for Management Information Systems* (with B. Baker).

Michael C. Jackson is Professor of Management Systems and Dean of the School of Management, Lincoln University Campus, University of Lincolnshire and Humberside. After studying politics, philosophy and economics at Oxford University, he spent four years in the civil service before returning to academic life. He has since studied and taught at Lancaster, Warwick and Hull Universities, being appointed a full professor at Hull in 1989. Professor Jackson has authored two books: *Creative Problem Solving* and *Systems Methodology for the Management Sciences,* and edited six others. He is editor of the journal *Systems Research*, the official journal of the International Federation for Systems Research, has published 70 articles in other learned journals, and contributed chapters to several books. As well as following intellectual pursuits, he has held managerial positions on the Council of the Operational Research Society, as Head of Department, Director of Research, and Chair of the UK Systems Society; and is currently a Dean of School and Vice-President of the International Federation for Systems Research. He has also undertaken many consultancy engagements with outside organisations, both profit and non-profit.

Matthew Jones is a Lecturer in Information Management in the Management Studies, Department of Engineering and Judge Institute of Management Studies at the University of Cambridge, England. He previously held postdoctoral research posts at the Universities of Reading and Cambridge where he was involved in the development of computer-based models for use in public policy decision-making. His current research interests are concerned with the social and organisational aspects of the design and use of information systems and the relationship between technology and social and organisational change. He has published widely on these issues.

Paul McGolpin is a senior manager within the IT function of Powergen Plc. His main responsibilities include corporate IT strategy and the development of external IT services business (UK and internationals). Paul has 15 years' experience in consultancy, projects and general management within the IT industry. His main interests are in strategic benefits management and organisational

IS/IT issues. He has a degree in economics from Birmingham University and an MBA from Bradford School of Management. This chapter is based on the work carried out for his PhD, obtained from Cranfield University in 1996.

John Mingers is Senior Lecturer in Operational Research and Systems at Warwick Business School, University of Warwick. He has published widely in a number of fields relating to information systems and OR, particularly within the area of methodology and the nature of information. He has published a book on the implications of the theory of autopoiesis - *Self-Producing Systems* - with Plenum. He is a recent member of the Council of the OR Society and is Chairperson of the UK Systems Society.

Michael Myers is Senior Lecturer in the Department of Management Science and Information Systems at the University of Auckland, New Zealand. He is the author of a number of published papers and co-author of two books, including *New Zealand Cases in Information Systems* (2nd edition, 1992). He is the editor of the *IS World Section on Qualitative Research*, an associate editor of *Information Systems Journal* and an associate editor of the *MIS Quarterly Special Issue on Intensive Research*. Dr Myers is also on the Editorial Boards of *Information Technology and People* and a new electronic journal called *Journal of Holistic Research in Information Systems*.

Stephen Probert is a Lecturer in Information Systems, Department of Computer Science, Birkbeck College, University of London. His research interests are in information systems methodologies and philosophical aspects of information systems. He has published a number of papers and book chapters in this field, and given presentations at many information systems conferences in both the UK and abroad. His current research is aimed at providing methodological guidelines for the development of information systems with emancipatory potential.

He began his career in the automotive and metallurgical industries, and has a wide variety of experience in the development and implementation of information systems in manufacturing organisations. He has acted as a consultant to companies such as Wiggins Teape, National Telecom and RTS International. He was previously at the University of the West of England, and prior to that he was at Newcastle Business School, University of Northumbria.

AUTHORS

Martin Spaul studied philosophy at Cambridge, completing a PhD on the impact of artificial intelligence on the philosophy of language when the world was still young enough to believe that AI was a promising research programme. After a period working in the aerospace industry specifying and designing real-time systems he moved to Anglia Polytechnic University, gradually migrating from software engineering to IS. His current research interests are in critical theory and the political effects of new communication technologies.

Ronald Stamper worked in hospital administration and then in the steel industry where he observed that technically good computer systems often served the business poorly. This prompted his interest in semiotics as a way of understanding organisations as information systems. His book, *Information*, on organisational semiotics appeared in 1973. He initiated research into organisations as systems of social norms which contributed to computers and law (the Legol language), database semantics (ontological mapping and the Semantic Temporal Database), methodology (MEASUR: Problem Articulation for soft systems, Semantic Analysis and Norm Analysis) and most recently telematics (open EDI). He is now Professor of Information Management at the University of Twente in the Netherlands.

Mark Stansfield is a Lecturer in Information Management in the Department of Business and Information Management at Napier University, Edinburgh. He holds a Masters degree in information systems and is currently completing his PhD at the University of Paisley into the use of computer-based technology in supporting a subjective method of inquiry. His previous research work has included the use of expert system technology in teaching soft systems methodology.

Frank Stowell is Professor and Head of Department of Computer and Information Sciences at De Montfort University, Milton Keynes. His area of research is concerned with methods of information systems development and the impact of IT on organisations. He is a long serving member of the executive committee of the UK Systems Society and edits the quarterly publication *Systemist*. He is a member of the editorial board of the journal *Systems Reseach* and a board member of the UK Academy of Information Systems and is active in a number of other IS related areas. He has written extensively about information systems and has published two books within the McGraw-Hill Information Systems series.

John Ward is Professor of Strategic Information Systems, and Director of the Information Systems Research Centre at Cranfield University. John's main interest areas are the strategic use of IS/IT and the integration of IS/IT strategies with business strategies. He acts as a consultant to a number of major organisations and is author/co-author of the books *Strategic Planning for Information Systems, The Principles of IS Management* and *The Essence of Information Systems*. Prior to joining Cranfield in 1984 he worked in industry for 15 years, the last three as Systems Development Manager at Kodak Limited. He has a degree in Natural Sciences from Cambridge and is a Fellow of the Chartered Institute of Management Accountants and is President of the UK Academy for IS.

Daune West is a Senior Lecturer in the Department of Computing and Information Systems at the University of Paisley. She graduated from the University of Wales, Aberystwyth, with an MA in Classics, after which she undertook a postgraduate diploma in information systems at Portsmouth Polytechnic. Her PhD, from Portsmouth Polytechnic, concerned an investigation into the development of a subjective approach to knowledge elicitation for the design of expert systems. Her current research interests include the use of systems concepts and tools in the development of information systems, particularly during the process of requirements analysis, and the role of information technology in the Higher Education system. She is the author and joint author of a number of journal and conference papers and is co-author of the text: *Client-led Design: a Systemic Approach to Information Systems Definition.*

Brent Work is a Senior Lecturer in Information Management at the University of Surrey. He has worked for many years as a management consultant, project manager, and systems analyst in a number of international organisations. His major interests are the analysis and modelling of systems, information systems planning and investment, the impact of IT on industrial structures, and the philosophy and practice of information systems education.

SERIES FOREWORD

The Information Systems Series is a series of student and postgraduate texts covering a wide variety of topics relating to information systems. The focus of the series is the use of computers and the flow of information in business and large organisations. The series is designed to fill the needs of the growing number of courses on information systems and computing which do not focus on purely technical aspects but which rather seek to relate information systems to their commercial and organisational context.

The term 'information systems' has been defined as the effective design, delivery, use and impact of information technology in organisations and society. Utilising this broad definition it is clear that the subject is interdisciplinary. Thus the series seeks to integrate technological disciplines with management and other disciplines, for example, psychology and sociology. These areas do not have a natural home and were, until comparatively recently, rarely represented by single departments in universities and colleges. To put such books in a purely computer science or management series restricts potential readership and the benefits that such texts can provide. The series on information systems provides such a home.

The titles are mainly for student use, although certain topics will be covered at greater depth and be more research oriented for postgraduate study.

The series includes the following areas, although this is not an exhaustive list: information systems development methodologies, office information systems, management information systems, decision-support systems, information modelling and databases, systems theory, human aspects and the human-computer interface, application systems, technology strategy, planning and control, expert systems, knowledge acquisition and its representation.

A mention of the books so far published in the series gives a 'flavour' of the richness of the information systems world. *Information Systems Development: Methodologies, Techniques and Tools*, second edition (David Avison and Guy Fitzgerald) provides a comprehensive coverage of the different elements of information systems development. *Information Systems Development: A Database Approach*, second edition (David Avison) provides a coherent methodology which has been widely used to develop adaptable computer systems using databases; *Structured Systems Analysis and Design Methodology*, second edition (Geoff Cutts) looks at one particular information systems development methodology in detail; *Software Engineering for Information Systems* (Donald McDermid) discusses software engineering in the context of information systems; *Information Systems Research: Issues, Techniques and Practical Guidelines* (Robert Galliers - Editor) provides a collection of papers on key information systems issues which will be of special interest to researchers; *Multiview: An Exploration in Information Systems Development* (David Avison and Trevor Wood-Harper) looks at an approach to information systems development which combines human and technical considerations; *Relational Database Design* (Paul Beynon-Davies) offers a practical discussion of relational database design. Other recent titles include *Business Management and Systems Analysis* (Eddie Moynihan), *Systems Analysis, Systems Design* (David Mason and Leslie Willcocks), *Decision Support Systems* (Paul Rhodes), *Why Information Systems Fail* (Chris Sauer) and *Transforming the Business: the IT Contribution* (Moreton and Chester).

Also of interest will be books from the Information Systems, Management and Strategey Series such as: *Understanding and Evaluating Methodologies* (Nimal Jayaratna), *Client-Led Design* (Frank Stowell and Daune West), *Information Systems Provision: the Contribution of SSM* (Frank Stowell), and *Constructing Systems and Information* (Malcolm Crowe *et al.*)

Information systems is indeed 'an emerging discipline' (if it is a discipline at all!). Only now are we considering such issues as 'what defines the subject?', 'what are the linking elements?', 'what should be left out as well as put in?', 'is it a science, social science or an engineering discipline?', 'what should be the relationship between theory and practice?', 'what research methods are appropriate?' .... the list goes on, this is truly an exciting time for information systems! These issues are only some of those discussed in this thought-provoking volume. For some time, we have needed this discussion to be contained in one book. John Mingers and

Frank Stowell have done an excellent job in bringing together some major figures in Information Systems who are proposing, debating and, to some extent, agreeing, and in essence forming discipline of information systems. The book will be of great interest to all those who identify themselves within the realm of information systems (whether they emphasise the computing, management, philosophical, or other aspects). It will be vital for those setting up curricula for information systems. It will be equally important for those researching the area as well as being a marvellous source material for undergraduate and postgraduate student studying information systems.

David Avison and Guy Fitzgerald

PREFACE

Information systems is a relatively new area of study having emerged over the past 20 years from domains including computer and business systems analysis, computing science, and management science. As with any newly emerging field there are many conflicting views about the appropriate subject matter, its boundaries and its relations to other disciplines. There are practical issues such as its institutional status with academe and a whole range of questions relating to the issues surrounding what it may mean to be recognised as a 'discipline'.

Questions such as those above have been discussed in a series of seminars organised by the UK Systems Society at Warwick University between 1992 and 1995. Each seminar had a particular theme relevant to the problems of the developing field of IS which attracted leading figures from the information systems community. Each contributor produced a paper which provided the basis for discussion by the members of the group.One outcome of the seminar programme has already provided the basis of a book (Stowell, 1995) concerning the contribution of soft systems to IS. This text provides a further contribution to the thinking and practice of the developing field of information systems from leading members of the European IS community.

The principal aim of the book is to raise and address fundamental questions arising from the debate concerning what some argue to be the emerging discipline of information systems (IS). The text should be seen as contributing to the debate, raising awareness of the practical and philosophical dimensions of the field as well as promoting discussion within both the academic and business communities. The text is particularly valuable for both undergraduate and postgraduate students studying information systems, business or management courses. The text also offers a view of what, typically, might be expected to be included in a programme of study, or research, which has been defined as information systems.

The book is divided into three sections each logically related by the common purpose of exploring the various dimensions of the emerging domain of information systems. The first section is dedicated to philosophical issues. The section will deal with questions such as 'what is the nature of a discipline?' and go on to critically examine the question of IS as a distinct discipline. The second section will address the research agenda of information systems and will cover both general research methodologies and research in particular aspects of IS. Finally, the third section will address issues of IS practice and education and explore the way that information systems as an area of specialism appears to be emerging within business and how this is reflected in the education system. A final chapter, considering the future of IS concludes the text.

Stowell, F.A., ed., 1995, *Information Systems Provision, The Contribution of Soft Systems Methodology*, McGraw-Hill, Maidenhead.

Chapter 1

INFORMATION SYSTEMS: AN EMERGING DISCIPLINE? - INTRODUCTION

Frank Stowell and John Mingers

1.1. Introduction

Fifteen years ago it would have been hard to find, within academia, any courses or departments using the title 'Information Systems', yet today business schools and management departments have professors, lecturers and courses in 'IS'. There are IS departments in organisations; professional bodies such as the UK AIS; and whole new areas of study, with attendant academic journals, such as *Information Management* and *Strategic Information Systems*. Paradoxically, however, academic IS groups often do not have a clearly defined identity, being subsumed in departments such as computer science. Moreover, IS was not recognised as a separate domain in the latest (1996) UK research assessment exercise (RAE). Dylan's lyrics seem quite apt: *something is happening here but you don't what it is, do you, Mr. Jones?*

The question of a separate existence for IS is not merely an academic one, but also a practical one at this time. Like many academics we believe that the engine which drives good teaching is research and one important difficulty for IS teachers is funding their research programme. The omission of IS from the RAE has left many IS researchers with a feeling that they are not being credited with recognition for their research. Moreover many researchers feel resentful that they are being 'forced' to work in research domains which fit more readily into the RAE definitions rather than in their areas of interest. The scarcity of research funding and formal recognition serves to exacerbate the problem rather than prevent the growth of the subject. Academics whose expertise and experience suggest to them that there are significant

1

problems surrounding the way that IT-based information systems are designed and implemented also feel starved of the funding that would allow them to carry out research – research, they argue, which might address important IS design problems. The lack of funding to undertake IS research may contribute to our failure to develop complex decision support systems which, we suggest, is often the result of old design methods being adapted or dressed up in an attempt to cater with what is effectively a new set of problems with new demands and new penalties for mistakes.

Information systems seems to be struggling to emerge, as a separate discipline, out of the shell of computing and computer science, and quite what will emerge is, as yet, unclear. Where will its boundaries be drawn? What will its distinctive contribution be? What will be its underlying paradigms and methodologies? These are the kind of questions that are raised by the contributors to this book.

1.2   The Emergence from Computer Science

There is a growing belief that information systems is different from computing. IS is argued to be concerned with wider issues and demand a different set of skills than those required for computer science. Many computer scientists seem to think that IS does not fit within the computer science domain and many IS academics and practitioners feel that there are aspects of their work which lie outside the technical confines of computing. The feeling is strong enough among IS academics for them to create a learned body to represent their interests and for that body to attempt to persuade government to recognise the difference. So what is it that makes IS different from computing science? There are many differences and these have inspired many definitions of the domain (Ciborra, 1987, p.261; Stowell and West, 1994, p.22; Galliers, 1995, p.60; UKAIS 1995; Stamper, Chapter 10 this book). One of the purposes of this text is to explore some of the differences which have lead many leading academics to raise the question 'is IS an emerging discipline?'.

1.2.1 Information Systems and Computing Science - Perceived Differences

Computer science has its intellectual roots in engineering and, not surprisingly, the design and development of computer systems has evolved within those traditions. The weakness of this approach became apparent as computers have become easier to use and more readily introduced into an enterprise. Technical difficulties of the 1970s and 1980s have given way to the significant problems associated with information distribution and the way in which the information is used. Technological devices make a fundamental contribution to the dissemination of information but these devices in themselves are not information. The technical process is concerned only with the translation, storage and transmission of signals but it is the understanding and interpretation (literal and contextual) of the resulting code by a human that makes it information (Stowell, 1995). We suggest that one major weakness which most of the popular IS development methods share is that they fail to differentiate between a data-processing system and an information system (Stowell and West, 1994). Each method seems predisposed to the underlying notion that the computer is the information system and consequently the boundary of the problem seems to be drawn around data and the technology that manages it.

Clearly information systems existed before the computer and do not require the computer to operate (Buckingham *et al*, 1987). However, the advent of the powerful and simple-to-use computer means that large amounts of data can be represented to the human as an aid to decision-making and in that sense information itself has become a tangible resource. Technology provides the infrastructure but it is the human that capitalises upon the data availability to make that data a powerful tool. In the past many considered an information system as the exclusive province of technology but it has become clear that it is not. The outcome of this is a growing realisation that those who develop information systems should be capable of differentiating between processing data and providing information.

In 1980 Methlie referred to the 'datalogical' and 'infological' approaches to computer-based information system design as one means of identifying two streams of thinking. Current practices of information systems design do not appear to have progressed since

1980 and it would appear that, what can be referred to as 1970s mainframe computer-based system thinking, still seems to persist. It appears that many of the more popular design methods are what could be described as datalogical, that is, they focus upon data definition as opposed to the investigation of the wider significance of information flows and needs. In the 1990s, with the increasing demands of organisational information systems and the increasing sophistication of the user and the power of computers, suggest that those who develop information systems require ideas and education that is based upon thinking that is appropriate to the complexity of information systems.

Many of the methods used in the development of computer-based information system subscribe to a particular and rationalistic view of 'organisation' (Winograd and Flores, 1987; Checkland, 1981) and it is only in the past decade that serious regard has been paid to the wider organisational implications (Stowell, 1987, 1995). As the demand to introduce technology has increased the design task has become specialist and increasingly more technically-biased and widened the cultural gap between the organisational management and the technologist (Methlie, 1980; Nelson, 1986; Ward and Peppard, 1996). The development of applications generators to speed up the design process has increased the pressure to provide a specification compatible with the needs of the development tool. One result of the pressure is a reduction in the time to understand the whole problem in favour of a quick and technically sound solution. Where a method explicitly encourages client involvement the client's role seems to be constrained either to the identification of data or to discussions about the way in which the computer could be used. It is rare that there is a stage in the method where the definition of the problem situation is other than that directly related to the strengths, constraints and limits of the computer. Despite attempts in several of the approaches to embrace the social aspects of an information system most seem to be based upon a functionalist view of information. (A similar view was expressed about socio-technical system approaches by Lyytinen and Klien, 1985.) The globalisation of business and the World Wide Web underlines the need for the wider interests of information systems to be considered at the time of design and development.

It may be that what we see as an increasing bias towards technological solution is one reason why some computer systems fail to fulfil client expectations. Despite this apparent poor record of customer satisfaction there is every indication that there is a division of concerns between CS and IS. Information systems is concerned with the task of designing information systems from a set of assumptions relevant to the socio-technical nature of the task. These assumptions relate to a particular epistemology about information systems and will determine the way in which the system is developed. We suggest that the fundamental difference between CS and IS is that CS is centred upon the functionalist paradigm and IS needs to consider alternative concepts.

There is little doubt that understanding organisational behaviour and culture are important considerations during the information definition and subsequent development process and in recent times this recognition has shown a move towards interpretivism by some researchers (Stowell, 1995; Walsham, 1995; Jayaratna, 1994). In order to gain the wider understanding that this assertion implies there has become a growing need to employ tools and introduce ideas other than those directly related to producing a technical specification. The way in which this is currently undertaken has a fundamental flaw, namely technological determinism. The whole development process seems to be dominated by the need to produce a technical specification. It is partially this dissatisfaction with the technical thrust of IS development that many IS professionals feel has precipitated the growth of IS as a distinct area of intellectual interest.

1.3   Is Information Systems a Distinctive Discipline?

Information systems is a relatively new area of study and is rightly concerned with its nature and status. What types of entities does or should it study? What other subject areas does it draw upon or relate to? In what way is it distinctive and separable from other disciplines or subjects? These are important questions, not only philosophically but also pragmatically, given that IS is not generally recognised as such by funding bodies, research assessment exercises, and HEFCE teaching appraisals, but at the same time has such a growing support at grass roots level.

6 INFORMATION SYSTEMS: AN EMERGING DISCIPLINE?

Discussion about the status of IS (or MIS) has been occurring spasmodically for some time. Banville and Landry (1989), in reviewing this issue, reject the suggestion that IS can be seen as a monistic, Kuhnian paradigm and instead argue that it is better seen as an example of what Whitley (1984) calls a 'fragmented adhocracy'. While Backhouse and Liebenau (1989) and Backhouse *et al.* (1991) suggest that such a fragmentation poses a threat to the study of IS as an academic domain. Although there have recently been practical and institutional moves in the direction of greater disciplinarity (e.g. the formation of the *Academy of IS* and the *Association of IS*) the underlying uncertainties concerning the intellectual characteristics of IS remain.

The question posed in the title of this section involves three inter-related levels. At the first level is the question of the disciplinary status of information systems. Is information systems already a discipline? Is it in the process of becoming one? Is it plausible or desirable for it to be one? These questions, of course, presuppose a more fundamental and controversial one - what is the nature of an academic discipline in itself? The second level question is that of the subject matter of information systems and boundary of IS. What kinds of objects or entities does IS study? What other disciplines or academic areas does IS draw upon? Can some boundaries be agreed that would constitute IS as a coherent whole? Finally, at the third level, is the question of the distinctive contribution, if any, of IS. What clearly distinguishes IS from other subjects and what value does it have? These are fundamental questions which, we believe, must be discussed, debated, and researched - not left unasked and unanswered.

In order to address these questions, we find that we must adopt an historical, indeed evolutionary, perspective and take the view that IS is actually the most recent stage in the development of that uniquely human characteristic, language and communication. It is generally agreed (e.g. Mead, 1934; Habermas, 1987; Maturana and Varela, 1987) that it was the development of language that marked the beginning of the separation of humans from other species. Language began to develop as a means of cooperation in practical activities – as a way of coordinating action. This provided evolutionary advantage and, with the concomitant enlargement of the brain and new domains of interaction within the nervous system, simple gestures and signs eventually resulted in symbolic activity, self-consciousness and language. This in turn opened the way for the development, beyond coordinating practical activity, to abstract reflection, thought and knowledge. This view is expanded by Stamper in Chapter 10 where he puts forward the argument that organisational semiotics provide a useful pathway towards gaining a satisfactory understanding of the concept information.

The development of written language opened up horizons in both time, storing and recording across the generations, and space. The advent of printing presented one major enlargement of possibilities, and that of telecommunications, first by telegraph and then via radio and television. Finally (so far), the invention of general multi-purpose computers and, most recently, of PCs, global networks and so on, has resulted in the emergence of what is known as information systems. The main implications of this brief historical sketch are: i) that information systems have come about at a certain historical time because of a combination of particular technological developments but are in fact part of a long term development; ii) that although technology is the immediate enabler, information systems is actually part of the much wider domain of human language and communication; and iii), that IS will remain in a state of continual development and change in response both to technological innovation and to its mutual interaction with human society as a whole.

1.3.1 IS as a Discipline

The question of the extent to which IS is or could be a discipline is complex and is worth further study and research. The first problem is the nature of a discipline itself. Is it to do purely with the academic integrity of the area? That is, there is general agreement about the domain of study, philosophical foundations (ontological and epistemological), educational programmes and appropriate research methods and methodology. Or, from a more Foucauldian perspective, is it about the institutionalisation of the subject (discipline?)? Is it the establishment of professional bodies; of codes of conduct and practice; of centres of tradition and influence; of gatekeepers and barriers to entry; that constitute a discipline?

To what extent does IS meet either, or indeed both, characterisations of a discipline? It appears to fall far short of a discipline with academic integrity. There is no agreed domain, nor even agreement about the nature of 'information' itself; substantively different philosophical stances; and a variety of different methodology/research approaches. On the other hand, in institutional terms the process is well established with IS departments, Chairs, Institutes, Academies. These issues are addressed particularly by Steve Probert (Chapter 2) and Matthew Jones (Chapter 4).

Equally, the educational programmes within IS are different and at first sight a critic might suggest that this is because the subject is not cohesive and comprises any topic that takes an academic's fancy. A closer inspection shows that the underlying theme common to all programmes is that IS calls upon many areas of knowledge and this knowledge is gained through the incorporation of topics from other domains of knowledge. This situation is not wholly satisfactory and it could be argued that it typifies a maturing domain of study. Current debates within the IS community includes views about an IS curriculum, the inclusion or exclusion of subjects, the balance between theoretical and practical training and issues that are felt to be appropriate to the IS professional. It is difficult to predict how or if there will be a common educational programme for IS in the near future but Work's (Chapter 12) argument for the return of a classical, or liberal education, may be one means of providing IS with the kind of educational foundation that is relevant for the IS professional of the 21st century.

1.3.2 The Domain and Boundaries of IS

What role is there, given the developments outlined above, for information systems if it were to be established as a discipline, and what might we include within the IS boundary? We would argue that, so far, IS is fulfilling a necessary but limited role, being largely concerned with developing more effective organisational information systems. However, the arguments put forward here and within the text suggest a much wider and more significant role. We believe that IS can become the discipline that concerns itself with the nexus of the varied domains outlined above (technology, information, mathematics, linguistics, semiotics, psychology, sociology, etc.) as they bear upon the evolution of human communications and society. It is when we remind ourselves of the artificiality of the boundaries between disciplines and begin to think about IS in terms of what areas of knowledge do we need to embrace in order to address the imensity of the field that we can begin to free ourselves from the present (and sometimes cosy) compartments of academic concerns. We suggest that it is only if we adopt a 'transdisciplinary' approach can we begin to understand both the evolving nature and impact of technology upon society, and consequently provide us with a chance of influencing what might emerge in the future rather than simply suffering it. The education and experience of the IS professional should reflect the spectrum of responsibilities that the information age seems to represent.

First, computer-based information systems (CBIS - we use the qualification 'computer-based' to signify the importance and ubiquity of computers currently, not to suggest that IS is only concerned with computers) do not represent something fundamentally new. Rather they result from an intensification of tendencies that have long been present. However, it may be that they represent a degree of change, in a relatively short time, that may herald a qualitatively different future. Second, CBIS are not confined to business information systems. Rather, information systems are inherently part of the very essence of humanity, that is linguistic and social interaction. CBIS are a particular mode or mechanism of such interaction. It is therefore of *fundamental* importance in that they will inevitably shape, possibly in undesirable way, our future. Third, CBIS have the potential to generate major transformations within communities and societies as a whole. They enable new ways of interacting, projecting, capturing, and communicating information and meaning, and will lead to the emergence of new domains of interaction between individuals, and within and between communities.

Given the above, a broad-brush demarcation of the possible domain of IS might be: 'the nature and development of linguistic and social information interchange in so far as it is technologically mediated'. This obviously draws on a wide range of disciplines, e.g. semiotics, psychology, sociology, linguistics, IT, etc., as has been suggested by many others. It would primarily be concerned with the *interaction* of all these different factors in the same way that a 'human science', if it existed, would be concerned with the interaction of biology, physiology, biochemistry, psychology, sociology, etc. in human beings. We do not intend this as a formal definition of IS, simply as a way of highlighting the very wide scope that the general study of information and information systems might have.

This is clearly much wider that other extant definitions of IS as a discipline such as that of the UKAIS, or of an information system such as that of Stowell and West (1994).

1.3.3 The Big Idea

At an early workshop at the University of Warwick, Checkland and Holwell (1995) presented a paper entitled 'Information Systems: What's the Big Idea?' in which the authors argued that the nature of IS as a field is elusive. While there are many practical examples of the need to develop thinking relevant to IS, they argued, IS had no big idea that would establish it as a distinctive department of knowledge. We venture to suggest that maybe we are overlooking the obvious perhaps IS is itself the big idea. There seems to be little doubt that information technology is facilitating a myriad of information systems which themselves are transforming the world and the lives of us all. Practical examples of the autopoietic character of IS can be seen from the dramatic growth of IS journals, conferences and the establishment of chairs in IS in many universities within the UK and the USA. There can be little doubt that in the opinion of many academics and managers there is, *de facto*, a discipline of IS.

It seems clear that Information System design necessitates the involvement of the IS practitioner into working practices and customs of the enterprise. Such intervention may alter the way in which the enterprise operates and the way in which the social networks interact. The IS practitioner is, in practice, a catalyst for organisational change because of the way in which new working practices may be created by the introduction of IT. The modern IS practitioner often becomes involved in the development of working procedures which go beyond the identification and specification of computer hardware and software. There is a general agreement that IS is something that is practised and the practice enriches the knowledge of the problem. This agreement suggest that we need to address the issues which relate to this assertion. Issues such as the practicalities of doing the job, doing the research, and reinvesting the knowledge. All features that other professions such as the legal and medical professions have embraced for centuries without great difficulty. We argue that IS runs into difficulties when we model ourselves on subject areas such as computing which are not appropriate to our concerns. Computing is a related subject area but it is not the big idea.

The relationship between practice and theory in IS are undeniable The practice is something we do in the 'real-world' and not merely in the classroom or laboratory. Information systems is 'different' to computing in that the IS professional is concerned not just with the exploitation of technology but with the effects of IT and the change and oranisational ramifications that IT will bring. The harnessing, manipulation of data to provide information is such a valuable resource that it is changing the fabric of society much in the way that oil and steam changed it over the past two centurys. It is only recently that we have begun to recognise the changes that are taking place and the wide range of knowledge, both practical and theoretical, that are needed to manage those changes. This text is about some of the implications of those changes and about the ways in which we are attempting to address them. The text is not the answer but an attempt to provide a record of work and a basis for those who wish to take up the discipline and further the thinking.

In recognition of the complexity of issues that the IS professional now needs to address leading academics have been investigating problem situations and commenting upon the evolution of the domain. Some of this research has been published in an earlier text (Stowell, 1995) which emphasised the need for a shift in thinking if the new problems and new opportunities that IS presents are to be addressed. Although the arguments expressed in the previous text were not claimed to be new they have, until relatively recently, been largely ignored or in many instances addressed only partially. The lack of progress is related in part to the way that IS has emerged and also because of the dearth of IS research funding. Many writers over the past decade have advocated the need to develop approaches that enable the practitioner to take into account the wider implications of introducing computing power into organisations. Increasingly writers have drawn attention to the differentness of IS when compared to computing (Stowell, 1985, 1995; Avison and Fitzgerald, 1988; Rzevski, 1988; Avison and Wood-Harper, 1990;

Pouloudi and Whiteley, 1996). The shift in thinking is characterised by an intellectual attitude exhibited by the advocates of 'socially aware' computer design. While there are arguments in support and in contention of this intellectual stance we argue that IS is based upon a fundamentally different paradigm and way of educating its practitioners than CS, which can be described in general terms as a move towards antipositivitism.

The basic thinking about computer development represented by traditional CS practice is not conducive to the way in which IS is developing globally. Boland argues that '...organisations are constituted by acts of communication and are fundamentally an interpretive problem,' (Boland, 1985). If we accept Boland's view then IS needs a paradigm shift and its practitioners need to be concerned with ways of appreciating the problem subjectively but, and this is the hard part, also need to be able to provide a functional translation of the IS definition.

The IS practitioner perceives the information system as a notional human activity system whose actors use, among other things, a computer as one source of business intelligence. Thus, an information system can be viewed as an assortment of intelligence-gathering devices used in a way specific to an individual so as to enable him or her to manage his or her environment. A computer, as Winograd and Flores remind us, is fundamentally a '...tool for human action' (Winograd and Flores, 1987).

There seems to be a consensus among IS academics that the skills of the modern IS practitioner are multifarious We suggest that to embrace the complexity of skills, a fundamental issue for IS academics to resolve is the underpinning philosophy upon which IS is based, and from that identify the core elements which the IS professional needs to embrace. The complexity and relative multidisciplinarity of the field makes such issues both contentious and difficult. This text attempts to address some of the issues and provides the reader with a basis for further thought.

1.4   Outline of the Book

In order to try to address the many issues and questions raised so far, the book is structured into four parts. The first part considers the most basic question of the extent to which IS is, or should aspire to be, a discipline. The contributions cover both the philosophical aspects of the nature of disciplines and the more pragmatic questions as to the context and nature of IS at this time. The second part considers research and scholarship in IS. It covers a variety of approaches such as interpretive, action research, semiotics, and critical systems in line with the arguments made above, that positivist, functionalist approaches alone are not sufficient for IS. The third part moves to the practice of IS, particularly considering educational curricular for IS courses. The book concludes with a chapter that presents a particular future scenario portraying the globalisation of business and the influence of IS/IT in that process

References

Avison, D. and Fitzgerald, G., 1988, *Information Systems Development: Methodologies, Techniques, and Tools*, Blackwell, Oxford.

Avison, D. and Wood-Harper, A., 1990, *Multiview: an Exploration in Information Systems* Development, Blackwell, Oxford.

Backhouse, J. and Liebenau, J., 1989, A need for discipline, *Times Higher Educational Supplement*, 31 March.

Backhouse, J., Liebenau, J. and Land, F., 1991, On the discipline of information systems, *Journal of Information Systems,* 1(1):19-28.

Banville, C. and Landry, M., 1989, Can the field of MIS be disciplined? in *Information Systems Research: Issues, Methods and Practical Guidelines*, R. Galliers, ed., Blackwell, Oxford, 61-88.

Boland, R.J., 1985, Phenomenology: a preferred approach to research on information systems, in *Research Methods in Information Systems*, E. Mumford, R.A. Hirschhein, G. Fitzgerald and A. T. Wood-Harper, eds., Elsevier, Amsterdam, 193-201.

Buckingham, R.A., Hirschheim, R.A., Land, F.F. and Tully, C.S., 1987, *Information Systems in Education: Recommendations and Implementation*, Cambridge University Press, Cambridge.

Checkland, P.B., 1981, *Systems Thinking, Systems Practice*, Wiley, Chichester.

Checkland, P.B. and Holwell, S., 1995, Information systems: what's the big idea?, *Systemist*, 17(1):7-13.

Ciborra, C.U., 1991, Research agenda for transaction costs approach to information systems, in *Critical Issues in Information Systems Research*, R.J. Boland and R.A. Hirschheim, eds., Wiley, Chichester, 253-274.

Galliers, R., 1995, Re-orienting information sytems strategy: integrating information systems into the business, in *Information System Provision*, F.A. Stowell, ed., McGraw-Hill, Maidenhead, 51-74

Habermas, J., 1987, *The Theory of Communicative Action Vol. 2: Lifeworld and System: a Critique of Functionalist Reason*, Polity Press, Oxford.

Jayaratna, N., 1994, *Understanding and Evaluating Methodologies*, McGraw-Hill, Maidenhead.

Lyytinen, K.J. and Klien, H.K., 1985, The critical theory of Jurgen Habermas as a basis for a theory of information systems, in *Research Methods in Information Systems*, E. Mumford, R.A. Hirschheim, G. Fitzgerald and A.T. Wood-Harper, eds., Elsevier, Amsterdam, 219-31.

Maturana, H. and Varela, F., 1987, *The Tree of Knowledge*, Shambhala Press, Boston.

Mead, G., 1934, *Mind, Self, and Society*, University of Chicago Press, Chicago.

Methlie, L.B., 1980, Systems requirements analysis-methods and models, in *The Information Systems Environment: Proceedings of the IDIPTET 8.2, Working Conference on Information Systems Environment*, H.C. Liveas, F.F. Land, T.J. Lincoln and K. Supper, eds., Noth-Holland, Amsterdam, 173-85.

Nelson, C., 1986, The design of well adapted and adaptable computer-based information sytems, *Journal of Applied Systems Analysis,* 13:33-51.

Pouloudi, A. and Whitley, E., 1996, Managing IS conflict: from the organisational to the interorganisational context, in *The Future of Information Systems,* Proceedings of UKAIS Conference, Cranfield, Day 2.

Rzevski, G., 1988, IT strategy and quality of information systems teaching: improving the practice, in *Proceedings of the Information Systems Association Conference*, Civil Service College, Sunningdale, 123-128.

Stowell, F.A., 1985, Experiences with SSM and data analysis, *Information Technology Training*, 48-50

Stowell, F.A., 1987, Information systems: a new discipline?, in *British Psychological Society Annual Conference, Wessex and Wight Branch publication No.2*, University of Sussex, Oct.:13-21

Stowell, F.A., ed., 1995, *Information Systems Provision, The Contribution of Soft Systems Methodology*, McGraw-Hill, Maidenhead.

Stowell, F.A. and West, D., 1994, *Client-Led Design: a Systemic Approach to Information Systems Definition*, McGraw-Hill, Maidenhead.

UKAIS, 1995, Information Systems subject definition and scope, *UKAIS Newsletter*, 1(3):3.

Whitley, R., 1984, *The Intellectual and Social Organisation of the Sciences*, Oxford University Press, Oxford.

Ward, J. and Peppard, J., 1996, Reconciling the IT/business relationship: a troubled marriage in need of guidance, *Journal of Strategic Information Systems*, 5:37-65

Walsham, G., (1995) The emergence of interpretivism in IS research, *Information Systems Research*, 6(4):376-394.

Winograd, T. and Flores, F., 1987, *Understanding Computers and Cognition: A New Foundation for Design*, Ablex, Norwood, N.J.

PART 1: PHILOSOPHICAL ISSUES

The central question that this book addresses is the extent to which information systems is, or is not, a discipline. At first sight it may seem very easy to answer this in the affirmative. After all, there are numerous undergraduate and postgraduate courses that have substantial amounts of IS; there are university departments that have IS in their title; there are professors of IS; and there are academic and professional associations concerned with IS, for example the UK Academy of Information Systems, and the British Computer Society.

However, a slightly closer look would reveal much debate and disagreement about fundamentals matters such as the subject boundaries of IS. For example, with respect to computer science or information technology; the appropriate research method(s) and underlying philosophies, and the other disciplines upon which IS may or should draw. There is not even a clear consensus on the nature (or even existence) of *information* itself.

These questions are, in turn, underpinned by a deeper and wider question, particularly raised by the work of Foucault, as to the actual nature of an academic discipline in itself. Is a discipline constituted by the existence of institutional and organisational bodies such as university departments and professional organisations? Or is it based on the academic and intellectual integrity of the subject as evidenced by general consensus about the object of study, and appropriate research methods? Or is a discipline to be seen, more negatively, as *disciplining* processes that govern and restrict the forms of knowledge and types of method that are accepted as legitimate? It is philosophical questions such as these that the chapters in the first section seek to address.

Steve Probert, in a detailed and comprehensive chapter, argues the case that Information Systems certainly *should* exist as an academic discipline, based on both social and technological underpinnings. He firstly deals with arguments against IS being seen as a discipline and points out three fallacies. The *essentialist* fallacy is that a discipline must have some universally agreed core theory or epistemology for it to count as a discipline. The *reductionist* fallacy is that IS is really just an amalgam of other disciplines. And the *epiphenomenalist* fallacy that academic subjects can only reflect underlying, unchanging reality, without actually impinging upon it. Probert next considers the *reality* of actual information systems in terms of the debates between positivism and interpretivism, which he considers have been over-simplistic.

The main part of the chapter puts forward Probert's own ideas of a new paradigm for IS research, drawing on the work of the critical theorist Adorno, who developed a comprehensive philosophical position encompassing technology, culture and administration. This section includes both a critique of interpretive views that information systems can never be more than subjective constructions; and consideration of authenticity in IS interventions, i.e, questions of ethics and morality.

Martin Spaul takes a much less committed position, seeking to question and probe the idea of IS as a putative discipline in order to provoke questioning and reflection. His particular rhetorical device is to consider the question through three different viewpoints, each associated with the work of the Frankfurt school of critical theory.

The first viewpoint, associated with Horkheimer, highlights the complex relations between science and ideology, raising the question of the interactions between a scientific endeavour and its constitutive social and political context. To what extent are the scientific and technological agendas shaped or even determined by historical contingencies? The question is pursued through a study of two approaches to information systems that have *not* become well established—Simon's generalised theory of information processing, and the study of formal semiotics, and concludes with an analysis of the social context of information systems at the moment.

The second viewpoint (relating to Habermas) focuses on the debates concerning purpose, rationality and values, and tries to map recent technological developments within a systems/lifeworld view of modernity. Three particular tendencies are analysed—the penetration of IT into the lifeworld; the rise of the 'information society'; and the convergence between previously discrete technologies such as computers, telecommunications, and the media.

The final perspective (again highlighted by Horkheimer) considers the problem of interdisciplinarity. Research in IS must surely be interdisciplinary, and yet this is clearly problematic, both at the level of the individual researcher, and at the structural level of the academic and institutional frameworks that both enable and constrain practical research.

Matthew Jones also points out problems with the nature of IS as a discipline, for example the seeming contradiction of debates about the disciplinary status of IS being carried on within academic journals and conferences that would usually be the mark of just such a discipline. He explains this through a consideration of the very different connotations of the term 'discipline'. Three in particular may be picked out—Discipline$_1$ as a normative definition of what *should* constitute the boundary and core components of IS; Discipline$_2$ as simply a description of what actually does get included in the label IS; and, more provocatively, Discipline$_3$ as a Foucauldian mechanism of control, structuring the reality of IS.

Jones argues that IS has not yet established itself as a coherent discipline in the first sense, although there are a number of current initiatives, such as the establishment of the Association of IS in the USA and the UKAIS in Britain, that can be seen as Discipline$_3$-type mechanisms trying to regulate the apparent disorder of the area. Despite not yet being a discipline, Jones does see IS as having a degree of unity, the twin focus on social systems combined with technology, and a distinctive character, its effects as an informating technology and the immateriality of information. Jones concludes with what he sees as the main implications of his position for IS research.

Finally, **David Avison** puts forward the most pragmatic line arguing that, in spite of the many difficulties in ordering such a multi-faceted area as information systems, its establishment as a discipline is important to avoid disadvantage in economic and political terms. This should involve the establishment of a broadly-based consensus on the scope of information systems, general curricula for information systems teaching, paradigms and methods for IS research, and approaches to IS development in practice. Avison recognises many of the barriers to the establishment of such a consensus, and it is just such a debate about these issues that this book is intended to encourage.

Chapter 2

THE ACTUALITY OF INFORMATION SYSTEMS

Stephen Probert

2.1   Introduction

In this chapter it will be argued that, as there real, genuine, problems concerned with many aspects of information systems (analysis, design, development, implementation, management, etc.), a *bona fide* academic discipline of information systems (IS) should exist. The argument put forward is that, firstly, IS is not unlike other academic disciplines; particularly those which, although they have been relatively recently established, have been extant for long enough to gain academic (and general) respectability. Secondly, it is argued that information systems are real socio-technical accomplishments (i.e. they are not mere mental constructions). From this analysis, the implications for studies in the discipline of IS are drawn. To begin with, some points concerning the social and technical aspects of IS are explored.

2.1.1   Socio-technical Considerations

The need for IS as a discipline arises from the nature of the problem-structuring (and 'solution-structuring') discourses in organisations; particularly those concerned with information accumulation, processing and dissemination. The problem-structuring discourses are greatly influenced by the economic and cultural environment in which organisations exist (i.e. the *social* environment). However, to be of real significance, IS research should also be concerned with the *technical* aspects of information systems, because the 'solution-structuring' discourses usually embody technological assumptions. In this respect there are many similar academic disciplines in which both social and technical aspects are highly relevant. Throughout history, certain discourses have emerged at certain times; often in response to changing circumstances. Such discourses make it possible to speak about things that had not really been spoken about hitherto. Although IS is a discipline which draws on subjects such as computer science, management sciences, organisational behaviour, and so on (the full list would be a large one), it will be argued that it is not a *branch* of any of these.

The need for a discipline of IS has arisen mainly as a result of there being many kinds of perceived problems in the organisations of the (Western) world. IS purports to solve (or at least ameliorate) some of these organisational problems. The problems of information accumulation, processing and dissemination, have become critical for organisations in this particular historical epoch (in which we find ourselves). As such IS is (or has been) *problem-driven*, and those problems have been ultimately problems of *management within organisations*, although many of these problems may in reality be delegated to the computer specialists employed by organisations. One group (management) generally set the problem agenda, but the other group (the computer specialists and related technologists), to a large degree, *make that agenda possible* (and pre-structure it to some extent). Of course, there has been an element of product-push associated with many IS developments. Managers have to make the decisions as to whether or not to go ahead with a proposed IS development, and such decision makers are often the targets of aggressive salespersons:

> As we all know the businessman is continually pressed to invest in the latest fashion, to keep ahead of the competition by possessing the latest new-fangled innovation. The vendor then becomes an important element in understanding implementation decisions. The vendor sells the product... (Winfield, 1991, p.41)

The IS development process (its legitimation at any rate) usually takes place in an economic and cultural environment which embodies (what can be termed) a set of *efficiency-maximisation imperatives*; these are determined both by managers' perceptions of impersonal market forces and by the ideological legacy of the enlightenment—which sustains the general belief that things can always be made more efficient:

...[At] a historical level, the development of technology and organisation alike has reflected the increasing pervasiveness of objective forms of knowledge through the 'rationalization' of society... And in this context, technology has long provided a model for the pursuit of objectively efficient forms of organisation. (Scarbrough and Corbett, 1992, p.18)

The solutions to problems with organisations' information systems often have far-reaching social consequences within organisations, and sometimes there are consequences which extend to the members of the wider society in which the organisations are embedded; a good discussion of such aspects can be found in Kling (1996).

All of these aspects are relevant for studies within the discipline of IS. However, technology also matters to IS because all solutions to IS problems invoke the use of some technology—even if the technology is a wax tablet and a sharp stick. However, it is only really with electro-mechanical reproduction, transmission and manipulation, that the technology creates new possibilities for organising (e.g. the VDU, the fax, or the photocopier), and many information systems invoke a wide variety of technological innovations (computers, microfilm, television, and so on); it is not only the computer that is relevant. One's perception of the capabilities of technology greatly influences one's perceptions both of the problems in organisations and the possible solutions to those problems. Put more abstractly: 'solution-structuring' discourses embody assumptions about technological capabilities.

Therefore, IS research should be concerned with both (relevant) social and technical aspects. As such it is similar to many areas of academic study. Some other examples of areas of study which link social and technical aspects would be environmental studies (global pollution and so on), housing, nursing, town planning, and media studies. Although the problems that IS practitioners have to try to solve are ultimately social or organisational problems, it is certain that the success of the proposed solutions, when implemented, depends crucially on making appropriate use of the available technologies.

But is there really such a thing as the *academic discipline* of IS (in the traditional sense)? In this chapter, it will be argued that there is. What arguments can be mounted to support such a position? Two basic kinds of supportive arguments will be developed. Firstly, factual comparisons with other academic disciplines will be made. Secondly, the nature of reality and its relationship to theory will be explored, and the nature of IS as a discipline will then be characterised. Essentially, it will be argued that academic disciplines and real-world practices constantly interact in a dialectical process; this creates both new *realities* (this should be understood literally), and new ways of thinking about those realities. Consequently, academic disciplines can, and will, be developed to cope with these new realities. To support this position (that the dialectical process constantly creates new *realities*), the argument put forward will, again, be partly 'factual', but philosophical considerations will also be important.

2.2   Arguments against IS as a Discipline

Of course there may be other ways in which arguments might be propounded to judge whether or not an academic discipline exists. In the case of IS, it is probable that some may feel that there is no such thing as a discipline of IS; three fallacious ways of arguing for such a view are outlined below. These fallacies have been entitled the *essentialist* fallacy, the *reductionist* fallacy, and the *epiphenomenalistic* fallacy. Examples from several disciplines (but mainly from economics, geography and sociology) will be given to demonstrate the nature of these fallacies.

2.2.1   The Essentialist Fallacy

An essentialist might want to claim that an academic discipline should have a core theory of some sort, or that there should be recognised procedures and methods for developing knowledge in that discipline, and so on. The problem with such arguments is simply that many established academic disciplines would probably fail some portion of any essentialist's tests.

Like many social science disciplines, economics contains disputes about exactly how to proceed to conduct economic studies. But, surely, economics is an established academic discipline (if it is not considered to be so then neither should IS). One important technical dispute in economics lies at its very core:

> The big dividing line in economics today is between new classicals and new Keynesians... it is not only what they think; it is also how they think. Their whole approach to economic theorizing and their choice of what to study is different. The first priority of the new-classical economists is theoretical rigour... Keynesians usually prefer relevance. (Pennant-Rea and Crook, 1986, p.164)

Furthermore, as is the case with most (if not all) social science disciplines, economics suffers from the impossibility of its researchers attaining value-freedom in their analyses:

> In fact, economics is far from value-free. Bias appears both in selection of the questions deemed to be legitimate subjects of economic analysis and in the ways in which those questions are treated... Economics claims to be value-free and is nothing of the sort. (Donaldson, 1978, p.12)

So any attempt to find a core of method or procedure for economic analysis would probably be in vain; therefore we should not necessarily expect to be able to find agreements about the nature of the core methods or procedures for conducting IS research either.

A similar situation occurs in geography, but for slightly different reasons. Surely, *geography* is an academic discipline! A brief, but insightful account of the early history of geography has been given recently by Livingstone (1994). The interplay of real-world events constantly affects the relevance, fruitfulness, etc. of different approaches to tackling geographic studies. Indeed, it can be argued that any academic discipline containing a social *component* should never be allowed to stand still, i.e. it should never be allowed to maintain a core of method or procedure which does not continue to evolve in response to changes in the actual circumstances it purports to explain. Furthermore, academic disciplines exist in an environment where bureaucratic contingencies exist (i.e. in universities); they have to be pigeon-holed somehow into faculties, departments, etc. Often, such decisions—while not being entirely arbitrary—can have a random appearance (to say the least!). Livingstone makes the following points:

> Disciplines do not possess some eternal, essential, core divorced from the mundane realities of cultural and social life. They are instead contingent affairs at least as likely to map on to the manoeuvrings of *fin-de-siecle* academic politics as on to the 'real-world'. No, geography's identity is not to be established by some static definition. It is instead to be found in an evolving tradition of inquiry—a conversation woven around such themes as map, place, space, region, landscape, and the relations between nature and culture. (Livingstone, 1994, p.15)

So, in IS, not only is the *search* for a core of method or procedure likely to be futile, the *demand* for one is also.

2.2.2   The Reductionist Fallacy

There are really two variants of this fallacy; these can be termed *simple* and *compound* reductionism. An advocate of simple reductionism would argue that discipline *x* was in fact a *branch* of discipline *y*. This approach could be called *subsumption* rather than *reduction*, if one prefers. An advocate of the compound approach would try to outwit someone who believes *x* to be an academic discipline by attempting to do something like reverse-engineering discipline *x*. The argument would be that discipline *x* is really an *amalgam* of other academically respectable disciplines. The problem with such arguments is that they fail to take into consideration the *emergent properties* that academic disciplines (should and do) attempt to describe.

In its early days, many critics argued that sociology was (or should be considered as being) merely a branch of either psychology, economics, biology, or education, i.e. other, better established, disciplines. (Indeed, the view that IS is a branch of either computer science or management science is institutionally embedded in most higher education institutions in the UK today.) Talcott Parsons (a notable sociologist in his own right) considered that:

> Emile Durkheim (1858-1917) may be called one of the two principal founders of the modern phase of sociological theory, the other being his somewhat younger contemporary Max Weber. (Parsons, 1974, p.xliii)

Weber will be considered shortly, but what was Durkheim's contribution and why should it warrant such an accolade? Again, according to Parsons:

> ...Durkheim used the framework of solidly established intellectual traditions—those of English utilitarianism, in certain respects of German idealism, and of his own French background—to formulate a theoretical framework that was both solidly grounded in those traditions and yet highly original. As grounded in tradition, it was capable of taking full account of established knowledge; but it went far beyond this... In his special conception of the nature of 'social reality', which emphasized the involvement of *normative components* in both social reality and, through internalization, the personality of the individual, Durkheim was following, along with a few others, the major line of development of social science. (Parsons, 1974, p.lxiii)

Of central importance in this characterisation is the notion of *transcendence*—of going beyond the simple amalgamation of existing ideas (from existing disciplines).

One particularly interesting attempt to reduce sociology (to biology) was made during Durkheim's time. A possible explanation for such an attempted reduction would be that biology (especially physiology), in nineteenth-century France, was going through what might be termed an expansionist phase—the many new discoveries made gave increasing influence and credibility to this discipline. An interesting application of biological ideas to society at large was provided by Saint-Simon (1760-1825):

> The name that Saint-Simon gave to his social theory ... [was] 'social physiology' ... Saint-Simon's ideal society consisted of a harmonious association of different individuals all of whom cooperated to ensure the efficient functioning of the whole society... It is also highly significant that the term *organisation* played a key role in Saint-Simon's social theory. In fact, it is around this time—from the second decade of the nineteenth century onwards—that this term began to shift from biological to common usage ... (Jones, 1990, pp.88-89)

In his early days, Durkheim was influenced by Saint-Simon's work:

> Durkheim made it quite clear that he regarded Saint-Simon as the inspirer of both sociology and socialism, although he gave Comte credit for having separated science from practice. (Thompson, 1982, p.33)

Saint-Simon's social theory—and similar variants—are usually termed 'organicist' theories (views, analogies, etc.). While there were powerful tendencies to adopt such a (biological) view of society in the late nineteenth century, Durkheim was to reject this; hence a new discipline, *sociology*, was required to study society:

> The organicist analogy served the function of implying that society was part of nature and should be studied by methods equivalent to those of the natural sciences. Although Durkheim made extensive use of the analogy in his early work ... Durkheim [later] maintained that sociology could not be reduced to biology because societies are united by ideal rather than material bonds, and the source of ideological unity is the collective conscience. (Thompson, 1982, pp.34-35).

Many might wish to reduce IS to computer science, management science, etc. However, it will be argued later that it is not reducible in this way, as the nature of the reality it purports to explain transcends the objects with which these disciplines interact.

A similar case can be found with geography. It is interesting, as it indicates that many of the problems that IS currently suffers were once problems for geographers too. According to Livingstone:

> As an academic discipline geography has been around since the professionalisation of the academic turf during the second half of the 19th century. Of course different figures with different agendas championed the subject in different places. But in Britain the name of Sir Halford Mackinder looms large... According to Mackinder, geography's *raison d'être* lay in its claim to bridge an abyss that was, he declared, 'upsetting the equilibrium of our culture'—namely the gulf between the natural sciences and the study of humanity. Thereby an experiment to keep culture and nature

(to use two abstractions) under one conceptual umbrella was institutionalised. (Livingstone, 1994, p.15)

But geography cannot be reduced to the study of purely natural or purely social phenomena. If one is in doubt about this, try to imagine explaining to a child how ports come to be located where they are without reference to both natural and social aspects! Clearly you would need to make reference to socio-economic aspects such as proximity to other nations/regions with which trade is conducted, but you would also need to make reference to natural aspects, such as the depth of the water, the possibility of shelter from storms, favourable tidal movements, etc. In this sense a port is a socio-technical accomplishment—as is an information system; the main difference being that while a port exploits (and modifies) natural conditions an IS exploits and modifies the capabilities of artifacts (usually computers, etc.).

Returning to sociology, both Durkheim and Weber experienced difficulties in establishing themselves as *sociological* academics, if only because of the newness of the discipline. One problem, common in IS no doubt, is that neither of them had, initially, an intellectual background (or formal qualifications) in *sociology*. Weber's university background was in law (and history and economics), and his doctoral thesis was entitled 'On the History of Medieval Trading Companies':

> In 1892 Weber got a minor position in law-teaching in Berlin ... In 1894 the University of Freiburg-im-Breisgau gave him a chair in political economy. In 1897 he succeeded the economist Knies at Heidelberg. During the 1914-18 war he worked in hospital administration. 1918 saw him return to teaching in a specially created chair of sociology in Vienna (MacRae, 1987, p.24)

Such is typical of the pattern of appointments to those in emerging disciplines. Durkheim has a similar *curriculum vitae*:

> Durkheim was ... of Jewish parentage ... and was expected to become a rabbi ... until he became an agnostic. (Parsons, 1974, p.xliv)

As is typical for an academic pioneering a new discipline, Durkheim had a varied early career. The early influence of religion was to have continuing significance for Durkheim (albeit in his entirely secular studies), and enabled Durkheim to get his early appointments in the academic world—although these appointments were not to be in sociology departments:

> The course on religion was only one of the courses he taught at Bordeaux [in 1894-5]. His appointment was in social science and education, and so he had to teach courses on moral and intellectual education, and the history of pedagogy. Both at Bordeaux and later at the Sorbonne in Paris the opportunity to teach sociology was only given on the basis that he would devote a substantial proportion of his time to teaching education courses. There was still formidable opposition to sociology in the universities and it virtually had to be smuggled in through the back door. When he moved to the Sorbonne in 1902 it was to a post in education, rather than sociology ... It was not until 1913 that his chair was made one in 'Education and Sociology'. (Thompson, 1982, pp.40-41)

Sociology had to 'pull itself up by its own bootstraps' in order to establish itself as a *bona fide* academic discipline—as many other academic disciplines have had to, no doubt. Although Comte had invented the phrase 'sociology', both Durkheim and Weber were crucial in establishing sociology as a *bona fide* discipline:

> Now sociology, in the late nineteenth century, was not—as it is now—institutionalised ... There was not, except in America, and even there only in a rather thin form, a community of sociologists in university positions and proudly legitimated by an appropriate training. The subject had indeed a long and ragged history... Neither the contents nor the methods of the enterprise were unambiguously defined... Weber, therefore was fortunate in that he gained academic advancement in other fields before becoming unequivocally committed to sociology, just as sociology as an institutionalised discipline has been fortunate in being able to claim for itself the legitimacy given by Weber's work and name. (MacRae, 1987, pp.43-45)

To return to geography, many interesting parallels with IS may be drawn. Concerning the question of whether IS is a social or a technical discipline, it can be seen that geographers once displayed similar angst:

> Perhaps on account of its historical occupancy of such an uncomfortable academic niche—straddling the worlds of the physical sciences, social studies, and humanities—geography in the middle decades of this century displayed its fair share of disciplinary angst. Many of its historians, accordingly, prosecuted their task with an apologetic fervour seeking hither and thither for some clear cut definition of the field. Of course such projects always were ill-fated. (Livingstone, 1994, p.15)

Those who would seek to reduce IS to some other discipline—or those that would suggest that IS is an amalgam (good, bad or indifferent) of other respectable disciplines would do well to observe Livingstone's comments concerning geography (and academic disciplines in general), as it seems reasonably clear that if geography is an academic discipline, so is IS (or so it should be at any rate).

2.2.3   The Epiphenomenalistic Fallacy

Epiphenomenalism is a philosophical argument (or a position) adopted to explain the mind-body problem. This problem, put simply, is concerned with trying to develop some understanding of how it is possible for physical things (such as brains) and mental things (such as sensations) to co-exist and/or be (causally) related to one another. Epiphenomenalism can be characterised as the view that mental phenomenon are merely (and it has to be *merely*!) by-products of physical occurrences in the world (see Horn, 1995, p.241). In terms of academic disciplines the epiphenomenalistic fallacy can be characterised as the notion that academic disciplines (and, for that matter, real-world practices) merely reflect and interact with an ontologically static and unchanging world; i.e. a world that has a *fixed* ontology. The problem with this argument is that the ontology of the world—at a fundamental physical level—may well be a fixed one (quarks, super-strings, or 'whatnots'), but most academic disciplines, as argued above, are concerned with the *emergent properties* of complex physical objects and systems (although, notably, mathematics apparently is entirely concerned with abstractions). However, academic disciplines can (and do) contribute to the *creation* of new ontological categories, and do not merely reflect actual occurrences in the real-world.

Economics has created a considerable variety of technical terms which have come to be used (if not necessarily understood) in common parlance; 'inflation', 'gross domestic product', 'money supply', and so on. The behaviour of ordinary people will come to be affected by their beliefs about the values ascribed to such terms, e.g. a decision as to whether or not to take industrial action will be influenced in part by the (perceived) rate of inflation. Such behaviour may well go on to affect the future values ascribed to such terms, and in economics such considerations are put under the label of 'rational expectations'—an important part of modern economic theory:

> Suppose that some theorists come up with a new idea about how the economy works. It is so persuasive that policymakers start to follow its prescriptions—and everybody believes that they will indeed do so. Will not that change by itself alter the way the economy works? And if it does, will it thereby cease to be a helpful guide for policymakers, since it had been derived from (and was therefore relevant to) the earlier performance of the economy? In short, ideas might be able to change economic variables, making the problem of aiming at a moving target ... tricky... (Pennant-Rea and Crook, 1986, p.162)

In the case of sociology, it was the very transformation from an agrarian to an *industrial* society that created the possibility of a new academic discipline. Until then, many had thought that sociology should be merely an *extension* of economics—a relatively well-established academic discipline; although some economists themselves had come to similar conclusions:

> The so-called 'economists of the chair' in Germany ... reacted against the orthodox liberal economics of the time, which deduced laws from an abstract model of the market-place, in which the individual made rational economic choices, and where the state should not interfere and ethical considerations were irrelevant. Against this they put forward theories that were inductive, social-ethical, and interventionist. The development of sociology at the end of

the nineteenth century was very much affected by this reaction against the old political economy, which now seemed inadequate to deal with the rise of big corporations, class conflict, national rivalries, and the need for national unity and reconstruction. Like Marx, Durkheim charged that the orthodox liberal economic theories that had been in the ascendent until the 1870s were ideological rather than scientific. They were ideological in that they took their basic concepts from the popular prejudices of the time, rather than developing them scientifically. Also, explanations of social events should be sought not in terms of individuals' motives and intentions, but in terms of social structural causes that often escaped consciousness. (Thompson, 1982, pp.35-36)

It is also for these reasons that Durkheim rejected the possibility of grounding sociology in biology. For Durkheim (and for later sociologists generally) the *sui generis* nature of industrial-social life was simply not to be confused or conflated with biological life and biological structures, etc. Interestingly, one could argue that this reductionistic (and arguably fallacious) tendency still remains influential today, via such vehicles as sociobiology, and 'totalitarian Darwinians'—who seek to explain all forms of social organisation by means of genetic mutations etc.

An example of a dialectical affect in IS would be the ubiquitous concept of the *systems development life cycle*. This was originally derived from an empirical (and essentially an *economic* study) by Barry Boehm (Boehm, 1976). However, the consequent life cycle model has been absorbed into nearly every structured IS method propounded ever since; if it is criticised, it is criticised as being a *prescription* that does not 'work' in practice (whatever the precise form of the criticism takes). However, it often seems to go unnoticed that the life cycle model can only be rationally defended as a *description* of *actual* IS practice (although this is only to say that it *might* be true, not that it *is* true), As soon as the life cycle is employed prescriptively in an IS method its essentially contradictory nature becomes apparent. The longer one takes to 'get the requirements right' the longer it takes to develop a system at all—and the greater the likelihood becomes that the requirements are out of date:

> The criticisms that are periodically made of the development life cycle concept ... mostly focus on its being a linear, sequential model in which each stage must be completed before the next is begun. This means that it relies heavily on the initial definition of the problem being complete and correct and that the users' requirements will not change in the time taken to progress to final implementation. In the case of modern complex information-systems neither of these assumptions can safely be made ... (Lewis, 1994, p.75)

Nevertheless the widespread use of life cycle methods for IS developments continues relentlessly (although numerous alternative approaches have been propounded).

These discussions are intended to show that ideas and practices can interact dialectically; if Boehm's life cycle model has influenced IS practice to a significant extent, then this is true, and indeed Lewis argues that this is the case:

> The legacies of hard systems thinking, such as the idea of the development life cycle, have become so deeply ingrained in IS thinking that only rarely is note taken of the constraints that they impose upon the way we view the development of information-systems. (Lewis, 1994, p.75)

Thus an academic discipline can do more than reflect or represent reality—it can influence (and thereby change) that reality over time.

This analysis implies that it is important to develop unique research methods for conducting IS research. One important reason for this is that many of the current approaches to information systems research have led to serious methodological and philosophical confusions; these confusions arise directly from the assumptions inherent in both positivistic and interpretivistic research approaches, and these are usually presented as binary opposites. Furthermore, these confusions manifest themselves acutely in information systems teaching material (and thereby information systems education itself). Therefore, an analysis of the current context in which information systems development takes place will now be conducted, and this is used to develop a set of requirements that a new information systems research method would need to satisfy. Two important areas for future research in information systems are described.

2.3   The Reality of Information Systems

In this section it will be argued that information systems are best treated as if they *actually exist*. Firstly, a discussion about the changing nature of information systems in organisations will set this discussion in its historical context. Secondly, a discussion concerning the epistemological and ontological notions, normally embedded within IS thinking, will indicate the improvements that are needed in this area.

2.3.1   Relevant Organisational Issues

Debates about the precise role of IS as an academic discipline are difficult to resolve without taking into consideration the historical (i.e. evolving) nature of IS practices. The old answers to these sort of questions were usually related to technological issues; more recent answers are usually related to management issues. As the price of hardware has fallen, and software has become easier to use, the agenda for IS problems has increasingly become user-driven, rather than being technologically determined, and users in the workplace have increasingly acquired their own PCs (the language is significant). Clearly managing this ubiquitous technology is one of the pressing problems facing management (generally) and therefore much of the IS agenda is management-driven; the problem is now often re-cast as being one of information management (Earl, 1989).

Looking back, over the past twenty or thirty years the shift of emphasis from technological issues to management issues, might (rather crudely) be explained by an *economic* relationship between *price* and *performance*. If the processing-power per dollar/pound continues to fall rapidly then changes to the IS agenda can be anticipated. (Typical anecdotal estimates of future price-performance suggest that by early in the next millennium the most powerful desktop computers in existence in the 1980s will be available on a credit-card, they will cost about £5.00—and they could therefore be thrown away when they fail.) The changes that have occurred in the IS agenda could be emphasised by the nature of the (managerial) questions that have been and will be asked, i.e.

1. e.g. 1970 'What can we do with computers in our organisation?'

2. e.g. 1985 'What ought we be doing with the information systems in our organisation?'
3. e.g. 2000 'What might people want to use information systems to do in our organisation (and can/should people be helped to achieve these aims)?'

The first sort of question needed a technological sort of answer—an example answer might be 'payroll'. However it is widespread knowledge that, despite the technical attractions of payroll systems, such systems are socially sensitive—for example they have to work correctly every week (or month)! But for as long as the question asked was, 'What can we do with computers in our organisation?' the answers would always be related to those things that appeared to be the most tractable:

> The cultural focus of much of the implementation of the 1970s and 1980s was on installing the answer, finding the quick solution, finding the quick 'technological fix'. The focus was on the technical capabilities of the machine and its promise ... (Winfield, 1991, p.19)

The second sort of question needed a managerial sort of answer (usually based on 'business need')—such answers are the dominant sorts of answers today, although there is a developing trend for these answers to take a more strategic view of the *possibilities for exploiting* the technology. This indicates a shift from the second sort of question to the third—although the strategic questions are essentially still management questions. What makes the third sort of question different from the first two sorts is that it presupposes that the employees themselves have a vision of what the organisation is trying to achieve, and that they share the value-system embodied in that vision; that is it implies the need for a shift from *management* to *leadership* (see e.g. Handy, 1989, pp.105-108). Much of the 'business process reengineering' literature stresses such elements:

> The fundamental error that most companies commit when they look at technology is to view it through the lens of their existing processes. They ask, 'How can we use these new technological capabilities to enhance or streamline or improve what we are already doing?' Instead, they should be asking, 'How can we use technology to allow us to do things

that we are *not* already doing?' Reengineering, unlike automation, is about innovation. It is about exploiting the latest capabilities of technology to achieve entirely new goals. (Hammer and Champy, 1994, p.85)

The 'information technology (IT) = possible solution' formula has given way to a 'IT = possible opportunity' formula:

> The increasing tendency for organisations to privilege innovation over efficiency ... places a particular stress upon the human qualities of flexibility and creativity which even the 'impersonal machinery' ... of IT hardware cannot yet provide. (Scarbrough and Corbett, 1992, p.19)

The end result of the shift in emphasis concerning the role of IT (from 'solution' to 'enabler') has two important implications for IS. Firstly, the role of people as *utilisers* (rather than *users*) of information systems is enhanced; secondly, it becomes more difficult to set a clear boundary between people and the IT with which they interact:

> ... [T]echnology and organisation are not ontologically separate categories, but rather mirror reflections of a mutual interchange of knowledge, meanings and political interests. (Scarbrough and Corbett, 1992, p.157)

However, this creates a number of problems which are not adequately dealt with effectively by current IS concepts; these problems—mostly philosophical in nature—will now be discussed.

2.3.2 The Epistemology and Ontology Underpinning Most Information Systems Concepts

In earlier times (1960-70) there was a tendency not to discuss these concepts at all. More recently, these concepts have been introduced in some IS texts but, often, they are not discussed in sufficient detail; consequently they can appear very confusing to students because coupled with a lack of detail comes a lack of clarity. However, these concepts are important for both educators and researchers. In this chapter it is not appropriate to explore all the various ways in which these concepts are treated in IS texts, but it can be stated that it is generally the case that contemporary IS methodologies assume that some *analysts/practitioners* are going to do most of the job (even on a facilitative model). This straight-away implies a *subject-centred epistemology* and—correspondingly—a *problematic ontology*—basically along the lines of the Cartesian model of scientific enquiry. Williams (1978) provides a thorough explanation of the Cartesian project, but in straightforward terms, the analyst starts from a position of subjective ignorance and has to use his/her wits to discover what is the case in a complex and often confusing social (and technical) situation:

> Analysts work with their wits plus paper and pencil. That's about it. (DeMarco, 1979, p.12)

Notwithstanding the introduction of CASE tools, this statement remains fairly typical of most statements about the situation faced by analysts today. Now, although such accounts might seem *prima facie* to be a realistic description of the real situation, the underlying epistemological assumptions embodied in such accounts are necessarily of a *subject-centred epistemology*. But various other accounts of epistemology exist; some of these are subjective in orientation, while others are both objective but unsympathetic to logical positivism (e.g. Popper, 1979). Therefore the standard epistemological model usually employed in IS texts is not 'definitely the case' (in philosophical terms); moreover, many of the versions of epistemology that accept that a subjective model for epistemology is the most appropriate (e.g. Quine and Ullian, 1978, Haack, 1995) are not discussed by most IS academics at all. On the one hand, this situation gives IS practitioners an impoverished view of the relevant possibilities for practice; on the other, it could actually mislead students as to the various possibilities for IS research. Everitt and Fisher (1995) provide detail as to the genuine wealth of possibilities in this field—most of which are largely ignored in the IS literature. However, the subject-centred model is, most probably, appropriate to questions of the first two types (discussed in Section 3.1), but is not so useful to the third type, essentially because the subject-centred model is, in a key sense, a *researcher-based* model. *Infusing the utilisers of information systems with a vision* is not normally considered to be a research activity, and is arguably not a very well-understood issue *per se*.

It seems likely that understanding the process of infusing people with a vision will be an important issue for both research and teaching in IS in the near future, and that 'the vision thing' will play a key role in determining the outcomes of IS developments in organisations. If so a new approach—new to many IS researchers at any rate—to understanding the relationship between epistemology and ontology will be needed. It is possible that the relationship that will most usefully be considered is a dialectical one; especially if IS developments are considered to be, in part, causally responsible for the actual nature (structure, processes, etc.) of the organisations of both the present and the future (as has been argued previously).

Much of what has been written about epistemology and ontology (in IS) comes under the rubric of (various) discussions about the differences between hard and soft systems approaches to IS development (e.g. Lewis, 1994). In such discussions, there exists a powerful tendency to simplistically equate hard systems approaches with the method of positivistic natural science, and to equate soft systems approaches with some other sort(s) of social methodology(ies) in IS texts. Here, the problem is twofold. Firstly, the arguments put forward are, in fact, often cryptic and confusing to would-be researchers; secondly, they are presented as being 'definitely the case'.

However, much recent philosophy of science (and sociology of knowledge) argues that *science has no definite method* (e.g. Feyerabend, 1993; Rorty, 1980). Feyerabend's argument can be summed up as follows:

> Philosophers of Science such as Popper or Lakatos have tried to define 'The Scientific Method'. But Feyerabend has shown that if scientists had followed their methodologies modern science would never have advanced a single step beyond its medieval predecessors. Galileo would have had to abandon Copernican astronomy, Einstein would have given up relativity. This is not to say that scientists never follow any rules or that science is completely irrational and subjective. Although Feyerabend admits his affinity to the irrational, his point has always been more subtle: there are no rules that apply to all science at all times. As science progresses, the criteria by which new theories and observations are judged change along with these theories and observations. (Weber, 1993)

Furthermore, all the homilies about the virtues of interpretivism (e.g. Stowell, 1993) tend to ignore recent - and arguably important—developments in philosophy which castigate the value of subjective immediacy (i.e. that which the analyst immediately perceives to be the case). This (critical) tradition can, in fact, be traced back to the 1930s (see Adorno, 1973a, 1982), although this tradition is now more generally associated with Foucault (e.g. 1982) and other postmodern philosophers. The discipline of IS has been impoverished by the over-simplification of some of these key issues. More importantly, placing so much emphasis on subjective immediacy may be positively dangerous in an environment in which leadership is a key concept; there are numerous examples of such dangers embodied in the views of extreme political leaders (and their followers) in the twentieth-century. To effectively criticise highly politicised views one would ideally need an objective standpoint—and, if this is not available, a dialectical position may be the best that can be attained in practical research terms.

Changes in the IS agenda clearly necessitate a re-think of some core IS concepts. In any case the temptation to present only *one* view of any controversial issue as being definitely the case should be resisted by both educators and researchers. In this respect, both educators and researchers in IS need, minimally, to be more circumspect.

2.4   Towards a New Paradigm for IS Research

This section will go some way towards outlining the epistemological and ontological notions that should be utilised in IS research, if such research is to be relevant to gaining an understanding of the nature of information systems in modern organisations. The background for the work in this section lies in part in the author's previous research work (Probert, 1992). In this work a hard and a soft IS methodology were both critically studied using *interpretive analytics* as a research method; this method is based on the work of Michel Foucault (Dreyfus and Rabinov, 1982). The hard or structured IS methodology chosen for the critical study was the National Computing Centre's (NCC) Systems Analysis and Design Methodology (NCC 1984a, 1984b). The soft IS methodology chosen for the critical study was Soft Systems

Methodology (SSM) (Checkland, 1981; Checkland and Scholes, 1990).

It is generally recognised that the implementation of information systems can alter the distributions of power in organisations (e.g. between managers and users, or between IS managers and functional managers, etc.). One of the main aims of this research work was to gain an understanding of the power effects (in terms of alterations in the distribution of power) caused by *using* these methodologies—both on the methodology practitioners themselves and on the recipients of the products generated by the use of the methodology.

In Probert (1992) it was concluded that the NCC methodology is based on acquiring an extraordinarily detailed knowledge of the functions of any particular organisation. These functions, and the people who perform them, become the objects of a highly disciplined examination. The purpose of computerising these functions being to provide for an increase (and refinement) in the disciplinary power of the owners and managers of the organisation. This change in the distribution of power need not be aimed at by the owners and managers who select an IS methodology, rather it arises directly from the use of the techniques themselves. It was also argued that SSM aims at acquiring knowledge of the subjective dispositions of the actors in organisations (rather than knowledge of the organisation's functions) with a view to facilitating the control of the actions of the subordinates by management. In using SSM the actors in the organisation will be treated as if they were free to choose to do whatever they will, and are capable of being 'improved'. However, it was argued that there are crucial differences, between the freedom of management to manage, and the freedom of subordinates to resist the will of management, which are obscured by the techniques of SSM. The key point to make in this context is that, in *both* of the methodologies studied, *bona fide* discussions of contemporary concepts of epistemology and ontology were either conspicuous by their absence (NCC) or highly partial, and thoroughly muddled (SSM). Both methodologies were more concerned with designing managerial control mechanisms for people in the relevant organisations than they were with analysing or studying a situation with a view towards designing appropriate and responsible solutions to real problems (Probert, 1996a, 1996b).

IS methodologies are necessarily theoretical and abstract, and are based on some implicit (or, in a few cases, explicit) philosophy—in the sense of a taken-for-granted set of assumptions about the way the world is and how it can be modelled, etc. Although it might be possible to improve IS methodologies by using an empirical technique to find out what the actual effects of using a particular methodology are etc., the philosophy behind the actual IS research methods themselves cannot really be analysed or challenged in this way, and yet it would seem *a priori* that, to be efficacious, an IS research method ought to be founded on an explicit and reasonably coherent philosophical base—even assuming that IS practitioners are concerned with purely practical matters. In the discussions that follow, two central *practical* issues in IS analysis and design are considered, and these have, as their corollaries, two *philosophical* issues (of course, there may be other aspects of philosophy relevant to these practical issues). The two practical issues can be characterised as: issues concerned with how the analysts acquire *knowledge* of the existing system and of the user requirements, and issues concerned with the analysts' *intervention*. These two issues are correlated by philosophers' concerns with *epistemology* and *authenticity*. Reflective considerations on these two aspects may be used to inform proposals for a new IS research method. These two aspects will now be discussed.

2.4.1   IS Research and Epistemological Considerations

It is important to acknowledge that an *appropriate* distinction can be made between scientific and interpretive approaches to research in many disciplines, and that each approach has its appropriate corresponding subject matter. Both approaches are relevant to aspects of IS research, owing to the nature of the IS discipline being concerned with both the social and technical aspects of organisations, although they are relevant in different ways. One philosopher who considered that both approaches had (appropriate) validity was Adorno (1903-1969). However, more importantly, Adorno's work enables a sort of 'unified theory' of technology, culture, and administration to be put to work on investigating IS problems. What useful IS methodology would not need to take into account aspects of the organisational environment concerning *technology*, *culture*, and *administration*? Adorno does not identify science with technology, and this is also important. Such features are relevant to IS research in that, in many aspects of IS research, it is difficult to isolate the social and technical components of the area under investigation; in any case, it is somewhat reductionistic to attempt to separate the area of investigation into two component parts (social and technical). Here, a sort of unified theory (of technology and society) might prove beneficial.

Adorno was a key member of the Frankfurt School. Habermas, a second generation member, has attracted quite a few followers in information systems (e.g. Lyytinen and Klein, 1985). If respectable information systems work can be based on the work of Habermas then it can plausibly be based on the work of Adorno. It would be a difficult task to summarise Adorno's ideas on the technology/culture dimension easily, but essentially Adorno thought that culture (generally) has become a matter to be administered, and that technology has made this possible. The relevance for IS research is that such a view would generate a new, possibly more appropriate (but inevitably more complex), theory of the role that technology plays in shaping the culture of organisations (and vice versa). As Scarbrough and Corbett note:

> ... [T]he relationship between technology and organisation is neither one of 'impacts' [of IT] nor of 'choice' [made by managers] *per se*. Rather, technology and organisation are closely intertwined through flows of knowledge and ideas which transcend the individual organisation but which find expression in, and are reinforced by, political interests and agendas at the organisational level. (Scarbrough and Corbett, 1992, p.157)

If Scarbrough and Corbett are even approximately right, then it would seem *prima facie* that simplistic distinctions between hard and soft systems approaches to IS development will not be adequate forms of conceptualisation for IS development *and* utilisation—two notions which themselves may be much more intertwined than is often acknowledged (see e.g. Fitzgerald, 1990, Paul, 1995). As Gardner *et al.* (1995) argue, the need now is for tailorable information systems to be put in place; in such systems the concepts of 'developer' and 'user' (and 'technology' and 'organisation') are increasingly blurred:

> A computer system is tailorable if it provides a user with control over its operation. This means a user should be able to regulate or operate the system, thus providing ultimate power to direct or manipulate a system's behaviour... A control is understood to be a device or interface widget that enables a user to regulate or operate a system and provides the user with the power to direct or determine its state. (Gardner, *et al.*, 1995, p.187)

Such considerations from the world of IS practice have important implications for IS research methods also. A 'binary opposition' view of the distinction between 'positivism' and 'interpretivism' is surely inappropriate when the 'objects' in the research area contain such 'intertwinings' between technical and social aspects; the *tailorability* of an IS is surely an *emergent property* of the possibilities (and the constraints) created by the definite technical 'configurations', and the actual social arrangements, pertaining in the situation.

However, although it would be possible to develop a more integrated theory of the social and technical aspects of information systems based on Adorno's *oeuvre*, it should not be thought that Adorno's ideas can be straightforwardly employed to develop IS research methods; numerous dangers would lie in store for a researcher taking such a simplistic approach:

> [Adorno's theses]... have a legitimate claim on the students of contemporary culture. In elaborating the nature and extent of that claim, two extremes need to be avoided. First, ... is the self-satisfied dismissal of Adorno as an unnecessarily gloomy and elitist dead German whose preoccupations might be understandable in biographical terms, but which 'we' have left behind. However, it would do no service to Adorno's conception of the critical analysis of culture to turn him into a public monument ... there should be no 'Adornoism'. The nature and extent of Adorno's claim to attention must always be contingent on the degree to which his work can illuminate contemporary developments in culture, polity and society ... an assessment must identify core themes in Adorno's analysis which continue to merit attention and to warrant further development. (Crook, 1994, p.18)

It should be noted that some other researchers' works are relevant to the work outlined herein. Some important 'new' researchers have emerged embodying (various degrees of) the Adornean tradition. Sloterdijk (1987) has written about the cynical condition (which in some ways links the concerns of Foucault to those of Adorno). Jameson (1990) also links the concerns of Foucault to Adorno, and this allows systemic connections to be made to the earlier work undertaken in Probert (1992). As it not appropriate to attempt to provide full details of Adorno's key ideas here (see Jay, 1984 for a useful summary), merely the essence of Adorno's epistemic considerations will be outlined below.

Adorno considers that there is a legitimate separation between the *subjects* (who carry out research) and the *objects* in the study, but generally this distinction is not made in an appropriate manner:

> The separation of subject and object is both real and illusory. True, because in the cognitive realm it serves to express the real separation, the dichotomy of the human condition, a coercive development. False, because the resulting separation must not be hypostatised, not magically transformed into an invariant. (Adorno, 1978, pp.498-499)

Adorno considers that 'the subject' makes possible the idea of critique—of a critical interpretation of reality. But the concept of 'the subject' is an intellectual construction—an abstraction— *derived from* (and not *prior to*) actual, real, living individuals:

> It is evident that the abstract concept of the transcendental subject—its thought forms, their unity, and the original productivity of consciousness—presupposes what it promises to bring about: actual, live individuals. (Adorno, 1978, p.500)

It should be noted that this was a Nietzschean argument (e.g. Nietzsche, 1956, pp.178-180), and this debt is acknowledged by Adorno (1982). Although we can treat the subject as real (or 'standing in for' real, live individuals), in Adorno's view the subject does not 'make the world up' (this is often termed 'constructivism'—Adorno uses the term 'constitute' instead of *construct*):

> While our images of perceived reality may very well be *Gestalten* [*Weltanschaunngen*—in SSM jargon], the world in

which we live is not; it is constituted differently than out of mere images of perception (Adorno, 1977, p.126)

However, Adorno does not argue for a return to vulgar objectivism, because this would deny the possibility of a critical interpretation of the objective circumstances. The objective world is real enough, but what we see is always *mediated* by concepts (although we may not be aware of this all of the time):

> What must be eliminated is the illusion that ... the totality of consciousness, is the world, and not the self-contemplation of knowledge. The last thing the critique of epistemology ... is supposed to do is proclaim unmediated objectivism. (Adorno, 1982, p.27)

In the earlier quotation (above) concerning 'perceived reality', what Adorno means by 'constituted differently' is that the world is, to a large extent, determined by economic realities, which he sometimes refers to using the term 'exchange':

> The living human individual, as he is forced to act in the role for which he has been marked internally as well, is the *homo oeconomicus* incarnate, closer to the transcendental subject than to the living individual for which he immediately cannot but take himself... What shows up in the doctrine of the transcendental subject is the priority of the relations— abstractly rational ones, detached from the human individuals and their relationships—that have their model in exchange. If the exchange form is the standard social structure, its rationality constitutes people; what they are for themselves, what they seem to be for themselves, is secondary. (Adorno, 1978, p.501)

For Adorno (as for IS professionals) the world of economic activity is very real:

> Somebody pays for what analysts and designers deliver. New systems have to be justified by the benefits that they deliver. It is easy to use terms like 'the users' and 'user management' ... and forget that they are subtitles for 'the customer'. (Yeates *et al.*, 1994, p.2)

In fact, the systems analyst should be seen *not* purely as some sort of enquiring transcendental subject, *but* as an economically-constituted actuality. Adorno argued that critique is only possible if some status is given to the subject who can become critically aware of these sort of circumstances. Therefore Adorno preserves a critical role for the subject:

> To use the strength of the subject to break through the fallacy of constitutive subjectivity ... Stringently to transcend the official separation of pure philosophy and the substantive or formally scientific realm ... (Adorno, 1973b, p.xx)

At the very least, the economic activities which generate systems development projects have a key determining role on the analysts' foci of attention in the project; systems analysts do not generate knowledge purely in the interest of advancing science.

Mark Poster summarises the 'economic/epistemic' problem for computer science research thus:

> Since computers are useful objects to industry and government, computer 'scientists' are especially sensitive to the question of the epistemological purity of their discipline. Louis Fein, writing to the *Communications of the Association for Computing Machinery*, insistently articulates his distress with the ambiguous status of his field: 'like other sciences, our science should maintain its sole abstract purpose of advancing truth and knowledge. It is not clear to me that an organisation can play simultaneously the role of a profession, of an industry, and of a science.' (Poster, 1990, p.147)

And the same is true for IS, as IS encompasses all three elements (a profession, and industry, and a sort of crypto-science). Therefore IS research needs a method that can tackle these three aspects. What is needed are techniques for analysing the actual relationships that appertain between the *subjects* conducting the analysis, and the *objects* in the study. Here, 'objects' should be understood as meaning all the various items that need to be analysed in the organisation; the term is not used here in the sense that it is used by the advocates of object orientation.

It has long been recognised that the interventions, made by systems analysts, themselves alter the current system in some way or other. What is currently lacking are the critical means to frame our understandings of these situations; owing to the tendency to adhere to a binary-opposition view of IS research methodologies as being positivistic or interpretivistic; most likely derived from the seminal work of Burrell and Morgan (1979). The problem with this binary view is that neither approach is adequate to analysing the actuality of IS practice, as experienced by IS professionals.

The positivistic approaches do not give sufficient emphasis to the active role of the analyst-as-intervener; the analyst is considered to be detached from personal concerns with the situation being analysed. The interpretivistic IS research methods have their history rooted in the phenomenological epistemological stance (usually associated with Edmund Husserl, see Bernet *et al.*, 1993, for details); such approaches effectively remove the possibility that the analyst might be able to stand back from the situation sufficiently to critically understand his or her role as intervener, as the analyst is considered as being both totally immersed in the situation and, simultaneously, condemned to an epistemological solipsism in which the very appearance of immersion is reduced to being purely a matter of his or her internal perception. Furthermore, it does nothing to improve matters to say that these internal perceptions are causal reflections of the analyst's own will (this argument is more fully developed in Probert, 1994). Consequently, a way out of this impass is clearly required. Although we are (often) totally immersed in organisational situations, nevertheless we are all sometimes able to see problems with the actually existing set of arrangements. By generating a philosophically robust technique for developing critical analyses of current IS practices, some greater clarity and precision can be brought to our understanding of those practices, and consequently the possibilities for improving the current arrangements will therefore be better informed.

2.4.2 Actuality and IS

Before discussing this issue fully, at this juncture it is worth discussing the facile tendency to treat information systems as, by and large, subjective constructs. This approach is largely a product of the SSM advocates (e.g. Checkland, 1981; Checkland and Scholes, 1990; Lewis, 1994). However, the supposed intellectual basis for such a manoeuvre does not seem to support such an endeavour. Husserl himself thought that to trivialise objective realities by (discursively) rendering them as social constructs was a wholly illegitimate move:

> ... [T]here is a certain disadvantage involved in saying, 'there is only absolute consciousness', as if one wished to say: all other being is only seeming... This would, of course, be *fundamentally false*. The objects of nature are evidently true objects. Their being is true being... It is fundamentally false to apply to such being a standard other [than] the one it itself requires in accordance with its category and to discredit something because it is 'constituted' or rooted in consciousness. (Husserl, cited in Bernet *et al.*, p.57)

No such attempt will be made herein to reduce information systems to subjective constructs, although subjective judgements clearly have a role to play within the discipline of IS, as will become apparent in the later discussion on *authenticity*. The constant lurching between the (supposed) binary opposites of subjectivism and objectivism, once again, lies at the root of the problem, and treating information systems as subjective constructs is certainly to fall into the trap of all subjectivist philosophy; the trap of needing to pose real-worlds behind the apparent world. Information systems are not purely subjective constructs—they have objective features such as processors, storage media, etc. (i.e. *hardware*); there is a good reason why they should not be construed as worlds behind mere appearances. To do so would give these features an almost magical unintelligibilty—and gives us a feeling of powerlessness in the face of the unknown (and, on a subjectivists view, unknowable):

> He who interprets by searching behind the phenomenal world for a world-in-itself (*Welt an sich*) which forms its foundation and support, acts mistakenly like someone who wants to find in the riddle the reflection of a being which lies behind it, a being mirrored in the riddle, in which it is contained. (Adorno, 1977, p.127)

It may well be a sensible strategy to treat the computer as a black box, if this results in an increase in the practitioners abilities to design new information systems with greater freedom than would otherwise be the case. But, if the final design is to utilise a computer, then surely it would be beneficial to understand (broadly) the capabilities of the technology that is to be utilised.

The question of the actuality of the academic discipline of IS is, though, not the same question as that of the actuality of information systems themselves. The former is a question of purpose, the latter a question of discourse and reality. There are probably as many definitions of information systems as there are texts on the subject. Recently, the UK Academy for Information Systems has tried to provide a general definition of the domain for academic study of information systems:

> The study of information systems and their development is a multi-disciplinary subject and addresses the range of strategic, managerial and operational activities involved in the gathering, processing, storing, distributing and use of information, and its associated technologies, in society and organisations. (UKAIS, 1995, p.3)

Although this is a broad definition, it can be seen that its subject matter is already assumed to exist. As has been argued previously, this seems fair—as people routinely refer to information systems (and this is not to be conflated with the way some people refer to unicorns or pink elephants). What is referred to (by managers, users, and information systems specialists), is referred to as *actual* (unlike unicorns and pink elephants). Therefore, the criterion for the existence of a *bona fide* academic discipline of IS depends on *its potential adequacy for being able to answer key questions concerning information systems* in the sense outlined by the UKAIS above, and not its actual ability to do so right now. If one considers medicine (as a discipline), then this criterion can be explicated somewhat. In medical research, it is not a case of whether or not it can prescribe cures for all diseases, but whether it is competent to search for cures for many presently incurable diseases.

Many (and perhaps most) philosophical problems remain unsolved, but most would agree that it is a respectable academic discipline. Adorno phrases the key question (concerning philosophy) thus:

> By 'actuality' is understood not its vague 'maturity' or immaturity on the basis of non-binding conceptions regarding the general intellectual situation, but much more:

whether, after the failure of the last great efforts, there exists an adequacy between the philosophic questions and the possibility of their being answered at all ... the question is in no way rhetorical, but should be taken very literally. (Adorno, 1977, p.124)

So, for information systems to have a *purpose* as an academic discipline it ought, minimally, to ask questions which have the potential to be answered. Given that information systems are created and managed it appears that questions related to the creation or management of information systems are *bona fide* questions, and that therefore information systems has a basic right to exist as a discipline. Although, one may well suspect that its current answers to such questions often seem inadequate, surely no other discipline is better-placed to provide such answers in the future. Of course, this is not to guarantee that answers to many IS research questions will be found, just as medical research may not be able to provide a cure for the common cold!

2.4.3   The Nature of Authenticity in IS Interventions

IS is complicated by the need to adopt positions on, and give recommendations about, IS *practice*. One key problem here is that IS analysts and designers have to *intervene* in organisations (and thereby intervene in the lives of the members of those organisations). Whether they choose to do in (what will be characterised as) an *authentic* manner is an important issue for IS research. Firstly, to characterise the concept of authenticity, a brief explanation will be given. Given that there is a lack of absolute guidance as to how one is to act in any given situation, the question of 'what should one do...?' raises severe difficulties. Some sorts of authenticity questions may be familiar to the readers of this chapter. As a consultant, the author experienced several authenticity problems, a few are given as example questions here:

1. Should I use a methodology which has embedded values that I do not agree with?
2. Should I use a methodology which, in my judgement, is wholly inappropriate to the circumstances pertaining in the organisation?

3. Should I attempt to improve organisation performance by introducing greater accountability in a low-wage organisation?

These are difficult ethical questions, and while some of these may be covered by the codes of conduct and practice of professional IS bodies, others may not be (see Walsham, 1996). Also, such decisions require degrees of interpretation, and therefore judgements about such matters are likely to vary from person to person. In any case, not all IS practitioners are members of professional societies, and not all those members may be aware of the codes of conduct and practice, and no doubt some will choose to ignore such things. More importantly, adherence to any such code is unlikely to be practically *enforceable*; adherence will therefore have to be granted voluntarily by the IS professionals concerned:

> In the scientific community the medical specialist has better defined ethical codes than most other groups... They are also enforced by powerful sanctions such as expulsion from the medical profession if serious infringements occur. Many other professionals, including the British Computer Society, have also drawn up ethical codes but these are often vague and difficult to apply and enforce... Ethical responsibilities will also vary both with the nature of work that is being carried out and the nature of the social environment where the work is conducted. (Mumford, 1995, p.6)

Ultimately, the value of ethical codes *per se* can be neatly summarised by an 1849 quotation from Thoreau (concerning the value of law itself):

> Must the citizen ever for a moment, or in the least degree, resign his conscience to the legislator? Why has every man a conscience then? I think that we should be men first, and subjects afterward. It is not desirable to cultivate a respect for the law, so much as for the right. The only obligation which I have the right to assume, is to do at any time what I think is right. It is truly enough said, that a corporation has no conscience; but a corporation of conscientious men is a corporation *with* a conscience. Law never made a man a whit more just; and, by means of their respect for it, even the well

disposed are daily made the agents of injustice. (Thoreau, 1995, p.4)

Because the value of ethical codes are limited, the sorts of questions characterised above (which all IS professionals must probably face from time to time) may best be understood as questions of *personal authenticity*, rather than being understood as strictly *ethical* questions. Indeed, it has been suggested that:

[T]he concept of authenticity is a protest against the blind, mechanical acceptance of an externally imposed code of values. (Golomb, 1995, p.11)

The concept of authenticity is often primarily connected to considerations put forward by Nietzsche (1844-1900):

There is a term Nietzsche himself rarely employs, but which is the most suitable label for a constant object of his philosophical concern—'authenticity'... Nietzsche's question could now be posed as follows: 'How to live authentically ... comfortable acceptance of inherited values, or comfortable evasions of questions of value, will both do the trick. But these are not authentic alternatives... (Cooper, 1983, p.2-3)

Cooper elaborates the concept of authenticity via some examples from teaching. He explicates the problems thus:

A familiar disturbance felt by the teacher arises when some of these [educational] policies, values, or whatever, are not ones to which he can subscribe... The disturbance produces a problem of authenticity, for unless the teacher resigns or is willing to invite considerable friction at work, he must simulate agreement to views that are not his. [Alternatively] ... The thought which may strike the teacher is not that he cannot subscribe to, or authoritatively transmit, various beliefs and values, but that he has slipped into, fallen into, unreflective acceptance of them. They have become part of the school's furniture; they go with the job like the free stationery. (Cooper, 1983, p.4)

Such questions are intensely personal, and researching how IS professionals deal (or should deal) with such questions as arise in IS practice will be necessary if real progress is to be made towards the aim of improving IS practice. Such considerations would need to be embodied within the philosophy of a new IS research method which would have to break the binary opposition of positivism and interpretivism, and allow for the causal influence of real economic factors while allocating a genuine role for subjective reflections and intentions. Again, a dialectical approach (and one that tightly connects the authenticity issues with the epistemic possibilities) might succeed here:

> Dialectically conceived 'subjectivity' is historically formed and yet not reducible to historical determinations; historical subjectivity is reconstructed from the framework of reflective critique in that the limits of constitutive synthesis establish the range of possible experience. Only in such reflective reconstruction of the genesis of subjectivity is it possible to distinguish between real possibilities and those modes of appearance that are but abstract illusions ... So conceived, the dialectical notion of subjectivity is a fundamental category of critical reason. In reflective reconstructions of self-formation processes, it is possible to show the pseudo-necessity of socially unnecessary motives and to thereby promote a reversal of consciousness that can dissolve the causality of these objective illusions. (Schroyer, 1973, pp.xii-xiii)

If there are any genuine possibilities for improving IS practice by (disseminating the results of) IS research it needs to be determined what these possibilities actually are, and how they can be realised by those who would have to achieve those possibilities in the real-world.

By adopting this approach a great deal of controversy about theory and practice in IS can be avoided. However, it will be worth conducting a brief analysis about this aspect to indicate why this is so.

2.4.4   The Dialectical Nature of Theory and Practice in IS

In many disciplines, there are *interactions* between theory and practice, e.g. economics:

> Some bits of economic theory have always remained just that—theory, interesting and no doubt clever, but with no

practical relevance. Other bits started out as theory but have become the bread and butter of practical economics. The role of prices in affecting both demand and supply is a central theme of all economic analysis, not just among economists but also politicians. (Pennant-Rea and Crook, 1986, p.159)

It seems clear that there should be similar interactions in IS, and there is no reason to see any great dichotomy between theory and practice in IS—neither could really exist without the other (except, possibly, practice). Theory and practice can also be seen as dialectically related.

Of course, such a conception of information systems as has been given may seem both over-elaborate and unnecessarily complex. It has been argued that such complexity is unavoidable, but adopting a dialectical position between both subjectivity and objectivity, and theory and practice, in IS, will probably make studies more difficult to carry out than they would be if a simplistic subjective or objective stance were taken. As discussed earlier, in the section entitled 'the epiphenomenalistic fallacy', there is an intertwining relationship between the subject matter of some academic disciplines and those disciplines themselves. The examples given were of social-scientific disciplines, however, even in physics such a view has been propounded—although the standard (common sense) view would be of a static conception of ontology, which can be described as *mechanistic materialism*, coupled with (what then turns out to be) a puzzling ontological realm of *free agents*:

> On this [standard, common sense] view physical facts do not possess 'meanings'—though we may still speak of clouds as 'ominous'... Such a picture of the world is strongly confirmed by our technological progress. Common sense also treats people as conscious agents, possessing beliefs and desires, and capable of acting freely. This sort of talk does not seem to fit in with the metaphysics of mechanistic realism... scientists conceive of themselves as designing experiments, carrying out tests and deciding whether to accept theories—conceptions that presuppose that they are free, conscious, rational agents. (Powers, 1982, pp.2-3)

In the earlier discussion, physics was used as an example to illustrate the possibility of a static conception of a discipline's subject matter. But even in this discipline, a dialectical approach has been proposed to overcome the inherent dualism (and the *prima facie* incompatibilism) of mechanistic materialism and free agency:

> The elastic and metaphysical scheme known as *dialectical materialism* attempts to overcome some of these difficulties. It differs from mechanistic materialism in asserting an inexhaustible variety of forms into which matter evolves and in insisting that at new levels of evolution new properties and new laws of behaviour 'emerge'. The general 'laws of the development of matter' proposed by dialectical materialism echo the laws of development of human history propounded by 'historical materialism'. This makes it possible to think of human beings as part of nature without reducing them to mere mechanisms, although this still leaves the puzzle of 'free will' unresolved. Methodologically it encourages scientists to study the different 'levels of matter', freeing them from the obligation to 'reduce' the behaviour of complex systems to the laws and properties of elementary particle physics. (Powers, 1982, pp.3-4)

An example of the dialectical emergence of a new reality would be *cyberspace*. According to Sterling (1992), the term *cyberspace* was invented by William Gibson, a writer of science-fiction. The term is used to describe the 'virtual world' (another neologism!) where electronic-informational activity is said to take place:

> ... [T]he world of electronic communications, now made visible through the computer screen, could no longer be usefully regarded as just a tangle of high-tech wiring. Instead it had become a *place*, cyberspace, which demanded a new set of metaphors, a new set of rules and behaviours. The term ... struck a useful chord, and this concept of cyberspace was picked up by *Time, Scientific American*, computer police, hackers, and even constitutional scholars. 'Cyberspace' now seems likely to become a permanent fixture of the language. (Sterling, 1992, p.247)

Whether it is permanent, or merely transitory obviously remains to be seen, nevertheless *cyberspace* is a reality that arises from the dialectical interactions between the social and technical aspects of life in this era. In a sense, new realities tend to annihilate older ones. In this respect it is important that IS as a discipline proceeds to critically annihilate older interpretations of reality; one example of such a change of interpretation would be that of Zuboff's attempt to persuade the managers of organisations to 'informate' rather than to 'automate' (Zuboff, 1988). In this respect, theory and practice will have to relate closely to one another—indeed they may be seen as two sides of the same coin, rather than being seen as binary opposites:

> The interpretation of a given reality and its abolition are connected to each other, not, of course, in the sense that reality is negated in the concept, but that out of the construction of a configuration of reality the demand for its [reality's] real change always follows promptly. The change-causing gesture of the riddle process—not its mere resolution as such—provides the image of resolutions to which materialist praxis alone has access. Materialism has named this relationship with a name that is philosophically certified: dialectic.... It is superfluous to separate out explicitly a conception of pragmatism, in which theory and praxis entwine with each other as they do in the dialectic. (Adorno, 1977, p.129)

Finally, in this context, it is important to note the political nature of information systems as a discipline. This arises from the fact that control of information has often been linked to the managerial control processes in organisations (e.g. Zuboff, 1988). It follows that, basically speaking, one's work in this field can either be motivated by a desire to liberate or a desire to enslave (or, perhaps, somewhere in between). Again, this raises questions of personal authenticity—in this case of the IS researcher. But as some of these issues have been discussed earlier (in the context of practitioner choices) it seems unnecessary to raise them again.

2.5   Conclusion

It has been argued that the nature of IS as a discipline implies that new approaches to IS research are required; this means that new IS research methods, capable of providing an adequate framework for the analysis of the key issues that arise in the discipline, need to be developed. Two problems arising in IS practice have been related to two aspects of philosophical investigation. The work of Adorno is introduced as providing a way forward for the endeavour of improving IS research methods. It has also been argued that IS researchers should be aware of the socio-political nature of their research efforts, and the concept of authenticity has been introduced as a means of interpreting these aspects of IS practice and research.

Furthermore, notwithstanding which particular approach to IS research is adopted by the researcher, it has been argued that IS *is an academic discipline*—and it is likely to remain so for some time to come. However, considerable work remains to be done before IS can be treated as an established discipline. Firstly, although it is unlikely that a single approach to the study of IS will emerge triumphantly, it will be necessary to develop research methods *unique* to IS; such methods should reflect the genuine ontological status of information systems in the world (both social and technical aspects; both subjective and objective features). Secondly, a number of contentious issues will need to be addressed, such as on whose behalf is IS research to be undertaken? It is unlikely that IS as a discipline will be seen as having a single *purpose* (this is one reason why a single *method* of IS research is unlikely to be triumphant). Is IS research to be conducted for owners of information systems, developers of information systems, or users of information systems (or other stakeholders)? These are open questions, and the authenticity of a particular researcher's motives can never be guaranteed in a complex and all too often coercive world.

References

Adorno, T.W., 1973a, *The Jargon of Authenticity*, Routledge and Kegan Paul, London.

Adorno, T.W., 1973b, *Negative Dialectics*, Routledge, London.

Adorno, T.W., 1977, The actuality of philosophy, *Telos* 31:120-133.

Adorno, T.W., 1978, Subject and object, in *The Essential Frankfurt School Reader*, A. Arato and E. Gebhardt, eds., Blackwell, Oxford, 497-511.

Adorno, T.W., 1982, *Against Epistemology: A Metacritique*, Blackwell, Oxford.

Bernet, R., Kern, I. and Marbach, E., 1993, *An Introduction to Husserlian Phenomenology*, Northwestern University Press, Evanston.

Boehm, B., 1976, Software engineering, *IEEE Computer.* C-25(12), 1226-1241.

Burrell, G., and Morgan, G., 1979, *Sociological Paradigms and Organisational Analysis*, Heinemann, London.

Checkland, P., 1981, *Systems Thinking, Systems Practice*, Wiley, Chichester.

Checkland, P., and Scholes, J., 1990, *Soft Systems Methodology in Action*, Wiley, Chichester

Cooper, D.E., 1983, *Authenticity and Learning*, Routledge and Kegan Paul, London.

Crook, S., 1994, Introduction: Adorno and authoritarian irrationalism, in *The Stars Down to Earth and Other Essays on the Irrational in Culture*, T. W. Adorno, Routledge, London, 1-33.

DeMarco, T., 1979, *Structured Analysis and System Specification*, Yourdon Press, Englewood Cliffs.

Donaldson, P., 1978, *Economics of the Real World* (2nd edition), Pelican, London.

Dreyfus, H.L., and Rabinov, P., 1982, *Michel Foucault: Beyond Structuralism and Hermeneutics*, Harvester, Brighton.

Earl, M.J., 1989, *Management Strategies for Information Technology*, Prentice Hall International, Hemel Hempstead.

Everitt, N., and Fisher, A., 1995, *Modern Epistemology*, McGraw-Hill, New York.

Feyerabend, P., 1993, *Against Method* (2nd edition), Verso, London.

Fitzgerald, G., 1990, Achieving flexible information systems: the case for improved analysis, *Journal. of Information Technology* 5:5-11.

Foucault, M., 1982, The subject and power, afterword, in *Michel Foucault: Beyond Structuralism and Hermeneutics*, H.L. Dreyfus and P. Rabinov, Harvester, Brighton.

Gardner, L.A., Paul, R.J., and Patel, N., 1995, Moving beyond the fixed point theorem with tailorable information systems, in *Proceedings of the 3rd European Conference on Information Systems*, Athens/Greece, 1-3 June, G. Doukidis, B. Galliers, T. Jelassi, H. Krcmar and F. Land, eds., 183-192.

Golomb, J., 1995, *In Search of Authenticity*, Routledge, London.

Haack, S., 1995, *Evidence and Inquiry*, Blackwell, Oxford.

Hammer, M., and Champy, J., 1994, *Reengineering the Corporation*, Nicholas Brealey, London.

Handy, C., 1989, *The Age of Unreason* (2nd edition), Arrow, London.

Horn, J., 1995, Epiphenomenalism, in *The Oxford Companion to Philosophy*, T. Honderich, ed., Oxford University Press, Oxford.

Jameson, F., 1990, *Late Marxism*, Verso, London.

Jay, M., 1984, *Adorno*, Fontana, London.

Jones, R., 1990, Educational practices and scientific knowledge: a genealogical reinterpretation of the emergence of physiology in post-revolutionary France, in *Foucault and Education*, S. J.Ball, ed., Routledge, London, 57-77.

Kling, R. ed., 1996, *Computerization and Controversy* (2nd edition), Academic Press, San Diego.

Lewis, P., 1994, *Information-Systems Development*, Pitman, London.

Livingstone, D.N., 1994, Lost in space, *Times Higher*, 11 March: 15.

Lyytinen, K.J., and Klein, H.K., 1985, The critical theory of Jurgen Habermas as a basis for a theory of information systems, in *Research Methods in Information Systems*, E. Mumford, R. Hirschheim, G. Fitzgerald, and A. T. Wood-Harper, eds., North-Holland, Amsterdam, 219-236.

MacRae, D.G., 1987, *Weber*, Fontana, London.

Mumford, E., 1995, Human development, ethical behaviour and systems design, in *Information Systems Development 1995*, N. Jayaratna, R. Miles, Y. Merali and S. Probert, eds., BCS Publications, Swindon, 1-15.

Nietzsche, F. 1956, *The Birth of Tragedy and the Genealogy of Morals*, Doubleday, New York.

NCC, 1984a, Systems Analysis Techniques, NCC Training, Manchester.

NCC, 1984b, Systems Design Techniques, NCC Training, Manchester.

Parsons, T., 1974, The life and work of Emile Durkheim, in *Sociology and Philosophy*, E. Durkheim, The Free Press, New York, xliii-lxx.

Paul, R.J., 1995, An O.R. view of information systems development, in *Operational Research Tutorial Papers 1995*, M. Lawrence and C. Wilsdon, eds., Operational Research Society, Birmingham, 46-56.

Pennant-Rea, R., and Crook, C., 1986, *The Economist Economics*, Penguin, Harmondsworth.

Popper, K.R., 1979, *Objective Knowledge* (2nd edition), Oxford University Press, Oxford.

Poster, M., 1990, *The Mode of Information*, Polity Press, Cambridge.

Powers, J., 1982, *Philosophy and the New Physics*, Methuen, London.

Probert, S.K., 1992, A Critical Study of the National Computing Centre's Systems Analysis and Design Methodology, and Soft Systems Methodology, Unpublished MPhil thesis, University of Northumbria.

Probert, S.K., 1994, On the models of the meanings (and the meanings of the models) in Soft Systems Methodology, in *Information Systems Methodologies 1994*, C. Lissoni, T. Richardson, R. Miles, A. T. Wood-Harper, and N. Jayaratna, eds., BCS Publications, Swindon, 185-194.

Probert, S.K., 1996a, Structured systems analysis and modern organisations: no space for systems integration, in *Systems Integration 96 Conference Proceedings*, J. Pour and J. Vorisek, eds., Prague University of Economics, Prague, 17-31.

Probert, S.K., 1996b, A genealogical study of managerial authority (as portrayed in Soft Systems Methodology) and its consequences for information systems analysis, in *Lessons Learned from the Use of Methodologies: Information Systems Methodologies 1996*, N. Jayaratna and B. Fitzgerald eds., BCS Publications, Swindon, 41-56.

Quine, W.V., and Ullian, J., 1978, *The Web of Belief* (2nd edition), Random House, New York.

Rorty, R., 1980, *Philosophy and the Mirror of Nature*, Oxford University Press, Oxford.

Scarbrough, H., and Corbett, J., 1992, *Technology and Organisation*, Routledge, London.

Schroyer, T., 1973, Foreword, in T. Adorno, *The Jargon of Authenticity*, Routledge and Kegan Paul, London, vii-xxii.

Sloterdijk, P., 1987, *Critique of Cynical Reason*, Verso, London.

Sterling, B., 1992, *The Hacker Crackdown*, Viking, London.

Stowell, F., 1993, Hermeneutics and Organisational Inquiry, *Systemist*, 15(2):87-103.

Thompson, K., 1982, *Durkheim*, Routledge, London.

Thoreau, H. D., 1995, *Civil Disobedience and Reading*, Penguin, London.

UKAIS, 1995, Information systems — subject definition and scope, *UKAIS Newsletter*. 1(3): 3.

Walsham, G., 1996, Ethical theory, codes of ethics and IS practice. *Info Systems Journal* 6(1):69-81.

Winfield, I., 1991, *Organisations and Information Technology*, Blackwell Scientific, Oxford.

Weber, M., 1993, The 'anything goes' philosopher, *Times Higher.*, Vol. 1101, 15.

Williams, B., 1978, *Descartes: The Project of Pure Enquiry*, Penguin, Harmondsworth.

Yeates, D., Shields, M., and Helmy, D., 1994, *Systems Analysis and Design*, Pitman, London.

Zuboff, S., 1988, *In the Age of the Smart Machine*, Heinemann, Oxford.

Chapter 3

DISCIPLINE AND CRITIQUE: THE CASE OF INFORMATION SYSTEMS

Martin Spaul

3.1 Introduction

Academic disciplines vary along many dimensions; one of the most important to those working within them is the degree of solidity that characterises a discipline, a sense that their work is both necessary and permanent. At one end of this spectrum lie disciplines that we feel could not help but exist; something very odd would have happened to our culture if, for example, physics ceased to exist as an academic study. Other disciplines seem solid from our current perspective, but are in fact the result of recent historical accident. It comes as a surprise to those who were thrashed through the study of the classics of English literature during their schooldays that—as a formal, critical discipline—it dates only from the beginning of this century, when the authorities of Oxford and Cambridge universities decided that the 'young ladies' who they were admitting in increasing numbers could not withstand the rigours of Classics and required a less taxing alternative. At the far end of this spectrum lie those disciplines that attract general scepticism, if not outright mock, as an illustration of the self-serving nature of academic institutions. The public pillorying which attended the recent creation of a media studies option in Oxford University's English literature degree—merely following a common, and lucrative, *zeitgeist*—is a case in point (Lawson, 1995). No one enjoys mockery and mistrust, and any would-be discipline, struggling at the far end of this spectrum, aspires to more security and respect and is prepared to expend the effort required to earn it. Thus it has been with information systems which, in a series of reflective publications (including Liebenau and Backhouse (1989), in the high-profile forum of the *Times Higher*) has directed considerable effort to establishing an intellectual territory to call its own, along with the public recognition as a profession that it is felt to warrant. Since this process has an almost inexorable logic that will be played out to exhaustion or success, this essay is an attempt to record some of the intellectual possibilities that may be lost or suppressed in the pursuit of disciplinary integrity—a process calculated to marginalise unconventional or nomadic forms of thought.[1]

The form taken by this chapter is that of the humanistic essay, rather than a rigorously academic argument. This form has been adopted in the belief that the consideration of something as nebulous as the formation of a discipline—especially by those normally immersed in the working practices of that discipline—is best pursued outside the normal constrictions of the academic process. This essay will, then, consider the would-be discipline of IS from a number of viewpoints; each identified by a figure of thought drawn from the 'critical theory' of the Frankfurt school (see, e.g. Kellner, 1989). No particular doctrinal attachment is intended by this process; it is adopted simply because critical theory has a quality that Rorty (1980) famously identified in Foucault: that of being an 'all-purpose subversive'. Critical thought serves to generate perspectives that upset customary assumptions and challenge the commonplace views of the world into which mass, bureaucratised academia is apt to fall. This essay attempts to tour a number of issues surrounding a disciplinary definition for IS: the tension between the attempt to create a 'well-founded science' as the basis of IS and the turbulent social forces—technological, economic and political that surround that attempt; the tension between the discipline's requirement for a commodified, exclusive expertise and the growing democratisation of information technology; and the possibility of a problem-oriented form of thought directed at information and information technology that resists codification. This tour will, of necessity, be impressionistic, partial and controversial; which is partly the point—its purpose will have been served if it generates argument.

Writing in a forum such as this seems to presuppose that, in some sense, the foundations of a discipline exist and have been

---

[1] This term bears more than an intuitive weight. See Deleuze and Guattari (1988), and later in the Chapter.

glimpsed by those working within it; and that the real task is to bring them to light for the purposes of curriculum development, the definition of professional competence, etc. Any expression of scepticism has to use the very term—information systems—which it doubts has a signification. This essay is written from a perspective that recognises that there are a set of overlapping themes and concerns that link the most hard-headed computer scientist, working in the laboratories of MIT or Yorktown Heights, through the most outrageous of cyberpunks celebrating the emergence of a society of cyborgs in the pages of *Wired* magazine, to the citizen who is the bemused victim or beneficiary of IT. What is done with these themes and concerns is a matter of conscious choice on the part of those with the power to shape academic, social and political agendas. Arguing for the formation of a discipline is a voluntary, consequential act; and one that should be examined, as far as possible, from a disinterested position.

3.2   Academia and a Science of Information

3.2.1   *Motif*: Science and Ideology

Max Horkheimer, in an essay setting out a programme and philosophy for the Institute for Social Research in Frankfurt (Horkheimer, 1976), made a distinction between two different understandings of enquiry which he labelled 'traditional theory' and 'critical theory'. 'Traditional theory' denoted a science with a self-understanding derived from Descartes; the idea that the human subject, through perception and rational reflection, could gain reliable knowledge of an external world. The discoveries of such a science are assumed to be timeless, and its method universally and permanently valid. These assumptions seemed to have served the sciences—especially the natural sciences—well for over four centuries; but, to Horkheimer, this period of success was a bounded period in history. In a quaintly dated Marxist phrase, he called this the period of 'bourgeois science'.

A fundamentally different form of theory—critical theory—was to have no such illusions of timeless validity; under its own particular version of historical materialism all knowledge and all practices of enquiry were embodied in concrete groups of human beings limited by historical circumstance. Knowledge had socially limited purposes and historically limited validity; a principle that extended to critical theory itself. Traditional theory, which operated without this awareness, could only be the unwitting agent of the powerful, understanding itself only in the unexamined terms of the status quo.

Horkheimer was not, despite these fundamental criticisms, dismissive of the findings and practice of 'bourgeois science'; on the contrary, he had an immense respect for their standards of rationality as a historical achievement. It was simply that these findings had to be understood and interpreted against their 'constitutive context': the background against which they were formed. Mutated forms of Horkheimer's distinction abound today. Rorty (1980) emphasised the pernicious influence that epistemology has had for disciplines that are methodologically uncertain, drawing them into an obsessive concern with 'secure foundations' at the expense of concrete, socially-involved practice. Studies of the social processes of science and technology (see, e.g. Jasanoff et al., 1995; Bijker et al., 1989) have shown the extent to which contingent, historical factors have served to shape a scientific and technological agenda which—on the self-understanding of those immersed in the relevant disciplines—is pursued in a technically neutral spirit.

3.2.2   Failed Sciences and their Constitutive Context

Those seeking to develop IS as a 'science', a well-founded practice with a distinctive and timeless subject-matter, have found fertile ground in established disciplines with an interest in human communication. This section looks at two sciences of information and their constitutive context: Simon's attempt to create a generalised science of information processing that would span human and artificial systems; and the study of semiotics, particularly in its more formal vein. Checkland has, on several occasions, lamented the fact that IS has lacked a Newton to bring it conceptual clarity and strong, unifying ideas (Checkland, 1990; Checkland and Holwell, 1995). One of the intentions of the histories below is to raise the question whether IS could expect a

Newton; and another is to ask what has conditioned the belief that it needs one.

Simon's Unified Science

Simon (1981) envisaged a research programme within a unified science of complexity and information processing in a range of systems spanning the natural and human worlds. All could be seen, he argued, as instances of general principles of decision-making under conditions of bounded rationality: working with limited information and processing capacity. The same basic model was to be applicable in economics, organisation theory, psychology and computer science. Simon's work was, and continues to be, heavily influential in IS. Mainstream textbooks (see, e.g. Kroenke, 1992) still repeat many of his basic assumptions. During the 1970s—with the maturation of 'classic' artificial intelligence and its convergence with psychology, the expansion of computer facilities in organisations, the development of industrial robotics, etc.—it seemed as though (the forerunner of) IS had found its Newton and that a whole class of problems had been permanently resolved.

It doesn't look quite the same now, as so many of Simon's assumptions have begun to unravel: classic AI has all but collapsed (Dreyfus, 1992); organisations have seldom less looked like formal decision-making structures (Handy, 1994); and the economics of rational choice stands accused of ravaging societies (Hutton, 1995). What is interesting in this case is the way in which a 'universal' science, justified by reference to abstract principles, has been exposed by historical development.

Winograd and Flores (1986) trace the roots of Simon's programme back to its Cartesian assumptions, but a more limited history is equally instructive. In the late 19th century Frege embodied two major concerns of his time: the formalisation of mathematical reasoning in a precise, logical system which removed the necessity for intuitive gaps in proofs; and bringing the same logical order to everyday language and reasoning. Frege's achievements in both of these projects (Frege, 1967, 1970) laid down a pattern of development pursued for half a century. The formalisation of mathematical proof became part of a search for a general specification of 'effective procedure' or computability, embodied eventually in Turing's conceptual computing machine and von Neumann's practical blueprint.

In parallel, first Wittgenstein and Russell under the banner of 'logical atomism', and then the Vienna Circle with their project of 'unified science' attempted to lay bare the formal structure which, they believed, had to underlie the chaotic surface of natural language (Coffa, 1991). In the background of this specific disciplinary study was a broader cultural current analysed by Weber (1948:196-266), who recognised that the formal administrative and industrial bureaucracies which were the cornerstone of modernity functioned under a culture of impersonality and abstract specification of duty. The occupant of an office in a bureaucratic organisation was merely a functionary; the executant of an exhaustive specification of actions, performed against the background of the information held by the organisation. Simon, who had developed this basic Weberian model (Simon 1976), was well-placed to draw these currents together into a general science of information-processing and decision-making. Such a science could seem inevitable because it had roots which went sufficiently deep into the culture of the century that it didn't seem a serious possibility that they could be questioned. From a later perspective that culture appears to be one of mutually-reinforcing forms of the order and discipline characteristic of high modernity; the precision of mathematics, the formalities of the bureaucratic organisation and a conformist popular culture could appear as a precondition of any viable existence.[2]

The unravelling of the pretensions to a general science does not, however, mean the abandonment of the basic ideas and achievements of Simon's model. A historically-located idealisation can still have a role to play if those using it are reflectively aware of the interests that it is capable of serving, and the intellectual agenda that it privileges. Thus, Simon's ideas survive in a pragmatic, rather than a foundational-scientific, form in organisational applications of 'expert systems' technology (see, e.g. Klein and Methlie, 1990), in domains in which some independent justification can be found for their use—such as the rule-governed, actuarial reasoning in the insurance sector. Failure to perform this kind of reflective exercise resulted in the over-selling of expert systems in the 1980s. When predictions of the rise of 'knowledge

---

[2] Poster (1990:28-29) analyses the connection between the 'laws' of cybernetics and the obsession with security in the hostile environment that marked the Cold War.

economies'[3] was at its height, the claimed future importance of expert systems seemed like a sober, scientific appraisal. With the benefit of hindsight it appears more as a self-defeating marketing hype that taints even those areas in which expert systems may have useful application.

Angell and Straub (1993) show that something similar has happened with the propagation of the 'tidy' development methods of an abstract information science. Such tidy methods have come virtually to define IS, and their limitations risk them being a source of future disillusion. Only an awareness of the limited assumptions on which such methods are based, and the interests that they serve (identified by Angell and Straub as those of an academia requiring a 'teachable' subject matter), can put supposed neutral methods in perspective.

Semiotics

Simon's programme for the logicist reduction of human behaviour and organisation to the principles of mathematical logic may now appear to be limited, and its ideological content dubious; but this does not, of itself, preclude the possibility that some other science might take on the tasks that Simon set, and do so in a more enlightened fashion. One candidate science that has emerged as a possible foundation for IS is that of semiotics ('the generalised science of signs and signification'; see, e.g. Eco, 1976) and the closely-related science of structural linguistics (see, e.g. Chomsky 1965). These traditions have developed with only remote connections with the technological base of IS, and with the organisational and administrative context that IS requires—and, hence, they do not come 'ready made' as a basis for IS in the way that Simon's programme did. They do, however, bring a rich perspective on the ideas of information and communication which indicates that their absorption into the IS tradition constitutes a promising research programme.

As Stamper (Chapter 10) shows, this programme has been underway, but marginalised, for many years. The question to be pursued here is whether semiotics can provide a 'scientific basis'

---

[3] The term 'knowledge economy' has inherent ambiguities. In its 1980s form it implied economies that produced commodified knowledge in a form detached from its human context. Its more recent meanings seem to emphasise the knowledge inhering in situated actors in the economy (see, e.g. Stehr, 1994).

for a discipline of IS, of the sort which Checkland's Newtonian imagery or Simon's programme envisaged; or whether its contribution can only be that of one more thread in a continuing chaotic situation. The particular value of this enquiry is that it takes place against the background of two disciplines—semiotics and linguistics—in which the debate on the value of an exclusively scientific outlook has already been played out.

Semiotics stems from two distinct traditions. The first, that of the American philosopher Peirce, for whom the study of the human use of signs was embedded into a larger study of the processes of enquiry (for an overview, see Habermas, 1978:91-112), is anything but 'scientific' in the classic sense. Peirce's remarks on semiotics are scattered through the body of his work and resist systematisation; something thoroughly in keeping with his belief that the growth of human knowledge is an open-ended, social and concrete process. The second tradition, stemming from the work of the Swiss linguist Saussure (for an overview, see Culler, 1976), provides a more systematic point of origin since he self-consciously set out to create a science of linguistics. Saussure inherited a discipline of linguistics marked by fragmentary enquiry, largely devoted to piecemeal language comparison ('comparative philology'); and to which he intended to bring order and precision. The process by which order was created, and the difficulties a reaction against that process (over the last couple of decades) has caused for linguistics and semiotics, provide an interesting object lesson in the difficulties of disciplinary definition that have a bearing on the case of IS.

The difficulty that confronted Saussure was that a bare brief to tackle human communication scientifically under-specifies both subject matter and starting point; there is an almost indefinite number of perspectives that can be brought to bear on something so rich. Saussure therefore had to be selective, and selective in such a way that the object of enquiry that he chose would be amenable to systematic treatment with the means at his disposal (the grammatical and phonetic apparatus of linguistics as it existed). He proceeded by a series of idealising steps (Hodge and Kress, 1988). Firstly, linguistic communication was separated from other forms of communicative interaction; the primary object of enquiry was language rather than the many phenomena that might accompany it: touch, gesture, bodily displays such as clothing or decoration, etc.

Saussure's study of linguistic interaction has thus become the primary model for a generalised semiotics: other forms of communication are understood through this model.

However, the separation of linguistic communication was still not sufficiently precise to get the required form of study underway, and a further division underlined the scientific intention behind the selection process. The second step separated the abstract system underlying language (langue) from particular situated acts of language use (paroles), since the latter seemed hopelessly arbitrary and beyond systematisation. A final step froze the abstract sign system in time, separating synchronic from diachronic study; again, with the latter not amenable to systematisation. The end point of this idealisation is a scientific semiotics with a precise content and clear boundaries: describable syntactic relationships with semantic issues (those pertaining to meaning) and pragmatic issues (those pertaining to appropriate situations of use) hived off as independent studies.

Each of Saussure's steps of idealisation carries a substantial theoretical commitment and serves to legislate the existence of a discipline rather than discover one. His legislative procedure systematically condemned the inconvenient and untidy contingencies of the human world to a 'rubbish bin' beyond the reach of science; but, simultaneously, the procedure made it difficult to define quite what human phenomena his science was meant to explain.[4] The questioning of each of these steps is also a questioning of the 'scientific status' which Saussure sought to establish; and each is the subject of active challenge in semiotics and linguistics.

Eco (1986:6-7), approaching the discipline of semiotics with formalist sympathies, questions whether Saussure's idealisation can be a general basis for the study of sign systems, in a manner analogous to the laws of physics. More radical internal critics (Hodge and Kress, 1988, championing the anti-Saussurean stance of Voloshinov's Marxist materialism) attempt to transform the discipline into a 'social semiotics', which recognises the deep influence of social and political context on the interpretation of

---

[4]   This problem is most obviously apparent in Chomsky's 'competence/performance' distinction. A methodological principle which can easily become an excuse that enables a researcher to avoid inconvenient data (see, e.g. Moore and Carling, 1982:48-88).

signs. Extreme context-dependence destroys the methodological base of a semiotic science dependent on a separation of concerns. The same dynamic has been at work within structural linguistics in which a counter-movement to Chomsky (Harris, 1987; Davis and Taylor, 1990) has attempted to reconstruct the 'discipline' of linguistics as an open-textured, socially and politically aware field of study which gives up scientific and territorial pretensions. Harris, in particular, grounds this appeal in a historical study which portrays the 'science of language' as a myth waiting to happen; an exercise in self-delusion rooted in the contingencies of post-Renaissance European culture: in printing, Cartesianism and the rise of the nation-state. Like Simon's science of information processing, the sciences of semiotics and linguistics now look like two more failed attempts to lever the basis of human thought and action outside of history. These failures are rooted in what has now become a commonplace in the social sciences: the impossibility of establishing an orderly science of human action on the model of the natural sciences. Any attempt to establish a single 'view from nowhere' from which enquiry can be conducted is always open to challenge from some other competing viewpoint (see, e.g. Dallmayr and McCarthy, 1977).

The Constitutive Context of Information Systems

Philosophy, and philosophically-inclined disciplines, are littered with attempts to give 'final' characterisations of human thought and communication. Wittgenstein's 'pictorial' view of language expressed in the *Tractatus* and the scientific phenomenology of Husserl's *Investigations* both attempted to give an ultimate grounding to language and thought; and the reductive attempts at sciences of signs and information discussed above are, in various ways, descended from them. While it is easy to appreciate the attraction of such grand schemes for philosophers, it is less obvious why they should surface in a pragmatic area of activity such as IS. Why should an orderly science have such an appeal to those immersed in the production of tools for the temporary satisfaction of localised information needs?

There seem to be two principal forces which impel IS in this direction; both the organisational climate of universities and the professional desire to delineate and control working practices favour the development of disciplines with stable methods and subject-matter. However, these are opposed by a major disruptive force: a commercial dynamic which drives the development of information technology as a consumer commodity, with a constant pressure towards radical innovation and the exploitation of new markets.

The process of 'vocationalisation' of the universities is commonly bemoaned as a recent trend which has served to overturn the Platonism of an academia pursuing the disinterested life of the mind, creating a crass commercialism (MacIntyre, 1990:216-236). Opening universities to the stringencies of a cost-benefit analysis measured only in terms of contribution to 'national prosperity' is, in popular perception, a phenomenon of the 'Thatcherite' 1980s. It is salutory to note that E.P.Thompson was able to complain about the control of academia by industry in 1970 (see Thompson, 1980); and even more salutory to learn that Oxford University was a centre for the teaching of business administration in the 14th century (Keen, 1990:232).

Universities have always commodified their products for a market-place, although the structure of that market-place may have changed, and the penalties for not succeeding within it may have been less dire in the past. IS exists in a space created by a market opportunity: with the proliferation of, and popular access to, IT a new sort of skill demand has arisen which is not catered for by existing computer science courses (themselves a recent and often grudging development within mathematics and engineering). The fact that this skill demand is yoked with the 'magic discipline' of the 1980s and 1990s, business studies, has served to heighten demand—and the logic of the market place dictates the response: business information systems, business information technology, information management, etc.

There is, of course, nothing ignoble about following enlightened self-interest, and teaching IS to undergraduates is an honest job of work; but the Platonic self-understanding of the academic and the dignities of academic life—professorships, departmental titles, research funding, etc.—demand more. A course requires a curriculum, a curriculum requires a discipline, a discipline requires a canon of 'great works' which must be produced by lecturers and researchers, and lecturers and researchers require some sort of self-belief: a science with a history and an ethos that can give meaning to their work. This science is immediately seen as independent from, and so much more worthy than, the fragile circumstances that drove its creation.[5]

Vocationalised universities exist within a commercial environment organised around a culture of professional expertise, with the patterns of entry, progression and privilege integral to the functioning of that culture. In one sense 'professionalism' implies a formal structure, with the mechanisms of the professional career overt and explicitly regulated by accreditation, membership, discipline and sanction; but a profession may have an informal face, more difficult to map, present in the subtle mechanisms of an unregulated job market. The new professions that cluster around IT have only been partially successful in establishing the disciplines and restrictions common in established professions such as medicine or engineering.

One explanation for this cites the laws of supply and demand, with the formal processes of education and accreditation having insufficient capacity to cope with the explosive growth of IT. Such an explanation provides ammunition for those who argue for an expansion of educational resources in the appropriate university departments. However, the establishment of an orderly profession requires a more fundamental level of agreement before the appropriate academic production lines can be set up: an agreement on the professional competence being regulated, and some means of representing it as a set of teachable principles. At this point the problems begin for any putative profession of IS, and hence the effort of which this volume is a part: an effort to draw a convincing boundary around a set of activities and competences which can attract sufficient agreement, and stay stable for long enough, for a profession to congeal. The definition of a discipline of IS, and the acceptance of that discipline as the basis of a profession, is a far from disinterested exercise on the part of the academic community. It has much to gain from the alignment of the logic of the job market place with its own—an alignment which is difficult to

---

[5] The dynamics of this process have been well-expressed by Harris (1990:23):

... once a new science is proclaimed, it inevitably and immediately acquires a history. Its birth is seen as the outcome of earlier views, which are retrospectively resurrected as progenitors ... Once a subject has retrospectively acquired a history, its practitioners are expected to situate their own practice with reference to it."

achieve without some conscious regulatory mechanism in which it has a role.

Professional structures demand a particular sort of commodified knowledge. In an early attempt to analyse the kind of education required for salaried officialdom Weber (1948:240-244) presents 'professional education' as being conditioned by the requirements of the organisational structures of his day—the hierarchical bureaucracy. The Weberian bureaucrat was assumed to perform a fixed set of duties that could be exhaustively prescribed, with the office-holder progressing on the basis of the acquisition of demonstrable, accredited skills. Such an education is heavily skewed towards an extreme specialisation and a prescriptive, examinable content. The official is, from the abstracted point of view from which he is perceived, only called upon to act within a restricted professional domain, and has no need of the forms of education that Weber found characteristic of other cultures (the humanistic cultivation of the Renaissance man, the stolid virtues of the empire builder, etc.).

It is doubtful whether any real bureaucracy, or the preparation for it, corresponded to Weber's 'ideal-type', and the hierarchical bureaucracy is in the process of being expunged from modern organisations; but the pattern of education that he describes is wearisomely familiar. Other forces also contribute towards an education based on commodified knowledge. Perkin's (1989) study of the transformation of British society from a principally class-based distribution of wealth and power to one based on professional merit traces the mechanisms on which this new order depends. The professional has to be able to claim some enduring basis on which to lay claim to the rewards of wealth and power. As a counter-claim to the established advantages of inherited wealth and aristocratic breeding the professional can advance 'merit'; but merit requires objectification. That objectification comes as the possession of abstract, transferable knowledge. Such a currency requires standard denominations, in the form of degree titles and professional accreditation, to represent a less stable underlying competence.[6] A vocational university education has to meet a dual requirement: of providing a competence that stands up to the

---

[6] A more abstract study of these mechanisms is provided by Hannerz (1992:100-125).

rigours of practice in an uncertain environment; but also to do so in a way that supports the commerce of professionalism.

This much of the constitutive context of IS is shared by any vocational discipline; but IS exists in a context that serves radically to disrupt the sedimentation of stable professional skills and university curricula. IS is yoked with a consumer technology whose development cannot be portrayed as a comprehensible progression from less useful to more useful technical instruments. As Grint (1995) argues, IT products can often be viewed as creating the problems that they are portrayed as solving; a process that is driven by an innovation and marketing logic only obliquely related to real human need. Roszak (1986) presents a radicalised form of this critique, in which 'information' has been raised to the status of a cult simply in order to sell repeatedly a technology that can be refashioned at will.

A fair assessment would probably have to conclude that the commercial exploitation of IT can neither be represented as a solidly need-driven process, nor as the cynical exploitation of the fashion victim; but it does ensure that the IS professional works in a world of radical instability. As Harvey (1990:105-106, 156-157) argues in his seminal study of postmodernity, the software industries show product lifetimes which mean that the models of steady 'creative destruction' of the Fordist industries of the mid-century—a comprehensible progression—no longer apply. Under conditions of repeated radical innovation there is little clear basis on which a vocationally-oriented discipline can establish the permanent principles of a science—if there were, then the innovators would be failing in their task. Postmodernity may be seen as the cultural reaction to the abandonment of permanent foundations; a cultural milieu in which IS must, of force, work.

3.3   Convergence, Expertise and Disciplines

3.3.1   *Motif*: A Map of Modernity

Weber provided one of the perennial themes of critical theory. In distinguishing 'purposive rationality' (the efficient pursuit of independently-identified ends) from 'value rationality' (the consideration of ends worthy of pursuit) he furnished himself with a means of describing what he saw as the over-riding pathology of modernity: an obsessive concern with the development of efficient instruments with which to pursue poorly-examined ends. When he looked at modernity he saw a world of 'specialists without spirit' locked in an 'iron cage of reason'. The Frankfurt School started from this Weberian premise and erected as one of its principal goals the achievement of a 'fully rational society' in which purposive and value rationality were in balance. The problem had both a theoretical and a practical dimension. Theoretically, it was necessary to develop an adequate characterisation of 'value rationality' since, *ex hypothesi*, it had a marginal and unexamined role in western culture. Practically, it was necessary to construct and propagate institutions and practices in which value rationality could flourish.

Both theoretical and practical achievements eluded the early Frankfurt school, but the recent work of Habermas provides a framework in which progress may be made in both dimensions. Habermas' *Theory of Communicative Action* (Habermas, 1984, 1987; White 1988) develops a 'two tier' theory of society in which Weber's balance of rationalities appears as a series of oppositions. Drawing on, and extending, social action theories Habermas distinguishes between two fundamental forms of action which are at the heart of his theory: strategic and communicative action. Strategic actions are performed by actors intent on maximising some medium—money and power are instances—calculated using the principles described by game theory. Communicative action is performed solely for the purposes of mutual understanding and accommodation, by actors operating outside all duress and extraneous influence.

The traditions of social theory furnish a second opposition: that between the systems theories of Parsons and Luhmann, and the hermeneutic studies of Schutz and Gadamer. Systems theories understand society in functional terms, with actors steered by media (see above) to preserve an abstractly-specifiable functional integration of society. Hermeneutics concentrates instead on the perspective of individual actors and the mechanisms by which the 'lifeworld' of those actors (reality as it is subjectively experienced) are maintained and communicated across the generations. Both theoretical oppositions blend in a map of modern societies divided into systems contexts, integrated by steering media and marked predominantly by strategic action, and lifeworld contexts, in which unforced communication and disinterested argumentation predominates. This map is highly programmatic: systems contexts are to be found in formal economic and administrative organisations; lifeworld contexts in domestic life and civil society.[7] This social map is not morally or politically neutral; for Habermas, a healthily functioning society is marked by a 'public sphere' (a forum for debate in the lifeworld) in which communicative action has the power to set political and economic agendas, bringing system and lifeworld into balance.

3.3.2   IT: Organisational and Social Change

Many images of movement have been used to describe the development and dissemination of IT. Organisations are said to have moved along an evolutionary path taking them from early practices of 'data processing' to an integrated use of IT in most of their activities. The whole of society is said to have evolved, in a short space of time, the new formations of 'information society'. Recently a whole range of technologies—telecommunications, information and broadcast—are said to have 'converged'. This section is an attempt to place these various trajectories, in a highly-programmatic fashion, on the map of modernity provided by *The Theory of Communicative Action*. The intention behind this is not to propose some 'grand theory of IS'—such a venture would be an absurd reversal of the stance of this chapter—but to suggest the breadth of issues which any discipline of IS has to confront, coupled with the suggestion that no bounded discipline is capable of fulfilling such a function.

In particular, reference is made to a range of social developments in order to forestall suggestions that a discipline of IS could be concerned principally with the world of 'business' or formal organisations. In this sketch three developmental tendencies in the use of IT will provide the primary focus: the penetration of IT into all areas of organisational life and the demand for analysis

---

[7] The precise delineation of these contexts is a matter of controversy (see, e.g., McCarthy 1991:152-180). Further exploration of these ideas is of particular importance for the participatory design tradition discussed below.

and design techniques capable of comprehending complex systems of human activity; the rise of 'information society' in which the experience of daily life is marked by encounters with knowledge and practices shaped by IT; and the recent phenomenon of 'convergence', in which previously-discrete technologies have merged to blur the distinction between computer-based information systems, telecommunications, the broadcast and print media, and a number of leisure and entertainment activities.

The cumulative effect of these changes, it is suggested, is that those working in IS will be forced to recapitulate the learning process undergone by planners and social systems practitioners and recognise that, just as the notion of a professional planner is almost a contradiction in terms and that 'there are no experts in the systems approach', the idea that there exists an abstractly-specificable body of expertise which might characterise the IS professional is in the process of becoming incoherent.

The Organisational Penetration of IT

One strand in the developmental history of IS begins in the technical mind-set of the professional expert, situated at the heart of the formal, systematic activities of large bureaucracies. The 'data processing' from which IS grew was the domain of the expert with arcane knowledge, progressing along a standard career path from the tortuous activity of programming to the highly-formalised analysis of whichever bureaucratic operations were amenable to automation on the mainframe computer systems of the 1950s to 1970s. The development of IS, recognised as being concerned with rather more than this mechanistic agenda, stems largely from the deeper organisational penetration of IT. This penetration is marked by a broadening of the tasks to which IT has been put, and in the range of people brought into intimate contact with IT in the workplace.

This transformation may be conveniently marked by the emergence of the PC, although this was simply a major step in the accessibility of IT. The eclipse of the 'priestly order' of the data processing department, capable of imposing its own definition on the organisational world and, simultaneously, protecting the boundaries of its own form of technical rationality, has been a gradual process. The challenging of the technical mind-set has several dimensions. As the exclusive possession of a narrowly technical knowledge begins to erode—there can be few 'IS experts' who have not experienced the embarassment of recognising that their 'users' have a firmer grasp on the arcana of some system than they have themselves—the professional is forced to seek other forms of self-definition, some other expertise that marks them as distinctive. At the same time, the professional IS expert has to respond to a demand for greater sensitivity towards the views and needs of those whom their systems serve.

These demands arise in the lifeworld and challenge the abstract imperatives that the system imposes. These demands fall into three principal categories. Firstly, there are demands for a recognition of the subjectivity of users, and the need for psychological satisfaction and comprehensibility in their experience of computer systems. A second set of demands focuses on social effects, on the disruption of existing patterns of work or employment, and a requirement to recognise this disruption during the design process. Thirdly, in a demand linked with the other two, a moral claim is made upon the professional expert that they be ethically accountable for the work that they perform or oversee.

One way in which a profession can respond to this situation is to reach for expertise from other existing 'disciplines' and bolt them onto the requirements for competent IS practice. During this process it is natural that disciplines, or tendencies within disciplines, that conform to the technical mind-set be adopted. Thus, to improve the usability of systems and improve interfaces IS reaches for cognitive psychology and models of human attention, perception and memory cast in terms that it antecedently understands. To understand the impact of IT, organisation theory and sociology are combed for the functional models that align with existing practices in systems analysis. In meeting claims for ethical accountability, codes and practices culled from the tradition of Anglo-American analytic philosophy provide the kind of calculative approach to ethics congenial to IS.

These appropriations have many of the characteristics of Simon's general science of information processing discussed above: they serve to confirm the existence of a coherent interdisciplinary field waiting to be discovered. Such a field now, moreover, seems wide-ranging, responsible and still eminently teachable as a set of tidy practices. What may, instead, have been discovered is—as Weber and the Frankfurt school claimed—that a narrow calculative rationality has been at work over the whole spectrum of society (a judgement shared, looking specifically at the realm of computer-related studies, by Weizenbaum, 1984).

A more thorough response to the demand that the human reception of IT be the subject of serious disciplinary study might be to look beyond those traditions most easily assimilated into a technical IS. When this is done, and it is a movement which has been underway for some years, serious cracks begin to appear in a disciplinary self-image of an IS founded on specifiable competences. Each of the disciplines from which IS has appropriated the more technical elements is—and perhaps this is inevitable—internally contested. One direction from which internal contest has come in psychology, social and organisation theory, and ethics is that of a tradition of study anchored in the lifeworld and hermeneutic techniques.

One of the earliest instances of the hermeneutic tradition impinging on the computer-related disciplines occurred in AI, to which Dreyfus brought critiques anchored in the work of Heidegger as early as the 1960s (see Dreyfus, 1992:xi). These critiques not only challenge cognitive psychology and its models of the decision-making process, but also the Cartesian image of the thinking subject interacting with an information-processing device which has been the source of much work in human-computer interaction.

An alternative perspective on HCI, and generally on the design of systems to be embedded in established areas of work—the 'tool perspective' (Winograd and Flores, 1986)—invites a different style of reasoning about the use of computer systems. An approach to design based on Heidegger's existential philosophy presupposes a form of education alien to that common on mainstream IS or computer science courses. A sensitivity to the way in which the artifacts which surround us are smoothly appropriated into unfolding human 'projects',[8] and are the subject of culturally-determined interpretation, requires an education characteristic of the artist or industrial designer.[9] A reflective engagement with Heideggerian design is, inevitably, a philosophical exercise which

---

[8] Heidegger's understanding of human action is expressed using an esoteric vocabulary. For a comprehensive and digestible introduction see Dreyfus (1991).

[9] For an expression of this re-orientation, see Laurel (1994) and later in the chapter.

demands active personal involvement. Such an educational process aims to develop embodied social skills, rather than the distanced 'looking on' of a 'traditional science' (to use Horkheimer's term).

A similar broadening of outlook is engendered by the soft approaches to organisational information systems design which have grown from the organisation as culture image (Morgan 1986) and its operationalisation in Soft Systems Methodology (SSM) (Checkland and Scholes, 1990). Although expressed more pragmatically, the action frame of practice and research which characterises SSM, when applied to IS (Lewis, 1994, Stowell and West, 1994), corresponds to a radical change in mind-set from that of the scientist or engineer.[10] This has a correspondingly radical effect on the conception of a discipline which could host such a mind-set. Checkland's characterisation of SSM as requiring a fleetness of foot and improvisatory ability—rooted in Vickers' resolutely experiential and undogmatic approach to planning—does not lend itself to prescriptive learning.

This requirement for a different form of engagement from the IS practitioner appears in its most radical form in Scandinavian approaches to IS development (Ehn, 1988, Greenbaum and Kyng, 1991) which couple an action approach to systems design with a recognition of the political significance of collapsing the distance between designer and user. The Scandinavian experiments in cooperative design, aided by a legal framework of compulsory worker consultation and participation in technological change, and theoretically underpinned by a range of political philosophies—including Critical Theory (Lyytinen, 1992; Lyytinen et al., 1991)—take the conventional practice of IS design and place it at the furthest distance from a domination by experts or managerial imperatives possible within formal organisational contexts.

To make the process of participation meaningful, it is necessary that it be conducted in terms which originate with the participating workforce; this demands a full-blooded interpretation of empowerment in which not merely the technical means to realise pre-given ends are the subject of participatory design, but the ends being pursued are also subject to democratic control by the workforce (for a clear definition of these distinctions, see Clement,

---

[10] It is supposed here that a soft approach to IS involves a radical re-thinking, on hermeneutic lines, of all aspects of IS analysis, design and use, rather than simply a revised approach to strategic IS planning.

1994). Design approaches of this sort presuppose, or argue for, the transformation of the workplace into an arena in which lifeworld influences play a part; and with these lifeworld influences comes a form of communicative rationality which can only be embodied in concrete debate between those involved in the situation. Abstract, transferable knowledge in the form of technical expertise has far less purchase in this form of IS practice. The skills of facilitation, of being prepared to open up technical expertise to the criticism of the supposedly 'uninitiated' requires a set of skills and democratic attitudes which are difficult to commodify; but they are a crucial component of participatory design.

A full development of this design approach places most of the assumptions of expertise, authority and specialised roles built into the patterns of employment in IS in question. Participatory design is not a process in which an 'expert' indulges or educates a group of potential users for the sake of an abstract democratic principle; it is a process in which what counts as 'domain expertise' is communicatively negotiated by all parties. A communicative process is one in which any knowledge claim on the part of an 'expert' is open to challenge, a challenge which may lead to the redefinition of expertise (Fischer and Forester, 1993, Ulrich, 1996).

The Rise of the Information Society

Over the same period that the use of computer-based systems in formal organisations has described the trajectory from DP to IS, the same dynamic of technological change has driven a related, more broadly social, movement: the growth of 'information society'. This term is loaded with ambiguities which must be unpicked before its full significance can be appreciated. In one sense, the rise of 'information society' may be seen as a phenomenon which adds weight to the argument for a thoroughly professionalised and socially valued vocation of IS. In this portrayal smoothly functioning information systems are the key to the efficient functioning of the economy and of the administration of society; and everyone has an interest in seeing that these tasks are carried out to the highest standards. This interpretation sees society as something passive, something impacted on by technological developments within the systemic sphere and served by trained professionals.

On a slightly broader interpretation 'information society' can also mean that a proportion of the population have opted to bring IT into their lives by the purchase of home computers or other forms of IT-based consumer good, thus becoming some kind of outpost of automation in the domestic sphere. There is, however, another way of conceiving the rise of information society which stresses that society is not something merely impacted on by technological change; it is instead an active component in a change process involving technology, but not solely directed by it. This conception sets up a counter-motion by which changes in the lifeworld help to condition the way in which technology is used within the systemic contexts of formal organisations, and which erodes the pivotal status of the information professional.

The starting point of this analysis is that modern actors have become reflexive (Giddens, 1991); that is, a modern actor does not simply live within an unquestioned world dictated by tradition, but consciously questions and determines that world in the unfolding of a 'personal project'. The lifeworld of the modern actor is thus 'rationalised'; the demand for explicit reasons for beliefs and actions itself becomes part of an inherited tradition. The way in which justifications are conceived and articulated is not something fixed; it depends upon the resources available in the world surrounding the actor—which now means a world soaked with information sources and forms conditioned by IT.

This does not mean that this conditioning only takes place by direct contact with IT, rather that information in a range of media is presented in ways derived directly or indirectly from IT. As examples one may consider a range of media which are not immediately experienced by the user as 'computer-based': the tendency of newspapers and magazines to present 'fact files' organised around keywords; the overlaying of sports broadcasts with tabulated information to help the viewer 'evaluate' performance; the highly segmented style of presentation of 'factual' publications, seen at its most developed in Dorling-Kindersley's educational books.

This experience helps to determine patterns of what is culturally accounted 'valid reasoning'; a conception more flexible than a normative standard of 'scientific reasoning', covering moral and aesthetic justifications as well as those of a more factual nature. The net result is a society of increasingly sophisticated manipulators of information (no longer simply 'mass consumers', McQuail, 1994:33-60) which inevitably impacts on the forms of reasoning and information provision within formal organisations. The sensitivity to user-expressed information needs within organisations may be read as a partial result of this trend. A formal information system within an organisation exists within a 'circuit' of meaning attribution which encompasses the lifeworld (which includes informal organisational, civil and domestic experience) of the actors accessing that system.

Technological 'Convergence'

A recent trend adds another layer of meaning to 'information society'. Another ambiguous term—'convergence' (see, e.g. Jameson, 1995)—signifies that yet more categories of our social experience are being transformed by technological change. 'Convergence' has one straightforward interpretation, an uncontroversial technological one in which distinct technologies have started to coalesce: information technology, the broadcast and print media, telecommunications, etc. now depend on a common base. The most visible evidence of this convergence is the mix of technologies that are experienced as the Internet, and the myriad information phenomena that have sprung up around it.

At a more challenging level 'convergence' means something else. It means a disruption of some of the basic categories of types of information and information source: reading a newspaper is like (or is?) accessing a database; sending a letter is like (or is?) composing on a word-processor; watching a video is like (or is?) running a software utility. It also means a disruption of our sense of place and space: domestic and work space is no longer so distinguishable and organisational and private life blurs; the world has a virtual geography overlaid on the real one (Graham, 1995). At its most far reaching it means that basic categories of experience— learning, entertainment, work, leisure, social contact, political process, etc.—no longer mean quite the same thing.

Convergence has been accompanied, almost inevitably, by calls for the creation of a new discipline, or at least an interdisciplinary area. Knight and Weedon (1995) began the task of defining such an area; a blend of skills and knowledges drawn from programming, design, psychology, architecture, etc. In addition to, perhaps, a sinking feeling of *deja vu*, those concerned with the definition of a discipline of IS may take from these developments the assurance that their own skill-set or curriculum will have to expand commensurately. As convergence phenomena begin to permeate the lifeworld new forms of reasoning and justification—based around pictorial, sound and motion-video information, as well as complex patterns of electronically-mediated interpersonal communication—will enter the repertoire of reflexive actors.

Again, radical innovation places in question attempts to throw a disciplinary net over the knowledge required to cope with it; and opens the possibility that a 'discipline', conceived in either its intellectual or institutionalised form can deal with such expansion or instability. In particular, it means that any attempt to create a restricted field of information systems for business or organisations—despite the professional cachet and lucrative possibilities it carries—is to create an artificially-restricted domain which is open to radical disruption by its environment. The sheer ubiquity of IT in modern societies forces a 'holism' on any would-be student of information phenomena; a holism which seems impossible to attain, since the scale of complexity is too great. The kind of study which might do justice to this complexity is the subject of the next section.

3.4   'Supradisciplinarity' and the Nomadic Intellectual

3.4.1   *Motif*: An Interdisciplinary Programme of Research

The early Frankfurt School had an idealised vision of what social research could be. In a brief outline of its research practice Horkheimer (1989) enunciated, *inter alia*, two principles. The first, that 'social concepts are integrative', meant that any social phenomenon could be explored using an open-ended collection of existing disciplines and their techniques, and that no single perspective, or even a closed collection of perspectives, could be adequate to the social object being studied. Trying to portray a living totality was a project which, in principle, could not be completed. What the researcher had to aim for was to be able to pass from discipline to discipline 'without being impeded by their boundaries'. How, exactly, this was to be achieved was never satisfactorily spelled out, save the assertion that historical materialism could provide a universal medium for study. The second principle was that 'social concepts are inductive'; meaning that, as society is a holistic system in which each of the parts reflect aspects of the whole, social research should proceed by the intensive study of particular social phenomena. The results of such intensive study would illuminate a whole which could not be tackled head-on. While the School's research programme is usually described as 'interdisciplinary', it aimed to be more than a bland commerce between different disciplines which might have useful things to say to each other. Its ambition, as Lowenthal expressed it (cited in Kellner, 1989:7), was to be supradisciplinary. Disciplinary boundaries were distortions which affected the validity claims made within them, and somehow social theory had to operate beyond all boundaries.

This desire is one that won't go away; and it has acquired greater resonance in the disciplinary confusion of postmodernity. Rorty (1980:357-394) has expressed the hope that philosophy could take on the role which Horkheimer had assigned to historical materialism. Deleuze and Guattari (1988) envisage a nomadic form of thought which has somehow become detached from the systematic disciplines of the past, operating without the firm roots of established knowledge. Their image—which has a metaphorical power but which is difficult to translate into the pragmatics of academic study—contrasts the 'arborescent', tree-like structure exhibited by traditional disciplines (exemplified by the taxonomy of knowledge that structures Diderot and D'Alembert's *Encyclopedie*) with a 'rhizomatic' structure: their term for the temporary forms of thought that emerge at the intersection of 'lines of force' created by shifting needs and desires.

3.4.2 IS as a Disciplinary Solvent

Interdisciplinarity was a relatively novel and daring aspiration for the Frankfurt School, requiring the establishment of an independent institute outside the highly conventional structures of the universities of the 1930s. In today's more liberal atmosphere interdisciplinarity appears to be an established educational principle; but today's institutional structures still militate against the kind of intellectual flexibility which the Frankfurt School sought.

Interdisciplinarity may be approached from two standpoints. Firstly, it may appear as an individual achievement; an individual researcher or practitioner (or a locally-coherent group) may succeed in personally integrating knowledge from different domains. This achievement may be expressed in a book rooted in a number of scholarly traditions, in a design which exemplifies distinct influences, or simply as a personal example recognised by colleagues, students or friends. Computer-related studies seem to have been fortunate in throwing up a large number of such individuals and teams (see examples below); something which may be due to the chaos and rootlessness of the computing disciplines and the lack, until relatively recently, of a formal educational process for them. Most established figures in the computing disciplines must, of necessity, have been formally educated in some other field and found 'crook'd and diverse ways' to their present roles.

Interdisciplinarity has a second aspect, which is apt to be overlooked: its embodiment in the enduring structures which constrain and direct the activities of education and publishing. The existence of university departments with titles and identities, the budgetary channels which sustain them, and the quality bodies which oversee them also serve—more powerfully than any individual—to define what counts as a valid academic pursuit. The publishing industry, and its reflection in the form of library provision, lives in a symbiosis with these structures; it assumes and reinforces the existence of particular 'client groups' for its products. Thus, any effort towards interdisciplinarity is not simply one of the individual will and intellect in breaking down abstract barriers, it is also a political process of institutional change.

To make these ideas more concrete, consider some of the 'landmark' achievements in interdisciplinarity which have appeared in computer-related fields in recent years. A particularly striking example is afforded by Laurel's *Computers as Theatre* (Laurel, 1994). This work is addressed (according to its Library of Congress data it is concerned with human-computer interfaces) to the computing community and urges them to abandon assumptions which differentiate work in technology and in the arts. It argues that the design of computer interfaces should be remodelled as an interaction between humans and computers, considered as an unfolding drama—human and computer are actors within a plot being played out to some conclusion. The theoretical background to the work is that of Aristotelian theory of drama, heavily laced with examples from modern drama and cinema which elide with discussions of computer use and design. Such a position is likely to be disturbing to the assumptions of those with an established technological mind-set; and Laurel erects elaborate defences against those who might argue that drama has nothing to do with the serious business of work, or is too fuzzy and imprecise to guide work in the hard world of technology (Laurel, 1994:22-28).

A contrasting example is that of Landow's *Hypertext: the Convergence of Contemporary Critical Theory and Technology* (Landow, 1992). The author, an established figure in literary criticism who 'got technology' through word-processing his work, is addressing a target group outside the computing community (according to the Library of Congress data, those working in criticism, literature and hypertext). His work is an attempt to persuade an established discipline that an engagement with IT is both a means of exploring tendencies already present in literary theory (textual deconstruction), and a way of extending the possibilities of writing and literary education. In the course of his argument he develops perspectives on the persuasive power of texts, and the political authority invested in them, which would not be lost on those thinking about the role of IS in organisational power structures. It is intriguing to speculate on how many in the IS community have digested Landow's work; or, indeed, how many in the theatre have encountered Laurel's.

It is difficult to see how work such as that of Laurel or Landow might be fully accommodated within existing university structures. To be sure, it is easy to conceive of a curriculum in which gestures are made toward such work; but saying to students 'you really ought to read this' or 'here's an interesting idea' is no substitute for an extended, reflective exercise in theatrical design and production, or learning and practising the techniques of literary deconstruction. Only the latter effectively say 'here is something to be treated very seriously'; but they are, not surprisingly, absent from IS curricula.

It must also be said that their addition wouldn't necessarily mark a major advance towards full-blooded interdisciplinarity, since indefinitely many other radically new perspectives also await exploration: serious work in the vein of Suchman's (1987) *Plans and Situated Actions* requires an engagement with anthropology and its field-work techniques; Mitchell's (1995) *City of Bits* suggests that architectural design provides a fruitful model for comprehending and designing the structures of cyberspace; and so on. In trying to find a form of education or institutional structure which can support such an anarchic, explosive growth of subject matter one is forced to turn to the kind of art-school education pioneered by the Bauhaus (Whitford, 1984).

The Bauhaus' educational project, devised by its first director Gropius, was founded on the principle that art and technology formed a unity which, during the processes of modernisation had been driven apart—and that these severed disciplines could be re-united. The method by which they were to be re-united was an eclectic form of educational practice: the students, assumed to be in an unformed state, were to be educated in workshops open to the influence of both technicians and artists. Workshop practice was project-driven and intellectually open-ended; once a concrete problem had been set any approach or technique which the students might use was considered potentially valid. The hope was that students trained in this way might become something essentially new; a form of artist-craftsman-designer which could not have been conceived before the Bauhaus' educational experiments were performed. The results obtained by the Bauhaus were ambivalent (Forgacs, 1995) but have had an enduring influence in art education.

The advent of multimedia—and the need for an 'electronic Bauhaus' form of education—has perhaps put this educational model on the agenda of the computer-related disciplines; but departments of IS, computing or business studies would have to evolve beyond recognition to accommodate Gropius' radical transformations of role and disciplinary assumptions. It is, however, worth noting that 'crazy' disruptions of role, and a fundamental challenging of assumptions about how organisations should work, have been entertained by some management gurus (see, e.g. Peters, 1992).

A pressure for a particular form of responsiveness to social need may also be used to support a case-centred and spontaneously expansive form of education for IS (and other, perhaps more fixed, disciplines). In the debate which has surrounded the need to meet 'skills shortages' and address 'worker obsolescence' attention has been focused on mechanisms to bring people back periodically into education in programmes of 'lifelong learning' (see, e.g. Cresson, 1996). In this debate it has been rather generously assumed that the basic disciplinary structure and research practices of the universities suit them for this task, and that the problem is largely one of access. A more serious probing of the disciplinary structure of universities may, as this chapter has repeatedly urged, find them ill-adapted to cope with the pace of knowledge turnover in the postmodern era. If that is found to be the case—and IT-related disciplines are among those most prey to knowledge obsolescence—then the pressing need will be to find ways of dissolving disciplines and their supporting structures, rather than constructing them.

3.5   Concluding Remarks

This chapter has been principally about the dangers of the many forms of exclusion and prescription that accompany disciplinary definition; exclusion and prescription by the abstract principles of a science, by professional accreditation, by model curricula, and by the simple desire for a distinctive group identity. None of these are necessarily bad in themselves—social life is founded on forms of identity and exclusion—but they are likely to become so when they are associated with potent technologies that are a source of power and privilege in modern societies. Perhaps the greatest service a putative 'information systems professional' might do for society is to ensure that a technology as malleable as the printed page becomes, or remains, a chaotic meeting place of all ideas and interests; and that professional access is not closed down in the name of some historically-located notion of 'best practice' or a 'sound' educational foundation.

References

Angell, I. and Straub, B., 1993, Though this be madness, yet there is method in't, *Journal of Strategic Information Systems*. 2(1):5-14.

Bijker, W., Hughes, T. and Pinch, T., 1989, *The Social Construction of Technological Systems*, MIT Press, Cambridge, Mass.

Checkland, P., 1990, Information Systems and Systems Thinking, in *Soft Systems Methodology in Action*, P. Checkland and J. Scholes, John Wiley, Chichester, 303-315.

Checkland, P.and Holwell, S., 1995, Information systems: what's the big idea, *Systemist*. 17(1):7-13.

Chomsky, N., 1965, *Aspects of the Theory of Syntax*, MIT Press, Cambridge, Mass.

Clement, A., 1994, Computing at work: empowering action by low-level users, *Comm. ACM*. 37(1):53-63.

Coffa, J.A., 1991, *The Semantic Tradition from Kant to Carnap*, Cambridge University Press, Cambridge.

Cresson, E., 1996, Adapt to survive in formidable form, *Times Higher*, 23 Feb.

Culler, J., 1976, *Saussure*, Fontana, London.

Dallmayr, F. and McCarthy, T., 1977, *Understanding and Social Enquiry*, University of Notre Dame Press, Notre Dame, Indiana.

Davis, H.G. and Taylor, T.J., *Redefining Linguistics*, Routledge, London.

Deleuze, G. and Guattari, F., 1988, *A Thousand Plateaus*, Athlone Press, London.

Dreyfus, H.L., 1991, *Being-in-the-World*, MIT Press, Cambridge, Mass.

Dreyfus, H.L., 1992, *What Computers Still Can't Do*, MIT Press, Cambridge, Mass.

Eco, U., 1976, *A Theory of Semiotics*, Indiana University Press, Bloomington.

Ehn, P., 1988, *The Work-Oriented Design of Computer Artifacts*, Arbetslivscentrum, Stockholm.

Fischer, F. and Forester, J., 1993, *The Argumentative Turn in Policy Analysis and Planning*, UCL Press, London.

Forgacs, E., 1995, *The Bauhaus Idea and Bauhaus Politics*, Central European University Press, Budapest.

Frege, G., 1967, *The Basic Laws of Arithmetic*, University of California Press, Berkeley.

Frege, G., 1970, *Translations from the Philosophical Writings of Gottlob Frege*, P. Geach and M. Black, eds., Blackwell, Oxford.

Giddens, A., 1991, *Modernity and Self-Identity*, Polity, Cambridge.

Graham, S., 1995, Cyberspace and the city, *Town and Country Planning*, August, 198-201.

Greenbaum, J. and Kyng, M., 1991, *Design at Work: Cooperative Design of Computer Systems*, Lawrence Erlbaum, New York.

Grint, K., 1995, Sisyphus and the social construction of computer user problems, *Information Systems Journal*, 5(1):3-18.

Habermas, J., 1978, *Knowledge and Human Interests*, Heinemann, London.

Habermas, J., 1984, *The Theory of Communicative Action Vol. 1*, Heinemann, London.

Habermas, J., 1987, *The Theory of Communicative Action Vol 2.*, Polity, Cambridge.

Harris, R., 1987, *The Language Machine*, Duckworth, London.

Harris, R., 1990, *On Redefining Linguistics*, in Davis and Taylor 1990.

Harvey, D., 1990, *The Condition of Postmodernity*, Blackwell, Oxford.

Handy, C., 1994, *The Empty Raincoat*, Hutchinson, London.

Hannerz, U., 1992, *Cultural Complexity: Studies in the Social Organisation of Meaning*, Columbia University Press, New York.

Hodge, R. and Kress, G., 1988, *Social Semiotics*, Polity, Cambridge.

Horkheimer, M., 1976, Traditional and Critical Theory, in *Critical Sociology*, P. Connerton ed., Penguin, London, 206-224.

Horkheimer, M., 1989, Notes on Institute Activities, in *Critical Theory and Society: A Reader*, S. Bronner and D. Kellner eds., Routledge, London, 264-266.

Hutton, W., 1995, *The State We're In*, Vintage Pub., London.

Jameson, J., 1995, *Convergence and the New Media: A Roadmap*, Institute for Public Policy Research.

Jasanoff, S., Markle, G., Petersen, J. and Pinch, T., 1995, *A Handbook of Science and Technology Studies*, Sage, London.

Keen, M., 1990, *English Society in the Later Middle Ages*, Penguin, London.

Kellner, D., 1989, *Critical Theory, Marxism and Modernity*, Polity, Cambridge.

Klein, M. and Methlie, L., 1990, *Expert Systems: A Decision Support Approach*, Addison-Wesley, Reading, Mass.

Knight, J. and Weedon, A., 1995, Editorial, *Convergence* 1,1:5-10.

Kroenke, D., 1992, *Management Information Systems*, McGraw-Hill, New York.

Landow, G.P., 1992, *Hypertext: the Convergence of Contemporary Critical Theory and Technology*, Johns Hopkins University Press, Baltimore.

Laurel, B., 1994, *Computers as Theatre*, Addison-Wesley, Reading, Mass.

Lawson, M., 1995, Please don't step on my blue pseud shoes, *The Guardian*, 7 Aug.

Liebenau, J. and Backhouse, J., 1989, A need for discipline, *Times Higher*, 31st Dec.

Lewis, P., 1994, *Information Systems Design*, Pitman, London.

Lyytinen, K., 1992, Information Systems and Critical Theory, in *Critical Management Studies*, M. Alvesson and H. Wilmott eds., Sage, London 159-180.

Lyytinen, K., Klein, H. and Hirschheim, R., The effectiveness of office information systems: a social action perspective, *Journal of Information Systems*. 1(1):41-60.

MacIntyre, A., 1990, *Three Rival Versions of Moral Enquiry*, Duckworth, London.

McCarthy, T., 1991, *Ideals and Illusions*, MIT Press, Cambridge, Mass.

McQuail, D., 1994, *Mass Communication Theory: An Introduction*, Sage, London.

Mitchell, W., 1995, *City of Bits*, MIT Press, Cambridge, Mass.

Moore, T. and Carling, C., 1982, *Understanding Language: Towards a Post-Chomskyan Linguistics*, Macmillan, London.

Morgan, G., 1986, *Images of Organisation*, Sage, London.

Perkin, H., 1989, *The Rise of Professional Society*, Routledge, London.

Peters, T., 1992, *Liberation Management*, Macmillan, London.

Rorty, R., 1980, *Philosophy and the Mirror of Nature*, Blackwell, Oxford.

Roszak, T., 1986, *The Cult of Information*, Lutterworth Press, Cambridge.

Simon, H.A., 1976, *Administrative Behaviour*, Free Press, New York.

Simon, H.A., 1981, *The Sciences of the Artificial*, MIT Press, Cambridge, Mass.

Stehr, N., 1994, *Knowledge Societies*, Sage, London.

Stowell, F. and West, D., 1994, *Client-Led Design*, McGraw-Hill, Maidenhead.

Suchman, L., 1987, *Plans and Situated Actions*, Cambridge University Press, Cambridge.

Thompson, E.P., 1980, *Writing By Candlelight*, Merlin Press, London.

Ulrich, W., 1996, *Critical Systems Thinking for Citizens*, Research Memorandum 10, Centre for Systems Studies, University of Hull.

Weber, M., 1948, *From Max Weber: Essays in Sociology*, in H. Gerth and C. Wright-Mills, eds, Routledge, London.

Weizenbaum, J., 1984, *Computer Power and Human Reason*, Penguin, London.

White, S.K., 1988, *The Recent Work of Jurgen Habermas*, Cambridge Univ. Press, Cambridge.

Whitford, F., 1984, *Bauhaus*, Thames and Hudson, London.

Winograd, T. and Flores, F., 1986, *Understanding Computers and Cognition*, Addison-Wesley, Reading, Mass.

Chapter 4

IT ALL DEPENDS WHAT YOU MEAN BY DISCIPLINE ...

Matthew Jones

4.1   Introduction

The attempt to define the discipline of Information Systems (IS) has been one of the enduring concerns of the IS literature. Indeed, the fact that it is felt that this volume can make a contribution to this debate in 1996 illustrates that, while the topic has aroused much heat and fury, it has, as yet, shown little sign of resolution. Such a state of affairs would seem to have an added mystery, since the fora within which much of this debate has taken place has been IS journals and conferences, the presence of which might seem to presuppose the existence of an IS discipline.

An explanation of this apparent conundrum, and of the persistence of foundational debate within the field, may be sought, at least in part, in the existence of three different meanings of the term 'discipline'[1], the confusion between which may have helped to delay the achievement of a clear understanding of the nature of IS as a subject area. As a result, the claims made for the IS discipline have often failed to match the actual status of the field and the institutions supporting it. In this chapter three alternative definitions of discipline will be considered and their implications for the nature of IS as a discipline will be explored. In particular it will be considered whether there are specific characteristics of the IS field that make it inherently prone to such ontological insecurity.

---

[1] It is worth noting that the multiple meanings of the word discipline, and the confusions that appear to arise from this, may be peculiar to the English language. In Finnish, for example, there are separate words for each concept.

4.1.1 Discipline$_1$, Discipline$_2$ and Discipline$_3$

The literature on IS as a discipline has generally taken one of two approaches to the issue: a normative one, seeking to set out, often on the basis of some first principles, what topics are to be included within its boundaries (e.g. Backhouse *et al.*, 1991); or a descriptive one, categorising what it is that IS teachers, researchers (and in some cases, practitioners) do (e.g. Culnan and Swanson, 1986). As is evident from this distinction, these approaches embody different interpretations of what a discipline is—either a distinctive area of academic study united by some common philosophy, or the combination of practices associated with a particular label. These two alternatives, however, do not exhaust the possible ways in which IS might be a discipline, since there is a third interpretation of the term that may also be helpful in understanding the current (and potential) status of IS. This is the view of discipline as a mechanism of control for the other two approaches.

These three interpretations may be seen to be present in the *Concise Oxford English Dictionary*'s definition of the term.

1. Branch of instruction or learning; mental or moral training, adversity as effecting this; system of rules for conduct, behaviour according to established rules.
2. Order maintained among schoolchildren, soldiers, prisoners etc; control exercised over members of church or other organisation.
3. Chastisement; (Eccl.) mortification by penance.
   ME f. OF, f. L *disciplina* (*discere* learn)

Ignoring, for the moment, the idea of discipline as a mortification by penance, the normative, descriptive and controlling character of the term are each evident. Taking them in order of the strength of the claims that they make about the coherence of the subject, the three perspectives will be called, for the purposes of this chapter, Discipline$_1$, Discipline$_2$ and Discipline$_3$.

Discipline$_1$, or the normative definition of discipline, emphasises the existence of established rules. In some cases this is also referred to as a paradigm (e.g. Ein Dor and Segev, 1981), with or without explicit reference to Kuhn (1970). It takes as its ideal a subject such as physics (Banville and Landry, 1989) which is seen as being united by a common set of methodological principles which in turn give rise to a consistent and coherent world-view which serves to clearly demarcate the boundaries of the subject. Thus physicists would generally be seen as sharing a realist ontology, believing that the phenomena they study exist independently of the observer, and a positivist epistemology for which traditional nomothetic methodologies, such as experiments, are appropriate. Leaving aside the question of whether physics, or any other subject, actually exhibits such unity and clarity of definition, such a viewpoint is widely accepted as being applicable to certain subjects, especially those within the natural sciences, and as such is invoked as a model to which IS can, and should, aspire.

The descriptive definition of discipline, or Discipline$_2$, adopts a more pragmatic approach to the issue. The question here is not whether there is necessarily a common perspective, but what is included under the banner of IS, however diverse the practices may be in terms of their philosophical stance. Avison and Fitzgerald (1991) justify the use of the term discipline in this context by reference to other 'disciplines' such as French or geography which would similarly fail the strong test of philosophical coherence. Evidence of IS as a discipline in this sense thus comes from the existence of university IS departments, professors and, recently a hot topic in the UK, from the presence (or not) of IS as a unit of assessment in the Research Assessment Exercise. The contents of IS journals and the activities of IS departments (both in teaching and research) are thus seen as primary indicators of the nature of the discipline and may be used to map the boundaries of the field (e.g. Buckingham *et al.*, 1987; Avison and Fitzgerald, 1991)

Discipline$_3$, the view that it is a mechanism of control, is somewhat at a tangent to the other two, but also links them together. Thus it is through the operation of Discipline$_3$ institutions, such as professional bodies, academies, accreditation systems and academic journals that the loose collection of individuals in Discipline$_2$ are brought into alignment, with varying degrees of success, with the rules provided by a Discipline$_1$. Discipline$_3$ therefore gives rise to Discipline$_1$, although it may also be argued that it is the strength of the Discipline$_1$ that affects the ability of Discipline$_3$ to marshal Discipline$_2$. The theoretical basis of this view derives from Foucault (1977) for whom discipline was an important concept in understanding the use of power in relationships of control.

4.2   What Sort of Discipline is IS?

Although there have been a number of attempts to develop a theory of IS upon which, it is argued, the discipline should be based (see for example Stamper, Chapter 10), the failure of these models, so far at least, to achieve general acceptance, would suggest that IS does not meet the requirements for Discipline$_1$. The weaker interpretation of Discipline$_2$ would thus appear to be a more appropriate description of the current state of the field. This would seem to be borne out by much of the literature on the discipline of IS which treats the term as simply a synonym for field or domain of study. But does IS deserve even this epithet? Does the field show enough coherence to justify its identification as a distinctive area of study, or are there characteristics of IS that make it even less of a discipline than other subjects?

Banville and Landry (1989), for example, argue that the IS field is 'essentially pluralistic' and that, following Whitley (1984) it may be best characterised as a 'fragmented adhocracy' with very limited intellectual and organisational cohesion or standardisation of methods. While it may be possible to disagree with the extent to which this specific characteristisation is an appropriate description of the IS field, there would seem to be general recognition that the field exhibits (growing?) methodological pluralism (Orlikowski and Baroudi, 1991), fragmented research efforts (Culnan, 1987), weak entry barriers (perhaps inevitable in a subject which did not exist when many of its current participants were starting their careers), and competing perspectives (Backhouse et al., 1991).

That IS lacks the cohesion of even some of the more poorly-integrated subjects might, however, be attributed simply to its novelty. Maybe it is just a matter of time before these alternative viewpoints are reconciled. For example, the recent acknowledgement by the editors of MIS Quarterly, traditionally a bastion of positivism (Emery, 1989), of the potential value of interpretive methodologies (DeSanctis, 1993), might seem to indicate the emergence of the sort of unifying framework advocated by writers such as Lee (1991).

An examination of the scale and scope of the differences between the contributors to the IS field, however, gives little grounds for optimism on that score. Thus, there is little sign as yet that *MIS Quarterly*'s new Editorial policy has led to a significant change in the nature of the papers that it publishes. Moreover, as Walsham (1995) discusses, despite their minority status within the IS field (95% of the papers identified by Orlikowski and Baroudi (1991) employed positivist methods), interpretive researchers are not necessarily any more conciliatory in their view of alternative methods than their positivist counterparts. Continuing divisions between different 'schools' of IS research would therefore seem likely to evade early resolution, if indeed, as Van Maanen (1995b) argues in relation to organisational studies, they can ever be reconciled at all.

This does not mean that attempts cannot, and in principle should not, be made to promote an IS discipline (by deploying the mechanisms of Discipline$_3$). Indeed authors such as Backhouse *et al.* (1991) argue that not to do so represents a 'threat to the study of IS as a valid academic domain' (Discipline$_2$). Such moves, however, should be made in acknowledgement of the weakness of the disciplinary status of IS and not seek to present a spurious cohesion where none currently exists. Moreover, as Van Maanen (1995a, 1995b) forcefully and entertainingly argues in rebutting similar claims of the strategic necessity of paradigmatic unity by Pfeffer (1993, 1995), disciplinary conformity may not be without its costs, in terms of 'style, breadth, [and] theoretical and methodological innovation' (Van Maanen, 1995b: 691)

In this respect it is interesting to note the simultaneous emergence in 1994 in both the UK and the USA of attempts to construct disciplinary structures in the form of the Academy, and Association of IS. In terms of Foucault's analysis (Foucault, 1977), these are not neutral institutions for mutual edification, but apparatuses of power through which unruly bodies may be controlled and proper standards of behaviour enforced (Discipline$_3$). If successful, these structures will help to define the members of the IS community, and hence, by implication, also those who are not.

Other mechanisms of control, such as conferences and journals also help to establish, through their refereeing processes and editorial policies, the boundaries and priorities of the discipline. As

Walsham (1995) discusses this can be effective in shaping at least the presentation of research in the field. From a Discipline3 perspective, however, the proliferation of journals (there are now more than a dozen with the term Information System in the title alone) and conferences in recent years may be considered to have hindered rather than helped the achievement of greater cohesion. It also raises the question of who speaks for the discipline, which of the journals and conferences should be seen as authoritative?

Seniority can be of some value in this respect, and may contribute to the influence of the annual *International Conference on Information Systems* which has run since 1980, and *MIS Quarterly*, established in 1977. Authority may also be bolstered by opinion surveys (Nord and Nord, 1995) and citation impact exercises (Social Sciences Citation Index, 1992), but journals and conferences face a continuing need to maintain their reputation through ever more rigourous reviewing procedures (provided that submission rates remain healthy) and by establishing alliances with other disciplinary systems. For example the Association of IS provides reduced price subscriptions for *Information Systems, The Journal of Organisational Computing* and *MIS Quarterly*, while the UK Academy of Information Systems has links with *The European Journal of Information Systems, The Information Systems Journal, The Journal of Information Technology, The Journal of Strategic Information Systems* and *Systems Research.*

A sign of the relative weakness of the IS field, however, is that its Discipline3 mechanisms are largely dependent on other structures for their influence. Thus the Association of IS in the USA is, in part, a defensive reaction against the decision of the American Association of Schools of Business to exclude IS from the core curriculum for accredited American Business Schools (Dickson *et al.,* 1993). The Association of IS is thus intended to provide a body that can argue the case for IS in such fora. Similarly in the UK, the treatment of IS in the forthcoming Research Assessment Exercise has provided a stimulus to the formation of the Academy of Information Systems as is shown by the attention devoted to this issue in its early newsletters (Avison, 1995). The expansion of IS journals may also be seen as having been assisted by the 'publish or perish' mentality of the US tenure system and the UK Research Assessment Exercise.

The creation of an IS discipline need not be wholly defensive though—there are positive incentives for such a move. Being recognised as a discipline confers a status on the field and its practitioners that can enhance career prospects, promote good practice, and, not unimportantly, provide opportunities for individual advancement through filling the various editorships, committee posts and expert advisor positions that the disciplinary structures create. A discipline can also have benefits even for less exalted members in terms of creating a community of people working on similar subjects who provide the opportunity for debate around topics of mutual interest. The importance of such a community for the majority of IS academics who are located outside the small number (in almost every country) of IS departments with more than a handful of staff, should not be underestimated.

In the light of the continuing debate in the field about its disciplinary status and the relatively recent nature of a number of the initiatives to provide more formal disciplinary structures, however, it would seem, at the very least, premature to regard IS as constituting a *distinctive* discipline, whose defining features can be set in terms of, for example, 'approved' syllabuses, certification of practitioners and criteria for membership of professional bodies. It would therefore seem more helpful to consider it as a 'field' or 'area of study' and to focus on its unifying features rather than its boundaries.

4.3   What Unifies IS?

Perhaps the only thing that unites the IS field is its subject matter, which, in general, is seen as involving a focus on systems that, increasingly, make use of information technology. There are significant differences of interpretation, however, on the nature of these systems (primarily technological or social), the interest in them (improving their effectiveness or analysing their effects), the level of analysis (individual, organisational or societal) and even about what *information* itself is (Mingers, 1995). IS also differs from most other 'disciplines' in lacking a unifying concept, such as space in geography, or the language in French.

Moreover, the main reasons why these systems constitute an important subject for study is not, it may be argued, because of their intrinsic interest or distinctive character, but because of their growing ubiquity (at least in the major industrialised economies), the scale of the investment in them and their consequent centrality to modern economic and social activity. As a result, it is widely argued that they are essential features of a new techno-economic paradigm, often characterised as the Information Society or Age.

While the relationship between IS and these, arguably very profound, social and organisational changes certainly suggests that they are potentially important topics for research, this does not mean that they are necessarily the dominant driving force behind these changes, as is often argued. For example, while IT-based systems have clearly played a major role in the growth of global corporations, the East India Company was able to operate a form of transnationalism long before the invention of the technologies that we call IT today. Globalisation is therefore not dependent on IT. Economic and social changes, such as rising labour costs in industrialised countries, and developments in international transportation systems have also provided a major stimulus to globalisation, largely independent of the influence of IS. It may therefore be more helpful to consider the social and organisational changes as making increasing use of IS developments which thereby help to reinforce their momentum, rather than as being IS-driven.

Seeing IS in the context of social and organisational changes, however, is both a danger and an opportunity for IS researchers. If we are to understand the role of IS, then we need to have a broad understanding of social processes, a subject in which relatively few of those currently involved in the field would consider themselves to be experts. There is therefore a risk of poor quality research as people struggle to operate in areas in which they are inadequately qualified (practically as well as academically). The opportunity, however, is that the role of the technological element in these changes is often poorly understood, even by otherwise subtle social theorists. There is therefore a distinctive contribution that IS researchers can make in such debates and it is this conjunction of the social and the technical that makes IS such a potentially demanding and important field.

There would be no case for IS as a distinctive field of research, however, if it was always simply an adjunct to work in other fields. Nor can the ubiquity and economic significance of its focal systems provide a sufficient justification. On such grounds, there would, historically, have been a case for a discipline of Steam Systems. While this might have been an interesting subject, the fact that it apparently never acted as a focus for concerted multi-disciplinary research may lead us to question whether this is simply a result of changes in academia over the past century, or if there are some additional qualities of IS that merit the attention directed at them.

4.4   The Distinctive Character of IS

While there have been a number of valuable contributions to the IS literature which have illustrated the potential of approaches such as socio-technical theory (Mumford, 1995), structuration theory (Orlikowski, 1992), critical social theory (Lyytinen and Klein, 1985) and hermeneutics (Boland, 1991) in the study of IS, these have not, it may be argued, depended upon any intrinsic character of IS *per se*. Thus their contribution could have been applied to other technologically-based systems, but addressed IS because of their current economic and social significance.

There are at least two characteristics of IS, however, that may be identified as distinguishing them from other technologically-based systems (such as steam power). The first of these is probably the most important: Shoshana Zuboff's concept of informating (Zuboff, 1988). This term has, unfortunately, become much misused in the IS literature, where it is often treated as little more than a synonym for certain organisational changes, usually presented (not least by Zuboff herself) as benign and emancipatory, or as an extension of automation into the realm of control (*cf* Blackburn *et al.* , 1985).

A more careful reading of Zuboff (1988), however, would suggest a different, and potentially more significant interpretation: that IT allows the textualisation of previously hidden work practices. For example, to take one of Zuboff's illustrations, the installation of computerised process control equipment in the Tiger Creek paper mill meant that a number of the operatives were able to develop a more explicit model of the performance of the equipment they were in charge of, and thus to take on greater responsibilities for managing their own work. On the other hand bar-code scanners in supermarkets can allow the monitoring of work-rates of check-out operators down to the level of the speed with which individual purchases are 'swiped'. As a result, some UK supermarket chains have started to include clauses in their work agreements which permit the use of such data in assessing employee performance. While this latter example, and a number of the others cited by Zuboff herself, suggest that informating can be a new means of management surveillance and contribute to work intensification, the important point here is not whether it is necessarily either a 'good' or a 'bad' thing, but that informating is a new development that results from the particular character of IS. Thus, informating is a significant and distinctive feature of IS, whether it enables the development of an information panopticon, in which every action of the individual is made visible to a controlling authority, or the opening up for participants of new realms of understanding of their work.

The second characteristic of IS that is novel, relates to the particular and unusual qualities of its essential resource, information (or perhaps strictly-speaking, data—the distinction between these offered by Liebenau and Backhouse (1990) is helpful, if not always widely recognised). The immateriality of information which means that it is not consumed when it is used, that its value exists only in its use (which also always depends on human interpretation), and that it is able to transcend normal time/space constraints, makes it very different from the commodities on which previous techno-economic 'revolutions' have been based. There are therefore a set of distinctive issues that IS research has to address. They do not, however, it may be argued, provide a *sufficient* case for treating IS as a separate discipline.

Thus most of the topics that IS researchers study might equally well be covered by other subjects. For example: strategy is usually dealt with rather better within management (as Jones (1995) discusses, traditional conceptions of strategy still widely employed in the IS field embody a formal-rational model of the strategy process that ignores signficant recent developments in the management strategy literature); information systems development within software engineering (or, more recently, anthropology—see for example Button, 1993); computer-mediated communication within social psychology (Galegher *et al.*, 1990); and the Information Society within sociology (see for example Webster, 1995). While such a list rather deliberately, tramples on some toes, its purpose is not solely provocative, but to question whether there is much beyond certain terms in particular people's job titles that justifies seeing their work as part of a single domain. Moreover, if the work in some other fields leaves much to be desired, for example much software engineering has a very impoverished, mechanistic conception of organisations, this does not mean that IS researchers necessarily have the answers by virtue of their different professional identity.

4.5   An Alternative Perspective

The position set out above would seem to have four important implications for IS as a discipline. First, if IS is not a discipline itself, then research in the field must be multi-disciplinary. No particular perspective can claim to have the 'right way' to understand IS (even if certain arguments are felt to be more persuasive by particular authors). Multi-disciplinarity, however, though widely advocated, often amounts to a dialogue of the deaf in which incompatible research approaches are pursued in parallel with little or no communication between them. The factionalism within economics would seem a salutary warning in this respect. Achieving multi-disciplinarity therefore requires a more reflective approach on all sides in which researchers maintain a critical awareness of the nature of their claims rather than seeking to establish the hegemony of their own viewpoint.

Second, this suggests that IS researchers need to engage with many disciplines, rather than assuming that the particular department within which they are located defines the boundaries of the subject. The openness of physics, for example, to mathematics may be seen to have substantially enriched both subjects. In principle, therefore, since there would seem to be no *a priori* limit on the number of possible reference disciplines, IS researchers need to remain receptive to a wide range of potential new perspectives on the issues with which they are concerned.

The third implication is possibly the most difficult to achieve, but is necessary none the less. This is that IS researchers should seek to do research which is good in terms of other disciplines. Quality IS research should be able to stand comparison with research in the discipline on which it is based, whichever that may be, and the specialised field of interest should not be used as a justification for IS becoming a backwater for substandard research.

One practical consequence of this is the need for IS researchers to go back to the original texts in the reference discipline (even if not necessarily in their original language) to gain a genuine appreciation of the arguments being proposed, rather than relying on the interpretations of secondary sources (the *Fontana Modern Masters* school of erudition), or regrettably often worse, of other IS scholars. The dangers of such second-hand scholarship are well illustrated in recent use of Giddens' structuration theory (Giddens 1984) in the IS field, where the adaptive structuration theory of De Sanctis and Poole (1994), itself arguably a significant misinterpretation of Giddens' ideas, has been taken up by others (for example Gopal *et al.*, 1992), without any reference to the original source of the concepts they are employing, as the basis for a positivist research programme that is almost the polar opposite of Giddens' position.

This is not to argue, following the dictum of A.N. Whitehead who claimed that the European philosophical tradition consists in a series of footnotes to Plato, that all IS researchers should commence their studies with a thorough grounding in the classics, but if IS researchers are to use concepts such as actor networks, to utilise critical methods, or to talk of discourse for example, they ought at least to have read some Latour, Habermas or Foucault to get an idea of what these writers were actually saying. It should not be pretended that this will be an easy process, unfortunately many of these luminaries express their complex ideas in a dense and convoluted style and employ their own particular usages of apparently familiar words (cynics might suggest that this might be the part of the reason for their cachet), but it is a necessary price if work in the field is to be taken seriously by others.

Even if IS researchers make this effort, though, there is no guarantee of acceptance: the resistance of mainstream studies to new perspectives, particularly where these come from 'unqualified' researchers, should not be underestimated. If it aspires to improve its disciplinary status, however, the IS research community needs to set itself such 'stretch goals' (to adopt a currently popular term). If IS researchers are careful and thoughtful in their work they may find that other disciplines are receptive to their ideas. They should have confidence in the importance of the issues that they seek to address and believe that this will be recognised by others. Moreover, IS researchers need not simply be passive partners in the relationship with other disciplines, but can seek opportunities for promoting mutual understanding for example through joint conferences, publications and courses.

Finally, it is necessary for those involved in the IS field to be aware of the processes that are shaping it. What networks are being constructed? For example, who is in (and out) of the Association (and Academy) of IS? What sort of papers get published in the leading journals (and which are they)? Where are the obligatory points of passage? Just because IS is not a 'discipline', doesn't mean that those involved in the field are not 'disciplined'.

4.6   Conclusions

The discussion in this chapter might seem to present an unduly pessimistic analysis of the prospects for IS as a discipline which would seem to be out of place in the current volume. If those involved in the field are so unconvinced of its merits then what hope is there of developing the sort of coherent approach that would help to establish it as a significant academic discipline. Examination of the title of this collection, however, reveals that it describes IS as an 'emerging discipline' and that it ends with a question mark, suggesting that the established status of the IS field is not to be taken as given.

More importantly, the analysis in this paper is not intended as a counsel of despair. What it seeks to question, however, in the face of growing attempts to promote the $Discipline_3$ control structures in the IS domain, are the claims about the disciplinary status of IS that underpin these developments. As has been argued in this chapter IS, as a subject area, is notable for the weakness of its integrating principles. Drawing up boundary conditions, such as 'approved' syllabuses, certification of IS professionals and researchers would seem, in such circumstances, to risk excluding much that is of value and that currently gives the field its vibrancy. The *Concise Oxford English Dictionary*'s third definition for discipline is 'chastisement (Eccl); mortification by penance'. It is hoped that these 'heretical' thoughts do not condemn this particular author to too much chastisement and may help to avoid the subject of IS becoming a mortification by penance for us all.

Acknowledgement

The ideas presented here have benefited from comments from members of the IS Forum at the University of Cambridge and in particular from Eija Karsten.

References

Avison, D., 1995, Information Systems: subject definition and scope, *UK Academy for Information Systems Newsletter,* 1(3):3.

Avison, D.E. and Fitzgerald, G., 1991, IS practice, education and research, *Journal of Information Systems,* 1(1):5-17.

Backhouse, J. and Liebenau, J., 1989, A need for discipline, *Times Higher Educational Supplement,* 31 March.

Backhouse, J., Liebenau, J. and Land, F., 1991, On the discipline of IS, *Journal of Information Systems,* 1(1):19-27.

Banville, C. and Landry, M., 1989, Can the field of MIS be disciplined, *Communications of the ACM,* 32:48-60.

Blackburn, P. Coombs, R; and Green, K., 1985, *Technology, Economic Growth and the Labour Process,* Macmillan, London.

Boland, R., 1991, Information systems use as a hermeneutic process, in *Information Systems Research: Contemporary Approaches and Emergent Traditions,* H. Nissen, H. Klein and R. Hirschheim, eds., North-Holland, Amsterdam.

Buckingham, R.A., Hirschheim, R.A., Land, F.F. and Tully, C.J., 1987, Information systems curriculum: a basis for course design. in *Information Systems Education: Recommendations and Implementation,* Buckingham, R.A. ed, Cambridge University Press, Cambridge

Button, G. *Technology in Working Order: Studies of Work, Interaction, and Technology,* Routledge, London

Culnan, M., 1987, Mapping the intellectual structure of MIS, 1980-1985: a co-citation analysis, *MIS Quarterly,* 11(3):341-353.

Culnan, M. and Swanson, E.B., 1986, Research in management information systems, *MIS Quarterly,* 10(3):289-302.

DeSanctis, G., 1993, Theory and research: goals, priorities and approaches, *MIS Quarterly,* 17(1): vi-viii.

DeSanctis, G., and Poole, M.S., 1994, Capturing the complexity in advanced technology use: adaptive structuration theory. *Organisation Science,* 5(2):121-147

Dickson, G.W., Emery, J.C., Ives, B., King, W.R. and McFarlan, F.W., 1993, Professional societies: a service to members and professional leadership, *MIS Quarterly*, 17(1):iii-vi.

Ein-Dor, P. and Segev, E., 1981, A Paradigm for Management Information Systems, Praeger, New York.

Emery, J.C., 1989, Editor's comments, *MIS Quarterly*, 13(3):xi-xii.

Foucault, M., 1977, *Discipline and Punish: the Birth of the Prison*, Allen Lane, London.

Galegher, J., Kraut, R.E. and Egido, C., 1990, *Intellectual Teamwork: Social and Technological Foundations of Cooperative Work*, Lawrence Erlbaum, London.

Giddens, A., 1984, *The Constitution of Society: Outline of the Theory of Structure*, Polity, Cambridge.

Gopal, A. Bostrom, R.P. and Chin, W.W., 1992, Applying adaptive structuration theory to investigate the process of group support systems use, *Journal of Management Information Systems*, 9(3):45-69.

Jones, M.R., 1995, Learning the language of the market: information systems strategy formation in a UK District Health Authority, *Accounting, Management and Information Technology*, 4(3):119-147.

Keen, P.G.W, 1981, MIS research: reference disciplines and a cumulative tradition, in E. McLean, ed., *Proceedings of the First International Conference on Information Systems*. Philadelphia, 9-18.

Kuhn, T., 1970, *The Structure of Scientific Revolutions*, Chicago University Press, Chicago.

Lee, A.S. 1991 Integrating positivist and interpretive approaches to organisational research, *Organisation Science*, 2(4):342-365.

Liebenau, J. and Backhouse, J., 1990, *Understanding Information: an Introduction*, Macmillan , Basingstoke.

Lyytinen, K. and Klein, H., 1985, The critical social theory of Jurgen Habermas as a basis for a theory of information systems, in *Research Methods in Information Systems,* E. Mumford, R. Hirschheim, G. Fitzgerald and T. Wood Harper, eds., North-Holland, Amsterdam, 219-232.

Mingers, J., 1995, Information and meaning: foundations for an intersubjective account, *Information Systems Journal*, 5,285-306.

Mumford, E., 1995, *Effective Systems Design and Requirements Analysis: The ETHICS Approach*, Macmillan, Basingstoke.

Nord, J.H. and Nord, D.G., 1995, MIS research: journal status assessment and analysis, *Information and Management*, 29(1):29-42.

Orlikowski, W.J. and Baroudi, J.J., 1991, Studying information systems in organisations: research approaches and assumptions, *Information Systems Research*, 2(1):1-28.

Orlikowski, W.J., 1992, The duality of technology: rethinking the concept of technology in organisations, *Organisation Science*, 3(3):398-427.

Pfeffer, J., 1993, Barriers to the advance of organisational science: paradigm development as a dependent variable, *Academy of Management Review*, 18(4):599-620.

Pfeffer, J., 1995, Mortality, reproducibility and the persistence of styles of theory, *Organisation Science*, 6(6):681-686.

Social Sciences Citation Index, 1992, Journal citation reports, Institute for Scientific Information, Philadelphia.

Walsham, G., 1995, The emergence of interpretivism in IS research, *Information Systems Research*, 6(4):376-394.

Webster, F., 1995, *Theories of the Information Society,* Routledge, London.

Whitley, R., 1984, *The Intellectual and Social Organisation of the Sciences*, Clarendon Press, Oxford.

Van Maanen, J., 1995a, Style as theory, *Organisation Science*, 6(1):132-143.

Van Maanen, J., 1995b, Fear and loathing in organisation studies, *Organisation Science*, 6(6):687-692.

Zuboff, S., 1988, *In the Age of the Smart Machine: the Future of Work and Power,* Heinemann Educational, Oxford.

Chapter 5

THE 'DISCIPLINE' OF INFORMATION SYSTEMS: TEACHING, RESEARCH, AND PRACTICE

David Avison

5.1 Background

This chapter is about establishing and furthering the academic discipline of information systems. By 'discipline' I mean 'a branch of instruction or learning'—I am somewhat nervous about 'mental and moral training', 'system of rules for conduct', 'behaviour according to established rules', 'order maintained', 'control exercise over members of an organisation', 'chastisement', 'mortification by penance', 'bring under control', 'train to obedience and order', 'drill', 'punish' or 'chastise' (all definitions from the *Concise Oxford Dictionary*). Indeed, I am also somewhat nervous about 'a branch of instruction or learning', because it might imply agreement on a limited field of study and perhaps some 'control', 'obedience' and too much 'order' about what we teach and research. This gives ground for concern, because information systems is a pluralistic field, founded on knowledge from other, more established, source disciplines. It should not be constrained to a narrow branch of learning, with limited research methods and domains.

We may respond by arguing that we should not worry about the question of the 'discipline' of information systems at all. It might be a concern only for those who wish to limit the areas taught and researched and the methods used. These people might indeed be trying to control, keep order and, perhaps, punish or chastise those who do not conform. We do not want this: the university sector would surely be poorer if we all taught the same material, used the

113

same texts, used the same teaching methods, pursued the same areas of research, used the same research methods and used the same case studies of 'good practice'.

Yet there have been many attempts to define a standard curriculum; a number of texts are marketed on the basis that they cover 'the' syllabus; some journals publish only one style of research paper; and there are case studies that are so widely used that few other 'stories' are told. While not suggesting that these are healthy, there are reasons why the move to establish a discipline might be positive. Unless a subject and its researchers achieve recognition, then it is difficult to gain funding for research. Further, it will be unlikely that it constitutes a research assessment panel or even be fairly represented in one. Its teachers and researchers will be unlikely to have the political clout to enable groups to expand and develop in universities. All these have financial implications which stifle research and teaching in universities. The news concerning practice is not much better, as information systems academics have made little impact.

As 'founding professor' in information systems at my own university, I used my inaugural lecture, What is IS? (Avison, 1995), to introduce information systems to the university. Few people in the university had knowledge of what the subject was about, what impact it had made and could make, what was researched, and how it was researched. Indeed, the widespread view was that information systems was another name for information technology. At my previous university, it was thought that it was another name for systems engineering (by which was meant, apparently, 'hardware'). This particular confusion is not helped by the British Computer Society referring to itself as the 'society for information systems engineers'. I have taught the same subject in departments of accounting, management, commerce, computer science and mathematics, and in faculties of science, social science, engineering and business. This suggests that the subject lacks focus and presents an image of incoherence.

This image of incoherence might be further exacerbated by the differing names for the academic field (and professors of the domain): information systems, computer information systems, information management, information technology, information resources management and management information systems.

These may not be synonyms, but the differences are not perceived consistently by everyone in the field.

Readers might be tempted now to limit the domain of information systems and argue against inter-disciplinarity, but, as we shall see, it is a pluralist discipline and many social science disciplines are inter-disciplinary as are some more established disciplines elsewhere, such as medicine. However, while it is important to recognise the plurality in the discipline, it is also important to establish some boundaries, but avoid narrow and rigid ones so as to maintain the richness of the subject.

In this chapter a domain for the discipline is suggested, followed by some guidelines for teaching, research and practice. Finally, we return to the topic of inter-disciplinarity, suggesting ways to overcome the problems that this might bring.

5.2   The Domain of Information Systems

The multi-faceted nature of the field is seen if we consider a definition of the central object of our discipline. Buckingham *et al.* (1987) define an information system as follows:

> A system which assembles, stores, processes and delivers information relevant to an organisation (or to society) in such a way that the information is accessible and useful to those who wish to use it, including managers, staff, clients and citizens. An information system is a human activity (social) system which may or may not involve computer systems.

This definition would seem to encompass a wide range of interests and underlying disciplines, for example, information theory (information), linguistics, psychology and semiology (delivers information), organisation theory and sociology (organisation and society), ethics and economics (impact on society) and computer science and engineering (computer systems).

The UK Academy of Information Systems (UKAIS) regards the subject's inter-disciplinary status as a cornerstone of their definition (UKAIS, 1996):

> The study of information systems and their development is a multi-disciplinary subject and addresses the range of strategic, managerial and operational activities involved in

the gathering, processing, storing, distributing and use of information, and its associated technologies, in society and organisations.

Both definitions suggest that information systems concerns the inter-relationship between people and organisations, on the one hand, and technology on the other. Although the former makes the point that computers may not be involved, 'the effective and efficient analysis, design, delivery, use and impact of information in organisations and society' (modified from Keen, 1987) is unlikely to be provided without modern information technologies, although the technology is surely not the essence of an information systems (just as a word-processing system is not the essence of a good novel). Computer technology may be seen as 'one management tool among many' (Davis, 1987).

Nevertheless, there may be some differences in view between the above 'European view' and a 'North American view'. For example, Cougar et al. (1995) define the scope of information systems as encompassing two broad areas:

1. Acquisition, development and management of information technology resources and services, which is referred to as the information systems function, and
2. Development and evolution of infrastructure and systems for information use in organisation processes, which is referred to as systems development.

In further defining these two major areas, it is the information technology that is stressed. For example, the former refers to the responsibility to develop, implement and manage an information infrastructure of information technology (computer and communications), data (both internal and external), and organisation-wide systems. It has the responsibility to track new information technology and support departmental and individual information technology systems. Systems development, the second part, is seen as involving creative use of information technology for data acquisition, communication, coordination, analysis, and decision support.

5.3   Information Systems Teaching

Information systems has been taught in university departments of computer science, where courses might reflect a technology-driven view of the world, and in business departments, where the teaching might stress applications and implications of the technology. The focus of many early business courses has been on training systems development practitioners. However, there are now some departments of information systems in the UK, and the teaching of information systems as being a balance of human, social and organisational factors on the one hand, and technological factors on the other, has gained pre-eminence in the UK. This is found in the suggested curriculum of Buckingham *et al.* (1987). It is also found in the draft curriculum of the UKAIS (1996):

1. Theoretical underpinnings of information systems (for example, theories of information, systems and organisation).
2. Data, information and knowledge management (theory and practice, including information resource management, database design and management, information and knowledge-based products/services).
3. Derivation, development and maintenance of information systems and processes (for example, theory, notation, conventions, modelling, processes, methods, techniques, technology and tools).
4. Capabilities, potential and limitations of technology as an intrinsic component of information systems.
5. Management of information systems and services (including the development and management of specialist professional skills, staff, related technologies and suppliers).
6. Information in organisational decision making (for example, decision and role theory and use of decision support and communication systems, management information systems, executive information systems, group decision support systems).
7. Strategic alignment (the role of information systems and technology in organisation strategies, planning, investment, risk, evaluation and benefit realisation).
8. Organisational and human impact of technology-based information systems.

9. Economic impacts of technology-based information systems (upon organisations, industries, including the information technology industry, and national and international economies).
10.Social and cultural effects of technology-based information systems (for example, at individual, organisational, national, international levels and implications for social policies, professional, legal and ethical standards, employment, education).

Although a number of correspondents have suggested modifications to this draft in the UKAIS Newsletter, they are ones of detail. This curriculum puts some boundaries on the subject without attacking the spirit of multi-disciplinarity or the balance of the discipline suggested by the definitions given in the previous section.

This curriculum is somewhat different to the joint one of the Association for Computing Machinery (ACM), Data Processing Management Association (DPMA), International Conference of Information Systems (ICIS) and the Association of Information Systems (AIS) in the USA, as seen in Cougar *et al.* (1995), prepared by academics and practitioners. This suggests courses as follows:

1. Knowledge work software tool kit
2. Fundamentals of information systems
3. Personal productivity with information systems technology
4. Information systems theory and practice
5. Information technology hardware and software
6. Programming, data, file and object structures
7. Telecommunications
8. Analysis and logical design
9. Physical design and implementation with DBMS
10.Physical design and implementation with programming environments
11.Project management and practice.

This curriculum does contain behavioural topics, such as creativity and empowerment, the effect of information systems on organisational structures, and ethical and societal issues in the detailed specification of the courses. This is nearer the wider UK AIS curriculum when compared to earlier US curricula in information systems (as found in, for example, DPMA, 1992 and Nunamaker *et al.*, 1992). Nevertheless, although possibly similar in the most part to a programme in information systems in a computer science department in the UK, this is certainly narrower and more computer-oriented than that suggested by the UK AIS.

Another aspect of information systems teaching concerns how the subject is taught, as against what is taught. Of course, lectures and tutorials are important, as in any subject. This is backed up by computer work and individual projects at most universities. However, case study work and action learning perhaps gain more emphasis in information systems teaching when compared to computer science and related courses.

There are two types of case studies. The first concerns a description of a case, usually with notes, supervisors' notes, videos and the rest, about what happened in an information systems project in the real-world. It is to be hoped that leaders of case study courses go 'behind' a case such as Otis Lifts, American Hospital Supply and American Airlines which are questionable versions of the reality described. The second is where an outline case is prepared for the students to 'develop a solution'. Again, there are warnings here. As Checkland (1994) points out, doing a case study and *pretending* to take decisions which, for example, might lead to the redundancy of workers, is very different from doing it.

Action learning (Avison, 1989) allows students who have already completed formal courses in information systems to practise using some of the techniques, tools and methodologies in a real-world situation. Students can gain experience of investigating, analysing, designing and prototyping information systems, working in teams, and in doing so experience people problems, making difficult decisions and so on. Case studies and action learning programmes suggest that the subject matter is steeped in practice, and in some university departments, driven by practice.

5.4 Information Systems Research

Keen (1987), in an overview of research in (management) information systems, critically examines particular areas of research. He points out that there has been a high proportion of 'hard' information systems research (that is, that relating to the technology, for example, design methodologies, computers, implementation, productivity tools, office technology and telecommunications); research looking for particular gains for businesses in an economically competitive environment (for example, economic and competitive implications); and also research looking for 'solutions' to perennial problems (for example, productivity tools, database management, personal computing and expert systems).

It is claimed (for example, Galliers and Land, 1987; Orlikowski and Baroudi, 1991) that the positivist research approach, which has its roots in the natural sciences, is the most commonly adopted because of a technological view of information systems. For example, Orlikowski and Baroudi (1991) found that 97% of the information systems literature they examined fell under positivist epistemology. These studies assume an objective reality, reducing information systems phenomena to their simplest elements, looking for causality and fundamental laws. These are seen as forming the basis for generalisable knowledge, often represented in mathematical models, that can predict patterns of behaviour, independent of time and context (for example, Foster and Flynn, 1984).

In recent years, however, social and organisational issues concerning information systems have been increasingly recognised. The work of IFIP Working Group 8.2 also reflects this (see, for example, Avison et al., 1993). This view is reflected in the use of non-positivist research approaches to study information systems. There are various strands among the non-positivist studies, depending of their views of the nature of information systems and the approach to inquiry. For example, interpretive approaches, aim to understand how members of a social group, through their participation in social processes, enact their particular realities and endow them with meaning (Walsham, 1993). Interpretive studies therefore view information systems as social constructions, focusing on shared interpretation around information systems and how meanings arise and are sustained (see, for example, Boland and Day, 1985). Within the interpretive studies, the role of theory in research also varies. For example, studies using a 'grounded theory' approach seek to develop new theory to explain information systems phenomena from the researcher's own interpretations (for example, Orlikowski, 1993). In these studies, theories are seen as emerging from the data. Other studies illustrate the potential of a theory to explain an information systems phenomenon (for example, Orlikowski and Robey, 1991; Walsham and Han, 1993; Jones and Nandhakumar, 1993). Another non-positivist approach to information systems research is critical epistemology (for example, Klein and Hirschheim, 1993), which takes account of structural contradiction within the social system.

There is also a range of research methods which are generally associated with the positivist and non-positivist approaches to information systems research. For example, much of the information systems research within the positivist traditions are primarily surveys investigating information systems phenomena within a single slice of time. This method is normally associated with scientific discipline and quantitative data.

Interpretive studies, on the other hand, tend to employ longitudinal field studies, seeking to obtain in-depth understanding on information systems phenomena. Most widely used techniques in information systems research are interviews, which are generally associated with qualitative data. Many other techniques are used in conjunction with interviews in the field, such as observation (Orlikowski, 1992) and participant observation (Jones and Nandhakumar, 1993). Interpretive studies tend to present detailed case studies from the field data to describe a version of events from which alternative interpretations can be made. Much of these techniques are commonly used in other disciplines, such as sociology and anthropology. For example, participant observation has its root in ethnographic research studies, where the researcher would live in tribal villages attempting to understand stage cultures (Easterby-Smith et al., 1991).

Other field methods used in information systems research are action research (for example, Avison and Wood-Harper, 1991). In this work, the use of action research led to the definition of the Multiview approach to information systems development, and was later used to refine the approach. In action research, the researcher seeks deliberately to intervene in the situation, often by employing specific techniques, in order to achieve a particular outcome. Action research is most frequently adopted in organisational development (Easterby-Smith et al., 1991)

The strength of the positivist research approach lies in its ability to provide a wide coverage of various situations and to be fast and economical, as well as in its rigour and replicability in the conduct of scientific research. However, Orlikowski and Baroudi (1991) claim that the existing dominance of positivism in information systems research provides a partial view and has implications on the understanding of information systems phenomena, theory building and thus for the practice of information systems work. The strength and weakness of the non-positivist approach are fairly complementary. Thus the main strength of the interpretive approach is its ability to look at change processes over time, to understand actors' meanings, to adjust to new issues and theories as they emerge, and to contribute to the evolution of new theories (Easterby-Smith *et al.*, 1991).

In researching information systems development, for example, field experiments, surveys, case studies and action research are particularly well used, but there are advocates of all the following research methods in information systems (Van Horn, 1973; Dickson *et al.*, 1977; Ein-Dor and Segev, 1981, Galliers, 1985; Benbasat *et al.*, 1987; Galliers, 1991):

- Conceptual study
- Mathematical modelling
- Laboratory experiment
- Field experiment
- Survey
- Case study
- Phenomenology
- Hermeneutics
- Participant observation
- Grounded theory
- Longitudinal study
- Action research.

I will attempt to give the briefest of overviews of the research methods used in information systems. Conceptual study is frequently referred to as armchair research. No actual on-site experimentation is carried out. It may precede other research. In mathematical modelling the degree of control is absolute: all variables are known, no human subjects are required and no context exists to affect the results. Objectivity is high. Some research in software engineering might be of this type. Phenomenology is concerned with meaning that gives sense and significance to our experience and attempts to find out what things are. The context is important (as it might be in any study of social action). Hermeneutics refutes the idea of an objective world alone, 'reality' is flavoured by our subjective perception. In laboratory experiments, one of the independent variables is manipulated by the researcher. Compared to action research, more control can be exercised by the researcher.

Action research is often confused with case study research, but whereas case study research examines phenomena in its natural setting with the researcher as independent outsider, in action research the researcher is participant. Grounded research might proceed through a series of interviews or observations to hypothesis formation. As no hypothesis is assumed, it attempts to avoid pre-judging the issues—it generates rather than tests theory. In participant observation, although there is active involvement by the observer, that person does not seek to influence the situation more than would be expected from other participants. Longitudinal studies, seeking to obtain in-depth understanding on information systems phenomena, add time as one of the important dimensions to the study. Action research is notable for the deliberate intervention of the researcher. Field experiments include field studies, field tests, adaptive experiment and group feedback analysis and demonstrate mixes of subjective and objective elements with a moderate degree of control. Surveys, or opinion research, concerns the gathering of data from human subjects on attitudes, opinions and beliefs as well as responses which are more 'cbjective'.

Survey research followed by case study research are, perhaps, the most well used approaches in information systems.

I wish to make some observations about research methods in the context of information systems. First, I have purposely 'mixed up' the list. They are often listed in a sequence that represents some continuum, say, from quantitative to qualitative; positivist to anti-positivist (Burrell and Morgan, 1979). Three observations here. First, there is a series of continua (for example, degree of involvement might form another) and also the research methods do not sit easily in their positions on the continuum (some aspects might be 'positivist' and other aspects 'qualitative'). Second, in any research project, several research methods can be used (and not only the same mix). The research that led to the definition of

Multiview was described as action research. Indeed, the cycle of theory, action, reflection, and theory modification using Multiview in a number of sites was carried out with researchers and practitioners involved in a cycle of action research. But this whole research included 'conceptual research' carried out when considering the various research methods in the literature; 'case study' research, when looking at the application of the alternative methodologies in context, and so on. Third, much research in information systems does not fit easily into a research category. These neat categories are the realm of texts and courses in research methods. To give one example, some research does not fit easily to being described as either case study or action research: the role of the researcher may have aspects in the project of both 'observer' and 'decision maker'.

The multi-approach and complex nature of information systems research is illustrative of information systems as a discipline: it is multi-disciplinary and multi-faceted, and one would expect there to be many appropriate research methods. If, however, we look at the range of research approaches, the emphasis in Europe is more and more on qualitative methods associated with the social sciences rather than with the more positivist approaches associated with the science and engineering disciplines. I would expect the 97% figure for positivist research that Orlikowski and Baroudi (1991) found in the USA to be lower than 50% in Europe by the end of the century.

5.5   Information Systems Practice

The multi-disciplinary nature of information systems practice can be seen by looking at one aspect, that of the approaches used to develop information systems. Avison and Fitzgerald (1995) suggest that information systems development methodologies can be compared on the basis of philosophy, model, techniques, tools, scope, outputs, practice and product, and they classify approaches within a number of broad themes including:

- Systems
- Strategic
- Participative
- Prototyping
- Structured

- Data
- Object-oriented.

General systems theory attempts to understand the nature of systems which are large and complex. Organisations are open systems, and the relationship between the organisation and its environment are important. Systems approaches attempt to capture this 'holistic' view, following Aristotle's dictum that 'the whole is greater than the sum of the parts'. By simplifying a complex situation, we may be reductionist, and thereby distort our understanding of the overall system. The most well-known approach of this type in the information systems arena is Checkland's soft systems methodology (SSM), found in Checkland (1981) and Checkland and Scholes (1990), although the most convincing account of relevance to information systems is found in Wilson (1990) and as part of a blended approach in Multiview (Avison and Wood-Harper, 1990).

Strategic approaches stress the pre-planning involved in developing information systems and the need for an overall strategy. This involves top management in the analysis of the objectives of their organisation. Planning approaches counteract the possibility of developing information systems in a piecemeal fashion. IBM's Business Systems Planning (IBM, 1975) is an early example of this approach and more recent examples are found in Bullen and Rockart (1986), Earl (1989), and Lederer and Mendelow (1989), and business process re-engineering (Davenport and Short, 1990; Hammer and Champy, 1993) is part of this movement.

In participative approaches, the role of all users is stressed, and the role of the technologist may be subsumed by other stakeholders of the information system. If the users are involved in the analysis, design and implementation of information systems relevant to their own work, particularly if this takes the form of genuine decision-making (as against lip-service consultation at the other extreme), these users are likely to give the new information system their full commitment when it is implemented, and thereby increase the likelihood of its success. ETHICS (Mumford, 1995) stresses the participative nature of information systems development, following the socio-technical movement and embodies a sustainable ethical position.

A prototype is an approximation of a type that exhibits the essential features of the final version of that type. By implementing a prototype first, the analyst can show the users inputs, intermediary stages, and outputs from the system. These are not diagrammatic approximations, which tend to be looked at as abstract things, or technically-oriented documentation, which may not be understood by the user, but the actual figures on computer paper or on terminal or workstation screens. Data dictionaries, fourth generation systems, CASE tools and workbenches of various kinds can all enable prototyping. These have become more and more powerful over the last few years. Rapid Application Development (Martin, 1991) is an example of a prototyping approach.

Structured methodologies are based on functional decomposition, that is, the breaking down of a complex problem into manageable units in a disciplined way. The development of structured methodologies in systems analysis and design stemmed from the perceived benefits of software engineering. These approaches tend to stress techniques, such as decision trees, decision tables, data flow diagrams, data structure diagrams, and structured English, and tools such as data dictionaries. Most of the techniques enable complex structures to be communicated using functional decomposition as the basic technique. Most of the documentation aids are graphic representations of the subject matter. This is usually much easier to follow than text or computer-oriented documentation. The approach adopted by Yourdon (1989) is typical of that school and follows the earlier works of DeMarco (1979) and Gane and Sarson (1979).

A methodology which incorporates formal methods uses mathematical precision and notation in the specification and design of an information system. Some systems requirements can be expressed mathematically rather than using natural language and this can be translated into computer language. This version of the specification can be tested for correctness. Software engineering approaches, which I have included in the structured school, aim at producing quality software and generally incorporate formal methods.

Whereas structured analysis and design emphasises processes, data analysis concentrates on understanding and documenting data. It involves the collection, validation and classification of the entities, attributes and relationships that exist in the area investigated. Even if applications change, the data already collected may still be relevant to the new or revised systems and therefore need not be collected and validated again. Information Engineering (Martin, 1989), for example, has a data approach as its crux.

Object-oriented information systems development has become the latest 'silver bullet'. Yourdon's (1994) exposition argues that the approach is more natural than data or process-based alternatives, the concepts of objects and attributes, wholes and parts and classes and parts are familiar to children, and also unifies the information systems development process.

In this brief tour around the various approaches to developing information systems, we see its potentially diverse nature. None of these approaches can be described as different flavours to well accepted approaches. They represent radically different approaches to information systems development and ways to perceive the information systems development process. They require different expertise: some emphasise people and stress the need for inter-personal skills; others require engineering skills and stress skills in the use of techniques; and yet others stress organisational issues.

If we consider the themes identified above as approaches to information systems development, disciplines relevant would seem to include, for example, computer science (prototyping tools and software engineering), mathematics (formal methods), sociology (participation) and business and management (planning).

5.6   Potential Difficulties of this Multi-Disciplinarity

We have seen, in our brief review of information systems teaching, research and practice, the inter-disciplinary nature of the subject area. Disciplines relevant to information systems include applied psychology, computer science, cultural studies, economics, ergonomics, ethics, linguistics, management, mathematics, politics, semiology, and sociology. Within these disciplines, different theories and philosophies exist and these may be mutually inconsistent. Consider, for example, the contrasting theories of systems theory, information theory, the theory of science and scientific method. They represent only some of the foundation theories of the disciplines listed.

All this leads to a perceived lack of coherence in the discipline. A particular fear is that the knowledge and understanding of work in the source disciplines of researchers working in information systems may be out of date or superficial. They are information systems specialists, not specialists in the source discipline.

It is true that many other disciplines (including French, geography, management and medicine) do not have a simple and single disciplinary status and can further be described as a collection of social practices. However, such disciplines can be seen by other academics as confused and lacking in coherence and academic rigour: information systems is often seen in the same light. In short, the 'discipline' of information systems appears to lack credibility. Indeed, Backhouse, Liebenau and Land (1991) state that: 'coming as it does out of computer science, management studies, and a variety of social and technical fields, it is hardly surprising that [information systems] does not have any theoretical clarity'.

They suggest that information systems lies firmly in the social sciences and not engineering or science. On the other hand, others disagree. For example, a technological emphasis is found in Gray (1992). This can be seen as confusion by many outside the discipline (and some inside it!), and the lack of an agreed and consistent theory is *potentially* disabling.

The choice of research method should depend on the area of concern. But in practice it also depends on other factors such as what type of research is acceptable to funding bodies, to university departments, and to assessors of various kinds. Non-positivist research can be rigourous and this extends to 'stories' (see Silverman, 1993), so there is no good reason for favouring one research method (applied appropriately and correctly according to its tenets) to another (applied equally appropriately and correctly). Likewise, the choice of information systems development methodology should depend on its appropriateness for the particular domain, but is more likely to depend on other factors, such as the dominant paradigm in the organisation or experiences of the actors (both of which may, in reality, be rule-of-thumb).

The emphasis and influence of practice on the 'discipline'—seen in the curricula and research methods—is also a potential weakness. There is a lack of theory in the field and what is practisd tends to be what is taught. The reverse impact, that of academics on practice, is rarer. Practitioners do not read (nor contribute) to information systems journals as much as in many other applied disciplines.

Academics in other disciplines regard information systems lecturers as able to bring in students who see university as a training ground for the few jobs available. They may therefore be favourable to information systems subjects being part of an MBA or computer science qualification. This is not a good academic reason and may be only a temporary phenomenon. Information systems academics are also used to teach fundamentals in data processing and computing (work that they do not necessarily find stimulating), and information systems is not often perceived as an 'academic' discipline in its own right.

This has meant that there are few stand alone university departments in information systems, especially in countries outside of the USA. Even in the USA and Canada, fewer than half of the 1,889 information systems faculty are found in stand alone information systems departments (DeGross et al., 1992). Most information systems faculty are found in business and management, commerce, computer science, mathematics, social science, and other departments. Sometimes, groups of information systems teachers can be seen as 'islands' off the main influential 'mainland' departments, and in other cases information systems faculty are split between two separate departments. This makes communications between information systems people difficult. Thus information systems faculty (and research students) may find themselves isolated.

The lack of stand alone university departments in information systems results in departments having a particular bias, such as a technology bias of most information systems academics in computer science departments or the practitioner bias of those in business schools. This means that the eclectic nature of information systems is not always reflected in academic information systems communities in any individual department. Worse, neither group seems particularly interested in theory: their concerns are with practical issues. Unlike information systems, most respected disciplines are built firmly on the rock of established theory. The potential gains of exploiting the source disciplines are not being made.

However, it is not the purpose of this chapter to suggest that such a discipline should give up our higher ideals for academic respectability, or that it should artificially restrict the scope of the discipline to fit in with an inappropriate monistic view of science (Banville and Landry, 1989). The inter-disciplinary nature of the subject provides richness and is a main reason for the interest shown by students on courses. It is also an important stimulus to researchers, witness the exciting debates in conferences which are inter-disciplinary. Different research processes and methods are relevant and add to the potential for progress and discovery. The emphasis on practice provides an exciting and relevant environment to try out ideas in their natural setting. Indeed, it is this that shows us that different situations do demand different approaches. Why should we not 'let many flowers bloom'? The potential weaknesses are also potential strengths and we need to address the issue so that their potential as strengths is realised.

Although it may be unrealistic to expect an agreed and consistent theory to emerge, it is important that more researchers work in areas that may establish the theoretical underpinnings of information systems. The inter-disciplinary nature of the subject is no excuse for a lack of rigour (Avison and Nandhakumar, 1995).

One of the problems with the use of concepts from another discipline is that they may be used uncritically (Avison and Myers, 1995). Researchers in information systems may be unaware of their historical development within the source discipline, and may gloss over the fact that there may be a range of perspectives that operate concurrently. The social sciences 'are marked by a plethora of "schools of thought," each with its own metatheoretic assumptions, research methodologies, and adherents.' (Orlikowski and Baroudi, 1991).

Although different intellectual traditions can lead to a patchwork of unrelated theories, practices and beliefs, there is a possibility that it exposes common ground. As Orlikowski and Baroudi (1991) point out, there is much that can be gained if a plurality of research perspectives is effectively employed to investigate information systems phenomena. They argue that any one perspective is always only a partial view, and unnecessarily restrictive. The fact that the theme for the International Conference on Information Systems (ICIS) in 1993 was *Valuing Diversity through Information Systems* would seem to suggest that

Orlikowski and Baroudi's valuing of a plurality of research perspectives is widely shared within the information systems research community.

5.7 Conclusion

It seems unlikely that there will be a merging of minds as to what discipline or set of disciplines is the most relevant to information systems, to the detail about what should be taught in undergraduate or graduate programs on information systems, and also as to which research methods are most appropriate. As we saw, to look at only one example of the practice of information systems, there is no commonly agreed approach to develop information systems and the differences in approaches are fundamental, not simply differences in nuance! But it is entirely appropriate that there is no agreement, because problem situations differ greatly. However, some disagreements are, perhaps, clashes of dogmas, such as those which occur between those taking a purely technical and technological view and those taking a purely social, human and organisational view.

Although a limited consensus between all information systems academics, researchers and practitioners may be unhelpful as well as unrealistic because information systems is multi-disciplinary and the different contributions enrich the discipline, there are strong reasons for agreeing a broadly-based definition for the discipline, a broadly-based curriculum, and an agreed set of teaching and research methods. In this way, information systems academics will be perceived as having a disciplinary status and having the influence that goes with such a status.

Acknowledgements

I would like to acknowledge the contributions of many friends who I have worked with in developing some of the ideas expressed in this paper, for example, colleagues on the Board of the UK AIS for the suggested information systems curriculum; Joe Nandhakumar and Michael Myers on research methods; Guy Fitzgerald on information systems development methodologies; and Trevor Wood-Harper, on the development of Multiview.

References

Avison, D.E., 1989, Action learning for information systems teaching, *International Journal of Information Management*, 9.

Avison, D.E., 1995, 'What is IS?', Inaugural Lecture, University of Southampton.

Avison, D.E., and Fitzgerald, G., 1991, Information systems practice, education and research, *Journal of Information Systems*, 1:1.

Avison, D.E., and Fitzgerald, G., 1995, *Information Systems Development: Methodologies, Techniques and Tools*, 2nd edition, McGraw-Hill, Maidenhead.

Avison, D.E., Kendall, J.E., and DeGross, J.I., 1993, *Human, Organisational, and Social Dimensions of Information Systems Development*, North-Holland, Amsterdam.

Avison, D.E., and Myers, M., 1995, Information systems and anthropology: an anthropological perspective on IT and organisational culture, *Information Technology and People*, 8(3).

Avison, D.E., and Nandhakumar, J., 1995, The discipline of information systems: let many flowers bloom, in *Information System Concepts: Towards a Consolidation of Views*, E. Falkenberg, W. Hesse and A. Olivé., eds. Chapman and Hall, London.

Avison, D.E., and Wood-Harper, A.T., 1990, *Multiview: An Exploration in Information Systems Development*, McGraw-Hill, Maidenhead.

Avison, D.E., and Wood-Harper, A.T., 1991, Information systems development research: a pragmatic view, *Computer Journal*, 34(2).

Backhouse, J., Liebenau, J. and Land, F., 1991, The discipline of information systems, *Journal of Information Systems*, 1(1).

Banville, C. and Landry, M., 1989, Can the field of MIS be disciplined? *Communications of the ACM*, 32(1).

Benbasat, I., Goldstein, D., and Mead, M., 1987, The case research strategy in studies of information systems, *MIS Quarterly*, February.

Boland, R.J., and Day, W.F., 1989, The experience of system design: a hermeneutic of organisational action, *Scandinavian Journal of Management*, 5(2).

Buckingham, R.A., Hirschheim, R.A., Land, F.F., and Tully, C.J., eds. 1987, *Information Systems Education: Recommendations and Implementation*, Cambridge University Press, Cambridge.

Bullen, C.V., and Rockart, J., 1984, A primer on critical success factors, CISR Working Paper 69, Sloan Management School, MIT, Boston, Mass.

Burrell, G., and Morgan, G., 1979, *Sociological Paradigms and Organisational Analysis*, Heinemann, London.

Checkland, P.B., 1981, *Systems Thinking, Systems Practice*, Wiley, Chichester.

Checkland P.B., 1994, Notes on teaching and researching IS, *Systemist*, 16(1).

Checkland, P. and Scholes. J., 1990, *Soft Systems Methodology in Action*, Wiley, Chichester.

Cougar J., Colter M.A., and Knapp R.W., 1982, *Advanced Systems Development/Feasibility Techniques*, Wiley, New York.

Cougar J., Davis, G.B., Dologite, D.G., Feinstein, D.L., Gorgone, J., Jenkins, A.M., Kasper, G.M., Little, J., Longenecker, H.E., and Valacich, J., 1995, IS'95: Guideline for undergraduate IS curriculum, *MIS Quarterly*, September.

Davenport, T.H., and Short, J., 1990, The new industrial engineering: information technology and business process redesign, *Sloan Management Review*, 31(4).

Davis, G.B., 1987, A critical comparison of IFIP/ECS information systems curriculum and information systems curriculum in the USA, in Buckingham *et al.* (1989).

DeGross, J., Davis, G.B., and Littlefield, R.S., 1992, *1992 Directory of Management Information Systems Faculty*, McGraw-Hill, Minnesota.

DeMarco, T., 1979, *Structured Analysis: System Specifications*, Prentice Hall, New York.

Dickson, G.S., Senn, J., and Chervany, N.L., 1977, Research in management information systems: the Minnesota experience, *Management Science*, 23(9).

DPMA 1992, *Information Systems: The DPMA Curriculum for a Four Year Undergraduate Degree*, Data Processing Management Association, Park Ridge, Illinois.

Earl, M.J., 1989, *Management Strategies for Information Technology*, Prentice Hall, Englewood Cliffs, New Jersey.

Easterby-Smith, M., Thorpe, R., and Lowe, A., 1991, *Management Research: An Introduction*, Sage, London.

Ein-Dor, P., and Segev, E., 1981, *A Paradigm for Management Information Systems*, Prager, New York.

Foster, L.W., and Flynn, D.W., 1984, Management information technology: its effects on organisational form and function, *MIS Quarterly*, 8(4).

Gane C., and Sarson T., 1979, *Structured Analysis: Tools and Techniques*, Prentice Hall, New York.

Galliers, R.D., 1985, In search of a paradigm for information systems research, in *Research Methods in Information Systems*, E. Mumford, R. Hirschheim, G. Fitzgerald and T. Wood-Harper, eds., North-Holland, Amsterdam.

Galliers, R.D., 1991, Choosing appropriate information systems research methods, in *Information Systems Research: Contemporary Approaches and Emergent Traditions*, H. Nissen, H. Klein and R. Hirschheim, eds, North Holland, Amsterdam.

Galliers, R.D., and Land, F.F., 1987, Choosing appropriate information systems research methodologies, *Communications of the ACM*, 30(11).

Gray, P., 1992, New directions for group decision support systems, in *The Impact of Computer Supported Technologies on Information Systems Development*, K. Kendall, K. Lyytinen and J. DeGross, eds., North-Holland, Amsterdam.

Hammer, M., and Champy, J., 1993, *Reengineering the Corporation: A Manifesto for Business Revolution'* Harper Business, New York.

IBM, 1975, Business Systems Planning, in *Advanced Systems Development/Feasibility Techniques*, J. Cougar, M. Colter and R. Knapp, Wiley, New York.

Jones, M. R., and Nandhakumar, J., 1993, Structured development: a structurational analysis of the development of an executive information system, in *Human, Organisational, and Social Dimensions of Information Systems Development*, D. Avison, J. Kendall and J. DeGross, eds., North-Holland, Amsterdam.

Keen, P.G., 1987, MIS Research: current status, trends and needs, in *Information Systems Education: Recommendations and Implementation*, R. Buckingham, R. Hirschheim, F. Land and C. Tully, eds., Cambridge University Press, Cambridge.

Klein, H.K., and Hirschheim, R., 1993 The application of neohumanist principles in information systems development, in *Human, Organisational, and Social Dimensions of Information Systems Development*, D. Avison, J. Kendall and J. DeGross, eds., North-Holland, Amsterdam.

Lederer, A.L., and Mendlelow, A.L., 1989, Information systems planning: incentives for effective action. *Data Base*, Fall.

Martin, J., 1989, *Information Engineering*, Prentice Hall, Englewood Cliffs, New Jersey.

Martin, J., 1991, *Rapid Application Development*, Prentice Hall, Englewood Cliffs, New Jersey.

Mumford, E., 1995, *Effective Requirements Analysis and Systems Design: The ETHICS Method*, Macmillan, Basingstoke.

Mumford, E., Hirschheim, R.A., Fitzgerald, G., and Wood-Harper, A.T., eds., 1985, *Research Methods in Information Systems*, North-Holland, Amsterdam.

Nunamaker, J., Cougar J., and Davis, G.B., 1992, Information systems curriculum recommendations for the '80s: undergraduate and graduate programmes, *Communications for the ACM*, 25(11).

Orlikowski, W.J., 1992, The duality of technology: rethinking the concept of technology in organisations, *Organisation Science*, 3(3).

Orlikowski, W.J., 1993, CASE tools as organisational change: investigating incremental and radical changes in systems development, *MIS Quarterly*, 17(3).

Orlikowski, W.J., and Baroudi, J., 1991, Studying information technology in organisations: research approaches and assumptions, *Information Systems Research*, 2(1).

Orlikowski, W.J., and Robey, D., 1991, Information technology and the structuring of organisations, *Information Systems Research*, 2(2).

Silverman, D., 1993, *Interpreting Qualitative Data: Methods for Analysing Talk, Text and Interaction*, Sage, London.

UKAIS., 1996, *UKAIS Newsletter*, 2(1).

Van Horn, R.L., 1973, Empirical studies of management information studies, *Data Base*, 5, Winter.

Walsham, G., 1993, *Interpreting Information Systems in Organisations*, Wiley, Chichester.

Walsham, G., and Han, C. K., 1993, Information systems strategy formation and implementation: the case of a central government agency, *Accounting, Management, and Information Technologies*, 3 (3).

Wilson, B., 1990, *Systems: Concepts, Methodologies and Applications*, 2nd edition, Wiley, Chichester.

Yourdon, E., 1989, *Modern Structured Analysis*, Prentice Hall, Englewood Cliffs, New Jersey.

Yourdon, E., 1994, *Object-oriented Systems Design, An Integrated Approach*, Prentice Hall, Englewood Cliffs, New Jersey.

PART 2: RESEARCH ISSUES

Notwithstanding the lack of funding for IS research in recent times there has been a significant increase in activity in IS related projects. There may be many reasons for this but it is likely that the spectacular failures of some computer-based projects over the past few years may have provided the motivation. This section of the text provides some examples of on-going research or lessons learnt from research which make a contribution to the thinking. The section includes chapters written by five authors who are concerned with different aspects of IS research including some of the practical difficulties in undertaking research as well as some fundamental questions that IS researchers might find worth addressing.

Bob Galliers refers to IS research as being an 'art' (rather than a science one assumes) in which he raises questions about the underlying philosophy of research and the choice of approach. In his view some research is more concerned with elegance and rigour than relevance which he illustrates with a discussion about field work and laboratory-based research. Using material obtained from Europe and the USA Galliers compares the topics that have been researched and concludes that European research can be characterised as being concerned with relevant issues and US research with rigour. The chapter provides the reader with some useful data as well as some stimulating discussion about the purpose of IS research itself.

Frank Stowell, Duane West and **Mark Stansfield** are concerned about the way that action research is used in information systems. The authors raise the issue that although there is a significant amount of literature advocating the value of action research (A/R) for IS the literature offers little guidance about the practice of A/R. The literature contains plenty of debate describing the difficulties and benefits of A/R versus positivist research but when it comes to how the researcher actually does it the accounts themselves are vague. Many researchers when presenting their doctoral thesis seem to assume that consultancy and action research are the same. This assumption often provides difficulties for the researcher and the examiner at the *viva* stage when it is fairly clear to the examiner that the individual has taken A/R to be any activity which takes place in a live environment. The authors attempt to differentiate between the underlying motivation behind field research and consultancy. Their differentiation is based upon lessons from three research projects in which the authors suggest that the fundamental difference between activities which are directly related to the *development* of an idea or 'theory' and those activities which are based *upon* an existing idea or 'theory' about a situation. In the latter case the lessons learnt from the encounter may help to enrich the theory which benefits both the researcher and the clients. In the former case the work may generate a statement about a situation which itself may be of value to some other research.. The authors look at the problem from the 'Ws' of a researcher and consultant-researcher which serves to provide some interesting observations about A/R.

Mike Jackson discusses the contribution of critical systems to information systems research. In some ways the author answers the questions raised by Galliers about the philosophy of the IS research process. Jackson argues that systems thinking is a natural approach to IS research and therefore lessons learned from the systems domain might be useful to IS researchers. For example, the rational methods applied to a complex world by Systems researchers may themselves be of practical and philosophical value to IS researchers. Jackson acknowledges that critical systems is a relative newcomer to systems thinking but believes that the concept offers the prospect of bringing various concerns into an integrated programme of research.

Michael Myers, in some respects, provides a useful link between the Chapters 7 and 8. Myers raises the issue about 'mixing' nomothetic methods with interpretative research which is fraught with problems but is also one which many IS researchers have to address. Interpretivism he feels is relevant where complexity prevents replication and in particular Myers suggests that the use of critical hermeneutics provides for the rigourous scrutiny of the processes of IS practices which can be used to supplement the more traditional approaches to IS research.

The final chapter in this section is written by **Ronald Stamper** who challenges the fidelity of objectivity in general and for IS in particular. Stamper argues that IS belongs to the social sciences which is a view he formed from his experience in industry and from the experience in the academic world and from teaching IS. Stamper's chapter raises the difficulties for IS which he argues has to adopt either a narrow technical view, with its impatience with human problems, or a softer approach which takes social aspects into account but cannot deliver a specification. Stamper's chapter provides a reader with the stimulating discussion of the relationship between semiotics and IS. By ridding ourselves of the vagueness of the term information systems and reverting to basic concepts Stamper argues we are able to create a 'truly scientific study of Information and Information Systems'. Stamper suggests that the use of a semiotic frame work may provide a basic check list for every IS problem. The chapter provides the reader with a valuable introduction into organisational semiotics as well as suggesting a means of operationalising these ideas.

Chapter 6

REFLECTIONS ON INFORMATION SYSTEMS RESEARCH: TWELVE POINTS OF DEBATE[*]

Robert Galliers

6.1　Introduction

This chapter provides some personal reflections on the state of the art of information systems research and poses a number of fairly basic debating points that arise from the argument as it unfolds. It attempts an evaluation of current research practice in the field both in the UK and the USA, with a view to establishing a more reflective attitude towards information systems research.

　　The use of the term 'reflections' in the chapter title is indicative of the limited evidence available regarding (i) the topics being researched and (ii) the research methods being employed. Hence, greater reliance has to be placed on personal reflections and questions than might otherwise have been the case had more empirical evidence been available at this point in time.[1]

---

[1] This situation will shortly be ameliorated, for the UK at any rate, as a result of survey research which is being undertaken by the Information Systems Research Unit at Warwick Business School. This research commenced in April 1995 and is designed to identify past, current and future research activity in the information systems field, both from the perspective of the methods being used and the topics being researched. The latter will be compared with the results from recent research into the views of British executives as to the major issues they face in managing information systems (Galliers, *et al.*, 1994)

---

[*] Earlier versions of this chapter have appeared as: Galliers, (1994a) and (1994b). Additional material is taken from Galliers (1995).

The analysis is undertaken in the context of (i) the usage of alternative research methods *vis à vis* the focus and objective of the research by utilising an existing taxonomy of research methods (Galliers and Land, 1987; Galliers, 1991, 1992), and (ii) the relevance of the topics of study *vis à vis* the issues deemed to be important to the practitioner community.

The intention is not to be prescriptive regarding the choice of research method or topic. It is to fuel a debate on this important subject with a view to improving research practice among the information systems academic community.

6.2   Background

This chapter has its genesis in a number of concerns I have held for the past decade or so regarding the state of the art of information systems research. These concerns include the following:

1. In examining PhD dissertations in a number of countries throughout the world, I have found that there is seldom any evidence of consideration of alternative research methods; indeed, the philosophy underpinning the method is rarely questioned.
2. In certain instances, there appears to be greater attention paid to the elegance of the design of the research instrument than to the relevance of the method given the topic under investigation, or indeed, the relevance of the topic itself.

> **Debating Point #1: To what extent do you clarify the underlying philosophy of your research in information systems? And to what extent do you explicate the arguments concerning the choice of approach(es) you have adopted?**

I am, of course, aware that elegance and rigour provide good indicators to assess the capabilities of the budding information systems researcher—and I am certainly not arguing that these particular 'babies' should be thrown out with the 'bathwater'. I am, however, asking whether you would agree with me that the question of methodological choice and topic relevance also provide an indication of research capability?

> **Debating Point #2: To what extent do elegance and rigour take precedence over relevance in the information systems research that you undertake?**

For example, the information systems literature is replete with articles describing well-designed laboratory experiments using undergraduate students as surrogates for executives and the classroom as a surrogate for the office. While elegant and rigourous in methodological terms, it may be argued that little new knowledge of practical import is gained as a result (see the debate between Galliers and Land, 1987, 1988 and Jarvenpaa, 1988 for more on this point). Conversely, it has been argued that laboratory experimentation and surveys, and the application of statistical techniques in analysing the data, are precisely the kind of research approaches that lend themselves to PhD study. They can be rigourous, self-contained and less open-ended and less risky than qualitative, interpretive work in the field.

> **Debating Point #3: To what extent should PhD students be exposed to interpretive fieldwork as opposed to more constrained analysis (such as survey work or laboratory experimentation) given their lack of research experience?**

6.3 Topic Selection

While I have focused attention in the previous section on some of the issues confronting doctoral students—and shall do so to some extent in this section as well, the argument I shall develop applies equally to more established researchers.

There are, of course, many factors that need to be considered when it comes to choosing a research topic. Personal interest; background knowledge and skills; the availability of appropriate supervision; questions of access; time availability—all these are important. Having said that, it would seem that while these are necessary conditions on which to base one's choice, they are not, of themselves, sufficient.

> **Debating Point #4: To what extent do you include arguments as to why it is important that we pursue research in your chosen topic area in reporting your research?**

In an applied discipline such as information systems, I would argue that it is important that we undertake research that is seen to be relevant by our colleagues in industry, government and commerce (and not just IS professionals either), as well as sufficiently scholarly by our colleagues in academia. This is the challenge associated with the term 'academic' in the field of information systems. While we wish to be scholarly, we do not wish to be labelled 'unpractical'.

It would seem appropriate, therefore, to compare and contrast the information systems topics actually being researched with the issues that have been identified as being crucial in the context of the introduction, utilisation, and management of information technology in society generally and in organisations in particular. Tables 6.1 and 6.2 attempt to highlight the two agendas.[2]

Table 6.1 provides an indication of the situation in the USA, while Table 6.2 provides similar evidence for the UK.[3] Note, however, that Table 6.1 relates to topics covered by PhD dissertations, while Table 6.2 provides summary information on the topics being researched by PhD candidates. In addition, the data are more recent in Table 6.2.

Notwithstanding the limitations of the available data, there does appear to be a different emphasis between the research agenda and the issues that are reported as being of concern to information systems managers.[4]

---

[2] It will be noted that the data presented are from 1989 and are therefore somewhat dated. This is indicative of the fact that it is often the case that we have to be reliant on older data and we often do not have a clear picture as to current concerns. This is, of itself, an issue which the IS community may—quite appropriately it seems to me—wish to take on board.

[3] The evidence is partial it is true, particularly for the UK where, as noted above, no data are currently available of the kind provided by Teng and Gallena (1990) regarding current research activity and the future intentions of the established IS research community.

[4] There is, of course, a danger in placing too much emphasis on the reported concerns of IS managers. In many studies, it may well be that the IS managers are simply feeding back the issues that have been identified for them by leading academics!

TABLE 6.1   *Key information systems issues and research topics in the USA*

Management Issues* (in rank order, 1989)	Research Topics**	(% of researchers)
1. Information architecture	1. DSS	(32%)
2. Data resource management	2. AI	(22%)
3. Strategic IS planning	3. DBMS	(21%)
4. IS human resources	4. MSS development	(19%)
5. Organisational learning	5. End-user computing	(15%)
6. Technology infrastructure	6. Human factors	(10%)
7. IS organisational alignment		
8. Competitive advantage		
9. Quality of s/w development		
10. Implementing telecomms		

*Source: Niederman *et al.* (1991)
**Source: Teng and Gallena (1990:3)

TABLE 6.2   *Key information systems issues and research topics in the UK*

Management Issues* (in rank order, 1997)	Research Topics**	(% of PhD students)
1. Strategic IS planning	1. IS development	(24.4%)
2. Distributed systems	2. Organisational impact	(17.0%)
3. Business process redesign	3. Object oriented design	(9.6%)
4. Managing data	4. Strategic IS planning	(7.3%)
5. Security and control	5. Requirements determination	(7.3%)
6. Competitive advantage	6. EIS	(4.9%)
7. DSS/EIS	7. IS evaluation	(4.9%)
8. Information architecture		
9. Measuring IS effectiveness		
10. Telecomms		

*Source: Galliers, *et al.*, (1994b), reprinted with permission of
        Elsevier Science, Amsterdam
**Source: 3rd UK IS PhD Consortium (1993).

This point may be illustrated as in Figure 6.1, which indicates that the two worlds of IS research and IS practice are, to some degree at least quite separate, closed systems. An alternative picture is provided by Figure 6.2, which illustrates the point that the two worlds could in fact be considerably more interdependent (see also Section 6.4).

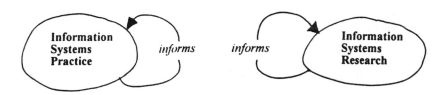

FIGURE 6.1   *The two worlds of information systems research and information systems practice* (Galliers, 1995:50)

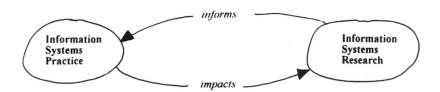

FIGURE 6.2   *The interdependency of the information systems research and information systems practice agendas*

> Debating Point #5: To what extent should your research agenda for information systems and the issues that are of most concern to practising IS executives be aligned?

6.4   The Question of Quality: Relevance or Rigour?

How might we define quality with regard to information systems research? And is the question of quality not perhaps more a matter of combining both relevance *and* rigour rather than emphasising one at the expense of the other? I have already touched on both these aspects of quality in this context in previous sections, but will look into this question in a little more detail here.

There would appear to be some informal evidence to suggest that European information systems research has a tendancy to emphasise relevance, while that of the USA has a tendancy to emphasise rigour. The point is illustrated in Figure 6.3.

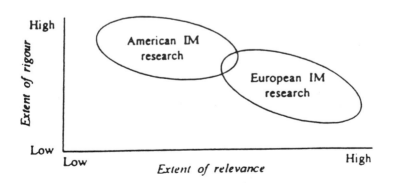

FIGURE 6.3   *Characterising US and European IS research in terms of relevance and rigour* (Galliers, 1995:49)

While illustrating the distinctive tendencies of the North American and European schools, Figure 6.3 should not be interpreted literally. It also begs the question as to who decides on these quality issues: who decides what is relevant? And what philosophical paradigm will we use in deciding which is rigorous?

In the previous section I ventured to suggest that there should be a closer linkage between the two worlds of IS theory and practice, with the one informing the other. I purposely stopped short of arguing that our research agenda should be dictated by the issues being confronted by IS executives, however. This is because:

1. There is some evidence to suggest that Information Sytems executives too readily follow the latest 'silver bullet' and are taken in by the hyperbole surrounding certain of the management fads (e.g. Niederman *et al.*, 1991). If we were to follow their lead, our research agenda would have to chop and change, with consequent diminution of relevant, quality output and virtually no longitudinal research (*cf.*, Pettigrew, 1985).
2. Some of the surveys tend to reflect the views of leading gurus in the field and are conducted among a relatively small community, who have been previously exposed to the gurus' latest pronouncements. The inevitable results: the views of the gurus are fed back by practioners to the gurus in a classic closed system.
3. Most of the surveys solicit the views of the IS practitioner community only, so that the views of users of IS are not compared (Galliers *et al.*, 1994b).

It would seem then that somehow we should take account of the views of the practitioner community (including IS users), and be ready to respond to changes in opinion, but at the same time not be swayed by temporary fads. Similarly, we should be proactive, with a view to informing our practioner colleagues as to the results of our efforts (see Figure 6.2).

The model looks simple enough, but we should not be fooled into believing that it represents reality, or is particularly easy to achieve. First, as we have seen, we do not have a clear picture of what the IS research community's agenda actually is at present. How then can we inform the practitioner community about it? Second, there is 'noise' in the data emanating from the practitioner community (*cf.* the arguments of Clark, 1992, and his call for more in depth, *in situ*, qualitative research).

Debating Point #6: What measures do you take already in ensuring that the results of your IS research are disseminated to the practitioner/user community? And how might dissemination be improved?

Debating Point #7: To what extent should the views of the practitioner/user community dictate your IS research agenda?

6.5 Methodological Choice

As this chapter aims to foster discussion and debate (rather than to report on rigourous research!) and, as has been noted, recent empirical evidence appears to be limited, I may be forgiven for providing anecdotal evidence in support of the contention that there is a tendency for particular institutions to favour certain research methods irrespective of the choice of research topic.[5,6] This is, of course, very much a generalisation and you will doubtless be able to identify certain institutions where this is definitely not the case. In some instances, of course, there will be a tendency to research particular topics in addition and the chosen method(s) may well be appropriate. Having said that, there may not always be such a rational reason for the approach(es) adopted.

Debating Point #8: To what extent should your institution focus its research efforts on a single (or very few) research method(s)? To what extent should there be a plurality of methods in use?

In earlier papers, a revised taxonomy has been presented that attempts to identify the likely suitability of a range of research methods in the context of the chosen IS research topics (Galliers

---

[5] Although the argument does appear to be supported by, e.g. Vogel and Wetherbe (1984).

[6] There is an argument that suggests that the choice of a particular research approach in a particular institution will mean that considerable expertise will be built in this method, and that there is just not sufficient time for doctoral students to become familiar with a range of approaches.

and Land, 1987; Galliers, 1991, 1993a). In developing this taxonomy, the idea was to (i) illustrate the range of available methods and (ii) provide a means by which suitable alternatives might be considered. An underlying principle was that alternatives might be considered in combination: methodological pluralism was the watchword, as also argued, for example, by Gable (1994). A variant of the taxonomy is provided in Table 6.1.

As a result of applications of the taxonomy, it has become clear that the taxonomy is also helpful in reviewing previous research in any given IS research topic area. For example, in undertaking this analysis, one might discover a particular method being employed almost universally. This might lead to a decision to attempt (an)other suitable approach(es) to discover whether similar results ensue, or alternatively, to utilise the same approach with a view to testing previous findings in different circumstances.

There are many weaknesses in the taxonomy. One could argue (as has Smithson, 1991:366) that the location of a particular method under either the positivist or interpretivist label is misleading or downright wrong. In addition, I personally have reconsidered the utility of certain methods in the context of individual topics so that Table 6.1 differs to some extent from the original taxonomy (Galliers and Land, 1987). In some respects, however, this is missing the point: if the framework[7] helps to raise such questions, then it is doing its job.

More serious concerns include whether: (i) the number of methods included is sufficiently comprehensive; (ii) different methods might be applied from different philosophical stances, and (iii) the methods listed are equivalent one to another. There is certainly a view that would answer (i) and (iii) in negative terms, while it is clearly the case that (ii) can be answered in the affirmative. For example, some have found difficulty in placing, e.g. structuration theory (Giddens, 1984) or ethnographic studies (Geertz, 1973) in the framework, while others might argue that, for example, forecasting should not be considered alongside the subjective/argumentative style of approach (the former being seen as a particular method, while the latter is seen more as a style of approach).

---

[7] Framework is a better description of the model than taxonomy.

TABLE 6.1 *A taxonomy of information systems research approaches* (from Galliers, 1993a:96, 1994:97)

Object	Modes for traditional positivist approaches (observations)						Modes for newer post-positivist approaches (interpretations)			
	Theorem proof	Laboratory experiment	Field experiment	Case Study	Survey	Forecasting and Futures research	Simulation & Gaming/ role play	Subjective/ argumentative	Descriptive/ Interpretive (inc. Reviews)	Action Research
Society	No	No	Possibly	Possibly	Yes	Yes	Possibly	Yes	Yes	Possibly
Organisation/ group	No	Possibly (small groups)	Yes	Yes	Yes	Yes	Yes	Yes	Yes	Yes
Individual	No	Yes	Yes	Possibly	Possibly	Possibly	Yes	Yes	Yes	Possibly
Technology	Yes	Yes	Yes	No	Possibly	Yes	Yes	Possibly	Possibly	No
Methodology	Yes	No	Yes	Yes	Yes	No	Yes	Yes	Yes	Yes

Another consideration relates to the location of the kind of research, prevalent in computer science and software engineering departments, that sees its major contribution as being the development of some new software or other, as against a contribution to theory *per se*. This was a matter of debate at the 1992 UK PhD Consortium (Galliers, 1993b). Where does one locate such research and development in the framework?

Debating Point #9: To what extent should research *and development* (the contribution being in the nature of a piece of software as opposed to a contribution to theory) be viewed as acceptable information systems research?

A further concern relates to the use of quantitative and qualitative analytical techniques and how this concern might be incorporated into the framework. Some would argue (see, e.g. Pervan and Klass, 1992) that quantitative techniques may be utilised irrespective of the research method being employed. The point is expanded by Yin (1993:57) when discussing case study research:

> ... case study research can be qualitative or quantitative. The characterisitics are not two competing types of research. Instead, they are attributes of types of data. Qualitative data are data that cannot readily be converted to numerical values. Such a focus ... avoids the unproductive debate between qualitative and quantitative research. Qualitative research can also be hard-nosed, data-driven, outcome-oriented, and truly scientific. Similarly, quantitative research can be soft and mushy and deal with inadequate evidence. These are attributes of good and poor research and not of a dichotomy between two types of research.

Debating Point #10: To what extent should quantitative analytical techniques be employed in interpretive research?

6.6   Towards a Revised Framework

Given the limitations of the earlier framework (cf., Table 6.1), some initial work has been attempted with a view to developing a revised framework which locates the range of methods in the context of the process of undertaking research, and which argues for the philosophical stance to be considered as a separate dimension, orthogonal to a hierarchical classification of approaches, methods and techniques (Galliers, *et al.*, 1992).

If we accept that the process of researching includes the gathering together of disparate information and the distillation or synthesis of this into a more readily understood format (cf. Boisot, 1987), we might be able usefully to relocate a number of 'approaches' (cf. Table 6.1) at different stages of this process. Figure 6.4 provides an illustration of this kind of thinking.

There is clearly a long way to go in developing the concept of Figure 6.4 into a framework that might provide the budding IS researcher with helpful advice as to the choice of research method(s) in any given context. What it does do, however, is indicate a direction for further thinking in this regard. Figure 6.4 omits the subject of the research effort it is true; it does, however, place research methods in the context of the research process and demonstrates the potential for an orthogonal relationship between research philosophy and method.

Debating Point #11: To what extent do you think that a framework depicting research methods in the context of the process of undertaking information systems research, and research philosophies as being orthogonal to research methods assist you in understanding the relevance of a given method for a particular piece of research?

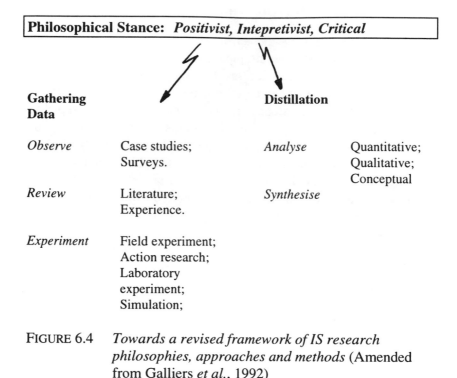

Philosophical Stance: *Positivist, Intepretivist, Critical*

Gathering
Data

Distillation

Observe   Case studies;   *Analyse*   Quantitative;
             Surveys.   Qualitative;
                                            Conceptual

Review   Literature;   *Synthesise*
             Experience.

Experiment Field experiment;
             Action research;
             Laboratory
             experiment;
             Simulation;

FIGURE 6.4   *Towards a revised framework of IS research philosophies, approaches and methods* (Amended from Galliers *et al.*, 1992)

6.7 Concluding Remarks

This chapter has attempted to raise a number of points for debate with a view to clarifying issues associated with research methods in the study of information systems. It has not attempted to present the results of empirical research, but has attempted to raise a number of concerns that arise as much from experience as they do from empirical data. The purpose has been to raise awareness and to provide a focus for debate.

Debating Point #12: To what extent do you think that there is a place for the subjective/argumentative style of research in the field of information systems?

It does appear that we IS researchers are pursuing somewhat different agendas than those of our colleagues in practice. It also appears that there is only limited concern regarding the choice of research method adopted in our research activities. Where debate tends to occur is in relation to the relative utility of quantitative and qualitative research and the extent to which our discipline is 'scientific'. As we have seen, this is a false distinction which is ultimately unproductive. It certainly appears to be the case that we have additional work to do if we are to develop frameworks that assist us in our understanding of what is meant by relevant research methods in our chosen context.

I do hope that this chapter has provided some food for thought that will engender further debate as our field of study develops. The debating points raised are deliberately posed at a fairly basic level since the answers that emerge will inform the more advanced debate that is undoubtedly necessary for our subject to develop further. This is certainly a debate which needs to ensue, and one which I eagerly await! Hopefully this chapter has been a useful starting point in that process.

References

Boisot, M., 1987, *Information and Organisations: The Manager as Anthropologist*, Fontana, London.

Clark, Jr., T. D., 1992, Corporate systems management: an overview and research perspective, *Communications of the ACM*, 35(2):61-75.

Gable, G.G., 1994, Integrating case study and survey research methods: an example in information systems, *European Journal of Information Systems*, 3(2):112-126.

Galliers, R.D., 1991, Choosing appropriate information systems research approaches: a revised taxonomy, in H.-E. Nissen *et al.*, eds., 1991, 327-345. Also in R. Galliers, ed., 1992, 144-162.

Galliers, R.D., ed., 1992, *Information Systems Research: Issues, Methods and Practical Guidelines*, Blackwell Scientific, Oxford.

Galliers, R.D., 1993a, Research issues in information systems, *Journal of Information Technology*, 8(2):92-98.

Galliers, R.D., 1993b, Doctoral information systems research in Britain, *Journal of Information Technology*, 8(2):118-120.

Galliers, R.D., 1994a, Points of debate in understanding information systems research, *Systemist*, 16(1):32-40.

Galliers, R.D., 1994b, Relevance and rigour in information systems research: some personal reflections on issues facing the information systems research community, in B. Glasson *et al.*, eds., 1994, 93-101.

Galliers, R.D., 1995, A manifesto for information systems research, *British Journal of Management*, 6, Special Issue, December, S45-S52.

Galliers, R.D. and Land, F.F., 1987, Choosing appropriate information systems research methodologies, *Communications of the ACM*, 30(11):900-902.

Galliers, R.D. and Land, F.F., 1988, The importance of laboratory experimentation in IS research: a response, *Communications of the ACM*, 31(12):1504-1505.

Galliers, R.D., Merali, Y. and Spearing, L., 1994, Coping with information technology? How British executives perceive the key information systems management issues in the mid-1990s, *Journal of Information Technology*, 9(3): 223-238.

Galliers, R.D., Ormerod, R.J, and Merali, Y. 1992, Towards an exploratory framework of information systems research philosophies, approaches and methods, *Working Paper (in manuscript)* Warwick Business School, Coventry.

Geertz, C., 1973, *The Interpretation of Cultures*, Basic Books, New York.

Giddens, A., 1984, *The Constitution of Society*, Polity Press, Cambridge.

Glasson, B.C., Hawryszkiewycz, I.T., Underwood, B.A. and Weber, R.A. eds., 1994, *Business process re-engineering: Information systems opportunities and challenges*, IFIP Transactions A-54, Elsevier, Amsterdam, 93-101.

Jarvenpaa, S., 1988, The importance of laboratory experimentation in IS research, , *Communications of the ACM*, 31(12):1502-1504.

Mumford, E., Hirshheim, R.A., Fitzgerald, G. and Wood-Harper, A.T., eds., 1985, Research methods in information systems, *Proceedings of the IFIP WG8.2 Colloquium*, 1-3 September, 1984, Manchester Business School, Elsevier, Amsterdam.

Niederman, F., Brancheau, J.C. and Wetherbe, J.C., 1991, Information systems management issues in the 1990s, *MIS Quarterly*, 16(4):474-500.

Nissen, H.-E., Klein, H.K. and Hirschheim, R., eds., 1991, *Information Systems Research: Contemporary Approaches and Emergent Traditions*, North-Holland, Amsterdam.

Orlikowski, W.J. and Baroudi, J.J., 1991. Studying Information technology in organisations: research approaches and assumptions, *Information Systems Research*, 2(1):1-28.

Pervan, G. and Klass, B., 1992, The use and misuse of statistical methods in information systems research. in R. Galliers, ed, 1992, 208-229.

Pettigrew, A.M., 1985, Contextualist research: a natural way to link theory and practice, in E. Mumford *et al.,* eds., 1985, 53-78.

Smithson, S., 1991, Combining different approaches, in H.-E. Nissen *et al.*, eds., 1991, 365-369.

Teng, J.T.C. and Gallena, D., 1990, MIS Research directions: a survey of researchers' views, *Data Base*, 21(3):3-14.

Vogel, D.R. and Wetherbe, J.C., 1984, MIS research: a profile of leading journals and universities, *Data Base*, 16(3):3-14.

Yin, R., 1993, *Applications of case study research*, Sage, Newbury Park, Ca.

Chapter 7

ACTION RESEARCH AS A FRAMEWORK FOR IS RESEARCH

Frank Stowell, Daune West and Mark Stansfield

7.1   Introduction

Action research has, for some time, been advocated as a useful way of conducting work in the field of information systems (IS) (Checkland and Scholes, 1990; Stowell and West, 1994), since it offers an alternative to the traditional positivist approach to inquiry. The majority of the action research literature appears to focus on the merits of action research as an alternative to positivist research in addressing social issues with the authors usually describing *what* comprises action research. However, to date authors seem to have paid relatively little attention to *how* an action research study can be undertaken particularly in terms of how the rigour of the research can be maintained. Those choosing to work within an action research framework soon become aware of the difficulties that the approach brings to bear upon the development and/or research processes involved. In an attempt to discuss some of the difficulties and implications involved in using action research as the basis for formal research, the authors distinguish between what appear to be two modes[1] of action research study within information systems research, namely a field study mode and a consultancy mode. Descriptions of studies illustrating each of these types of study will be provided, with the final part of this chapter, focusing on the issues arising from the different studies.

---

1 In using the term 'mode' the authors are attempting to describe what appears to them to be two potentially interesting directions that might be found within IS research that adopts an action research perspective.

159

7.2 The Role of Action Research in Social Inquiry

The term action research is widely credited to Lewin (1948) whose work at the University of Michigan developed through a concern for dealing with what he considered to be critical practical social issues that were not being resolved through traditional positivist scientific methods. Lewin's work highlighted the need to bridge the gap between social action and social theory in which the researcher, rather than being an outside objective observer, becomes a visible and active participant in the social group under investigation. This practical involvement is a means of initiating a process of change within the social group as well as generating knowledge concerning ways in which attitudes are developed and changed.

Parallel but independent work to that of Lewin's took place at the Tavistock Institute of Human Relations in London which, according to Levin (1994), made a substantial contribution to the reindustrialisation of England. Examples of such work include studies into large-scale social systems such as the coal mining industry (Trist and Bamforth, 1951), as well as work into socio-technical systems (Trist, 1953). Although both Lewin and the Tavistock Institute were committed to solving important social problems through the active engagement of the social sciences (Susman and Evered, 1978), the emphasis of Lewin's work, which Rapoport (1970) terms the Group Dynamics stream of action research, is more concerned with individual and smaller groups than larger scale social systems. In some respects Lewin's work appears to be more academically orientated than that of the Tavistock group, which was more professionally orientated, with industrial organisations being a prominent area of application in which cooperative relationships between members were encouraged to bring about a consensus among participants in which specialists worked together in teams.

Other developments in action research have included collaborative links between the Tavistock Group and Norwegian researchers in the area of Norwegian working life (Emery and Thorsrud, 1976; Elden, 1979), in which Norway was viewed as a more fruitful area than Britain for closer cooperation between employers and trade unions (Levin, 1994). Other researchers closely aligned with the tradition of action research include those associated with work on cooperative experiential inquiry (Reason and Rowan, 1981; Reason, 1988) which is concerned with research which breaks down the distinction between researcher and subject in which collaborative relationships are established as a means of knowing-in-action.

Over the last fifty years action research has been applied to a wide range of application areas (e.g. education, politics, manufacturing), and incidents where the need to change has been paramount. Recent special editions of the journal *Human Relations* demonstrate the wide range of applications which are discussed under three main headings illustrating the applicability of action research at all levels of inquiry: the company (or organisation), community, and country (or region) (Elden and Chisholm, 1993, p.131).

7.2.1   Defining Action Research

Action research is generally accepted as being a diverse concept with many different strands with different meanings being attributed to the concept over many years (including: Hult and Lennung, 1980; Peters and Robinson, 1984; Mansell, 1991; West, 1991; Levin, 1994). One of the most commonly quoted definitions of action research in the literature is based upon that of Rapoport which emphasises the overall aims of action research which he views as contributing:

> .. both to the practical concerns of people in an immediate problematic situation and to goals of social science by joint collaboration within a mutually ethical framework (Rapoport, 1970, p.499).

The reason for the importance of this definition is that it draws a sharp distinction between applied research and action research, since applied research is not concerned with contributing to the goals of social science (Clark, 1972). To these two aims, Susman and Evered (1978) add a third which emphasises the notion that action research should also develop the self-help abilities of those people facing problems, since the participants should benefit from the collaborative learning experience as a result of the social inquiry (Susman and Evered, 1978; Hult and Lennung, 1980). For Lewin, action research was both a means of researching into various forms of social activity and a means of initiating social action through research which he regarded as 'research for social management' (Lewin, 1948, pp.202-203). Social management as described by Lewin proceeded in a 'spiral of steps' in which each step comprised a circle of explicitly defined activities of 'planning, action and fact-finding about the result of the action' (p206). This cyclical process which comprises action research has been further developed and modified by Susman and Evered (1978) who distinguish five iterative phases: *diagnosing, action planning, action taking, evaluating* and *specifying learning,* which are carried out to varying degrees collaboratively between the researcher and the client. Elden and Chisholm (1993) make the point that many recent reports of action research projects and reviews of the field do share a broad definition of action research which encompasses in some form the points already highlighted in this section. However, they do add that recent reports seem to show a focus upon the 'self development capacity' within the areas of application so that learning still continues after the researcher's role within the engagement has been completed (p.125).

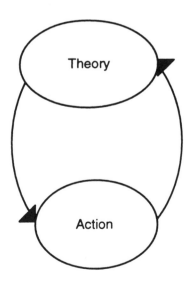

FIGURE 7.1. *The theory-action cycle of action research*

Checkland and Scholes offer a more recent description of the type of output that is sought through action research which also underlines the difficulties of adopting the approach:

> Action research, not being based upon the hypothesis-testing model from natural science (which is so slippery a concept in the investigation of social phenomena) has to be judged by the even application of two criteria which relate, respectively, to the 'action' and to the 'research': practical achievements in the problem situation and the acquisition of process knowledge concerning problem solving....... It is in general harder to achieve the latter than the former... (Checkland and Scholes, 1990, p.182).

Checkland and Scholes' description draws our attention to the practical difficulties of action research. While action research may appear to be an attractive option for information systems (IS) research there are practical difficulties of carrying out the research. The catalytic potential of IS may create unimagined issues which the researcher may have to address. The issues may be relevant to the research but equally they may not. The learning experience of the project itself may be useful to research at some future stage but there is the danger for the researcher that when they attempt to piece together the lessons after the project has finished they may be accused of bias. One danger is that of convincing a dispassionate reader of the validity of the argument which may have been constructed after the event with little evidence to support it. Some may argue that provided the method of action research is declared at the start this is sufficient to give the research credibility. There may also be times when it is difficult to sustain an argument with little more than a personal analysis of the situation. One difficulty for the action researcher, then, is how to plan and how to manage the research in the kind of complex and unpredictable situations that precipitate its use.

7.2.2   Action Research and Information Systems Research

An interest in thinking about the theoretical foundations of information systems and appropriate paradigms goes back at least to the work of Methlie (1980). It has been charted by Hirschheim (1985) who described the trend away from the pure scientific foundations of computing towards social science of post-positivism and 'the need to do away with the physical science model as the only acceptable vehicle for knowledge acquisition...' (p.60). Other strong advocates of the necessity to move away from the more traditional scientific model of research in computing include Winograd and Flores (1986), Stowell and West (1994), Walsham (1995).

The trend towards the interpretive paradigm is becoming increasingly important to IS research. In Britain, soft systems work and the interest, both theoretical and practical, of the relevance and use of this work in IS (e.g. SSM), stems from this interpretive perspective. A result of this work is that IS is advocated as being as much in the domain of social science as it is in computing science (Stowell, 1995). However, in rejecting the realist, positivist, deterministic, and nomothetic framework of empiricism (Burrell and Morgan, 1979), an alternative mode of inquiry is required to take its place. Action research has, therefore, become a popular means of conducting non-positivist inquiry, which has been taken up by those in IS. In practice this has led to action research being used as a framework for designing, developing and implementing IS (Avison and Wood-Harper, 1990; Stowell and West, 1994), as well as a means of conducting IS research.

The fundamental requirements of action research as adopted by researchers at Lancaster University in a 25 year programme of action research has been the declaration in advance of the epistemology within which the findings will be expressed (Checkland, 1991; 1995). This vision of action research which helped the thinking behind SSM is based upon the hermeneutic cycle which is operationalised through a framework of ideas using systems thinking to tackle an area of application (perceived real-world problem situation). As well as action being carried out to improve the perceived real-world problem situation, reflection based on the framework and methodology is carried out by the researcher in order to extract lessons from the experience. This version of action research has been primarily aimed at attempting to tackle ill-structured 'management problems' which also includes the provision of information in IS.

Bubenko (1986) criticises many academic IS methodologies which have not been tested or evaluated by applying them in demanding cases. He also states that the take up of academic research ideas in industry is very low and slow. Avison and Fitzgerald (1995) explain how some researchers have attempted to address this problem through using consultancies as a means of infiltrating the use of methods into industry as well as using action research as a means of developing ideas within practical situations. Other means they identify include adapting academic methodologies into commercial methodologies as well as combining techniques of academia and industry. Examples of such attempts include Multiview in which '...the methodology itself has been refined using "action research" methods, that is the application and testing of ideas developed in an academic environment into the "real-world"...' (Avison and Fitzgerald, 1995, p.375). The difficulties inherent in both planning and in undertaking any action research study are well recognised by those who have used this mode of inquiry. Furthermore, undertaking IS research by means of action research brings its own problems to the difficulties of research and it is towards these difficulties that the rest of this chapter is directed.

7.3   Three Experiences of Using Action Research for Information Systems Research

We have selected three studies which we will use to represent, which is for us, different problems which seem to be created by adopting action research for IS research. We will identify key issues that are significant across all three for action research and for IS research generally.

7.3.1   STUDY A

The area of interest for the first study to be described is that of knowledge elicitation for expert systems. (A full description of this research can be found in West, 1991.) When attempting to develop an expert system to be used to help identify and catalogue archeological remains the process of knowledge elicitation was seen to be a particular weakness in the expert system development process. The literature on expert systems and knowledge elicitation (KE) seemed to support this contention and much can be found on the problems of KE and the various KE techniques available dating back to early AI work of the late 1960s. The research entailed the identification of weaknesses in current KE practice and the development of a set of key elements of a KE approach that might address these weaknesses. A means of operationalising these key elements in a KE approach was then derived and a field study conducted to apply the ideas.

The field study involved undertaking a KE study in a large UK company. The company was in the process of developing an expert system within the personnel department that would help assist personnel staff assess company members, develop training and personal development programmes, and help to develop succession planning. Progress on the expert system had slowed due to difficulties over the KE process and the need to qualify concepts used and to assemble clear, unambiguous descriptions of such things as 'good managers'. Although the expert system development team had originally identified concepts and terms by reference to management literature and personnel proforma and tests, it was felt that the content of the expert system would be more appropriate and management acceptance would be greater if the description contained within the expert system was specific to that particular organisation (which was felt to have a unique culture and history that accounted for its people and their way of working) and its people.

The key elements relating to the KE approach were put into practice with participants of manager and executive manager level across the organisation. Participants were identified by the 'champion' of the expert system project and, on the whole, participation was wholehearted. The study enabled the researcher to experience the research ideas in practice and to reassess both their theoretical and practical foundations. On the client's side, the realities of the expert system project and the aspirations of its champions were reflected upon. Involvement of staff from personnel resulted in an executive manager reconsidering the way in which personnel issues had been adressed. The lessons gained by him from this exercise provided a new perspective of personnel issues which he considered to be richer than the view he held previously. Feedback from the individual mangers involved in the study illustrated that the KE process undertaken had provided a way of thinking through and verbalising the way they saw and tackled their jobs as managers. This new awareness and knowledge was considered by those involved to be a valuable personal and organisational resource.

Use of the research ideas in this study enabled reassessment of the participants' ideas and the way in which they were operationalised, and provided lessons about the use of the KE approach which enabled a further KE study to be undertaken. The clients of this second study was the software house that had produced the expert system shell used by the organisation in the first study. The software house invited participants from among their own clients who had reported difficulties in using the expert system shell due to the complication of the KE process. Participants (12 senior managers from the UK, Italy and Germany) attended a two-day workshop during which time they were introduced to the research ideas and encouraged to put them into practice. In terms of the research the study provided an important setting in which to explore the way in which the ideas were taught, received, and used and thereby provided a valuable input to the process of learning about the research ideas. For the software house (clients of the study), the workshop offered an opportunity to address (or at least to be seen to be addressing) some of the reported difficulties surrounding the use of their product. It is believed that further workshops were conducted by the software house.

The final study in this research was of a rather different nature. In this study the client of the research could be said to have been the researcher, in the sense that the research ideas were being used to promote discussion and criticism of the research from KE practitioners in the field. This time the participants were three individuals who were involved in knowledge engineering: one was from a well-known expert system software house, one from a multinational company manufacturing business computers and one was an academic who had a strong background in computing, psychology and KE. The research ideas which had continued to be reassessed and developed were used on the three individuals to elicit their ideas about knowledge elicitation. The output from this exercise not only provided expert feedback on the evolving approach to KE but also provided a first-hand account of the problems of KE which were then fed back into the research ideas development process.

7.3.2   STUDY B

The second example built upon the lessons learnt from the research reported in study A. The main objective of this research was to explore the effect of computer-based technology upon the process of learning initiated by a subjective method of knowledge elicitation (KE), namely the Appreciative Inquiry Method (AIM) (West, 1995). Over the last decade a number of conventional computer-based approaches to knowledge elicitation have been developed from manually applied KE approaches in an attempt to overcome certain problems within the KE process. The focus of this research appears to have been upon structured aspects of domain knowledge. Moreover, it is arguable whether these computer-based KE approaches actually enhanced the manual approaches from which they are derived. In study B the research was concerned with (i) developing a computer version of AIM (ii) learning what the effect technology might have upon the process of learning that the manual AIM seems to facilitate and (iii) drawing out some lessons with respect to the key elements upon which AIM was developed (West, 1991). Using a computer-based version of AIM was a means of attempting to learn about how an automated AIM might affect the interpretive approach to KE.

The field research was undertaken as a piece of action research using AIM to facilitate the cycle of learning. The collaborators agreed that learning about 'marketing for small enterprises' would be of value to them which provided a suitable focus for the research. Marketing was accepted by the researcher as a complex messy domain because it appeared to an external observer that marketing in small businesses is ill-structured, experiential and subjective. The researcher approached a number of host organisations which included small business advice agencies, small business consultancies, small businesses and university departments in which a number of domain experts agreed to provide their time and expertise in assisting the researcher to explore the research ideas. A number of domain experts used AIM in its computer-based and manual-based versions to aid them in their understanding of their chosen domain and allowed the researcher the opportunity to reflect upon the process of inquiry.

At an early stage in the action research, the researcher had a problem of trying to set up a series of interviews from which lessons about the underlying concepts of AIM would be learnt. Because the number of employees in each company involved were small (e.g. one or two people) there was a practical problem of how to get views about AIM at each stage in order to learn from the exercise. The problem was addressed by attempting to create a virtual group. That is the grouping was transparent to the clients and used by the researcher in order to undertake sessions which would allow the differences in application of AIM to be observed. Each set of interviews was taken as being similar to single interviews from a larger group. The collaborators had the advantage of learning about marketing from the experiences gained by the group as a whole. Some of the collaborators also had the opportunity to comment upon the usefulness of the two versions of AIM in facilitating the process of learning. The design of the research project included considerations about ways of enabling the collaborators to learn about marketing and to provide them with an opportunity to comment upon the usefulness of the versions of AIM that they used. Great care was taken to ensure that the process of learning that was essential to the research was unaffected by the conduct of the study.

Through a collaborative learning process, the field studies attempted to provide the researcher with knowledge about a particular approach to KE, and the problem domain, from within the subjective experiences of a number of domain experts. At the end of each phase of AIM the collective views of the collaborators were considered and the lessons learnt informed both the researcher about the use of AIM and about the clients' reactions to their use of AIM. The action research approach contrasted with the more common laboratory-based methods of comparing computer/manual-based KE on relatively simple domains in which the role of the researcher is that of a detached observer.

7.3.3   STUDY C

We have argued above that action research can enrich two groups of people involved in a field study. First, those interested in research and second, the client group. It is to the second group that this section is dedicated. Stowell and West (1994) refer to a case study that was carried out at a company euphemistically called Waverley Randall. This case study was based upon a real field study from which a number of valuable lessons were learnt. In addition to the contribution that the study made to the research programme there appear to have been tangible benefits for the clients which can be attributed to the process of action research itself.

As described elsewhere (Stowell and West, 1994), Waverley Randall had a number of interrelated problems which necessitated changes to working procedures, products, and its skill base. There existed at the time a requirement for staff to change working practices and this depended upon the willingness of the staff to embrace that change. The company was facing industrial unrest at the time of the study in the manufacturing area which related to a number of possible causes but the common problem seemed to be a requirement for staff to change important and traditional ways of working. The particular study was initially confined to the working of the Commercial Department, the staff of which were not directly involved in the industrial unrest.

At the time of the study the Commercial Department had developed into identifiable managerial areas which in turn broke down into sub-sections. This seemed to have happened where the office staff had developed their own ways of working with different individuals in the organisation. For example, some of the sales and marketing staff worked directly to a particular clerk in the Commercial Department rather than go through any of the managers of that department. The clerk and the individual sales person even worked out discounts and ways of treating particular customers. This kind of approach meant that in the Commercial Department there were personal records kept and maintained without other people in the department being aware of what the records contained. Although there were records that should have been a common source of data they were not always shared between individuals. The so called 'general' records were maintained and stored in a personal filing system with each individual having their own version.

Initially the research was confined to the Commercial Department although at a later stage the study embraced Manufacturing and Stock Control. This report will be confined to the development of the work in the Commercial Department. The purpose of the research was to learn more about organisational change and the impact of organisational power upon the change.

The lessons learnt from this aspect of the research can be found elsewhere (Stowell, 1989), but the benefits of the process of action research were apparent to the clients.

The study was carried out using soft systems methodology as the practical method of action research. The research involved a number of staff from the Commercial Department (see Stowell and West, 1994, pp.162-163) who met at regular intervals to agree about problem themes and initiate ideas which were considered to be useful in addressing these problem themes.

Membership of the group was on a 'voluntary' basis from the department as a whole but, naturally, the directors expected this group to include relevant Managers. However, the way in which the group developed, arguably because of the approach used, was one in which very soon the discussion and development of ideas were highly interactive and developed from within an atmosphere of free and open discussion.

The group discussion led to the production of a series of models which the group believed represented the existing situation and, at a later stage, a desirable way in which the Commercial Department should operate. At regular intervals these models were presented to the department as a whole who were given the opportunity to comment. Any member of the department who wished to contribute to the development of the models was invited to the smaller group meetings. The process seemed to enrich the deliberations and level of the models as the problems became openly discussed. Those members of the department who had been responsible for the small personalised methods of working were encouraged to bring to the group problems which they felt were special and could not be managed by an all-embracing departmental system. Once these 'special' problems were raised within the group, the group members found ways of building the means of handling these differences into the model: in this way the group took ownership of the developing models. However, the group did not always accept the argument for special treatment for certain tasks and often arrived at the conclusion that the differences could be handled in a more generic way. It soon became clear to the group that the special sub-sections in the department were, in fact, unnecessary. In some instances the difficulties were seen as examples of inefficiency or bad practice and the group dealt with these problems themselves in a practical and constructive way.

The lessons learnt from the exercise served to help the client appreciate the problem situation as a whole which, in turn, helped to better inform the way in which they should manage their situation. For example, the client group took ownership of the situation and went on to develop ways of addressing these problems. The client group went on to present these ideas to the Board of Directors for formal acceptance arguing for the viability of their proposals. The prime benefit of conducting the field study in this way appears to be the control that the client group exercised over the situation. Interestingly, this was in sharp contrast to previous, more traditional studies that the department had been involved in. Action research seemed to have provided a platform for the problem to be openly discussed by all members of the department and for the problems to be managed by the group as a whole. Moreover, although there were members of the departmental management present the way that the research was conducted enabled all members to participate. The focus of attention seemed to be upon producing a feasible model of the way that the department should work. The model provided an agenda for the department as a whole and appears to have been the vehicle which enabled the members of the department to take ownership of the problem/opportunity. The cycle of learning enabled by action research provided both the researcher and the clients with the opportunity to learn about their particular area of interest.

The equal participation of clients provided an opportunity for information to be fed into the group by experts from a number of different areas (e.g. technical (IT), strategy, and marketing) as well as allowing general points from individuals to be made without any one individual or area dominating the proceedings. For the researcher lessons were learnt about the way in which the group gained, first, an appreciation and then ownership of the problem and its 'solution'. The researcher was also able to consider the robustness of the approach used and to offer suggestions about how its weaknesses might be addressed.

7.3.4   Key Issues Arising from the Three Studies

The studies described above provided the opportunity to consider some of the practical difficulties of undertaking action research. The main issues can be summarised as follows:

- Domain—complex situations with a number of uncontrolled variables which negated the adoption of a positivist research approach.
- Conduct of the study—interviews took place in all of the reported studies over a number of months. A common problem was how to carry out the studies within a reasonable period of time.
- Collaborators/collaboration—the clients in each study were volunteers but in each case the circumstances placed different demands upon client and facilitator.
- Rigour—should records be maintained or should reporting the study be based upon the author's recollection of what happened? If records are to be kept what form should they take and how should they be maintained?
- Expectations—are all concerned aware of the nature of action research and the unpredictability of its outcome?
- Initiating the lessons—there are a number of problems which need to be considered in advance including how to initiate an atmosphere of learning in a hectic workplace environment. The different kinds of problems that manifest between one-to-one and one-to-many situations, the research and the consultancy/research type situation.

From the three studies reported above we can identify two different starting points, or catalysts, for research: the researcher may embark upon action research to investigate an initial concern - either to explore an idea or theory related to methodology (theory-initiated) or to use an existing approach to help clients learn about their problem situation and its ramifications (action-initiated). These two starting points seem to pose different challenges to the researcher and present different practical difficulties in terms of action research. In the next section we consider these challenges and difficulties using the headings of the key issues outlined above as a way of structuring the debate.

7.4 Two Action Research Scenarios

From our own work, summarised above, we can identify two significant differences of emphasis in an action research project. For the purposes of discussion we will refer to the two different modes of action research. This is not to suggest that we are dealing with two different types of action research, merely different emphasises due to different initial concerns and interests. In the first approach, which we will refer to as the 'field Study' mode, action research is adopted as an appropriate way of carrying out field studies in order to learn about ideas that have been formulated previously as a result of critical evaluation of the literature and practice. The aim of this mode of study is, first and foremost, to learn about the nature of the research ideas in a practical situation by gaining an understanding of their use. This allows reflection upon the original ideas and may encourage the researcher to make practical changes or re-evaluate the theoretical grounds of the research ideas. While the focus is upon the research ideas it is expected that the organisation hosting the field study will also benefit. In such a study we argue that action is theory-led since the researcher is interested, primarily, in learning about the research ideas from their practical application. It may be useful, therefore, to consider the researcher as both a researcher and a client of the study since they have a personal reason (e.g. MPhil/PhD) for conducting the study, a reason which should not be overlooked.

Some of the emphases and priorities of the field study mode can be seen to differ from those of the action research study where the researcher takes advantage of a real-world problem situation as a means of obtaining research material. Such a study might be one in which the client(s) is helped to address a perceived problem/opportunity but there is also the chance to learn about the relevant research ideas through the live study. We shall refer to this type of study as the 'consultancy' mode. A prime purpose of the consultancy mode is to feed the lessons learnt from previous action back into the problem situation with the intention of bringing about change.

7.4.1. Issues for the Field Study Mode

There are a number of issues to be considered for the field study mode which can be problematical if the process of action research is to be maintained. In each of the studies described above the chosen domain was within a business environment and concerned complex issue-based problems. In the first two cases (studies A and B) the research element was the focal point since the catalyst to the studies had been the wish to explore interesting theoretical implications for information systems practice.

The first two studies, therefore, suggested what we have called the 'field study' mode from which the following points for discussions were drawn:

(i) The choice of a suitable domain

One of the issues in an action research field study is the selection of an appropriate domain through which to explore particular themes, theories and ideas. The initiation of the field study will usually be by the researcher who will have approached some organisational member within the chosen domain. The researcher has targeted the particular domain because it is seen to contain issues which are apposite to the research. Many researchers will recognise that, while in theory the selection of a suitable domain is quite straightforward, in practice recruiting willing collaborators is not always easy.

The chosen domain needs to offer sufficient depth and complexity to allow the research themes to be explored rather than to act simply as a pre-defined vehicle through which to sell research ideas. In study A, criticisms of knowledge elicitation (KE) processes and techniques in the literature (West, 1991), suggested that it would be worth while researching key elements of a KE approach that was consistent with statements about the subjectivity of expertise. In this case an industrial partner was sought who also had a reason for being interested in the process of KE. Senior management agreed to collaborate because the difficulties in developing an expert system had proved more problematic than they had been led to believe. In this study the collaborators and researcher shared an interest, namely, how to develop the expert system. In order to explore this problem the clients and researcher agreed upon a subject that would provide some interesting lessons for both parties. The subject was 'management training'. The clients benefited from an increased understanding about 'management' and 'management training', as expressed by their managers, and the difficulty of formalising such concepts while the researcher learnt valuable lessons about eliciting expertise.

In study B, the researcher wished to learn about how a developing method of KE could support practitioners in exploring and expressing thoughts about their domain of interest compared to an approach which had been researched previously. Both methods of KE in study A and B were based upon interpretative systems thinking and the research was conducted as a piece of action research. In study B the quest for a single collaborator proved to be unsuccessful. The end result was a group of people with a common belief that marketing was an important issue for small businesses but who rarely had the opportunity to consider their marketing strategies and practices. The researcher, therefore, had the task of managing the practical problem of how to carry out action research with a number of collaborators, each of whom were in a different small company: although they were geographically and organisationally separate they represented a single group with a common concern.

> *Lesson:*
> *Obtaining willing collaborators within a chosen domain can be difficult but the researcher needs to be mindful of the danger of selecting a domain purely on the basis of access to willing collaborators. The researcher must be sure that the domain is an appropriate one from which to explore their research ideas while also maintaining an acceptable learning experience for their collaborators. The researcher must, therefore, have an awareness of the possible learning outcomes (their type and direction) and be mindful that researcher and collaborators may not have shared interests.*

To summarise, in study A the focus of interest of the researcher and the clients was the same but for different reasons. In study B the domain problem was the unifying interest for the collaborators, although for the researcher the domain problem was incidental: it provided a suitable complex situation upon which to focus the research. In both cases, then, the collaborators benefited from the lessons learnt from the study and the researchers were able to learn some useful lessons from their own particular research interests.

(ii) Planning and implementing the field study

In case studies A and B the researchers had an element of control in as much as they could plan what they intended to do and make appointments with the clients with an estimated time for each meeting. In both these studies the encounters were usually on a one-to-one basis which was a marked difference from the third project where group meetings were the norm and the element of planning was much reduced. Each of the three studies took place within the organisations concerned in surroundings which were familiar to the clients (e.g. their office). This policy was adopted because it was considered to be one way of facilitating concentration upon the problem situation and reducing the impact of the researcher's presence.

The dilemma that researchers face concerns the degree of planning that can and/or should be undertaken for an action research project. Our experience suggests that if criticisms of anecdotal or commonsense results are to be avoided then detailed consideration about the way in which the action research study is planned and implemented should be given. Checkland (1981) recognises this point as being one of the main issues of undertaking action research when he explains: 'The problem with action research arises from the fact that it cannot be wholly planned and directed down particular paths.' (p.153). Eden and Huxham (1996), however, argue that even with action research: 'A high degree of method and orderliness is required in reflecting about, and holding on to, the emerging research content of each episode of involvement in the organisation' (p.81). These two comments help to explain how action research, by its very nature, is a different mode of inquiry to that of positivist science and as such cannot be planned in the same way as a piece of empirical experimentation. However, if we are to avoid criticisms of lack of standards then an action research study still needs to be managed in as much as research aims are considered and expressed as 'hopes' (Checkland, 1981. p.153). Some degree of planning, therefore, needs to take place but will be concerned with process and method as opposed to attainment of desired outcomes.

The planning of an action research study depends upon the reason for undertaking the study but a number of questions are likely to need consideration whatever the particulars. The question that might be worth considering at the start (as the study progresses the answer to these questions may change significantly) include:

1. What is an appropriate time span for the study?
2. How many participants should there be?
3. Who should be included? (and who decides upon this?)
4. Should interviews be undertaken with groups or individuals?
5. Should the views expressed in a one-to-one situation be treated in a similar fashion to the views expressed by a larger group?
6. How can the knowledge gained from one cycle of action be reinvested?
7. How can/should the encounters be recorded?
8. How can a description of the situation be 'validated'?

An important part of any action research study is noting what happens in order to try and record the development of ideas or changes in practice or attitude. If records are to be maintained and we are to avoid criticisms of bias it seems that we should consider ways of recording observations so that they can be revisited by any interested party both for validation purposes and to support critical reflection and learning. Keeping records of the process of the study is an important aspect of action research which requires careful consideration and planning.

> *Lesson:*
> *A useful way of approaching the planning of action research is to focus upon the approach used in order to undertake the study (rather than concern ourselves with predicting and testing the outcomes), since we cannot (and would not care to) predict the direction that the study may take.*

Discussing this issue, Somekh (1995), points out that commercial companies undertaking action research produce careful research designs to ensure that the action research process is fully documented. Our experience suggests that it is important to plan the process of the field study, as far as is possible, in advance and to consider fact finding and fact recording tools and techniques appropriate to action research. The choice of tools, techniques and methods should be revelant to the epistemological basis of the research in order to allow the emergent lessons to be related to a particular intellectual framework (Checkland, 1991; Stowell and West, 1994).

(iii) Engaging collaborators

Collaborators involved with field research should be made aware of the researcher's intentions at the outset. That is to say the researcher's prime interest is in learning about a particular aspect of research from which they, the collaborators, may benefit. Benefits of the research may be gained directly through the domain under investigations, as in case B, or indirectly from the outcome of the study, as in case A, which may be of use to them. This is in contrast to the consultancy mode where the consultant-researcher has been invited into the enterprise in order to aid them in addressing an organisational situation.

Finding willing collaborators is directly related to the problem of identifying a suitable domain. While potential collaborators may accept that a research experience may be valuable not all feel this way and are justified in asking 'what is in it for me?' Moreover, as in the case of study A the collaborators had been 'volunteered' by their line managers and needed to be convinced personally of the value of the study to them.

Because information technology is likely to make a significant contribution to the organisation much IS research requires us to work with the busiest members of the organisation and, consequently, time commitment is often a problem. A further practical problem is that of maintaining consistency in the body of collaborators throughout a long study which spans 18 months or so. It is not unusual for members of the organisation to move on or for new members to join the project. The involvement of new members or the loss of willing collaborators may create a number of problems for the researcher. Given that collaboration and learning are fundamental to action research the prospect of a key member being replaced three-quarters of the way through the study may have serious consequences for the research programme.

For example, the new collaborators may wish to widen or even re-orientate the study in order to align it more closely with work they have been involved with previously. Such developments need to be considered carefully against the projected research aims (e.g. what effect will such action have on the study and can we allow for what appears to be a deviation that will cause extra work?). In studies A and B described above, the researchers found themselves in situations in which a particular member from the host organisations withdrew from the research (e.g. due to work commitments, moving jobs, illness, disinterest) which had an immediate effect upon the field studies. In this respect it may be difficult to maintain the joint learning process that plays such a central role in action research.

> *Lesson:*
> *The value of the contribution of field research is dependent upon willing and able collaborators. There is a need for the researcher to consider how changes in personnel during the study may influence and affect the study. These considerations will become part of the overall learning experience.*

It should be recognised from the outset that members of a host organisation are free agents and, therefore, it is not possible to protect the study against the withdrawal of key players. The action researcher should be aware of the likelihood of such a situation developing and consider how this may affect the research (e.g. how will this new person become immersed in the study which may have been progressing for a number of months? What is the effect of losing one member from the group? Will the new member have new ideas and if so how can these be pulled into the study?). While such difficulties are natural and largely unavoidable they do need careful consideration, particularly in terms of how they may affect the research.

(iv) The rigour of action research

It is the responsibility of the IS researcher to maintain the rigour of the research and the way in which action research is presented if criticisms concerning the validity of the lessons learnt are to be avoided. This is particularly important in IS where many practitioners have been brought up in the tradition of positivist empiricism. Elden and Chisholm (1993) discuss this point:

> In conducting research, the action researcher engages in a form of scientific inquiry and must follow the basic rules of the social sciences to support conclusions. Since action

research is change oriented, it requires data that help track the consequences of intended changes. So, action research must have data collected systematically over time (p.128).

This is particularly important in terms of formal research since material must be presented in a form that can be understood at a later date rather than depend upon the recollection of events. In order to be able to use the lessons learnt from a field study for others to use at a later date some appropriate means of presenting the research needs to be considered. This is difficult to achieve, mainly because of the tendency of the work to become anecdotal (Checkland, 1995). Knowing what to record and what not to is an on-going problem for the action researcher. The material serves as a reservoir of information that can be referred to and used at any point in the study.

> *Lesson:*
> *While it may be valid for an action research study to call upon positivist methods and other forms of social research, if deemed appropriate in gaining an increased understanding of a particular aspect of the problem situation (Lewin, 1948; Peters and Robinson, 1984; Ledford and Mohrman, 1993), the researcher needs to address at the outset how to incorporate other forms of research within a programme of action research without compromising the principles upon which action research is based.*

In all three projects the field research took place over several months and, consequently, the researchers found it necessary to keep some form of record of each encounter. The primary record was the wealth of diagrams that were produced by the clients in the process of the different exercises. The diagrams themselves varied in each case but included rich pictures, maps (Venn convention) and rudimentary data flow diagrams (Stowell and West, 1994, pp.54-90). The records themselves were not seen by the researchers as 'proof' in a positivist sense but as a source of information which could be used to enrich learning at the time of the study and subsequently. For example, records kept from Study A provided some useful lessons for study B without in any way acting as a constraint.

(v) False expectations

In the first two reported projects the clients were aware that the researcher wanted to learn about the approach being used to explore the domain of interest but the clients also expected to gain some insight into the chosen topic which they considered to be important to their organisational role. Given that for the researcher the primary concern is with exploring the research ideas and themes, how much of the study can be directed towards solving the problems within the host organisation? For example, in study A, the collaboration was based upon the premise that both parties would benefit from exploring the process of KE with respect to the domain of management training, albeit that the interests and emphasis of those involved were different.

> *Lesson:*
> *The researcher may avoid false expectations if the nature of the research method and its potential outcomes are discussed with the host organisation at the beginning of the study, but given the nature of action research, client expectations may change as the study progresses which means that a wise researcher needs to consider how such a situation can be managed. Having a strategy for dealing with possible outcomes helps to prevent unrealistic expectations on the part of the host organisation as well as making the researcher's role clearer.*

In this study there was no formal agreement that at the end of the study the host organisation would have an expert system. At regular intervals care was taken to discuss progress with the clients (where they were different from the collaborators) and the lessons learnt. In study B, there was no emphasis on solving problems relating to small business marketing, although the difficulties experienced by small businesses to find the opportunity to consider their marketing practices and strategies were recognised. Therefore, an agreement was made that exploring the domain of marketing in small businesses using a particular approach to KE would benefit the researcher and the process of learning that it entailed would aid the collaborators in thinking about the domain itself.

(vi) Identifying useful lessons and knowing when to bring the study to a close

The lessons learnt from each of the reported studies were gained in similar ways. In each study the method chosen was used to create an agenda as a means of structuring the debate. The discussions and the social interaction provided ideas which were discussed and validated by the clients themselves. The validation of the lessons and the outcomes were achieved by the clients' acceptance of the definition of the problem situation. The way that this was achieved varied between the studies. In the first case the clients were given the opportunity to accept/reject a pictorial representation of the problem situation which itself generated discussion and opportunities for learning. For the researcher, lessons were learnt about the usefulness of the method in structuring a debate. In the second study the clients were asked if the methods used for the action learning process had provided them with a clearer understanding of the problem situation (in this case marketing). The researcher was able to learn about the value of the two variations of KE used both in terms of their usefulness in enabling the expert to divulge their expertise and use in engendering the process of learning.

Since the field study mode involves exploring the research ideas in a predefined and appropriate domain the research is, to a greater extent, under the control of the researcher and is unlikely to be deflected by a problem that surfaces which is not directly related to the research itself. This observation suggests that as long as an appropriate type of domain can be found then the ideas can be explored and the lessons reinvested to produce a framework of an approach that might inform other, similar, situations.

The issue of identifying useful lessons is also related to the question of knowing when to draw the research to a close (e.g. how do we know when we have learnt enough to critically evaluate our ideas?). The question itself can be argued to be in conflict with the underlying principle of action research which states that the learning cycle is never ending. Although these questions cannot be easily answered in a practical sense we suggested that it is the participants, including the researcher, of the study who decide when enough learning has taken place so that the next stage can begin or the research be concluded. For example, in case study A, the first of the three field studies conducted was large-scale and provided the majority of the lessons learnt about the approach used. In terms of the researcher's intentions, the second study was conducted to provide the opportunity to consider the use of the approach with groups and with less involvement from the researcher. By the third study, fewer new lessons about the approach were to be found and instead the learning experience tended to support the outcomes of the previous two studies. Consequently, the researcher deemed this an appropriate time to conclude the field studies. Another consideration may be that the tolerance level of the collaborator(s) is such that a strategic withdrawal is the most prudent course of action!

> *Lesson:*
> *The notion of 'useful' lessons is often something that cannot be determined at the time of the action from which the lessons are later derived. This difficulty means that rigourous documentation, awareness of the process of interaction, and continuous reflection are required to ensure that useful lessons are identified. Each action research project is unique and it is difficult to state when sufficient has been learnt to satisfy the research demands, saying that the researcher should assess the situation in terms of their needs and the tolerance level of the collaborators. However, it should be possible for the researcher to recognise a point when the learning experience begins to support and repeat previous experiences with only small or imperceptible differences. This situation may indicate an appropriate time to draw the study to a close.*

7.4.2 Issues for the Consultancy Mode

In the third study described above (case study C), the prime motivation was to aid the clients to 'solve' their problem using an approach which seemed likely to be successful given previous experience. The study had been initiated as a piece of consultancy but, after a short time, it seemed that the study would support formal research since the opportunity had arisen for the researcher to explore some previously identified research aims. We have referred to this type of approach to research as a 'consultancy' mode. This reflects the view that we consider the researcher's first loyalty to be to the consultancy with the requirements of research being met only if they can be incorporated, seamlessly, within the consultancy. In the following sections the issues arising from the consultancy mode approach will be discussed using the same 'key issue' headings identified above.

(i) Choosing a suitable domain

A number of different scenarios for the inception of a consultancy mode approach may be given. The first scenario is akin to the field study mode in that an investigation of the literature and practice has promoted some research ideas. In order to explore these ideas the researcher engages upon some consultancy which has been initiated by a client. The decision to take on the consultancy will be determined by a number of factors but in particular, for the serious researcher, it is the suitability of the domain in relation to the research issues that will be the deciding factor. Like the field study mode the researcher does have a certain amount of choice and flexibility in the selection of a domain but unlike the field study mode does not have the problem of convincing the client that the problem is a valid area for investigation. A second possibility is that an on-going consultancy may, at some point in its process, seem able to support previously identified research interests (as was the case with study C). Other consultancies may, themselves, initiate research issues which can then be explored.

Lesson:
The consultant-researcher has to weigh the balance between satisfying the client's needs and the requirements for the research. Of prime importance, before the project is accepted, is for the consultant-researcher to be sure that the clients problems can be addressed. The consultant-researcher should also consider whether the consultancy (given its constraints and demands) is a suitable vehicle for formal research.

In whatever way the consultancy mode has been initiated, there are a number of issues that are generally applicable. For example, there is the ever present danger that the direction of the study might move away from the area that the researcher is interested in which may force the researcher to abandon his or her original intentions, and perhaps the research altogether. Too strong an adherence to the research 'hopes' may result in the consultancy being a failure (and thereby the research since the desire for change will not have taken place in the organisational setting). Alternatively, it is possible that the study may inform the research in a negative way particularly if the study is based upon a method which is unsuited to the problem situation.

(ii) Planning and the conflict created between consultancy and research

To a large extent the planning of the research within the project will be determined by the problem situation and by the demands of the client. This was particularly so in study C. In the later stages of the study the clients determined what they were going to do and how long they were prepared to spend on the task. Although the consultant-researcher attempted to take a less active role in the development the clients wished to have the presence of the consultant at every meeting. In this particular study this appeared to have no adverse effect upon the research element but it is conceivable that there may be situations where such demands on time would cause significant problems for the research element of the study.

Lesson:
There should be a conscious effort on the part of the consultant-researcher to accept that the client demands may make it difficult to follow their preferred interests. An awareness of this possibility may allow the researcher to consider potential strategies for action prior to the event and thus may limit the damage that client demands might otherwise cause to the research.

We have learnt that the day-to-day requirements of a project may make it difficult for the researcher to step back from the study and reflect upon research which may not be directly related to the activities of the clients. For example, the cycle of learning engendered by action research may involve the consultant-researcher in a number of time-consuming activities which may have little to do with the specific research issues and more to do with addressing the operational activities of the organisation. Unlike the field study mode the consultant-researcher cannot guarantee to pursue his or her direct research interests and should be mindful of the possibility of 'shaping' the clients' problems to fit the research.

(iii) Engaging willing collaborators

Given the fact that the clients from the host organisation have a personal interest in the study and that they have been responsible for its commission, it is not unreasonable for the consultant-researcher to expect to start the project with supportive clients. Experience shows that there are situations where it may be difficult for organisational members to remove themselves from the study. The organisational representative might have been put into the position because of pressure from influential members of the organisation. An action research project has the potential to empower the clients by enabling them to take ownership of the problem situation (Stowell, 1994; Eden and Huxham, 1996) but it is not unusual to find that some clients have firm ideas about the approach that they wish to be adopted and the kind of outcome that they expect from the project: the action research consultant needs to be prepared to react in any appropriate way as dictated by the situation. In some instances appropriate action might consume all the consultant-researcher's effort.

> *Lesson:*
> *Collaborators may have their own agenda for the project which may be counter productive both for the consultancy and the research. The consultant-researcher needs to be able to note and consider the movements and concerns of collaborators and to place this information within the context of both organisational problem solving and the research ideas.*

In study C it was rare for there to be one-to-one encounters and each session was with at least six members of the organisation which meant that had the research element not been concerned with the kinds of problems that such encounters generate then the research element may have had to give way to the needs of the clients. One of the traps that it is easy for the consultant-researcher to fall into is to attempt, retrospectively, to piece together events that have taken place during the project in the hope that they will contribute to the research dimension. It is possible that the study might reveal an interesting path but it is equally possible that the outcome of the project may yield little contribution to the intended areas of research.

(iv) The rigour of action research

Perhaps the first question that should be addressed is should action research be rigourous? We suggest that action research shares much in common with scientific research in terms of the need to uphold quality and a desire to provide a contribution to the body of knowledge of a particular area of human interest. In order to achieve this researchers need to have a clear understanding about how they intend to set about the research and about the method that they intend to use. We can agreed with Eden and Huxham (1996) who argue that important issues for action research include '.. the pragmatic focus of action research, designing action research and the validity of action research'. While great emphasis is placed upon the collaborative process of action research for the clients and the consultant in as much as it provides the basis for appreciating and then learning about the problem, when the consultant becomes researcher there is a shift in emphasis where, at times, the researcher needs to be able to 'stand outside' him or herself and observe the action research process. This situation is perhaps best described by Torbet when he speaks of 'consciousness in the midst of action' (Torbet, 1976, 1991).

If the outcome of an action research consultancy is to be used as part of formal research material then, we would argue, that there must be as much rigour attached to its provision as would be expected from scientific research: the difference between the two modes of inquiry is not one of rigour but of epistemology: 'Action research constitutes a kind of science with a different epistemology that produces a different kind of knowledge, a knowledge which is contingent on the particular situation, and which develops the capacity of members of the organisation to solve their own problems' (Susman and Evered, 1978).

In the previous section reference has been made to the difficulty of a consultancy-based study when the project develops along lines not directly related to the original expectations of the researcher. A second problem appears to be when the consultant-researcher decides, retrospectively, that the consultancy undertaken may provide the basis of research which can be presented under the umbrella of action research. It is not unusual for attempts to write a thesis based upon consultancy activities which are then offered as action research to run into difficulties (e.g. there is no evidence for the assertions made about the work other than the consultant-researcher's remembrance of it; the cycles of learning cannot be identified because at the time the action research process was not clearly conceived). Research which is submitted on this flimsy basis creates difficulties and not the least of these is how to counter criticism by a sceptic about the rigour of such work.

Given the nature of a consultancy type of action research project it is difficult to predict what records to keep and how best to keep them. For the researcher this is less of a problem since they will have an idea in advance about the direction in which they are heading but for the consultant the priority is helping the clients and their own research interests takes second place: for the consultant-researcher this situation represents a potential clash of interests. While it is possible to combine the two quite separate tasks successfully this can only happen where there is a genuine concatenation of circumstances. It seems to us that the consultancy/research area is at most risk of criticism for lack of rigour. The corollary to this potential danger is that the work itself ceases to be action research because of the restrictions placed upon the work by the record-keeping. There is, however, a good argument for a clear approach to be declared at the outset of the project and for some form of record of the progress of the research to be maintained.

> *Lesson:*
> *The consultancy-research project, in particular, is at risk from criticisms of lack of rigour which need to be addressed at the outset. Using past consultancies, even if well documented, as material for action research is inadvisable.*

(v) False expectations

In project C the focus of attention was the clients' desire to understand their problem situation and to reach an accommodation about how it might improved. For the researcher the project provided an opportunity to reflect upon the strengths and weaknesses of the chosen method for problem appreciation and to consider how the weaknesses might be addressed. Here the appreciation gained from the process of action research enabled the client group to bring about change. In this situation the clients' prime purpose was to gain an understanding of the problem situation but that did not prevent the researcher from learning about the usefulness of the research method in a dynamic social environment. However, within the consultancy mode, problems may arise from clients having false expectations. For example, the client may suggest at the start of the project that the problem is 'X' and all that is required of the consultant is to introduce the antidote to 'X' and the problem will disappear. The nature of an action research project suggests that the outcome is not always clear but and may produce an unexpected result—a potential situation which the consultant-researcher may be wise to explain to the client. We suggest that the consultant-researcher attempts to reduce the possibility of false expectations by establishing a clear agreement with the clients at the outset, explaining the nature of the approach and that the outcome might reveal 'X' merely as the manifestation of the problem and not the problem itself (as occurred in case study C). Furthermore, the learning process undertaken during the study may develop along unexpected and perhaps even undesirable lines as far as the client is concerned.

As far as the research element of the project is concerned there are situations where the client is willing to accommodate the research element of the project provided it will make a contribution towards addressing the problem perceived by the organisational members. For example, the researcher may wish to explore the usefulness of certain ways of facilitating discussion which will provide useful lessons for the researcher and will also contribute to the interactions between the collaborators themselves. The researcher should be prepared to modify or even abandon the research element if it seems to be getting in the way of helping the clients. It is important to recognise that the consultancy may not always be able to contribute much to the research and in such a case the distinction between consultancy and action research should be made. Failure to achieve this leads to the possibility of a study which is 'all action and no research' and so while the affinity between some form of consultancy and action research may be close, it would be a mistake, as is implied by Ormerod (1994, p.47), 'to simply declare that a consultancy undertaken is action research'.

> *Lesson:*
> *It is possible for both the clients and the researcher to have false hopes about the outcome of the study. The consultant-researcher's first duty is to facilitate a process of learning which will help the clients in addressing their problem situation. However, consultancy which cannot make some contribution to the body of knowledge, or theory, is not action research.*

(vi) Identifying useful lessons and knowing when to bring the study to a close

A carefully considered approach to the project can provide an opportunity for both clients and researcher to learn about the problem situation. Since the client may have commissioned the study and many of the lessons may be directed towards addressing specific organisational problems there may be much to be gained for the researcher too. However, there may be projects where it may be difficult for the researcher to extract the wider, more theoretical lessons from the research given the complexity and the practical nature of the situation.

In study C the clients took ownership and advocated changes that they wished to make to their methods of working. The situation whereby the clients take ownership may provide the consultant-researcher with an opportunity to reflect upon the strengths and weaknesses of the method used and to use those lessons as part of the research programme.

From a practical point the project will cease when the clients consider that their problem situation has been addressed and there is little more to be gained in continuing, or perhaps more commonly, the project completion date is agreed in advance. The problem for the researcher may be that while such a study may have satisfied the clients, the needs of the researcher may be left wanting. The latter is likely to occur if the demands of the project have pulled the study in a direction away from the interests of the researcher or if the lessons coming out of the study have been particularly rich. Additionally, while the lessons gained from a consultancy will be of undoubted value they may not be directly related to the research that was intended by the researcher. The researcher should respect this development and if further collaboration is not possible then there is no alternative but to accept that the project has yielded little for their research.

> *Lesson:*
> *Consultancy may provide an interesting problem domain but, equally, it may not provide the sufficient research material. The consultant-researcher should be aware of the usefulness of the lessons for the clients and for the research. The consultant-researcher may need to accept that the consultancy has not fulfilled requirements in terms of (i) action research and/or (ii) the original research 'hopes' expressed by the researcher.*

7.5   Reflections

The arguments in this chapter have been put forward on the premise that action research is an appropriate means of carrying out formal information systems research. The reason for the focus upon formal research was to explore how the demands of an MPhil/PhD might influence the interaction between researcher and organisational members and the way in which the study is conducted. From our own work two types of study, both using action research as the research approach, have been identified and explored to try and extract lessons about conducting such action research studies. It is not the intention to claim that we have different types of action research but to demonstrate and discuss two different ways of carrying out a collaborative study which conforms to the ethos of action research while providing sufficient material and scope to satisfy the demands of formal research.

7.5.1   General Reflections about the Field Study Mode

In the field study mode the investigation of research ideas is of primary importance. There is no attempt to discourage the collaboration of participants from the field study organisation, but the very nature of this type of research means that the researcher often assumes the role of an academic practising and doing research on the host organisation, which supplies resources and expertise. The researcher often approaches an organisation that seems to offer the type of scenario that the researcher is attempting to address. The researcher hopes that the host organisation will be able to gain from the experience in terms of a greater understanding of the situation under exploration and this, if achieved, may be considered as a valuable and worthwhile reason for them to agree to take part in the study. Practical results may also be forthcoming that may benefit the host organisation. However, the clients' urgency and commitment to the study is unlikely to be the same as one which has been instigated by the clients themselves who then work in collaboration with the researcher to help understand and solve their own difficulties or need for change. It is reasonable to suggest that at times researchers undertaking an action research study as part of their MPhil/PhD research have been anxious that they will be able to maintain their host organisation's interest and cooperation for the duration of the study.

Figure 7.2 represents an attempt to illustrate the theory/action cycle of action research as practised in the field study mode. The life of such a study may be something like this: some recognition of a real-world problem leads to an investigation of how this problem (or ones similar to it) has been dealt with to-date (as represented through the literature and practitioners). This growing appreciation of the problem situation may have suggested some potential ways of working to alleviate the problem and, so, some research ideas evolve. An organisation which is deemed to contain the type of problem domain being researched is contacted and a field study agreed. The research ideas are put into practice and the process and outcome are carefully documented. The researcher's focus of attention is likely to relate to the usefulness of the ideas that can be argued as a result of their practice (i.e. what do we think about our ideas now that we have seen them being used in a practical sense? Do they act as we expected? Have they been shown to be consistent with the theoretical standpoint from which we claimed they were derived?) A practical example of this is described in case A where, at the time, there appeared to be no method of KE suited to complex domains of expertise. The research was dedicated to exploring a method which might prove to be useful in such areas. In this way the action provides materials to allow reflection upon the theory which will enrich the theory prior to further action.

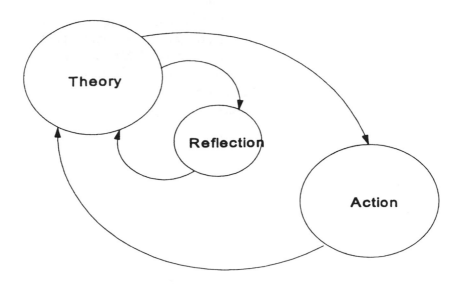

FIGURE 7.2 *A representation of the theory-action cycle of action research in the field study mode showing how reflections tend to take place around the theory activity*

Figure 7.2 illustrates how reflection takes place away from the action and how it is directed at the theory and preparation for action. This type of study is not a once-through experiment but is a continuous learning cycle. In some respects the emphasis upon the reflection of the theory and the approach taken to put the theory into practice is a result of formal research demands (e.g. tried and trusted, commercially available methodologies are not usually the subject of MPhil/PhDs). In order to illustrate the focus of attention upon evolving theory through action, Figure 7.2 shows how a cycle of reflection may take place around the cycle of theory evolution.

7.5.2   General Reflections about the Consultancy Mode

In comparison, Figure 7.3 illustrates the role of reflection in a consultancy mode of action research where the emphasis is upon addressing the client's problems. From the consultant-researcher viewpoint the attraction to take on the consultancy mode may be the same as for the field study mode, namely a perception of some real-world difficulty encouraging exploration of this difficulty and the ways in which it might be overcome. An equally plausible scenario is that organisational management seeks help to alleviate some problem situation and engages a consultant as problem solver. The field study mode of Figure 7.2 was managed to some extent by the researcher through planning and reflection away from the field of action but it is unlikely that this degree of control is possible in the consultancy mode.

The very nature of the consultancy mode means that there is the desire to bring out organisational change: the need to respond to the live situation results in the reflection being closely associated with the action activity of the theory-action cycle of action research as illustrated in Figure 7.3. Consequently, although theory underpins the action, it is the action which then predominates. Eden and Huxham (1996) raise the difficulties of being both action researcher and consultant: 'notably both reflect a practical orientation and both are focusing on the generality of ideas expressed...but they are meeting different needs and satisfying different audiences'. We would argue that the consultant-researcher who uses a method based upon action research does so in order to initiate both the learning cycle for the clients and for themselves. The consultant-researcher focuses upon the problem and the lessons learnt but with a different priority than the researcher: the researcher focuses upon the theory and the practice, the consultant upon the practice and the theory.

In study C, the action research, and the method chosen to facilitate it, had enabled the consultant-researcher to become first facilitator/teacher and then to become part of the group itself. The consultant-researcher initially provided expertise on the method of approach used and, when the clients had become confident in their abilities at problem solving, then moved on to offer advice about IS. As a researcher, the consultant-researcher, had to consider aspects of the work relevant to the area of research.

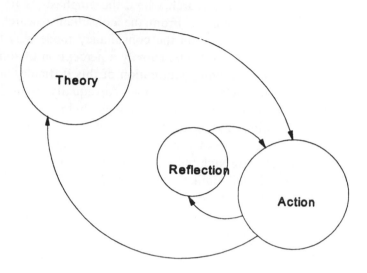

FIGURE 7.3 *A representation of the theory-action cycle of action
research in the consultancy mode showing how
reflection tends to take place around the action
activity*

This was undertaken after each encounter when the researcher
took the opportunity to reflect upon the method of action research.
In this instance the prime area of interest was how the chosen
method of action research was influenced (corrupted?) by the way
that individuals used their 'commodity' of power (Stowell, 1989) to
influence outcomes. It is important to note here that there is a dual
role of consultant and researcher with the latter being subordinate
to the former during the encounters with the clients themselves and
only after the event can the researcher reflect upon what has taken
place.

    Plans for action may be developed and it is hoped that at some
point along the way there is time for the researcher to reflect upon
this action and re-inform and reconsider its intellectual basis if
necessary. The pressures of such a study mean that reflection needs
to take place at the time of acting (e.g. as a result of needing to
react to immediate circumstances), and so in Figure 7.3 the

reflection cycle is shown circling the 'action' activity. Ideally, this reflection will then later be translated, explained and formalised through the theory.

7.5.3   Endnote

It is the nature of action research that the cycle of learning is never-ending; this is also true of the lessons reported here. These lessons are not intended to be definitive but to offer some ideas about some practical problems of undertaking action research.

We recognise the dangers of making a distinction between a field study and a consultancy approach but these headings have been used to categorise the different approaches adopted in our own work and have provided us with a useful way of discussing the problems of undertaking action research. We are mindful of extracting lessons from three individual research studies and recognise the possible context-dependency of many points highlighted. However, the lessons drawn out during the discussion seem to be relevant to promoting an awareness about some practical difficulties of undertaking formal information systems research based upon action research.

The issues relating to action research as a method for conducting IS research merits far more detailed treatment than can be offered in one chapter but the aim here has been to raise awareness of the problems and issues of adopting action research as a method for conducting IS research. The authors fully recognise that the two modes suggested may be extreme cases but our purpose for suggesting them is to provide an agenda for discussion about the practicalities of carrying out this kind of research. The modes raise important issues relevant to current IS research which we believe need to be recognised and addressed if action research is to be accepted as a framework for IS research.

References

Avison, D.E. and Fitzgerald, G., 1995, *Information Systems Development: Methodologies, Techniques and Tools*, McGraw-Hill, London.

Avison, D.E. and Wood-Harper, A.T., 1990, *Multiview: An Exploration in Information Systems Development*, McGraw-Hill, Maidenhead.

Bubenko, J.A., Jr., 1986, Information systems methodologies - a research view, in *Information Systems Design Methodologies: Improving the Practice* T.W. Olle, H.G. Sol and L. Bhabuta, eds., North Holland, Amsterdam.

Burrell, G. and Morgan, G., 1979, *Sociological Paradigms and Organisational Analysis*, Gower, Aldershot.

Checkland, P.B., 1981, *Systems Thinking, Systems Practice*, Wiley, Chichester.

Checkland, P.B., 1991, From framework through experience to learning: the essential nature of action research, in *Information Systems Research: Contemporary Approaches and Emergent Traditions*, H.E. Nissen, H.K. Klein and P.Hirschheim, eds., Elsevier, Amsterdam, 1-7.

Checkland, P.B., 1995, Soft systems methodology and its relevance to the development of information systems, in *Information Systems Provision: The Contribution of Soft Systems Methodology*, F.A. Stowell, ed., McGraw-Hill, London, 1-17.

Checkland, P.B. and Scholes, J., 1990, *Soft Systems Methodology in Action*, Wiley, Chichester.

Clarke, P.A. 1972, *Action research and Organisational Change*, Harper and Row Ltd, London.

Eden, C. and Huxham, C., 1996, Action research for management research, *British Journal of Management*, 7:75-86.

Elden, M. 1979, Three generations of work democracy experiments in Norway, in *The Quality of Working Life in Western Europe*, G. Cooper and E. Mumford, eds., Associated Business Press, London.

Elden, M. and Chisholm, R.F., 1993, Emerging varieties of action research: Introduction to the special issue, *Human Relations*, 46(2):121-142.

Emery, F. and Thorsrud, E., 1976, *Democracy at Work*, Martinus Nijhoff, Leiden.

Hirschheim, R., 1985, Information systems epistemology: an historical perspective, in *Research Methods in Information Systems*, E. Mumford, R. Hirschheim, G. Fitzgerald and A. Wood-Harper, eds., Elsevier, Amsterdam, 1199-1214.

Hult, M. and Lennung, S., 1980, Towards a definition of action research: Notes and a bibliography, *Journal of Management Studies*, 17(2):241-250.

Ledford, G.E. and Morhmam, S.A., 1993, Looking backward and forward at action research, *Human Relations*, 46(11):1349-1359.

Levin, M., 1994, Action research and critical systems thinking: Two icons carved out of the same log?, *Systems Practice*, 7(1):25-41.

Lewin, K., 1948, Action research and minority problems, in, *Resolving Social Conflicts*, G.W. Lewin, ed., Harper, New York, 201-220.

Mansell, G., 1991, Action research in information systems development, *Journal of Information Systems*, 1:29-40.

Methlie, L.B., 1980, Systems requirements analysis methods and models in the information systems environment, in *Proceedings of the IDIPTET 8.2, Working Conference on Information Systems Environment*,. H. Bonn, ed., West Germany, 1979, North Holland, Amsterdam, 73-85,

Ormerod, R.J., 1994, Combining management consultancy and research, *Systemist*, 16(1):41-53.

Peters, M. and Robinson, V., 1984, The origins and status of action research, *Journal of Applied Behavioural Science*, 20(2):113-124.

Rapoport, R.N., 1970, Three dilemmas in action research, *Human Relations*, 23(6):499- 513.

Reason, P. and Rowan, J., eds, 1981, *Human Inquiry: A Sourcebook of New Paradigm Research*, Wiley, Chichester.

Reason, P., ed., 1988, *Human Inquiry in Action*, Sage, London.

Somekh, B., 1995, The contribution of action research to development in social endeavors: A position paper on action research methodology, *British Educational Research Journal*, 21(3):339-355.

Stowell, F.A., 1989, Change, organisational power and the metaphor 'commodity', Unpublished PhD Thesis, Department of Systems, University of Lancaster.

Stowell, F.A., 1993, Hermeneutics and organisational inquiry, *Systemist*, 15(2):87- 103.

Stowell, F.A., ed, 1995, *Information Systems Provision: The Contribution of Soft Systems Methodology*, McGraw-Hill, London.

Stowell, F.A. and West, D., 1994, *Client-Led Design: A Systemic Approach to Information Systems Definition*, McGraw-Hill,London.

Susman, G.I. and Evered, R.D., 1978, An assessment of the scientific merits of action research, *Administrative Science Quarterly*, 23(4):582-602.

Torbett, W.R., 1976, *Creating a Community of Inquiry: Conflict, Collaboration, Transformation*, Wiley, New York.

Torbett, W.R., 1991, *The Power of Balance: Transforming Self, Society and Scientific Inquiry*, Sage, Newbury Park, CA.

Trist, E., 1953, *Some observations on the machineface as a sociotechnical system*, Tavistock Document Series, London.

Trist, E. and Bamforth, K.W., 1951, Some social and psychological consequences of the long wall method of coal getting, *Human Relations*, 4:3-38.

Walsham, G., 1995, Interpretive case studies in IS research: nature and method, *European Journal of Information Systems*, 4:74-81.

West, D., 1991, Towards a subjective approach to knowledge elicitation for the development of expert systems, Unpublished PhD Thesis. Department of Information Science, Portsmouth Polytechnic.

West, D., 1995, The appreciative inquiry method: A systemic approach to information systems requirements analysis, in *Information Systems Requirements Analysis, The Contribution of SSM*, F.A. Stowell, ed., McGraw-Hill, London.

Winograd, T. and Flores, F., 1986, *Understanding Computers and Cognition: A New Foundation for Design*, Ablex Publishing, New Jersey.

Chapter 8

CRITICAL SYSTEMS THINKING AND INFORMATION SYSTEMS RESEARCH

Michael C. Jackson

8.1 Introduction

This chapter discusses the contribution that critical systems thinking can make to the emerging discipline of information systems and, consequently, to the practice of information systems development. It begins by arguing that systems thinking provides a natural underpinning for work in information systems research and a theoretical platform which should ease the growth of the emerging discipline towards maturity.

One facet of the assistance that systems thinking can give is that being a related applied discipline, but also somewhat older than information systems, it has already experienced some of the growing pains that lie ahead for information systems. In particular it has been through the trauma of seeing its traditional, 'rational' methods and models come to grief when applied to the increasingly complex and turbulent world of social organisation; it has lived the proliferation of different systems intervention methodologies, often based on alternative paradigms; and it has weathered the increased difficulty of grounding claims to knowledge and legitimacy in the context of postmodern thinking. All these challenges are clearly visible now to many working in the field of information systems research. If they can be convinced that at least some of the responses offered by systems thinkers are valid, then they will be able to save themselves and the discipline considerable wasted energy and be empowered to move rapidly onto the many pressing problems that still confront systems thinkers as well as information systems researchers.

Critical systems thinking is a relative newcomer in the systems tradition of thought, but it is the strand of systems thinking that has sought most explicitly to address some of the key issues that are now coming to confront information systems researchers. It offers the greatest hope to those wishing to move information systems rapidly forward to a high level of theoretical sophistication. This chapter, therefore, is concerned to demonstrate the necessity for critical systems thinking, to explain the nature of critical systems thinking and its response to the significant challenges haunting applied disciplines, and to show how it can help channel information systems research in a manner conducive to rapid progress in theory and in the contribution it can make to practice.

Having established the significance of systems thinking, and especially critical systems thinking, for information systems, the critical systems approach is shown being employed in an information systems strategy project with an English county police force. This project required rethinking the nature of the police force under review—the kind of 'system' it was—in order to facilitate information systems design; the use of different systems methodologies in combination to assist information systems development; and the creation of a trust relationship with employee organisations. In short, it called into question the value of traditional models, it involved working with intervention methodologies based on different paradigms, and it confronted questions concerning the legitimacy of the recommendations eventually provided. The project followed the guidelines of 'Total Systems Intervention', a preliminary attempt to operationalise, in a meta-methodology, the important features of critical systems thinking (see Flood and Jackson, 1991a, for an account of 'Total Systems Intervention'). What is more important for our purposes in this chapter, however, is that it was conducted in the true 'spirit' of critical systems thinking and demonstrates the value of that approach in the information systems arena of work.

8.2 Systems Thinking as a Theoretical Prop

It would, of course, be preposterous to claim that systems thinking has well worked out answers to all the problems an emerging, applied discipline like information systems is likely to encounter. For a start, the systems approach itself has been subject to severe and damaging criticism. Silverman's (1970) demolition job on the use of the traditional systems approach in organisational analysis was so successful that, to this day, organisation theorists have closed minds regarding the possibility of anything useful emerging from the systems tradition of thought (see Checkland, 1994). Habermas (in his debates with Luhmann), from the point of view of critical social theory, and Lyotard in his postmodern critique of the attempt to enhance 'performativity' through any systematic or systemic approach (see Jackson, 1991, for a discussion), have poured even weightier theoretical scorn on the systems endeavour. Add to this the fact that systems thinkers often seem hopelessly divided among themselves, as 'soft' systems thinkers attack 'hard' systems thinkers and 'cyberneticians', critical systems thinkers attack soft systems thinkers and vice versa, and the example provided by systems thinking to other applied disciplines may not appear particularly inspiring. Nor can systems thinking, any more than information systems, boast the theatrical props of wide acceptance as an independent field of study in universities or significant support from research councils.

The claims made for systems thinking must be more modest and must be carefully substantiated in each case. It is nevertheless the argument of this section that, partly because of the external challenges faced and partly because of the intense internal debate, systems thinkers have been forced to pose to themselves questions that are of critical import to information systems as well and in seeking to provide answers, however tentative these may be, they have undertaken work that can greatly assist the emergence of information systems as a discipline.

The case for systems thinking as a theoretical prop for information systems research rests upon four interrelated arguments. First is the progress that systems thinking has made in questioning the nature of the 'systems' it seeks to understand and intervene in. Second is the fact that systems thinking has undergone, and managed to come through, a period of crisis when different conceptualisations of the field of study fought one another for hegemony. The third argument is that systems thinking, of all the applied disciplines, has demonstrated the greatest potential for linking theory and practice. Finally, there is the utility of the 'boundary' concept which, as Cooper (1990) has persuasively argued, must be a notion more fundamental to systems thinking than even 'system' itself. We shall try to tease out the main points in these four arguments in turn.

The first argument depends on the assumption that, in order to develop information systems properly, a designer must possess some sort of appropriate appreciation of the nature of the 'system' the information system is being designed to serve. As I have argued elsewhere (Jackson, 1987a), if organisations are treated as being like machines then the task of information systems development is rendered relatively straightforward. Unfortunately, as the organisation theory literature constantly reminds us, and as those concerned with information systems increasingly recognise, there are many different 'metaphors' which can be used to look at organisations, each of which yields understanding as to their nature and functioning. Morgan (1986), in his well-known work discussing different 'images of organisation', considers organisations as 'machines', 'organisms', 'brains', 'cultures', 'political systems', 'psychic prisons', 'flux and transformation' and 'instruments of domination'. Choosing to take an organisation to be like any of these things will clearly affect the approach adopted to the design of information systems.

In these circumstances there may appear to be no obvious guidelines or consistent theoretical support for the work of information systems specialists. The traditional model of the organisation as a machine performing some well defined function, which has in the past often been employed to guide the process of information systems design, is revealed to be of limited application. Organisation theory is enlightening as to the existence of alternative paradigms but is hardly specific enough in its recommendations to be easily translated into use. In any case, its findings seem to be at best inconsistent and, at worst, contradictory. Information analysts risk lapsing into a state of anomie.

Fortunately, it can be argued, there are various systems models available for supporting information systems design in organisations even when these are not conceived of as being machines. Systems thinking, broadly defined, is able itself to deploy different strategies each dependent upon a particular perspective on the nature of organisations. The systems approach is not limited simply to using the machine metaphor. For example, it can be demonstrated that 'hard', 'organisational cybernetic', 'soft' and 'emancipatory' systems methodologies correspond respectively to the machine, organismic, cultural and coercive views of organisation (see Jackson, 1987a). It is therefore possible for information systems to draw on systems thinking to question the nature of the 'systems' it is seeking to serve. At the same time, as will be discussed below, the systems approach retains its commitment to assisting practical intervention in real-world problem situations, and so offers specific guidance to those involved in information systems development.

Our second argument concerns the paradigm crisis that systems thinking can be said to have successfully weathered. That such a crisis was inevitable will be recognised from arguments made so far because, in order for systems thinkers to break out of machine thinking and explore alternative conceptions of organisation, they had to question and challenge the prevailing orthodoxy in the field. The prevailing, 'hard' systems orthodoxy in systems thinking lasted from the time of the Second World War, when approaches such as operational research (OR) were born, up until the 1970s. During the 1950s and 1960s hard systems approaches, such as OR, systems analysis and systems engineering, experienced rapid growth and development. They were increasingly used in civilian, as well as military, organisations, became established in the universities and institutionalised with the foundation of professional societies and journals. At this time there was considerable unanimity about the nature and function of systems thinking and general optimism about future prospects. To use the popular Kuhnian terminology (Kuhn, 1970), the dominant paradigm—the set of ideas, assumptions, and beliefs—guiding the activity of systems thinkers went unchallenged, and facilitated the practice of 'normal science'. This paradigm was based upon positivism and functionalism, and advocated a transfer of the methods of research felt to operate in the natural sciences to human affairs. On the basis of this paradigm a typical methodology emerged which brought success over a relatively narrow range of management problems—problems of allocation, inventory, replacement, queuing, sequencing, routing, etc.

In the 1970s, however, the confidence that many systems thinkers had in their work and its purpose began to wane. Failures began to accumulate as researchers started to push beyond the narrow range of problems of initial concern, to tackle more complex problem situations with strong behavioural and social aspects. The failure of traditional, hard systems thinking to come to terms with problems found at the strategic level in organisations and in social systems led to a spate of criticisms of the approach from researchers such as Ackoff, Churchman and Checkland; the main faults identified being summarised by Jackson (1991) as an inability to cope with multiple perceptions of reality, to handle extreme complexity, and to escape from conservative bias. The feeling of something akin to a crisis was reinforced by the increasing influence of various alternative systems approaches that challenged the traditional functionalist orientation. During the late 1970s and 1980s, organisational cybernetics, soft systems thinking, and critical systems thinking were successful in establishing themselves as important currents in the systems tradition of thought. In terms of sociological paradigms, the functionalism of hard systems thinking was being challenged by the structuralism of organisational cybernetics, the interpretivism of soft systems thinking, and the radical perspective of emancipatory systems thinking (see Jackson and Keys, eds., 1987). By 1981, Dando and Bennett were able to suggest that OR (perhaps the most important strand of hard systems thinking) was going through a period of paradigm crisis similar to the kind Kuhn describes as taking place in the natural sciences.

An alternative interpretation of events soon opened up, however, championed by Jackson and Keys (1984) through their 'system of systems methodologies'. Jackson and Keys challenged Dando and Bennett's assumption that different approaches in management science were competing for exactly the same area of concern and with the same purpose. They presented alternative approaches as suitable for the different types of situation in which systems practitioners are required to act. Each approach could be seen as useful in certain defined areas of work, according to its underlying assumptions and logic, and should only be used in appropriate circumstances. According to this perspective, the diversity of approaches heralds not a crisis but increased competence and effectiveness in a variety of situations and in addressing a variety of purposes. The 'system of systems methodologies' by matching different systems approaches to 'ideal-type' problem-contexts, according to the assumptions they make, gave coherence to this pluralist interpretation.

The 'pluralist' or 'complementarist' interpretation of developments in systems thinking, with its explicit prescription to use systems methodologies in combination, has been subject to much debate and development since 1984. It is from this debate and this work that information systems researchers, facing their own paradigm crisis, can benefit. This will become clearer in the discussion of critical systems thinking, which has embraced complementarism, in the next section.

We have demonstrated that systems thinking can provide a link for information systems researchers back to different 'images' of organisation, thus making it possible for them to be critically reflective about the particular model underlying their own favoured information systems design approach. This is one example of the capacity of systems thinking to link theory and practice, the basis of our third argument for information systems to employ systems thinking as a theoretical prop.In the same way, the attention that modern systems thinking has paid to social theory can be taken advantage of by information systems researchers to reflect on their efforts in the light of different sociological paradigms, Habermas' theory of human cognitive interests, and the modernism versus postmodernism debate (see Jackson, 1991, for guidance). It is also the case, and this is particularly significant for an applied discipline like information systems, that systems methodologies can assist in the task of translating the findings of social theory into a practical form and encapsulating those findings in well-worked-out approaches to intervention.

It must often be the case that information systems researchers ask themselves, like systems thinkers once did, what real differences the fine theoretical distinctions drawn by social scientists make when applied in practice in the world. Not all do make any difference, but some have considerable import and must be regarded as crucial in information systems as in systems thinking. The case can perhaps best be made by considering how Beer's 'viable systems diagnosis' (his implied methodology for using the viable systems model) and Checkland's soft systems methodology (SSM) closely reflect very different traditions of social inquiry (Jackson, 1993).

Beer's (1985) viable systems diagnosis (VSD) is most convincingly understood as based upon 'structuralist' assumptions. It serves to develop explanations of observable phenomena in social systems based upon cybernetic principles and laws governing the behaviour of all systems under control. It seeks exploration of perceived surface occurrences in organisations in terms of processes at work at a deeper, structural level. For example, the cybernetic law of requisite variety can generate explanations as to why delegating control to autonomous work groups can lead to increasing efficiency and effectiveness. The sociological home of Checkland's (Checkland and Scholes, 1990), SSM, by contrast, lies in the 'interpretive' paradigm. SSM concentrates on systems as the mental constructs of observers rather than as objective features of the outside world. Its subjectivist orientation means that it seeks understanding of systems from the point of view of those involved in creating and maintaining them; seeks to engage participants in trying to shape their own future; and uses expertise sparingly, if at all. At the same time SSM demonstrates a concern with regulation rather than radical change; with understanding how order is achieved rather than with disrupting established social cohesion.

VSD and SSM are relatively pure representatives of their respective paradigms. They demonstrate how extremely subtle philosophical and sociological judgements can be incorporated into tools for practical action and what a significant difference such judgements make to interventions in organisations. Information systems researchers are, of course, aware of Beer's and, especially Checkland's work but they have not yet, perhaps, taken full advantage of the ready access these and other systems methodologies can provide to the most relevant social scientific theory.

To complete the argument for systems thinking we shall briefly consider the significance of the notion of 'boundary'. Like Cooper (1990) many modern systems thinkers would regard this concept as more powerful than 'system' itself. The idea that existing organisational boundaries need to be questioned in any proper systems study is a commonplace in systems approaches as diverse as Beer's and Checkland's. Checkland's SSM can, indeed, be seen as an exploration of the consequences of drawing system boundaries in different places according to different world views, and much of its attractiveness to information systems researchers seems to lie in the manner in which SSM allows them to consider the different information requirements in the various 'human activity systems' constructed on the basis of different boundary definitions. The real credit for developing our understanding of the boundary concept, and how usefully to employ it, must however be attributed to that strand of systems thinking derived from the work of Churchman (1979, for example). Important in the development of this strand has been the work of Mason and Mitroff (1981; see also Mitroff and Linstone, 1993), and Ulrich (1983).

Mason and Mitroff demonstrate that a clear indication can be gained of the nature of the boundary assumed by any proposed systems design by considering what is being taken for granted about the system's stakeholders in drawing the boundary in a particular way. Ulrich, giving Churchman's thinking an explicitly critical turn, argues that boundary judgements inevitably enter into any social systems design as presuppositions. These presuppositions can be unearthed and challenged by posing 12 boundary questions, based on 12 critically heuristic categories, in an 'is' mode and an 'ought' mode; for example, 'who is the actual client of the systems design?' compared to 'who ought to be the actual client of the systems design?' Once brought to the surface by Mason and Mitroff's or Ulrich's techniques, the boundary judgements supporting particular proposals for a systems design can be challenged. The ability to unearth and challenge the boundaries being assumed in information systems design would seem to be an extremely powerful skill which information systems can learn from systems thinking.

We have, hopefully, redeemed our claim that systems thinking can act as a useful theoretical prop for information systems research and greatly assist the emergence of information systems as a discipline. As mentioned earlier, of all the strands of systems thinking currently extant, it is critical systems thinking that has most self-consciously tried to build on the strengths of the systems movement while accepting, and responding to, the challenges to systems thinking that have come from outside that tradition. It is to critical systems thinking, therefore, that we now turn in the expectation that it will provide the best catalyst for rapid progress in information systems.

8.3   The Critical Systems Turn

There are two significant versions of critical systems thinking which have not yet found a comfortable way to live with one another. The first version derives from the work of Churchman as developed by Ulrich (1983). As noted it employs as its primary device the critical potential present in the concept of boundary. Any proposal for a systems design will rest upon certain 'boundary judgements' which are often not made explicit. Ulrich's work enables us to unearth and challenge those boundary judgements by counterposing to them equally defensible alternatives. The current drive in this version of critical systems thinking (Ulrich, 1995) is to so simplify the idea of boundary as a critical device that it becomes available for all 'citizens' to employ in challenging the design proposals of so-called experts. We mentioned, in the previous section, the importance of 'boundary' in information systems as well and would reiterate here the value to information systems researchers of following and contributing to the debates surrounding this concept in the systems literature.

We shall concentrate in this chapter on the second version of critical systems thinking because it has more immediate resonance with contemporary developments in information systems. The second version was a purely UK development and embraced the specific criticisms aimed at particular systems approaches, the explicit call for a systems approach that recognised 'coercive contexts', the attempt to reconstruct systems thinking upon complementarist foundations, and the preliminary operationalising of critical systems ideas in a meta-methodology (Total Systems Intervention—TSI) by Flood and Jackson (1991a).

A reasonable starting point for understanding this version of critical systems thinking is Checkland's (1981) assault on hard systems thinking. Checkland showed that hard systems thinking represents the world as made up of systems that can be studied objectively and have clearly identifiable purposes. He argued that very few real-world problem situations actually present themselves in terms of systems with clearly defined goals and objectives. In these circumstances hard systems thinking will prove ineffective in the great majority of situations.

Checkland was trying to establish a space for his own 'soft' version of systems thinking and it was not clear that anything 'critical' was about to be born. This only became obvious with Mingers' (1981) examination of the links between critical theory and SSM and Jackson's (1982) full-frontal attack on the ambitions of soft systems thinking as expressed in the work of Churchman, Ackoff and Checkland. Jackson argued that the assumptions made by these authors about the nature of systems thinking and social systems constrained the ability of their methodologies to intervene, in the manner intended, in many problem situations. Soft systems thinking, too, had a limited domain of application. For example, in situations of fundamental conflict or unequal access to power resources, soft systems thinking either has to walk away or fly in the face of its own philosophical principles and acquiesce in proposed changes emerging from limited debates characterised by distorted communication.

Once it was obvious that all systems approaches had their limitations, their weaknesses as well as their strengths, a number of avenues of critical inquiry presented themselves. One possibility was to take each strand of systems thinking, reveal its assumptions, subject it to rigourous critique and confirm (in the best examples) that the conclusions could be substantiated from study of actual cases of use. This culminated in Jackson's (1991) review of five strands of systems thinking (organisations as systems, hard, cybernetic, soft, critical) from the point of view of some relevant social theory. Another possibility was to identify problem situations for which no currently existing systems approach seemed appropriate. The most obvious candidates were coercive contexts and this led Jackson (1985) to make an explicit call for a 'critical approach' which would take account of such contexts. It also encouraged the somewhat unhappy, if understandable, attempt to represent Ulrich's work as the solution to this problem—something for which Ulrich's work was unsuited and, in retrospect, led to its misrepresentation. Finally, if all systems approaches have different strengths and weaknesses why not recognise this and use them, in combination, as a complementary set to address different problem situations and different purposes? This was the thinking behind Jackson and Keys' (1984) 'system of systems methodologies' which related various strands of systems thinking to an 'ideal-type' grid of problem-contexts, seeking to demonstrate the assumptions about the nature of problem-contexts underlying the different systems methodologies. A 1987 article by Jackson (1987b) was explicit in declaring for a 'pluralist' developmental future for systems thinking as opposed to the 'isolationist', 'imperialist' and 'pragmatist' tendencies also in the field.

Out of this ferment of ideas a critical systems movement, with a particular 'spirit' and particular concerns of its own, began to take shape. The book *Critical Systems Thinking: Directed Readings* (Flood and Jackson, eds., 1991b) is recommended to readers who feel the need for a fuller understanding of this development. We must pass on to briefly mention Total Systems Intervention (TSI) (Flood and Jackson, 1991a), an attempt to give guidelines for the use of critical systems ideas in practice.

TSI was built around three phases—creativity, choice and implementation. The creativity phase gave recognition to the many different views that were possible of organisations and their problems, and encouraged managers and analysts to explore these through the use of metaphors, particularly the machine, organism, brain, culture and coercive system metaphors. The aim was to take the broadest possible initial look at the problem situation but gradually to focus down on those aspects most crucial to the organisation at that point in its history. Worthy of note is the attention paid in 'creativity' to the possibility that the problem situation could be coercive. Having identified the crucial problems for the organisation, a 'choice' had to be made of a suitable systems methodology or systems methodologies to address the problems. This was done on the basis of a review of the strengths and weaknesses of the different methodologies available conducted using the 'system of systems methodologies'. 'Implementation' of change could then proceed by employing appropriate methodologies either singly or in combination. As intervention proceeded the problems that had earlier seemed to be crucial might fade into the background and new ones emerge. This could be catered for by continually cycling around the three phases of TSI, with different systems methodologies assuming the role of 'dominant' and 'dependent' in leading the intervention at particular times. The whole methodology was said to be governed by an emancipatory commitment which was broadly defined to include improving the human condition by increasing efficiency and effectiveness as well as 'liberating' individuals from subjugation.

TSI has attracted a lot of comment both favourable and unfavourable (e.g. Tsoukas, 1993). As an attempt to capture the 'spirit' of critical systems thinking it was possibly successful, but as an effort at systematising critical systems ideas, to make them more useable, it was a failure. This failure becomes even more obvious in later attempts to 'improve' TSI (such as Flood's *Solving Problem Solving*, 1995) by seeking to further systematise and mechanise (in unfathomable ways) the employment of critical systems thinking. In this mélange the critical idea gets reduced to providing appropriate tools to address the various strategic contingencies that organisations face; 'organisations as systems' functionalism is reborn.

By about 1991 critical systems thinking seemed to have settled down somewhat, and various writers tried their hands at summarising its key elements. Schecter (1991) argued that critical systems thinking is defined by three commitments: to critique, of all schools of thought; to emancipation of human beings to realise their potential for full development; and to pluralism, which is a commitment to develop a broad framework encompassing the advocates of different approaches. Flood and Jackson (1991a) represent the philosophy of critical systems thinking as embracing complementarism, seen as making use of all types of systems approach as appropriate; sociological awareness of the pressures to choose particular methodologies and the social consequences of use of the different methodologies; and human well-being and emancipation, broadly defined. Jackson (1991) sees critical systems thinking as built upon the five pillars of critical awareness, social awareness, complementarism at the methodological level, complementarism at the theoretical level, and dedication to human well-being and emancipation. To complete this section, and to take us forward to consideration of how critical systems thinking can benefit information systems research, I will reinterpret Jackson's fuller list in the light of some newer thinking.

Critical awareness primarily concerns understanding the strengths and weaknesses and the theoretical underpinnings of available systems methods, techniques and methodologies. It is here that critical systems thinking has drawn most heavily and successfully on social theory and thus helped advance systems thinking as a whole as a field of study. Clearly, interrogating the various systems approaches old and new, to see what they have to offer, will remain central to the critical systems endeavour. In the 1991 formulation another form of critical awareness was said to involve closely examining the assumptions and values entering into actually existing systems designs or any proposals for a systems design; in other words Ulrich's contribution. It now seems that more thought than this needs to be given as to how the two 'versions' of critical systems thinking can be properly integrated.

Social awareness involves, as one of its aspects, considering the organisational and societal 'climate' which determines the popularity of use of particular systems approaches at particular times. This must incorporate consideration of the effects that power at the micro-level can have on the formation and development of knowledges. Although present in most descriptions of the nature of critical systems thinking, this key element has been little developed, and Brocklesby and Cummings (1995) are right to insist that more attention be given to the 'cultural constraints' preventing easy combination of hard, soft and critical methodologies. Another side of social awareness was stated (Jackson, 1991) to be attention to the social consequences of use of different systems methodologies. This second aspect is probably best considered as an element contributing, or not, to human well-being and emancipation.

Complementarism at the level of methodology originates, as we have seen, from Jackson and Keys' (1984) 'system of systems methodologies' and received its fullest expression as a set of procedures for combining methodologies in Flood and Jackson's (1991) TSI. The popularity of the idea of combining methodologies continues to grow but there is much debate about the form such combinations should take—parts of similar methodologies, parts of different methodologies, whole methodologies, etc. This debate can only be usefully advanced by considering the next commitment of critical systems thinking.

The commitment to complementarism at the methodological level requires, according to critical systems thinking, an equal commitment to the complementary and informed development of all varieties of the systems approach at the theoretical level. This is because the different strands of the systems movement express different rationalities stemming from alternative theoretical positions. It still seems to me logical that to get the most out of combining different methodologies it is necessary to combine methodologies expressing different theoretical rationalities rather than methodologies formulated from within the same paradigm.

Paradigm incommensurability has remained a hard nut to crack, however, and it is now less clear that Habermas' apparently complementary human-species-dependent interests can be employed to ground complementarity at the level of theory (see Jackson, 1991). Perhaps, in line with postmodern thinking, it is best to see systems approaches as standing in a 'pluralist' rather than complementary relationship to one another, often throwing up contradictory suggestions for systems improvement. An even heavier burden is then put on the fifth tenet of critical systems thinking, human well-being and emancipation, because it necessarily becomes the basis for following recommendations stemming from one methodology rather than another.

Critical systems thinking has long made vague statements about being dedicated to human emancipation and seeking to achieve for all individuals the maximum development of their potential. Putting this item on the agenda was a real achievement of the approach— no systems methodology used to intervene in human affairs can claim neutrality. Sensible statements about what is meant by this commitment are, however, few and far between. The issue is even more crucial now that methodology choice (because different systems methodologies have different social consequences of use) and choice between the recommendations of methodologies used in combination (because these may be contradictory) can be seen to depend upon some kind of resolution to this problem. If as postmodernists such as Lyotard (1984) argue, the 'grand narratives' constructed around increased performativity or personal liberation can no longer command our respect, then it appears we are left with 'local improvement', a dangerously unsystemic notion, or ethical choice, and systems thinkers are unlikely to come up with instant solutions to problems that have phased moral philosophers for thousands of years (see Jackson, 1995, for a fuller discussion).

The purpose of this section has been to outline the development of critical systems thinking which is the most theoretically sophisticated strand of the modern systems approach. It has also been possible, hopefully, to indicate the sorts of questions it is concerned to ask and to suggest some of the answers it is able to provide and those that it is still struggling with. On the basis of this discussion, in the following two sections, we can map out more clearly the contribution that critical systems thinking can make to information systems research and information systems practice.

8.4   Critical Thinking and Information Systems Research

The task is to show how information systems, as an emerging discipline, can benefit from work in critical systems thinking. We have already argued that critical systems thinking can function as an effective conduit, channelling relevant social theory to the applied disciplines. And we have suggested that many of the arguments already worked on by critical systems thinkers are now being taken up, or will soon have to be taken up, in information systems. We shall now seek to develop this last point beyond mere suggestion by demonstrating that information systems researchers have, at one time or another, shown an interest in each of the commitments of critical systems thinking previously outlined. The argument can then be further developed to show that critical systems thinking can yield an *integrated* programme for information systems researchers. Research in information systems would benefit greatly if critically inclined scholars were to become conscious, as have critical systems thinkers, of the integrated nature of their various endeavours and were to establish an integrated programme to coordinate and guide future research. As suggested, the argument proceeds by relating work in information systems to each of the five commitments of critical systems thinking. For a fuller account see Jackson, 1992.

In the information systems field of study critical awareness has tended to take the form of attacks upon the accepted way of conceiving of and undertaking research. Thus Hirschheim (1985a) has argued that it is a mistake to view office systems as purely technical systems. Rather they should be seen as social systems and more participative approaches should be used in their design. Boland (1987) wants to reject Simon's imagery, of the organisation as a calculating machine and information as a commodity, that currently dominates information systems research and concentrate information systems professionals' minds on their proper task, which should be about supporting the emergence of meaning through interpersonal dialogue in a human community. Information as meaning is a skilled human accomplishment, not a commodity. Klein and Lyytinen (1985) criticise the 'scientism' which they see as constituting the current orthodoxy in information systems. Scientism is bound to fail because it conceives information systems too narrowly, as technical systems to be engineered, and it ignores social factors and the need to improve the sharing of meaning necessary to tackle ill-structured problems. They advocate exploring other neglected paradigms as a basis for information systems research and as alternatives to scientism. Mingers (1994) concludes a review of information systems as a discipline by stating that much work in information systems has been overly dominated by technological and technical considerations at the expense of recognition of the human context in which information systems are used.

Some information systems researchers have, however, been prepared to advance alternatives to the orthodoxy and to explore other paradigms. Boland (1985) puts forward phenomenology as a preferred approach to research in the field. Checkland (1988) wants an approach based on soft systems thinking and this particular way forward has produced some excitement and gained considerable support, particularly in the UK (see the papers in *Systemist*, 14.3, 1992; also Stowell., 1995). Other perspectives are explored by Espejo and Watt (1978) who seek to construct information systems around the cybernetic logic of Beer's viable system model, and Mumford (1983) who advocates a participative approach centred on socio-technical systems thinking. This proliferation of alternatives would be a healthier development if each of the alternatives was itself subject to critical review—as has happened with alternatives to 'hard' systems thinking in the critical systems literature, but as yet little of this has taken place. Some useful taxonomies of information systems approaches exist (e.g. Wood-Harper and Fitzgerald, 1982; Hirschheim, 1985a; Avison and Fitzgerald, 1988; Hirschheim and Klein, 1989) but these lack the necessary critical bite. Of greater potential, perhaps, is Jayaratna's (1994) NIMSAD, a framework which it is claimed can be used to evaluate any methodology.

Social awareness, the second commitment of critical systems thinking, has been given some attention in the information systems field by Klein and Hirschheim (1987). They argue that the 'image' of society presented in popular texts is changing. The nature of work is changing as is the way organisations are regarded; power holders are subject to increasing anxiety; and knowledge, especially as derived from science and technology, is viewed with much greater scepticism. All in all, it is reasonable to assume that broad social change is on the way and this should affect the way information systems research is developed. At the more micro-level we also have Markus' (1983) work on the relationship between the power structure of organisations and the introduction of new information technology and information systems.

There is considerable clamour for complementarism in methodology use in information systems research. Hirschheim (1985b), for example, seeks to make the case for 'methodological pluralism', claiming that there are many methods of science, and choice of the 'correct' one in any instance will depend upon matters such as the problem to be studied and the type of knowledge required. Klein and Lyytinen (1985) call for 'affirmative pluralism'. They want to see the phenomenological-interpretative, the radical-structuralist, and the critical social theory paradigms explored as resources for information systems research which offer alternatives to the prevailing scientism. Walsham (1991) argues that future information systems research would benefit from a pluralist approach in which different methods or methodologies are used simultaneously to provide richer insight, or particular approaches are selected on the basis of the relevance they bring. In his view information systems has been dominated too long by the metaphors of the organisation as a machine and as an organism.

Despite this clamour the attempt to provide guidelines for actually combining methods in practice has scarcely got beyond first base. There has been much debate about the benefits of joining Checkland's SSM and various 'functionalist' information systems methodologies but no agreement has been reached about whether this is possible or desirable, let al.one about how it should be done (see the papers by Fitzgerald, Prior, Wood, Omerod and Lewis in *Systemist* 14, 3, 1992; also Savage and Mingers, 1996). Wood-Harper (1985) proclaims the 'Multiview' approach (Avison and Wood-Harper, 1990) as a realisation of information systems as a multi-perspective discipline using a pluralism of research methods. We must be careful, however, before accepting this conclusion. Multiview fuses the work of Checkland and Mumford with ideas from harder methodologies. We might reasonably ask, however, on the basis of what rationality this fusion of apparently contradictory approaches takes place? Wood-Harper (1985) in fact makes clear that Multiview has to be understood as conditioned primarily by hermeneutic philosophy. This is supported by his contention that the 'ideal' use of the methodology is in the sequence as prescribed—essentially moving from softer to harder approaches. Accepting this, it is easy to see that 'soft' rationalities will be distorted by the expectation that they will lead to a more structured intervention, and 'hard' rationalities because they are operating in an hermeneutic climate and are front-ended by a soft logic. The further refinement of Multiview, as with the further development of complementarism or pluralism in critical systems practice, must await the resolution of certain difficulties plaguing complementarism at the level of theory.

Turning to complementarism at the theoretical level, we find Walsham and Han (1991) suggesting that Giddens' 'structuration theory' might offer a useful meta-theory within which other theories and methodologies can be contained. The worry must remain that structuration theory itself leans too heavily on one rationality at the expense of others. More in line with the approach favoured in critical systems thinking, Symons and Walsham (1987) recommend using different perspectives in parallel in order to provide a rich evaluation of information systems. They analyse their data using the 'formal-rational' 'structural', 'interactionist' and 'political' perspectives. Again, as in critical systems thinking, the work of Habermas has appealed to information systems researchers as a means of developing pluralism at the level of theory. Lyytinen and Klein (1985) believe that Habermas' work on knowledge constitutive interests can be used to both classify existing work in information systems and to support the need for a broader approach to research in the area. At present most work in the field supports the technical interest and aims at increasing organisational effectiveness. It is equally necessary to look at information systems as a means of increasing human understanding and as a means to emancipate people from constraints imposed by distorted communication and misapplied power. Lyytinen and Klein want to see a critical social theory view of information systems fully developed and believe that this squares with their proposal for a 'multi-paradigm' research community in information systems. As a further development, Lyytinen *et al.* (1991) have called upon Habermas' social action theory to develop a new framework for understanding and judging the effectiveness of office information systems. This gives a much broader perspective on office activity. We see, in all this work, information systems researchers struggling with the same issues that have bothered critical systems thinkers in seeking to construct and justify complementarism at the theoretical level. In relying to a large extent on Habermas they must, in the future, face up to the same challenge from postmodern thinking. What is certain is that information systems research, just as systems research, cannot and should not remain aloof from these debates.

Nissen (1985) poses the right question, as far as the fifth commitment of critical systems thinking is concerned, when he asks 'for whom and for what reason are we acquiring knowledge?' A number of scholars in information systems have been keen that their work be used to design and implement information systems in a way which promotes human well-being and emancipation. Hirschheim (1985a) wants to see information technology adopted in offices only if it can be shown to yield a plurality of benefits, including demonstrating a high degree of social and ethical responsibility; if an authentic consensus can be reached about its use and objectives; and if a participative approach is used during design and implementation. Boland (1987), from his phenomenological perspective, argues that:

> The only information system designs which are morally acceptable are those ... which take dialogue, interpretation and an individual's search for meaning as sacred.

Klein and Lyytinen (1985) are convinced that scientism leads to information systems which are too narrowly conceived and implemented without regard to how they affect the quality of life of the humans who have to live with them. Lyytinen and Klein (1985) argue that information systems should be designed with attention given to all three of Habermas' human species imperatives. They must serve the technical interest, but also the practical and emancipatory interests. An article by Klein and Hirschheim (1987) is, however, the most explicit call in the information systems field for a research strategy founded on the pursuit of human well-being and emancipation. Reviewing possible futures for information systems research, they call for an 'emancipatory information systems research programme'. This would seek to transcend existing powerful interest groups and work independently towards improving the situation in each particular instance, with an eye, ultimately, to bringing about a better society. Its aim would be to reshape 'society in accordance with democratic ideals'.

I have demonstrated, I hope, that each of the commitments on which critical systems thinking stands has been addressed, at one time or another, by scholars in the information systems area. Our further argument is that identifying these commitments as separable but closely interrelated aspects of research, as has happened in critical systems thinking, can greatly assist the development of an integrated programme of research in information systems. Pursuing critical and social awareness is what makes possible complementarism or pluralism at the level of methodology. The whole project is justified on the basis of complementarism at the level of theory and guided by some form of commitment to human improvement. There are obviously other important relationships between the five commitments.

It is time to turn to how critical systems thinking can assist information systems development in practice.

8.5   Critical Thinking and Information Systems Development: A Case Study

To demonstrate the usefulness of critical systems thinking in guiding information systems development, I am going to use, as a case study, a project carried out in North Yorkshire Police in 1991. Perhaps because it was in the very early days of trying to use critical systems ideas in practice, and because we were very consciously developing and using strategies which later became second nature, the project clearly illustrates a number of the significant benefits that can be derived from taking a critical approach. Overall the project was successful but there were some hiccups along the way. Interestingly, at the point where the intervention nearly came to grief, the blame could be laid at our door for *not being critical enough*.

The intervention was carried out by a senior officer in the North Yorkshire Police Force, Steve Green, under my supervision over a five month period, as part of an MA degree in Management Systems. The original reporting on the project is available to interested readers (Green, 1991) and the case has also been written up as an exercise in the use of the Total Systems Intervention meta-methodology (Green, 1992). I shall emphasise and highlight those aspects of the project where critical systems thinking seems to have been decisive in determining what occurred. The earlier accounts of what happened can be consulted to check that I have not overly exaggerated the significance of these moments.

North Yorkshire Police is, in terms of geographical area, the largest English, single county, force and extends over approximately 3200 square miles. It covers a largely rural area and includes, as part of its territory, the beautiful area of the North Yorkshire Moors shown in the popular television series *Heartbeat*—a series which captures, apparently, what policing was like in the area in the 1960s. Also in its boundaries are urban settlements such as York and Scarborough. In 1991 North Yorkshire Police (NYP) employed some 1400 police officers, supported by around 500 civilian staff, and had a budget of more than £55 million for the year. In 1991 it had to cope with almost 170,000 separate incidents of crime, the predominant offences being burglary and thefts of and from motor vehicles.

At the time of the project the North Yorkshire force was undergoing a major reorganisation of its structure. Its headquarters are based in Northallerton and dealt with matters of policy, finance, personnel, complaints against the police, and research and development. Beyond headquarters, it had traditionally been divided into four divisions, centred on York, Harrogate, Richmond and Scarborough, and these divisions then further divided into a total of ten sub-divisions. The reorganisation was to see the disappearance of one level in this hierarchy and the amalgamation of a number of sub-divisions, leaving only seven territorial divisions of the force (based at York, Selby, Harrogate, Skipton, Richmond, Malton and Scarborough) reporting to headquarters. These changes were explicitly designed, by the Chief Constable, as a step towards forcing decision making down the hierarchy of the organisation. Managers of the various territorial divisions were henceforth to have considerable local autonomy.

The study of communications within NYP which we were undertaking was seen as a part of the overall change programme. It was important to ensure that the information that flowed around NYP supported the new structure, and aims and purposes, and not the old. Apart from that most important aspect of the brief, our remit was to produce a workable strategy for communications within NYP which would rationalise information flows, and improve the quality of policy making and dissemination through the provision of accurate and timely information.

The project began with a series of interviews of a cross-section of individuals at all levels in the organisation, civilian support staff as well as police officers, headquarters staff as well as staff from one selected territorial division. This was the start of the 'creativity' phase of the intervention, according to the logic of Total Systems Intervention (TSI) which was the specific methodology employed to operationalise critical systems thinking in this study. The interviews were allowed to be fairly general and wide-ranging but did make some use of the 'cognitive mapping' technique, developed by Eden *et al.* (1983), and the metaphor analysis, proposed in TSI, to assist with the generation of creativity.

The impression gained from the interviews was of very general dissatisfaction with the existing communication and information flows. All interviewees recognised that the impending reorganisation required new and improved information systems. The higher ranks in the organisation were primarily concerned that the spirit of their policy initiatives seemed to get lost in the existing communication system and, therefore, implementation on the ground was never as intended. They could, to some extent, communicate the detail of what they wanted but not why they wanted it. The Chief Constable commented that:

> It is apparent from a number of changes I have made that, frequently, the letter of an instruction is complied with but, clearly, the philosophy has been lost (from Green, 1991).

He provided the example of an attempt to control vehicle expenditure by imposing a cut in the overall mileage travelled. This was implemented in many sub-divisions by allocating a target mileage to each vehicle on a 'per shift', weekly or monthly basis. One officer was instructed to use a Land Rover, which still had mileage to spare, rather than a Ford Fiesta which had exceeded its target miles. The senior ranks were particularly critical of middle managers which they saw as bureaucratic and unwilling to make decisions.

Middle managers themselves complained about the confusing nature of the various media of communication employed since these seemed to mix up important policy matters with minor administrative details. They also saw the executive as being secretive and excluding them from decision making but, at the same time, failing to provide them with instructions in a timely and accurate manner. The lower ranks were frustrated by their inability to get what they saw as important information passed upwards and acted upon. Organisational communication in NYP was compared to a game of 'snakes and ladders'; information would get so far up the hierarchy but before it reached its destination it would hit a 'snake' and tumble down again. Civilian employees saw problems of communication as closely intertwined with their perceived status as second-class citizens in the organisation compared to police officers. A final point worthy of note was the feeling among staff representatives that the consultative processes of the force were not useful or meaningful. The staff associations representing the police officers and the trade union (NALGO), representing the civilian support staff, seemed only to be called in once decisions had been taken. They were used to disseminate information about decisions rather than as bodies to be consulted about the views of staff before decisions were taken.

TSI calls for a problem situation to be analysed using systems metaphors and this was the next task undertaken. It was clear, and was openly stated by many interviewed, that NYP operated like a bureaucratic machine. There was a functional division of labour at headquarters and in the divisions, a prevalence of charts showing the organisational hierarchy, detailed job descriptions, a formal discipline code, a recognisable 'officer class' and, of course, uniforms and badges of rank. Many felt that this form of organisation was inappropriate in a situation which required police officers to act flexibly to cope with an increasingly unpredictable and turbulent environment. It seemed, indeed, that the main source of the organisation's problems, including communication problems, lay in its adherence to the machine model and machine thinking. As Green (1992) argues:

> Such perceived problems as middle management's adherence
> to bureaucratic methods and refusal to be more responsive
> and decisive, the organisation's refusal to treat its members
> as individual human beings, the gulf which existed between
> the territorial divisions of the force and its headquarters, and
> the compartmentalization of specialist departments could be

explained in terms of the shortcomings of the machine metaphor.

Use of the organism metaphor led to reflection on how little attention NYP gave to its environment and to communication with the public it sought to serve. The brain metaphor revealed how little suited were the organisation's current information flows to the promotion of local autonomy, and what significant changes would be necessary if decision-making was to be delegated to lower levels, if information was to be conveyed in a manner suitable for learning, and if the organisation as a whole were to become responsive in the face of its environment. Cultural analysis tended to support the findings of employing the machine metaphor, especially highlighting the bureaucratic values of middle managers. It was clear enough that changing the culture of the organisation, to ensure proper use of information flows based on a more decentralised structure, would be no easy task. The political metaphor revealed no open conflict in NYP about the aims of the organisation but drew our attention again to the issue of proper involvement of staff through the consultation process.

What critical analysis allowed us to recognise at this stage was that the kind of improvements sought could not be brought about by designing more efficient and effective information systems on the basis of the machine model. Making NYP a better machine would lead to things getting worse not better. We were able, using critical systems thinking, to draw in findings from the social sciences to reconsider the nature of the organisation for which we were designing the information systems. Instead of making NYP a better machine we needed to rethink it as an 'organism with a brain' and put in place information systems that supported local autonomy and decision-making, learning, responsiveness and the ability to adapt. Without critical systems thinking, I would suggest, it would have been easy to fall into the trap of employing an information systems development approach, premised on the machine model, that would not have addressed the real issues; would indeed have made things worse.

We were now on to the 'choice' phase of TSI. Choice is about selecting a systems methodology, or methodologies, best able to deal with the types of problem revealed in the creativity stage. We were aware of the difficulty of changing the organisation's culture and aware of the political issues surrounding consultation, but we became obsessed with the notion that rapid progress to improving things could be made if we designed the communication and information systems to support a vision of NYP as an 'organism with a brain'. This was especially the case since this approach seemed to have senior management support. Critical systems thinking (the system of systems methodologies) told us that Beer's (1985) viable system model (VSM) was exactly what we needed for designing information systems on the basis of the 'organism' and 'brain' metaphors. We proceeded apace to the implementation phase of TSI and to the application of the VSM as our 'dominant methodology'.

For those not familiar with the VSM, Figure 8.1 shows, in very broad outline, NYP pictured as a viable system. The analysis we conducted and the recommendations that we were led to make then became very much standard VSM fare. Each of the seven new territorial divisions was to be given autonomy, developing its own statement of purpose and its own environmental scanning and planning capabilities. In VSM terms each had to become a viable system in its own right.

Figure 8.2 shows the Selby Division as a viable system. Whereas previously coordination had been achieved by strict adherence to commands from headquarters, this was no longer possible if the divisions were to develop their own identities. The nature of 'force orders' was therefore clarified by separating out orders requiring strict adherence, policy guidelines (which the divisions could interpret according to their own local circumstances) and coordination matters. The coordination function should indeed, it was suggested, cease to be controlled by the centre. If it could be set up and maintained by the divisions it would truly be seen as a service to them and not an authoritarian element of command.

Removing direct control from headquarters of so much of the divisions' activities might be seen, by senior management, as a recipe for anarchy unless they could at least be sure of control over the outcomes. To this end attention was given to the establishment of 'monitoring channels' which let senior management know how the divisions were doing in terms of some key performance indicators. Senior management should henceforth exercise control on the basis of goals obtained but would not (generally) interfere in specifying the means used to achieve the goals.

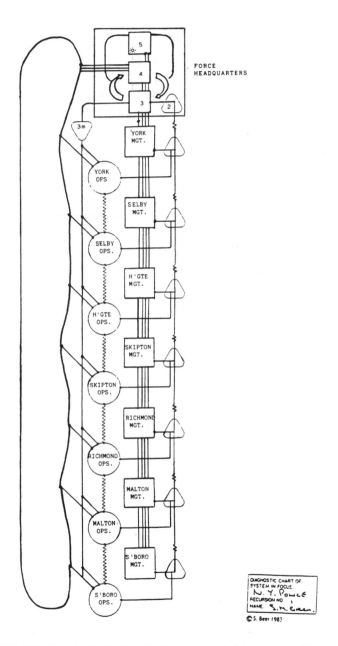

FIGURE 8.1 *North Yorkshire Police as a viable system* (from Green, 1991)

Information on performance, according to the indicators, should also be freely available to the divisions themselves so that they could adjust their own behaviour. Finally, it was recommended that policy making at the top level of NYP could best be supported by the creation of a development function which might be formed by merging the current 'operational conference', which dealt with internal matters, with the 'information technology conference' which showed some rudimentary interest in monitoring external affairs. This was necessary if the organisation was ever to be appropriately responsive to the changing environment it faced.

The recommendations outlined were written up in a discussion document, 'Divisional Autonomy—The Viable System Perspective', which was circulated to force senior management prior to presentation to members of the Steering Committee overseeing the reorganisation, and consisting of the Chief Constable, the Assistant Chief Constable Operations, the Chairman of the Police Authority, representatives of the Staff Associations and members of the Implementation Team. We were unperturbed at a trickle of feedback before the meeting suggesting that the document had not been well received. We felt that, logically speaking, the VSM provided exactly the information flows NYP needed; giving the divisions autonomy and the information to make their own decisions, ensuring coordination, and providing senior management with the means to ensure proper internal control and to see that NYP was adaptable to external developments. It was disturbing, however, when Steve Green was asked by one middle manager, on the morning of the meeting, whether he had 'gone mad'.

The project was lucky to survive this meeting. It was clear that there was no general understanding of how local autonomy could work in an organisation like NYP, how coordination could be maintained, or why the headquarters meeting structure should be rearranged to ensure responsive policy making as we envisaged it. There was no doubt also that the distrust that had grown up, because of the history of lack of consultation over important decisions, continued to poison the atmosphere. It was probably only the fact that the Chief Constable had not read the report before the meeting, and was impressed by some of the points made in discussion, that saved the day.

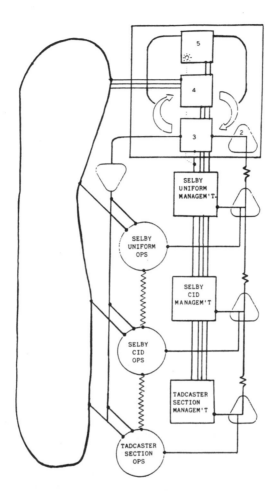

FIGURE 8.2 *Selby Division as a viable system* (from Green, 1991)

As critical systems thinkers we knew about the strengths and weaknesses of the VSM, but we had not been *critical enough* of how its weaknesses would detract from the success of this project. In particular, the VSM did not keep us alert enough concerning whether the changes recommended would be culturally and politically acceptable. The intervention had taken too much of an expert-driven form with insufficient participation from those whose minds had to be won if change was to be accepted. Furthermore it had not provided us with the means to address the consultation issue. It was just as well we were forced to think again. Even if we had been allowed to design the information systems suggested they would have been sabotaged.

Re-entering the choice phase of TSI, we felt we now needed a methodology that would bring about sufficient cultural shift in NYP, through learning, to make feasible the kinds of changes that seemed necessary. We were also determined that it be able to address the consultation issue. To these ends Checkland's (1981; Checkland and Scholes, 1990) soft systems methodology was selected. This methodology was followed through in fairly conventional, Mode 1, form. Rich pictures of the problem situation and of important aspects of the problem situation were drawn (see Green, 1991). Four relevant systems were eventually chosen for consideration:

1. a system to develop a concept of local autonomy appropriate for implementation in NYP;
2. a system to provide for the coordinated implementation of policy;
3. a system to make policy in a manner which balances the demands of the present with the needs of the future;
4. a system to provide a consultative style of decision-making.

Three of these were directed at issues that had troubled participants in the meeting on the recommendations derived from the VSM; the fourth was aimed at improving consultation. Root definitions and conceptual models were constructed. Conceptual models 'to provide for coordinated implementation of policy' and 'to provide a consultative style of decision making' are included here, as Figures 8.3 and 8.4, for the interest of readers.

Following the philosophy of our new 'dominant methodology', SSM, all stages were conducted in as participative a way as possible. The original interviewees (with one or two notable additions) were revisited, the various issues were discussed, on the basis of the root definitions and conceptual models, and the models amended either in the presence of the interviewees or, later, in the light of the discussions. Considerable debate was generated among those involved as they began to learn their way to their own understanding of matters such as what autonomy might mean in NYP.Finally a consultancy report was prepared containing conclusions expressed in simple, real-world, terms. It has to be said that the recommendations in this report were little different from those in the previous one, but the reception of the report was completely different. If anything the response now was 'yes, very good, this is obvious, what have you been spending your time doing?' This is a response that is disturbing to inexperienced users of SSM, but is actually just about the highest level of praise an SSM analyst can receive. When something is 'obvious' it has become part of the culture of the organisation; people act according to the obvious and things get implemented.

The intervention was successful and brought about considerable change in NYP (see Green, 1992). I am pleased to say that we have continued to work with NYP, in the years since 1991, on a number of engagements that stemmed from this original project. The point here, however, is to argue that it was a project, in the information systems area, that made full use of critical systems thinking and would not have been as successful if it had not made use of critical systems thinking. The project demonstrated critical awareness of the strengths and weaknesses of the methodologies used, and what they could most appropriately be employed to do—even if, initially, we were carried away with what the VSM seemed to be able to offer.

Had we been more socially aware we might have recognised that it was not sensible to try to push through the conclusions derived from the VSM study even if these did seem to command senior management support. There was complementarism in the use of systems methodologies—cognitive mapping, VSM and SSM were all employed. There was complementarism at the theoretical level in that two methodologies (VSM and SSM) were at different times chosen as dominant and, once chosen, the distinctive rationale of each was strictly followed. The project should certainly not be read just as a case study on the need for effective participant involvement in change processes (as secured using SSM). The coherence of the recommendations produced on the basis of the VSM diagnosis and design contributed equally to overall success. That said, we were perhaps lucky that the VSM and SSM converged on similar conclusions and we were spared from having to chose between contradictory recommendations derived from alternative rationalities.

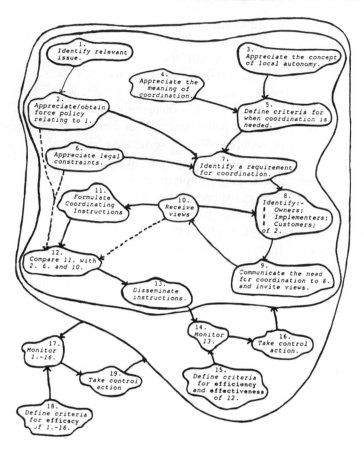

FIGURE 8.3 *Conceptuual model to provide for coordinated implementation of policy* (from Green, 1991)

Finally, if nobody was 'liberated' or 'emancipated' according to any reasonable usage of those terms, then at least attention was given to improving the involvement of ordinary staff in decision-making through new consultative procedures which had the support of the staff associations.

8.6   Conclusion

The argument that critical systems thinking can contribute to information systems research and practice has proceeded through a number of stages. We began by setting out various reasons why systems thinking could be seen as a valuable theoretical basis for the applied disciplines and especially information systems. Critical systems thinking was then introduced as the most theoretically sophisticated strand of the systems approach and as, therefore, the most likely to offer the greatest help to information systems in responding to the challenges that it, as well as systems thinking, inevitably confront.

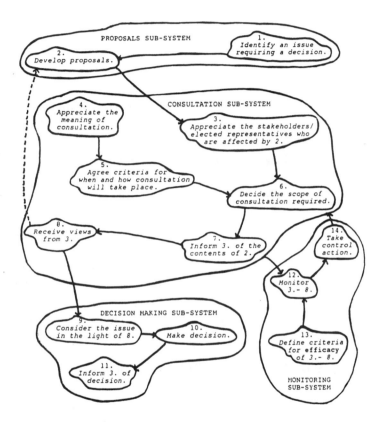

FIGURE 8.4 *Conceptual model to provide a consultative style of decision making* (from Green, 1991)

The benefits that critical systems thinking can bring were then further outlined by demonstrating that it offers the prospect of bringing various concerns which information systems has already demonstrated an interest in, into an integrated programme of research. Finally a case study was presented, and it was suggested that the outcome of the information systems project described would not have been as successful if it had not been guided by critical systems thinking. I hope the argument has been convincing. I think that critical systems thinking can provide a strong impetus to the emergence of information systems as a coherent discipline. It will also ensure that Nissen's (1985) question, addressed to information systems researchers, is never forgotten: 'for whom and for what reason are we acquiring knowledge?'.

References

Avison, D., and Fitzgerald, G., 1988, *Information Systems Development*, Blackwell Scientific, Oxford.

Avison, D., and Wood-Harper, A., 1990, *Multiview : An Exploration into Information Systems Development*, Blackwell Science, Oxford

Beer, S., 1985, *Diagnosing the System for Organisations*, Wiley, Chichester.

Boland, R.J., 1985, Phenomenology: a preferred approach to research on information systems, in *Research Methods in Information Systems*, E. Mumford, R. Hirschheim, G. Fitzgerald and A.T. Wood-Harper, eds., Elsevier, Amsterdam.

Boland, R.J., 1987, The in-formation of information systems, in *Critical Issues in Information Systems Research*, R.J. Boland and R.A. Hirschheim eds., Elsevier, Amsterdam.

Brocklesby, J., and Cummings, S., 1995, Combining hard, soft and critical methodologies: the cultural constraints, *Systems Research,* 12:239.

Checkland, P.B., 1981, *Systems Thinking, Systems Practice*, Wiley, Chichester.

Checkland, P.B., 1988, Information systems and systems thinking : time to unite?, *International Journal of Infomation Management,* 8:239.

Checkland, P.B., 1994, Conventional wisdom and conventional ignorance: the revolution organisation theory missed, *Organisation,* 1:29.

Checkland, P.B., and Scholes, J., 1990, *Soft Systems Methodology in Action*, Wiley, Chichester.

Churchman, C.W., 1979, *The Systems Approach and its Enemies*, Basic Books, New York.

Cooper, R., 1990, Organisation/Disorganization, in *The Theory and Philosophy of Organisations*, J.Hassard and D. Pym, eds., Routledge, London.

Dando, M.R., and Bennett, P.G., 1981, A Kuhnian crisis in management science, *Journal of the Operational Research Society*, 32:91.

Eden, C., Jones, S., and Sims, D., 1983, *Messing About in Problems*, Pergamon Press, Oxford.

Espejo, R., and Watt, J., 1978, Management information systems: a system for design, Working Paper 98, University of Aston Management Centre.

Flood, R.L., 1995, *Solving Problem Solving*, Wiley, Chichester.

Flood, R.L., and Jackson, M.C., 1991, *Creative Problem Solving: Total Systems Intervention*, Wiley, Chichester.

Flood, R.L., and Jackson, M.C. eds., 1991, *Critical Systems Thinking : Directed Readings*, Wiley, Chichester.

Green, S.M., 1991, Total Systems Intervention : organisational communication in North Yorkshire Police, Unpublished MA Thesis, University of Hull.

Green, S.M., 1992, Total Systems Intervention: organisational communication in North Yorkshire Police, *Systems Practice,* 5:585.

Hirschheim, R., 1985a, *Office Automation : A Social and Organisational Perspective*, Wiley, Chichester.

Hirschheim, R., 1985b, Information systems epistemology : an historical perspective, in *Research Methods in Information Systems*, E. Mumford, R. Hirschheim, G. Fitzgerald and A.T. Wood-Harper eds., Elsevier, Amsterdam.

Hirschheim, R., and Klein, H.K., 1989, Four paradigms of information systems development, *Communications of the ACM* 32:1199.

Jackson, M.C., 1982, The nature of soft systems thinking : the work of Churchman, Ackoff and Checkland, *Journal of Applied Systems Analysis* 9:17.

Jackson, M.C., 1985, Social systems theory and practice : the need for a critical approach, *International Journal of General Systems* 10:135.

Jackson, M.C., 1987a, Systems strategies for information management in organisations which are not machines, *International Journal of Information Management,* 7:187.

Jackson, M.C., 1987b, Present positions and future prospects in management science, *Omega* 15:455.

Jackson, M.C., 1991, *Systems Methodology for the Management Science*, Plenum, New York.

Jackson, M.C., 1992, An integrated programme for critical thinking in information systems research, *Journal of Information Systems,* 2:83.

Jackson, M.C., 1993, Social theory and operational research practice, *Journal of the Operational Research Society*, 44:563.

Jackson, M.C., 1995, Beyond the fads: systems thinking for managers, *Systems Research,* 12:25.

Jackson, M.C., and Keys, P., 1984, Towards a system of systems methodologies; *Journal of the Operational Research Society*, 35:155.

Jackson, M.C., and Keys, P., eds., 1987, *New Directions in Management Science*, Gower, Aldershot.

Jayaratna, N., 1994, *Understanding and Evaluating Methodologies : A Systemic Framework*, McGraw Hill, London.

Klein, H.K., and Hirschheim, R., 1987, Social change and the future of information systems development, in *Critical Issues in Information Systems Research*, R.J. Boland and R.A. Hirschheim, eds., Wiley, Chichester.

Klein, H.K. and Lyytinen, K.J. 1985, The poverty of scientism in information systems, in *Research Methods in Information Systems* E. Mumford, R., Hirschheim, G. Fitzgerald and A.T. Wood-Harper, eds., Elsevier, Amsterdam.

Kuhn, T.S., 1970, *The Structure of Scientific Resolutions*, second edition, University of Chicago Press, Chicago.

Lyytinen, K.J. and Klein, H.K., 1985, The critical theory of Jurgen Habermas as a basis for a theory of information systems, in *Research Methods in Information Systems*, E. Mumford, R., Hirschheim, G. Fitzgerald and A.T. Wood-Harper, eds., Elsevier, Amsterdam.

Lyytinen, K.J., Klein, H.K. and Hirschheim, R.A., 1991, The effectiveness of office information systems : a social action perspective, *Journal of Information Systems,* 1:41.

Lyotard, J.-F., 1984, *The Postmodern Condition: A Report on Knowledge*, Manchester University Press, Manchester.

Markus, M.L. 1983, Power, politics and MIS implementation, *Communications of the ACM*, 26:430.

Mason, R.O., and Mitroff, I.I., 1981, *Challenging Strategic Planning Assumptions*, Wiley, New York.

Mingers, J.C., 1980, Towards an appropriate social theory for applied systems thinking: critical theory and soft systems methodology, *Journal of Applied Systems Analysis*, 7:41.

Mingers, J.C., 1994, Information systems as a discipline : problems and possibilities for research and teaching, *Systemist* 16(1):70.

Mitroff, I.I., and Linstone, H.A., 1993, *The Unbounded Mind*, Oxford University Press, New York.

Morgan, G., 1986, *Images of Organisation*, Sage, Beverley Hills, CA.

Mumford, E., 1983, *Designing Human Systems*, Manchester Business School.

Nissen, H.E., 1985, Acquiring knowledge of information systems - research in a methodological quagmire, in *Research Methods in Information Systems*, E. Mumford, R., Hirschheim, G. Fitzgerald and A.T. Wood-Harper, eds., Elsevier, Amsterdam.

Savage, A., and Mingers, J., 1996, A framework for linking Soft Systems Methodology (SSM) and Jackson System Development (JSD), *Information Systems Journal*, 6:109.

Schecter, D., 1991, Critical systems thinking in the 1980s: a connective summary, in *Critical Systems Thinking : Directed Readings*, R.L. Flood and M.C. Jackson, eds., Wiley, Chichester.

Silverman, D., 1970, *The Theory of Organisations*, Heinemann, London.

Stowell, F., ed., 1995, *Information Systems Provision: The Contribution of Soft Systems Methodology*, McGraw Hill, London.

Symons, V. and Walsham, G., 1987, Evaluation of information systems: a social perspective, Research Paper, No. 1/87, Management Studies Group, Cambridge University.

Tsoukas, H., 1993, The road to emancipation is through organisational development: a critical evaluation of Total Systems Intervention, *Systems Practice*, 6:53.

Ulrich, W., 1983, *Critical Heuristics of Social Planning*, Haupt, Bern.

Ulrich, W., 1995, Critical systems thinking for citizens: a research proposal, Research Memorandum No. 10, Centre for Systems Studies, University of Hull.

Walsham, G., 1991, Organisational metaphors and information systems research, *European Journal of Information Systems*, 1:83.

Walsham, G. and Han, C.K., 1991, Structuration theory and information systems research, *Journal of Applied Systems Analysis*, 18:77.

Wood-Harper, A.T., 1985, Research methods in information systems: using action research, in *Research Methods in Information Systems*, E. Mumford, R., Hirschheim, G. Fitzgerald and A.T. Wood-Harper, eds. Elsevier, Amsterdam.

Wood-Harper, A.T., and Fitzgerald, G., 1982, A taxonomy of current approaches to systems analysis, *The Computer Journal*, 25:12.

Chapter 9

INTERPRETIVE RESEARCH IN INFORMATION SYSTEMS

Michael Myers

9.1   Introduction

There has been growing interest in interpretive research methods and their application to information systems in recent years. The interest shown is a direct result of the emergence of a certain dissatisfaction with the state of information systems research in the late 1980s and early 1990s. At that time the most common research methods used in information systems were surveys, laboratory experiments, and descriptive case studies (Alavi and Carlson, 1992), which led some researchers to charge that IS research suffered from a lack of diversity (Galliers and Land, 1987; Orlikowski and Baroudi, 1991). Other researchers claimed that IS research was often superficial and somewhat faddish (Banville and Landry, 1989), which is disturbing given the importance and impact of information technology in contemporary society.

Out of this situation came a call for methodological pluralism in information systems (Avison and Myers, 1995; Galliers, 1991; Landry and Banville, 1992). Landry and Banville (1992) suggested that no single method could ever capture all the richness and complexity of organisational reality, and that a diversity of methods, theories, and philosophies was required (Landry and Banville, p.78). Orlikowski and Baroudi (1991), likewise, argued that there was much that could be gained if a plurality of research perspectives was effectively employed to investigate information systems phenomena. They argued that any one perspective is always only a partial view, and unnecessarily restrictive.

In line with these calls for methodological pluralism, interpretive research methods have gained prominence and been increasingly accepted by the IS research community in the last few years (Walsham, 1995b). Other reasons for the growth of

239

interpretive research include a general shift in IS research away from technological to managerial and organisational issues (Benbasat *et al.*, 1987), a desire to study problems in the richness of their real-life setting as contrasted with the artificial context of laboratory studies, and the ability to address issues of causality and human purpose in their complex real-life setting. Prominent among the variety of interpretive research strategies which have been suggested in the research literature are interpretive in-depth case studies (Walsham, 1993, 1995b), grounded theory (Glaser and Strauss, 1967), ethnography (Harvey and Myers, 1995), phenomenology (Boland, 1985), hermeneutics (Lee, 1994), and critical hermeneutics (Myers, 1994, 1995).

9.2   The Nature of Interpretive Research

In the social sciences the differences between positivist and interpretivist research have been characterised as objective versus subjective (Burrell and Morgan, 1979), quantitative versus qualitative, nomothetic versus. idiographic (Luthans and Davis, 1982), as aimed at prediction and control versus aimed at explanation and understanding, as taking an outsider (etic) perspective versus taking an insider (emic) perspective, and so on (for a fuller discussion see Morey and Luthans, 1984). Considerable controversy continues to surround the use of these terms because of disagreement about what qualifies as positivist or interpretive, and how the various research methods and approaches should be classified (see also Kaplan and Maxwell, 1994; Lacity and Janson, 1994; Miles and Huberman, 1984). In the IS research community in particular, a common misconception has been to equate qualitative with interpretive research and to confound the differences in methods.

For example, Lee (1991) said that the interpretive approach 'refers to such procedures as those associated with ethnography, hermeneutics, phenomenology, and case studies', whereas the positivist approach 'refers to such procedures as those associated with inferential statistics, hypothesis testing, mathematical analysis, and experimental and quasi-experimental design'. (Lee 1991, p.342). I believe this categorisation, while useful as an initial characterisation, is unsatisfactory. I agree with Visala (1991) that it is possible to have case studies which are positivist (e.g. Yin, 1989) or interpretivist (e.g. Walsham, 1993) and mathematical analyses or statistical methods can be used in interpretive research (e.g. Kaplan and Duchon, 1988; Kaplan and Maxwell, 1994) even though they tend to be more applicable and frequent in research which follows the positivist canons of science. It is incorrect to equate qualitative research with interpretive research, and vice versa.

Klein and Myers suggest that a more useful way of categorising the research into positivist or interpretivist is by looking at its *underlying ontological and epistemological assumptions* (see Klein and Myers, 1995). Ontological assumptions are concerned with beliefs about 'reality' and epistemological assumptions with beliefs about what counts as knowledge and how it can be obtained. The question is then not one of deciding if the research study uses numbers or not, but determining what is the underlying philosophical position. According to this view, the actual methods of data collection and analysis (survey, experiment, case study, etc) are, to some extent at least, independent of the underlying epistemology. This view of the fundamental nature of interpretive research means that it is not limited to the exploratory phase of the research process (as was suggested for case studies by Benbasat *et al.*, 1987, p.371).

The basic ontological assumption of positivism is that reality is objectively given and can be described by measurable properties which are independent of the observer (researcher) and his or her instruments. In practice it is often assumed that the units of analysis which make up reality can be classified objectively into subjects and predicates (subjects are also often referred to as entities or objects). In interpretivism, one may or may not assume that an independent reality exists, hence an interpretivist can also be a realist, but she or he need not be. What is foundational is that all interpretivists assume that access to reality (given or socially constructed) is only through social constructions such a language, consciousness, shared meanings and instruments. None of these are neutral and all have a profound impact on 'what one can see and measure' (Klein and Myers, 1995, p.7).

The difference in ontological position produces very different attitudes towards epistemology which are summarised in Table 9.1. Positivist studies generally attempt to test theory, in an attempt to increase the predictive understanding of phenomena. In line with this Orlikowski and Baroudi (1991, p.5) classified IS research as positivist if there was evidence of formal propositions, quantifiable measures of variables, hypothesis testing, and the drawing of inferences about a phenomenon from the sample to a stated population.

In their study they found a clear preference for positivist research in information systems, which is somewhat disappointing given that positivist studies tend to depict an a-historical and a-contextual view of information systems phenomena.

In distinction to this interpretive studies generally attempt to understand phenomena through the meanings that people assign to them and interpretive methods of research in IS are 'aimed at producing an understanding of the *context* of the information system, and the *process* whereby the information system influences and is influenced by the context' (Walsham, 1993, p.4-5). Interpretive research does not predefine dependent and independent variables, but focuses on the full complexity of human sense making as the situation emerges (Kaplan and Maxwell, 1994).

Both positivist and interpretivist research aim at improving the understanding of phenomena, but differ in how this can be achieved. Both can contribute to suggesting normative interventions through engineering or action research, but a discussion of the relationship between interventionist strategies (such as policy design, social work, action research etc.) and interpretivism is beyond the scope of this chapter.

9.3   The Applicability of Interpretive Research

The output from IS research has consistently shown that it is the social and organisational contexts of information systems design, development and application which lead to the greatest practical problems (e.g. see Hirschheim and Newman, 1991; Newman and Robey, 1992; Walsham, 1993). This area has attracted increasing attention in information systems research and has led to the realisation that all aspects of any information system have a highly complex, and constantly changing, social context. It is in the exploration of that social context where interpretive research comes into its own. The goal of interpretive field research is to improve our understanding of human thought and action through interpretation of human actions in their real-life context.

TABLE 9.1 *Differences between positivist and interpretivist epistemology*[1]

Epistemological assumptions of positivism	Epistemological assumptions of interpretivism
1. Experience is taken to be objective, testable, and independent of theoretical explanation	1. Data are not detachable from theory, for what counts as data is determined in the light of some theoretical interpretation, and facts themselves have to be reconstructed in the light of interpretation
2. Theories are held to be artificial constructions or models, yielding explanation in the sense of a logic of hypothetico-deduction (if T is true, phenomenon x follows)	2. In the human sciences theories are mimetic reconstructions of the facts themselves, and the criterion of a good theory is understanding of meanings and intentions rather than deductive explanation
3. Law-like relations (generalisations) are derived from experience and are independent of the investigator, his/her methods and the object of study	3. The generalisations derived from experience are dependent upon the researcher, his/her methods and the interactions with the subjects of study. The validity of the generalisations does not depend upon statistical inference 'but on the plausibility and cogency of the logical reasoning used in describing the results from the cases, and in drawing conclusions from them' (Walsham, 1993, p.15).
4. The language of science can be exact, formalisable and literal	4. The languages of the human sciences are irreducibly equivocal (because of multiple, emergent meanings) and continually adapt themselves to changing circumstances
5. Meanings are separate from facts	5. Meanings in the human sciences are what constitute the facts, for data consist of documents, intentional behaviour, social rules, human artefacts, etc., and these are inseparable from their meanings for agents

---

[1] This figure is mostly adapted from Bernstein (1983), who summarizes Hesse. In the original context, Bernstein reviews the commonly assumed differences between the natural and social sciences, and argues that all of the epistemological assumptions which supposedly distinguish the human sciences apply equally well to the natural sciences. Bernstein points out that there is a necessary hermeneutical dimension to all science. Kuhn's historical analysis of the nature of paradigm shifts in science supports this view (Kuhn, 1970). Other interpretivists, however, believe that the methods of natural science are appropriate for the study of the natural world and are inadequate only for the study of social reality.

For an interpretivist, the preferred way of contributing to a realistic understanding of information systems in organisations is to investigate how they affect social interaction and the creation of shared meanings. Whereas hypothesis testing requires abstracting from the richness of real-life and experimental situations in order to achieve a measure of controllability and precision, interpretive research focuses on the full complexity of human sense making as the situation emerges. As Kaplan and Maxwell (1994) point out, the goal of understanding a phenomenon from the point of view of the participants and its particular social and institutional context is largely lost when textual data are quantified.

In summary, interpretive research is applicable especially in real-life situations where complexity prevents replicability and thereby statistical significance testing in the positivistic sense. The situations identified and studied are sufficiently varied, complex and emergent as to make experimental replication of the observed human behaviours unlikely if not impossible (Klein and Myers, 1995, p.10).

9.4 Interpretive Field Research

In more traditional positivist techniques, context is treated as either a set of interfering variables that need controlling, known as noise in the data, or other controlled variables which are experimentally set up in order to seek for cause and effect relationships. The context of a situation is seen as something which can be factored out of the analysis or operationalised as a variable. In interpretive approaches, however, context is treated as the socially constructed reality of a named group, or groups, of social agents and the key task of observation and analysis is to unpack the webs of meaning transformed in the social process whereby reality is constructed. For an interpretivist, the context is what defines the situation and makes it what it is. In positivist techniques, cause and effect are the main objects being searched for, while in interpretive techniques, meaning in context is the most important framework being sought (Harvey and Myers, 1995).

Because context is crucial to interpretive observations and analyses, techniques which explore contextual webs of meaning are important. The two most common interpretive field research methods for doing this are interpretive in-depth case studies

(Walsham, 1993) and ethnographies (Hutchins, 1995; Star, 1995; Suchman, 1987; Wynn, 1979, 1991; Zuboff, 1988). Although there is no hard and fast distinction, the principle difference between the two depends upon the length of time that the investigator is required to spend in the field and the extent to which the researcher immerses himself or herself in the life of the social group under study. In a case study, the primary source of data is interviews, supplemented by documentary evidence such as annual reports, minutes of meetings and so forth. In an ethnography, these data sources are supplemented by data collected during participant observation on the part of the researcher over an extended period of time. The ethnographer 'immerses himself in the life of people he studies' (Lewis, 1985, p.380) and seeks to place the phenomena studied in its social and cultural context. As Yin explains,

> Ethnographies usually require long periods of time in the 'field' and emphasise detailed, observational evidence. . . In contrast, case studies are a form of enquiry that does not depend solely on ethnographic or participant observation data. One could even do a valid and high-quality case study without leaving the library and the telephone . . . (Yin, 1989, p.21-22).

The difference between an interpretive case study and an ethnography can be illustrated from the IS research literature. The ethnographic research method was used by Orlikowski and Baroudi (1991) who studied a large, multinational software consulting firm over eight months. Data was collected via participant observation, interviews, documents, and informal social contact with the participants. The in-depth case study method was used by Walsham and Waema (1994), who studied a building society for a period of two years. The principal method of data collection was in-depth interviews with a range of organisational participants. The researchers did not use participant observation.

In an interpretive field study, primary or secondary sources of data can be used. Primary source material can be collected by the investigator by methods such as participant observation, interviews, tape recordings of meetings, diaries and so forth. Primary source material also includes unpublished written materials created by the participants independently of the researcher, such as memos, correspondence, minutes of meetings, reports and so on. Secondary source material includes any previously published documents by scholars or practitioners.

Although almost all ethnographic research can be characterised as interpretive, there are many different schools or views within anthropology about ethnographic interpretation and there is critical debate within anthropology concerning the ethnographic research method (Van Maanen, 1989). These different views about ethnographic research are relevant to the ethnographic study of information systems as they show the variety of approaches already being adopted within the source discipline. Although I am unable to discuss this critical debate within anthropology in depth, one of the landmark publications in this debate is Clifford and Marcus' (1986) work (see also Clifford, 1988; Marcus, 1992).

Sanday (1979) divides ethnography into the holistic, semiotic, and behaviouristic schools of thought, and she further divides the semiotic school into thick description and ethnoscience. Each school of thought has a different approach to doing an ethnography. For example, most ethnographers of the holistic school say that empathy and identification with the social grouping being observed is needed; they insist that an anthropologist should 'go native' and live just like the local people (e.g. Evans-Pritchard, 1950; Cohen, 1985). The assumption is that the anthropologist has to become like a blank slate in order fully to understand local social and cultural practices. The anthropologist acts like a sponge, soaking up the language and culture of the people under study.

On the other hand, Clifford Geertz, the foremost exponent of the 'thick description' (semiotic) school, says that anthropologists do not need to have empathy with their subjects (Geertz, 1973, 1983, 1988). Rather, the ethnographer has to search out and analyse symbolic forms—words, images, institutions, behaviours—with respect to one another and to the whole that they comprise. Geertz argues that it is possible for an anthropologist to describe and analyse another culture without having to empathise with the people. He says that anthropologists need to understand the 'webs of significance' which people weave within the cultural context, and these webs of significance can only be communicated to others by thickly describing the situation and its context.

An alternative to the above is the adoption of a critical perspective on ethnographic research. For example, Forester (1992) used the critical social theory of Habermas in the development of an approach called critical ethnography. Forester used critical ethnography to examine the facetious figures of speech used by city planing staff to negotiate the problem of data acquisition. Myers (1987) used critical hermeneutics to illuminate the ethnographic research process in his study of the independence movement in the Melanesian nation of Vanuatu (see also Marcus and Fischer, 1986).

The critical hermeneutic approach to interpretive field research, which I advocate, is discussed below. Critical hermeneutics can be used with the interpretive in-depth case study (e.g. Myers, 1994) or ethnography (e.g. Forester, 1992; Myers, 1987).

9.5 Critical Hermeneutics

Critical hermeneutics is an integrative theoretical framework, combining interpretive and critical elements (Thompson, 1981). Like structuration theory (Giddens, 1984; Orlikowski and Robey, 1991), critical (or dialectical) hermeneutics is an attempt to dissolve the boundaries between the interpretivist and critical research traditions, which have usually been seen as quite distinct (Orlikowski and Baroudi, 1991). The philosophical basis for integration is provided by Bernstein (1983), who argues that there is common ground between the critical theory of Jurgen Habermas and the hermeneutics of Hans-Georg Gadamer. Hoy (1988), likewise, argues that it is possible to integrate the interpretive and critical approaches. Hoy finds that the writings of Paul Ricoeur provide such an integrative framework.

Walsham (1993) argues that constitutive process theories, which emphasise both the importance of subjective meaning for the individual actor and the social structures which condition and enable such meanings, provide a new approach to research on the social aspects of computer-based information systems. Critical hermeneutics is one such constitutive process theory; it is in effect a meta-theory, and provides principles to guide the interpretation process and a framework for the integration of multiple perspectives.

What follows, then, is a description of critical hermeneutics as an integrative perspective; in this discussion critical hermeneutics will be distinguished from 'pure hermeneutics' and from critical theory as it has been traditionally represented.

Hermeneutics is the science of interpretation, concerned with analysis of the *meaning* of a text or text-analogue. The basic question in hermeneutics is 'What is the meaning of a text?' (Radnitzky, 1970, p.20). Taylor says that

> Interpretation, in the sense relevant to hermeneutics, is an attempt to make clear, to make sense of an object of study. This object must, therefore, be a text, or a text-analogue, which in some way is confused, incomplete, cloudy, seemingly contradictory—in one way or another, unclear. The interpretation aims to bring to light an underlying coherence or sense. (Taylor, 1976, p.153).

The idea of a hermeneutic circle refers to the dialectic between the understanding of the text as a whole and the interpretation of its parts, in which descriptions are guided by anticipated explanations (Gadamer, 1976b, p.117). As Gadamer explains,

> It is a circular relationship.. . The anticipation of meaning in which the whole is envisaged becomes explicit understanding in that the parts, that are determined by the whole, themselves also determine this whole.

It follows from this idea of the hermeneutic circle that we have an expectation of meaning from the context of what has gone before. The movement of understanding 'is constantly from the whole to the part and back to the whole' (Gadamer, 1976b, p.117). Ricoeur points out that:

> Interpretation. . . is the work of thought which consists in deciphering the hidden meaning in the apparent meaning, in unfolding the levels of meaning implied in the literal meaning. (Ricoeur, 1974, p.xiv)

The idea of the hermeneutic circle can be applied to the way in which we understand an organisation as a text-analogue. The more interviews we conduct and the more information we gather, the more we understand the organisation as a whole and its constituent parts. This hermeneutic process continues until the apparent absurdities, contradictions and oppositions in the organisation no longer appear strange, but make sense.

Hermeneutics is used to explore the socially constructed contexts of institutions and organisations (Berger and Luckmann,

1967) and, as an approach to meaning analysis, it has been used in many disciplines, including education, medicine, anthropology, sociology and architecture (Vattimo, 1988). It has also been taken up by researchers in the information systems area (e.g., Winograd and Flores, 1987; Lee, 1991; Boland, 1991; Myers, 1994, 1995). The principles of hermeneutics have been applied to the analyses of the metaphorical nature of theories of information (Boland, 1987) and of systems development (Hirschheim and Newman, 1991). Hermeneutics is a recognised framework for the analysis of organisations (Bryman, 1989), in particular when looking at organisational culture (Frost, *et al.*, 1985), and has been applied to the analysis of socio-technical interactions (Barley, 1986). This makes it a potentially important approach to the analysis of information systems in organisations.

There are different forms of hermeneutics, all concerned with the textual treatment of social settings, but not all concern themselves with reflective critique of the meaning of interpretations derived from textual analyses. The early hermeneuts such as Dilthey advocated a 'pure hermeneutics' which stressed empathic understanding and the understanding of human action from the 'inside'. As Radnitzky points out, however, pure hermeneutics is uncritical in that it takes statements or ideologies at face value (Radnitzky, 1970, p.20ff.). He cites Gadamer as saying that 'we don't have to imagine oneself in the place of some other person; rather, we have to understand *what* these thoughts or the sentences expressing them are *about*' (Radnitzky, 1970, p.27).

More recently, critical hermeneutics has emerged following the debates between Habermas and Gadamer (Gadamer, 1976a; Ricoeur, 1976; Thompson, 1981; Myers, 1995). There is a potential tendency to view interpretation as a closed and exact form, but critical hermeneutics recognises that the interpretive act is one which can never be closed as there is always a possible alternative interpretation (Taylor, 1976). In critical hermeneutics the interpreter constructs the context as another form of text, which can then, of itself, be critically analysed so that the meaning construction can be understood as an interpretive act. In this way, the hermeneutic interpreter is simply creating another text upon a text, and this recursive creation is potentially infinite. Every meaning is constructed, even through the very constructive act of seeking to deconstruct, and the process whereby that textual interpretation occurs must be self-critically reflected upon (Ricoeur, 1974).

Critical hermeneutics also recognises that 'prejudice', pre-judgement or prior knowledge plays an important part in our understanding. In positivist social science, 'prejudice' or pre-judgement is seen as a source of bias and therefore a hindrance to true knowledge; objectivity, according to positivism, is best attained if a social scientist adopts a value-free position and does not let biases interfere with his or her analysis. By contrast, hermeneutics recognises that prejudice is the necessary starting point of our understanding. The critical task of hermeneutics then becomes one of distinguishing between 'true prejudices, by which we understand, from the false ones by which we misunderstand' (Gadamer 1976b, p.124). Of course, the suspension of our prejudices is necessary if we are to begin to understand a text or text-analogue. But as Gadamer points out, this does not mean that we simply set aside our prejudices. Rather, it means that we, as researchers, must become aware of our own historicality (Gadamer, 1976b, p.125). This awareness of the dialogue between the text and the interpreter is peculiar to contemporary hermeneutics. The earlier hermeneutic philosophers such as Dilthey ignored this dialogical relationship between the text and the interpreter and attempted to understand the objective meaning of a text in its own right.

As an integrative approach, then, critical hermeneutics emphasises both the subjective meanings for individual actors and the social structures which condition and enable such meanings and are constituted by them. The theory can be used as a meta-theory to integrate research emphasising subjective meanings (Boland, 1985) and research which focuses on the institutional character of information systems (Kling and Iacono, 1989). The advantage of the critical hermeneutic approach is that it enables one to portray the real complexity of organisations as social, cultural and political systems. A critical hermeneutic analysis of information systems and IS development requires a researcher to look at information systems from many different perspectives: we have to look at the meaning of information systems for the various stakeholders in an organisation and the real value conflicts that there may be; we also have to look at the objective social impacts of information systems.

Although the critical hermeneutic approach is critical and not purely 'subjective', there are differences between critical hermeneutics and critical theory. Unlike most critical theorists, who have focused their research on a critique of class-based societies and capitalist forms of production, a researcher informed by critical hermeneutics does not assume from the outset what the most important oppositions, conflicts and contradictions are in contemporary organisations (see Poster, 1989, 1990). Rather, the interpretive hermeneutics must go hand in hand with a critical analysis of organisations and societies. There is, then, a dynamic interplay between a hermeneutic analysis and theoretical critique, where the critique is firmly grounded in social reality. A summary of the differences between the three theoretical frameworks is shown in Table 9.2.

TABLE 9.2 *Summary of three theoretical approaches*

Theory	Primary focus	Description
'Pure' hermeneutics	meaning, intentions	interpretive, 'subjective'
Critical theory	contradictions, unintended results	critical, 'objective', historical
Critical hermeneutics	social reality, intended and unintended results	interpretive and critical, subjective and objective, historical

Adoption of the critical hermeneutic perspective leads to criticism of non-dialectical views of interpretive research. One such non-dialectical position is that of the holistic school in ethnography. Ethnographers of the holistic school, in their attempt to 'go native' and understand other cultures 'in their own terms', in effect deny the glossing of those views by the interpretive act of the analyst. The end result is tantamount to a recourse to objectivity due to a taking for granted of the need for the critical analysis of the dialectics of the interpretive process. The role of the observer is treated as context-free, ignoring the fact that every interpretive exploration leads to a new understanding, thus rendering history as the most vital attribute of ethnographic analysis, the history of the material and the history of the interpretation. Zuboff's study of computer-mediated work (Zuboff, 1988) took the dialectical process of historical critique as fundamental to the ethnographic work being carried out. She argued that 'history would offer only a brief window of time during which such data could be gathered' (Zuboff, 1988, p.xiv).

I would argue that another non-dialectical view of interpretive research is that of grounded theory. According to Martin and Turner (1986), grounded theory is an inductive, theory discovery methodology that allows the researcher to develop a theoretical account of the general features of a topic while simultaneously grounding the account in empirical observations or data. But whereas most grounded theorists recommend that the researcher should not let his or her preconceptions interfere with the interpretation of the data (Glaser and Strauss, 1967)—in fact some of the leading figures of this movement go so far as to suggest that grounded theorists should not even write a literature review before starting data collection—critical hermeneutics suggests that prejudice is the necessary starting point of our understanding. Recognition of the dialectical nature of research requires the researcher to confront the data which emerge through the research process with the preconceptions (prejudices) which guided the original research design (i.e. the original lenses).

The critical hermeneutic perspective thus openly recognises that understanding of an institutional context is not gained by the researcher suspending her or his prejudices. Rather, the ethnographer is encouraged to become critically aware of them, making them explicit in the process of learning about cultural differences, a process not unlike the behaviour of practitioners who have to traverse a variety of sub-cultures within organisations (Orlikowski and Baroudi, 1991). This cultural bridging process is typically one attributed to systems analysts and business analysts in the information systems field, where they have to mediate between the users in the various business units and the more technically-oriented IS staff. This implies that the critical hermeneutic approach to interpretive field research also has great potential for helping this group of practitioners to conduct their work in an informed and rigourous manner (although a discussion of how critical hermeneutics could be used by IS and business analysts is beyond the scope of this chapter).

The critical hermeneutic perspective leads to the recognition that any interpretive field research is a form of historiography. The researcher is essentially situated in history, the history of the situation and of the interpretation, and is also part of a wider set of social, economic and political relationships. One of the key tasks of a researcher is to be aware of the historical context in which research takes place and to critically reflect this onto the research process itself. In arguing for a reflexive anthropology, Kahn (1989) points out that the interpretation of culture(s) 'is in fact part of a process of construction' and says that anthropologists themselves 'are similarly part of a broader socio-historical process' (p.22; see also Scholte, 1972).

> To put the argument in another way, when I, or any other anthropologist, produces in text an account of another culture, what I am in fact doing is engaging in a process with a history. That history is the cultural product of a longstanding relation between 'us' and 'them' within which I and my 'informants' are embedded. At the same time, the knowledge which I/we produce out of that relation—in my case for example the knowledge I might choose to term 'Minangkabau culture', or 'the meaning of mosque symbolism in a West Sumatran village', or whatever—is new knowledge in the sense that it does not pre-exist in West Sumatra, hard-wired as it were in the brains of the Minangkabau from time immemorial. It exists, and can only exist, in the relationship between Minangkabau and the West (Kahn, 1989, p.16).

This awareness of the importance of history leads to criticism of the 'ethnographic present', a standard device used by many anthropologists to describe social and cultural practices. The ethnographic present gives the (false) impression that the activities being described have always existed from time immemorial. The use of such phrases as 'The development process starts out each September' or 'All the members of the development team do not participate' gives the distinct impression that such activities have taken place since the world was created. The ethnographic present is thus a-historical, and neglects to mention when these activities were instituted. The ethnographic present ignores how human actions are always situated in history.

9.6   Examples of Interpretive Research

Although interpretive research has received relatively little attention in the IS literature so far (Walsham, 1993, p.34), more research work employing a variety of interpretivist perspectives is now starting to appear (Walsham, 1995b).

Boland (1979, 1985, 1987) was one of the first IS researchers to suggest hermeneutics and phenomenology as a means of looking at the sense-making process in information systems development. Klein and Hirschheim (1983) also provided a brief introduction to the hermeneutic approach to IS research.

More recently, Rathswohl (1991) has suggested Idhe's phenomenology as an IS research framework. Idhe's phenomenology, based in part on Heidegger's work, emphasises the basic idea that tools become extensions of ourselves (embodiment relation) which changes both how we experience the world and how we represent it (hermeneutic relation). Both Lee (1994) and Myers (1994, 1995) have used hermeneutics in their studies of information systems, although the two latter authors tend to use hermeneutics in a different way to Boland; Lee and Myers' usage is more sociological than phenomenological. Lee (1994) looked at richness in email communications by exploring the wider social and political context within which the email communications took place, while Myers (1994, 1995) examined the implementation of information systems from a critical hermeneutic perspective.

A number of researchers have used the speech-act theory of Searle (1979). Two examples are the work of Winograd and Flores (1987), and Lehtinen and Lyytinen (1986). The latter view an IS as an artefact which replaces more conventional forms of communication (such as telephone calls or meetings). Another example of the application of language analysis philosophy to IS research is Dietz and Widdershoven's (1991, 1992) work. They argue that Habermas' classification of speech acts is a useful starting point for the analysis of information systems requirements.

Other researchers to use interpretive methods are Feldman and March (1981), who analysed how information in organisations is embedded in social norms, and Hirschheim and Newman (1991), who analysed the role of myth, metaphor and magic in IS development, and Barley (1986).

Walsham (1993, 1995a, 1995b) has been one of the leading advocates of using the interpretive in-depth case study. In one of his articles with Waema (Walsham and Waema, 1994), the IS strategy formation and implementation process in a medium-sized UK building society was analysed. One of their conclusions was that the IS strategy formation and implementation process is a dynamic one, involving time-varying relationships, multilevel contexts, and cultural and political aspects.

In recent years a small but growing number of information systems researchers have recognised the value of the ethnographic method for IS research (Bentley *et al*. 1992; Harvey and Myers, 1995; Hughes, Randall and Shapiro, 1992; Lee, 1991; Lee, Baskerville and Davies, 1992; Orlikowski, 1991; Preston, 1991; Suchman, 1987; Wynn, 1991; Zuboff, 1988). Some of the early ground-breaking work was done by Wynn (1979) in her study of office conversations, Suchman (1987) in her study of the problem of human-machine communications, and Zuboff (1988).

Since then ethnography has become more widely used in the study of information systems in organisations, from the study of the development of information systems (Hughes *et al.*, 1992; Orlikowski, 1991; Preston, 1991; Orlikowski and Robey, 1991; Suchman, 1995) to the study of the use of information technology forms (Yates and Orlikowski, 1992), also including the study of aspects of information technology management (Davies, 1991; Davies and Nielsen, 1992). Ethnography has also been discussed as a method whereby multiple perspectives can be incorporated in systems design (Holzblatt and Beyer, 1993) and as a general approach to the wide range of possible studies relating to the investigation of information systems (Pettigrew, 1985). Bentley *et al.* (1992) conclude that ethnographic studies 'are helpful in informing the systems design process and may produce insights which contradict conventional thinking in systems design' (p.123). Orlikowski (1991), likewise, found that, contrary to the theoretical position of much of the IS research literature which assumes that information technology will transform existing bureaucratic organisational forms and social relations, the use of new information technology led to the existing forms of control being intensified and fused. Her research, which was informed by Giddens' theory of structuration, used the ethnographic research method to study a large, multinational software consulting firm.

In the area of the design and evaluation of information systems, some very interesting work has been taking place in a collaborative fashion between ethnographers on the one hand, and designers, IS professionals, computer scientists and engineers on the other. This collaborative work is especially strong in the UK and Europe and is growing in the USA. In the UK and Europe this work includes what is being done at Lancaster (Hughes, Shapiro and Rodden), Manchester (Bowers, Lea, Church and Lee), Oxford (Goguen), Surrey (Heath and Luff), Rank Xerox EUROPARC in Cambridge (Anderson, Sharrock, Button, Harper and McKay) and Vienna (Wagner). In the USA this work includes what is being done at Texas AandM (Henderson), Pittsburgh (Forsythe), Virginia (Downey), Carnegie Mellon (Kiesler and Monarch), Xerox PARC at Stanford (Suchman), Boston (Sproull), Illinios (Bowker, Star) and Irvine (Kling, King, Kraemer, Grudin and Ackerman). One of the main projects of the Lancaster group has been to use the ethnographic method to gain an understanding of human cooperation in air traffic control (Bentley *et al.*, 1992; Hughes *et al.*, 1992).

9.7   Evaluating Interpretive Research Manuscripts

Since interpretive research is relatively new to the information systems field, criteria for evaluating research of this kind have yet to be developed and agreed upon by the IS research community (Klein and Myers, 1995). Therefore, the following criteria for evaluating interpretive research manuscripts are offered as suggestions only; they are not intended as being in any way definitive.

Interpretive research manuscripts can be evaluated in terms of theory and in terms of data. With regard to theory, one of the key issues to be considered is whether the paper is a contribution to the field. Has the author developed or applied new concepts or theories? These concepts or theories do not have to be completely new, but it helps if the theory is new to the IS research community eg. Orlikowski (1991) adapted Giddens' structuration theory from sociology. Alternatively, the author may be able to make a contribution to the field by applying a well-known theory in a new or unique way.

Another key issue is whether the author offers rich insights. One of the marks of a good piece of interpretive research is that it should give us rich insights into the human, social and organisational aspects of information systems development and application.

Another theoretical issue is whether or not the manuscript contradicts conventional wisdom, e.g. Bentley *et al.* (1992) found that their ethnographic studies contradicted conventional thinking in systems design. They found that the conventional principles normally thought of as 'good design' could be inappropriate for cooperative systems.

In terms of data, a sufficient mass of data must have been collected for significant insights to emerge. Does the real complexity of the organisation as a social, cultural and political system come out? Does the manuscript tell us about real people with their different agendas, problems and so on? Is the subject matter set in its social and historical context? In interpretive research all of these questions are crucial, since context is crucial. It is the context which constitutes and gives meaning to the situation, and therefore it is important that the broader social and historical context is explored in interpretive studies.

As part of that broader context one would expect that a good piece of interpretive field research would present multiple viewpoints and alternative perspectives. Are there hidden agendas? Are there unintended consequences of people's actions? For an anthropologist, there is nothing more suspicious than being presented with the 'official line'. Unfortunately, many IS case studies are of this kind, where the only people who have been interviewed are from management. In an interpretive field study, one would expect to see the author adopt a more critical perspective than is usual in descriptive, positivistic case studies.

Another issue relating to data is whether sufficient information about the research method and the research process has been presented. Is the researcher aware of his or her historicality? I believe it is important to know how the data was gathered, when the research took place, and how the research developed over time.

Perhaps the most important question relating to the quality of the contribution overall is, are the findings significant for researchers and/or practitioners? If the answer is in the affirmative, then the results of the interpretive field research should be regarded as a contribution to the field, and as such, merit publication in one of the leading journals in information systems.

9.8   Conclusion

Interpretive field research offers a rigourous approach to the analysis of the institutional contexts of information systems practices, with the notion of context being one of the social construction of meaning frameworks. Both the interpretive in-depth case study and ethnography, as research methods, are well suited to providing information systems researchers with rich insights into the human, social and organisational aspects of information systems development and application. When the form of interpretive research known as critical hermeneutics is used (although this is not the only one), the findings can be rigourously scrutinised to allow for a thorough analysis of the processes of information systems practices, thus supplementing the more traditional approaches which tend to concentrate on content rather than process.

Because interpretive field research deals with actual practices in real-world situations, it allows for relevant issues to be explored and frameworks to be developed which can be used by both practitioners and researchers. It also means that researchers can deal with real situations instead of having to contrive artificial situations for the purpose of quasi-experimental investigations. Knowledge of what happens in the field can provide vital information to challenge and explore some of the assumptions gained from a mainly experimental-based body of knowledge. In-depth interpretive research points our attention to the non-instrumental appropriation of IT systems, and their ultimate embeddedness in local workplace cultures.

Another reason for using interpretive field research to study actual practices in real-world situations is that it enables a researcher to study organisations as the complex social, cultural and political systems that they are. An interpretive analysis requires a researcher to consider many different perspectives: to look at the views of the various stakeholders in an organisation and the real value conflicts that there may be, and to look at the objective social impacts which may result from the implementation of new information systems. Interpretive studies can also show differences in how information technologies tend to be used in different contexts.

The use of interpretive research methods means that opportunities which arise from contextual situations can be built upon, instead of avoided. As Zuboff (1988) argued, a 'window of opportunity' can be found to explore particular issues, for example where 'people who are working with technology for the first time were ripe with questions and insights regarding the distinct qualities of their experience' (Zuboff, 1988, p.13). By applying an interpretive approach to the analysis of such situations, a rigourous body of knowledge can be developed, which contributes directly to the support of the practical knowledge developed by practitioners. This can only enhance information systems research, allowing for practically relevant, rigourous research to be conducted in an effective way.

Information systems research is different from traditional scientific research in that the discipline is an applied discipline. It is generally agreed that the information systems discipline has to develop a body of knowledge which enhances the practical knowledge of workers in the institutional contexts under investigation. This leads to problems for researchers who may choose to give up rigour for relevance or the reverse of sacrificing relevance for rigour. Interpretive field research offers a research opportunity to conduct rigourous research which is of direct practical relevance. When supported by perspectives such as critical hermeneutics, the rigour is strengthened and more is discovered of the situation, leading to more knowledge with high potential for relevance to practitioners. This makes interpretive field research a worthy vehicle for facilitating scholarship and practice to develop in collaborative coexistence.

References

Alavi, M. and Carlson, P., 1992, A review of MIS research and disciplinary development, *Journal of Management Information Systems*, 8(4):45-62.

Avison, D.E. and Myers, M.D., 1995, Information systems and anthropology: an anthropological perspective on IT and organisational culture, *Information Technology and People*, 8(3):43-56.

Banville, C., and Landry, M., 1989, Can the field of MIS be disciplined? *Communications of the ACM* 32(1):48-60.

Barley, S.R., 1986, Technology as an occasion for structuring: evidence from observations of CT scanners and the social order of Radiology Departments, *Administrative Science Quarterly*, 31(1):78-108.

Benbasat, I., Goldstein, D.K. and Mead, M., 1987, The case research strategy in studies of Information Systems, *MIS Quarterly*, 11(3):369-386.

Bentley, R., Rodden, T., Sawyer, P., Sommerville, I., Hughes, J., Randall, R. and Shapiro, D., 1992, Ethnographically-Informed systems design for air traffic control, in *CSCW '92: Sharing Perspectives*, ACM Press, New York, 123-129.

Berger, P. and Luckman, T., 1967, *The Social Construction of Reality: a Treatise in the Sociology of Knowledge*, Penguin Publishers, London.

Bernstein, R.J., 1983, *Beyond Objectivism and Relativism*, University of Pennsylvania Press, Pennsylvania.

Boland, R., 1978, The process and product of system design, *Management Science,* 28(9):887-898.

Boland, R., 1979, Control, causality and information system requirements, *Accounting, Organisations and Society,* 4(4):259-272.

Boland, R., 1985, Phenomenology: A preferred approach to research in information systems, in *Research Methods in Information Systems*, E. Mumford, R.A. Hirschheim, G. Fitzgerald, and A.T. Wood-Harper, eds., North-Holland, Amsterdam.

Boland, R., 1987, The in-formation of information systems, in *Critical Issues in Information Systems Research*, R.J. Boland, and R.A. Hirschheim, eds., John Wiley and Sons, New York.

Boland, R., 1991, Information system use as a hermeneutic process, in *Information Systems Research: Contemporary Approaches and Emergent Traditions*, H-E. Nissen, H.K. Klein, and R.A. Hirschheim, eds., North-Holland, Amsterdam.

Bryman, A., 1989, *Research Methods and Organisation Studies*, Unwin Hyman, London.

Burrell, G., and Morgan, G., 1979, *Sociological Paradigms and Organisational Analysis*, Heinemann, London.

Clifford, J., 1988, *The Predicament of Culture: Twentieth-Century Ethnography, Literature and Art*, Harvard University Press, Cambridge, MA.

Clifford, J. and Marcus, G.E., 1986, *Writing Culture: The Poetics and Politics of Ethnography*, University of California Press, Berkeley, CA.

Cohen, A.P., 1985, *The Symbolic Construction of Community*, Ellis Horwood, London.

Davies, L.J., 1991, Researching the organisational culture contexts of Information Systems strategy, in *Information Systems Research: Contemporary Approaches and Emergent Traditions*, H-E. Nissen, H.K. Klein, and R.A. Hirschheim, eds., North-Holland, Amsterdam.

Davies, L.J. and Nielsen, S., 1992, An ethnographic study of configuration management and documentation practices in an Information Technology centre, in *The Impact of Computer Supported Technology on Information Systems Development*, K.E. Kendall, K. Lyytinen, and J. De Gross, eds., Elsevier/North Holland, Amsterdam.

Dietz, J.L.G. and Widdershoven, G.A.M., 1991, Speech acts or communicative action? *Proceedings of the Second European Conference on Computer-Supported Cooperative Work*, Kluwer Academic Publishers, Dordrecht, 235-248.

Dietz, J.L.G. and Widdershoven, G.A.M., 1992, A comparison of the linguistic theories of Searle and Habermas as a basis for communication support systems,' in *Linguistic Instruments in Knowledge Engineering*, R. Van der Reit and R. Meersman, eds., North-Holland, New York.

Evans-Pritchard, E.E., 1950, *Witchcraft, Oracles and Magic among the Azande*, The Clarendon Press, Oxford.

Feldman, M.S. and March, J.G., 1981, Information in organisations as signal and symbol, *Administrative Science Quarterly*, 26(2):171-186.

Forester, J., 1992, Critical ethnography: on field work in an Habermasian way, in *Critical Management Studies*, M. Alvesson, and H. Willmott, eds., Sage Publications, London.

Frost, P.J., Moore, L.F., Louis, M.R., Lundberg, C.C. and Martin, J., eds., 1985, *Organisational Culture*, Sage, Beverly Hills.

Gadamer, H-G., 1976a, *Philosophical Hermeneutics*, University of California Press, California.

Gadamer, H-G., 1976b, The historicity of understanding, in *Critical Sociology, Selected Readings*, P.Connerton, ed., Penguin Books Ltd, Harmondsworth.

Galliers, R.D. and Land, F.F., 1987, Choosing appropriate information systems research methodologies, *Communications of the ACM*, 30(11):900-902.

Galliers, R.D., 1991, Choosing appropriate information systems research methods, in *Information Systems Research: Contemporary Approaches and Emergent Traditions*, H-E. Nissen, H.K. Klein, and R.A. Hirschheim, eds., North-Holland, Amsterdam.

Geertz, C., 1973, *The Interpretation of Cultures*, Basic Books, New York.

Geertz, C., 1983, *Local Knowledge: Further Essays in Interpretive Anthropology*, Basic Books, New York.

Geertz, C., 1988, *Works and Lives: The Anthropologist as Author*, Polity Press, Cambridge.

Giddens, A.., 1984. *The Constitution of Society: Outline of the Theory of Structure*, University of California Press, Berkeley, CA.

Glaser, B.G., and Strauss, A., 1967, *The Discovery of Grounded Theory: Strategies for Qualitative Research*, Aldine Publishing Co, Chicago, IL.

Harvey, L. and Myers, M.D., 1995, Scholarship and practice: the contribution of ethnographic research methods to bridging the gap, *Information Technology and People*, 8(3):13-27.

Hirschheim, R. and Newman, M., 1991, Symbolism and information systems development: myth, metaphor and magic, *Information Systems Research*, 2(1):29-62.

Holzblatt, K. and Beyer, H., 1993, Making customer-centered design work for teams, *Communications of the ACM*, 36(10):93-103.

Hoy, T., 1988, *Praxis, Truth, and Liberation*, University Press of America, Lanham.

Hughes, J.A., Randall, D. and Shapiro, D., 1992, Faltering from ethnography to design, in *CSCW '92: Sharing Perspectives*, ACM Press, New York, 115-123.

Hutchins, E., 1995, *Cognition in the Wild*, MIT Press, Cambridge, MA.

Kahn, J., 1989, Culture: demise or resurrection? *Critique of Anthropology* 9(2):5-25.

Kaplan, B. and Duchon, D., 1988, Combining qualitative and quantitative methods in information systems research: A case study, *MIS Quarterly*, 12(4):571-587.

Kaplan, B. and Maxwell, J.A., 1994, Qualitative research methods for evaluating computer information systems, in *Evaluating Health Care Information Systems: Methods and Applications*, J.G. Anderson, C.E. Aydin and S.J. Jay, eds., Sage, Thousand Oaks, CA.

Klein H.K. and Hirschheim, R., 1983, Issues and approaches to appraising technological change in the office: a consequential perspective, *Office: Technology and People*, 2:15-24.

Klein, H.K. and Myers, M.D., 1995, *The Quality of Interpretive Research in Information Systems*, Department of Management Science and Information Systems Working Paper Series, No. 89, University of Auckland, Auckland.

Kling, R., and Iacono, S., 1989, The institutional character of computerized information systems, *Office: Technology and People,* 5:7-28.

Kuhn, T., 1970, *The Structure of Scientific Revolutions*, University of Chicago Press, Chicago.

Lacity, M.C. and Janson, M.A., 1994, Understanding qualitative data: a framework of text analysis methods, *Journal of Management Information Systems,* 11(2):137-155.

Landry, M. and Banville, C., 1992, A disciplined methodological pluralism for MIS research, *Accounting, Management and Information Technologies*, 2(2):77-97.

Lee, A.S., 1991, Integrating positivist and interpretive approaches to organisational research, *Organisation Science,* 2:342-365.

Lee, A.S., 1994, Electronic mail as a medium for rich communication: an empirical investigation using hermeneutic interpretation, *MIS Quarterly*, 18(2):143-157.

Lee, A.S., Baskerville, R.L. and Davies, L., 1992, A workshop on two techniques for qualitative data analysis: action research and ethnography, in *Proceedings of the Thirteenth International Conference on Information Systems*, 305-306.

Lehtinen, E. and Lyytinen, K., 1986, Action based model of information system, *Information Systems,* 2(4):299-317.

Lewis, I.M., 1985, *Social Anthropology in Perspective*, Cambridge University Press, Cambridge.

Luthans, F. and Davis, T.R.V., 1982, An idiographic approach to organisational behavior research, *Academy of Management Review,* 7(3):380-391.

Marcus, G.E., 1992, *Rereading Cultural Anthropology,* Duke University Press, Durham, NC.

Marcus, G.E. and Fischer, M.M., 1986, *Anthropology as Cultural Critique,* Chicago University Press, Chicago.

Martin, P.Y. and Turner, B.A., 1986, Grounded theory and organisational research, *The Journal of Applied Behavioral Science,* 22(2):141-157.

Miles, M.B. and Huberman, A.M., 1984, *Qualitative Data Analysis: A Sourcebook of New Methods,* Sage Publications, Newbury Park, CA.

Morey, N.C. and Luthans, F., 1984, An emic perspective and ethnoscience methods for organisational research, *Academy of Management Review,* 9(1):27-36.

Myers, M.D., 1987, Independens Long Vanuatu: The Churches and Politics in a Melanesian Nation, Unpublished PhD thesis, University of Auckland.

Myers, M.D., 1994, A disaster for everyone to see: an interpretive analysis of a failed IS project, *Accounting, Management and Information Technologies,* 4(4):185-201.

Myers, M.D., 1995, Dialectical hermeneutics: a theoretical framework for the implementation of information systems, *Information Systems Journal,* 5(1):51-70.

Newman, M. and Robey, D., 1992, A social process model of user-analyst relationships, *MIS Quarterly,* 16:249-266.

Orlikowski, W.J. and Baroudi, J., 1991, Studying information technology in organisations: research approaches and assumptions, *Information Systems Research,* 2(1):1-28.

Orlikowski, W. and Robey, D., 1991, Information technology and the structuring of organizations, *Information Systems Research,* 2(2):143-169.

Pettigrew, A.M., 1985, Contextualist research and the study of organisational change processes, in *Research Methods in Information Systems,* E. Mumford, R. Hirschheim, G. Fitzgerald, and A.T. Wood-Harper, eds., North Holland, Amsterdam.

Poster, M., 1989, *Critical Theory and Poststructuralism,* Cornell University Press, Ithaca.

Poster, M., 1990, *The Mode of Information*, The University of Chicago Press, Chicago.

Preston, A.M., 1991, The 'problem' in and of management information systems, *Accounting, Management and Information Technologies*, 1(1)43-69.

Radnitzky, G., 1970, *Contemporary Schools of Metascience*, Scandinavian University Books, Goteborg.

Randall, D., Hughes, J. and Shapiro, D., 1994, Steps towards a partnership: ethnography and system design, in *Requirements Engineering: Social and Technical Issues*, M. Jirotka and J. Goguen, eds., Academic Press, London.

Rathswohl, E.J., 1991, Applying Don Idhe's phenomenology of instrumentation as a framework for designing research in information science, in *Information Systems Research: Contemporary Approaches and Emergent Traditions*, H-E. Nissen, H.K. Klein and R.A. Hirschheim, eds., North-Holland, Amsterdam.

Ricoeur, P., 1974, *The Conflict of Interpretations: Essays in Hermeneutics*, Northwestern University Press, Evanston.

Ricoeur, P., 1976, Hermeneutics: restoration of meaning or reduction of illusion? In *Critical Sociology, Selected Readings*, P.Connerton, ed., Penguin, Harmondsworth.

Sanday, P.R., 1979, The ethnographic paradigm(s), *Administrative Science Quarterly*, 24(4):527-538.

Searle, J.R., 1979, *Expression and Meaning, Studies in the Theory of Speech Acts*, Cambridge University Press, London.

Scholte, B., 1972, Toward a reflexive and critical anthropology, in *Reinventing Anthropology*, D. Hymes, ed., Random House Inc., New York.

Star, Susan L., 1995, *Cultures of Computing*, Blackwell. Oxford.

Suchman, L., 1987, *Plans and Situated Actions: The Problem of Human-Machine Communication*, Cambridge University Press, Cambridge.

Suchman, L., 1995, Making work visible, *Communications of the ACM*, 38(9):56-64.

Taylor, C., 1976, Hermeneutics and politics, in *Critical Sociology, Selected Readings*, P.Connerton, ed., Penguin Books Ltd, Harmondsworth.

Thompson, J.B., 1981, *Critical Hermeneutics: A Study in the Thought of Paul Ricoeur and Jurgen Habermas*, Cambridge University Press, Cambridge.

Van Maanen, J., 1988, *Tales of the Field: On Writing Ethnography*, University of Chicago Press, Chicago.

Vattimo, G., 1988, Hermeneutics as koine, *Theory, Culture and Society*, 5:2-3.

Visala, S., 1991, Broadening the empirical framework of information systems research, in *Information Systems Research: Contemporary Approaches and Emergent Traditions*, H-E. Nissen, H.K. Klein and R.A. Hirschheim, eds., North-Holland, Amsterdam.

Walsham, G., 1993, *Interpreting Information Systems in Organisations*, Wiley, Chichester.

Walsham, G., 1995a, Interpretive case studies in IS research: nature and method, *European Journal of Information Systems*, 4:74-81.

Walsham, G., 1995b, The emergence of interpretivism in IS research, *Information Systems Research*, 6(4):376-394.

Walsham, G. and Waema, T., 1994, Information Systems strategy and implementation: a case study of a building society, *ACM Transactions on Information Systems*, 12(2):150-173.

Winograd, T., and Flores, F., 1987, *Understanding Computers and Cognition, A New Foundation for Design*, Addison-Wesley Publishing Co. Inc., New York.

Wynn, E., 1979, Office Conversation as an Information Medium, Unpublished PhD Dissertation, University of California, Berkeley.

Wynn, E., 1991, Taking practice seriously, in *Design at Work*, J. Greenbaum, and M. Kyng, eds., Lawrence Erlbaum, New Jersey.

Yates, J. and Orlikowski, W.J., 1992, Genres of organisational communication: a structurational approach to studying communication and media, *Academy of Management Review*, 17(2):299-326.

Yin, R.K., 1989, *Case Study Research, Design and Methods*, Sage Publications, Newbury Park.

Zuboff, S., 1988, *In the Age of the Smart Machine*, Basic Books, New York.

Chapter 10

ORGANISATIONAL SEMIOTICS

Ronald Stamper

10.1 Introduction

Our conventional education teaches us that scientists should write in a depersonalised style which projects the image of objectivity. I reject this stance as misleading, even dishonest. Scientists must take responsibility for their assertions and hypotheses, their observations and how they report them. Depersonalising their reports, removing mention of the responsible agents, expunges the record of who takes responsibility. This educational convention has impeded our attempts to make a scientific study of information systems.

Taught to believe in the necessary objectivity of all science, we persuade ourselves that information and information systems fall into the same pattern as the natural sciences. But, as I aim to persuade you, our new discipline belongs centrally to the social sciences in such a fundamental way that its basic concepts have no existence apart from human attitudes and behaviour.

My own philosophy of information systems was formed while working in industry where computer systems met the high technical standards placed on them but then failed to match our expectations of how they would serve the organisation. Their technical excellence did nothing to compensate for their organisational failure because they only had any value when they succeeded in meeting the needs of people in their work with others to produce results that society values. (This does not count the pleasure derived by the technical people through building the technical system, often the only visible benefit!) In the 1960s technical people simply assumed that installing computers would deliver value as day follows night; sadly the same attitude prevails in most computer departments in industry and universities today.

My journey into organisational semiotics began in the 1960s when commissioned to write a book on designing information

systems. I found myself saying on every other page in footnotes
and parentheses 'In this context, when I use the word 'information'
I mean . . . '; so I gathered all these remarks together in a first
chapter, which turned into Part I, which, at over 350 pages,
appeared in 1973 as *Information in Business and Administrative
Systems* (Stamper 1973) and will reappear soon in an updated form
(see also Nauta, 1992). The quest for a satisfactory understanding
of the concept 'information' set me on the road towards
organisational semiotics, or the understanding of organisations
through their use of signs.

10.2   Why Semiotics? The Sign as a First Primitive Concept

Semiotics, the doctrine of signs (Locke, 1700), has many benefits
for the information systems field, among them, for example, the
relational methods used now in database design, created as a part of
C.S. Peirce's massive corpus of work that forms the foundation of
modern semiotics (Peirce, 1931-1935). Foremost, it allows us to
dispense with 'information' as a basic technical term, and so rid
ourselves of its incomparable vagueness. We cannot build a body
of cumulative scientific knowledge on a vague terminology,
because no one can guarantee that the next idea will not use the
terms in a slightly different and incompatible way. Looking at the
use of 'information' and the attempts to define the term in our
current literature, makes me feel embarrassed to realise that I
belong to a profession so unwilling to exercise self-criticism. Look
at the books on your own shelves for some typical examples (I cite
no authors out of courtesy to colleagues for whom I have great
respect); they nearly all run on the following lines:

- 'Data is the raw material from which information is distilled by
  processing it.'
- 'Information is the meaning that people give to data in some
  context.'
- 'Information is data that are relevant to making decisions.'
- 'Information is what we use to convey knowledge to one
  another.'
- 'Information is the process of creating form or structure.'

The vague metaphors implied by words like 'distilled' and 'convey' suggest a quite useful 'plumbing' model for information. I guarantee that you will find examples where authors base their definitions of 'information', as above, on even vaguer, even more contentious concepts such as 'meaning' and 'decision' and 'knowledge'. Vague words beget vague words; and the use of the verb 'to be' compounds the problem, as I shall explain later.

We can escape from the verbal merry-go-round by doing what the physicists do: relying on primitive concepts (*object* and *event*, in their discipline) which anyone can be taught to understand without recourse to verbal definitions. In our discipline, as counterparts to object and event, we need the notions of *token* and *signal*, the permanent and transitory forms of signs. Anything can function as a sign if it can stand for something else for the people in some community. Take your students into the town and show them endless examples: traffic lights, price tags on goods, people waving to friends, advertisements, car horns, books, a model of the new town hall and so on. The idea of a sign, defined in this 'ostensive' mode puts our other words on a firm foundation relating them to the actions we can perform.

Upon the primitive concept of a sign we can build a truly scientific study of information and information systems. As physicists learn about the properties of physical objects and their behaviour from many different aspects, we need to study the properties of signs. I shall try to sketch, though all too briefly, some of the main branches of semiotics and the aspects of signs with which they deal. As we make a close inspection of the properties of signs, we find that some of them correspond, in precisely definable ways to the various, incompatible notions we have about 'information'. For a scientific treatment of information systems, we must carfully distinguish each precise meaning of 'information' .

Classical semiotics explains how physical tokens must function on three levels to perform successfully as signs: the syntactic, the semantic and pragmatic levels. Embedded within philosophy, semiotics could content itself with these questions respectively about the structure, meaning and use of signs but, in a business situation, as I found myself at the time of writing on this subject, they failed to raise questions about either the cost or the value of information. A brief examination reveals that the costs of information relate strongly to the physical resources used and the efficiency with which they encode the information, while the value of the information always depends on the social effects elicited. Hence, I decided to add to the semiotic framework the physical and empiric levels below the syntactic, semantic and pragmatic, and to place the social level above them all.

10.3   Technical Properties of Signs

Ask anyone to show you some information and they will have to point to something physical: a signal or token which stands for something else. However, at this level we do not care what the sign stands for, we have some basic engineering problems to solve. At the physical level we want to make signals and tokens that have minimum cost, minimum size, use the minimum of energy or material, have maximum robustness and maximum speed of transmission, with other physical properties, depending upon the application. Notice that it seems quite natural to answer the enquiry, 'How much information do you have now?' by saying '10 Gigabytes'. a large number of physical tokens, so that 'information' in this simplest sense just means the quantity of tokens or signals involved. We also say, diagnosing a problem, 'The appearance of that signal on the monitor *means* that a connection exists', thus using ' x means y' in the sense of 'y causes x'. These definitions reflect our concern on the physical level only with such aspects as hardware, energy and materials and their costs.

Once we have the physical means to produce, store and transmit sign-tokens we can concentrate on their *empirical* properties. First of all, we have to create a repertoire of tokens that people can reliably and repeatedly recognise (the paradigm, in de Saussure's (1949) terminology), and the hardware should store and transmit them without deterioration caused by noise or random perturbations. (Incidentally, one often gives the *meaning* of one paradigm or set of codes in terms of another.) This level of empirics concerns only the statistical properties of the paradigm in use, such as: how often do the various tokens accidentally get confused with others, how many of them can a channel carry per second and how to calculate the effective channel capacity. Telecommunications engineers who created this branch of our subject must answer such questions without any concern about the language, the meaning or the purpose of the signal transmitted. At this level, the idea of information translates into the idea of variety, so that messages that have a low frequency of occurrence convey most information and sources which behave in the least predictable way emit the most information, for which Shannon devised the 'entropy' measure of variety (Shannon and Weaver, 1945), a kind of analogue of disorder not unlike the entropy of thermodynamics. So by 'empirical properties' we mean those based on the equivalence of codes and on the observing and counting of relative frequencies of sign-events.

Using physical tokens that behave with empirical reliability we can construct complex signs with the *syntactic* structures which mathematics, logic and software engineering deal with. These disciplines concern themselves with formal structures and how to manipulate them: tasks well suited to machines, especially computers. Computer science concerns the manipulation of electronic sign-tokens; designing records, files, software and databases has nothing intrinsically to do with the contents of the information represented or processed. On this level, we define *meaning* in terms of the equivalence of one lot of sign-structures to another—just the right interpretation for the investigation of form rather than structure; for example, model theory (Tarski, 1935) does this by mapping logical expressions onto set-theoretical structures. One of the several syntactic definitions of information measures sign-tokens relative to the formal language to which they belong, by counting how many other formulas of the language they can exclude from consideration: the more exclusive, the more informative (Carnap and Bar Hillel, 1953 and Bar Hillel, 1964). Syntactic information increases with structure—just the opposite of empiric information which increases with randomness.

If you want to communicate then you must stand on a technical platform with the appropriate physical, empiric and syntactic properties (roughly speaking, the right hardware, communications and software in the most general sense). Improving them can have profound effects on society. For example, science as we know it today could not be practised on the platform of a script technology; monks copying manuscripts in penny numbers multiplied the errors because in most cases they did not really understand the text, and even less so the accompanying diagrams; so the critical examination of theories and methods, on which scientific progress depends, had no chance to proceed until printing made possible the rapid dissemination of exact multiple copies *under the control* of the author, for discussion and constructive criticism. Technology reduced the costs and so improved aspects of quality from which the pay-off appeared on the social level in the form of modern science.

10.4   Social Properties of Signs

Technology has nothing to do with some properties of signs; these depend entirely on human social abilities. For most practical purposes we want to take the technology for granted. When we use the telephone we want to press on with the conversation, making our meanings and intentions clear in order to agree something with the person on the other end; we do not want to fiddle with loose wires, say everything twice because of noise on the line, or have to negotiate complex software. The value of the telephone comes from human conversations which share meanings, change attitudes and make relationships between people. Sadly, our emerging discipline of information systems has yet to learn how to deal with these properties of the information resource. Although at the core of our emerging discipline, they receive less of our attention than the technical properties of information which belong more appropriately to computer science.

Given the ability to form complex signs reliably, we can use them to represent things in the world and the world's complex structures. The *semantic* properties of signs deal with meaning in the special sense of how signs relate to reality, how they represent, designate and signify things. Philosophers have battled for millennia over semantic problems, but while their fight continues, we, acting as engineers, need information with reliable meanings to run organisations or solve problems. In our field we must face these issues and choose one unequivocal philosophical position or another. Of those available, two stand out: the objectivist position, favoured by most information systems professionals and the subjectivist. The objectivist assumes that words, numbers and other signs have fixed meanings which simply map them onto things that exist in an objective reality, independently of everyone. The subjectivists, among whom I count myself, recognise that we can know nothing without involving some agent or agents who create the meanings of signs and maintain them by removing the misunderstandings that arise when signs and actions do not mesh. Objective meaning approximates successfully to subjectivist meaning but only in the special cases of uncontentious, routine work, whereas in all other cases people make meanings and, in doing so they exercise power and we had better know about these meaning-makers to make sense of their information, especially in business, design, the frontiers of science, government and law. In many information systems we cannot take semantics for granted in the objectivist manner, because they play key roles in making and maintaining meanings. In the days of small computer-based information systems, within a single organisation, objectivism did no harm; today, with electronic commerce and other huge global systems that fall under no jurisdiction, or complex systems in ethically sensitive areas of social, health and medical policy, the crude approximation of objectivist semantics does do harm. The popular objectivist position plays straight into the hands of hidden prejudices which subjectivists expose by placing the responsible agents in full view. Subjectivism sounds complex and expensive compared with designing systems from an objectivist position but our experience proves quite the contrary (Ades, 1994). On the semantic level, we see that information systems do not merely report about the world, they actually play a major role in making it.

Incidentally, you may not have noticed an unusual feature of the prose style I have adopted (called 'E-prime' by Borland, R.J., 1974): it makes absolutely no use of the verb 'to be' (the words in quotes I only *mention*). Doing this I intend to underline two points: first that English and most European languages have the objectivist position built into them by virtue of the verb 'to be' which allows us to say 'x is y' (for example: 'British beef is safe' the statement from every minister during 1996) without mentioning who should take responsibility for the connection (not, for example: 'I believe that British beef is safe because we ministers together with all the scientific experts and our families confidently eat it', which would have been false!); and second that we can say anything of practical import without using the dreaded verb provided that we talk in terms of some agent doing something. In fact I always recommend my students of requirements engineering to use this style because it results in better analysis and design (Borland, K.L.R., 1974). Hirschheim, Klein and Lyytinen (1995) label these two semantic positions 'fact-based' and 'rule-based' and they show how they lead to quite different ways of specifying information requirements. One can use the formal equivalent of this no-verb-to-be discipline in a formal specification language (Stamper, 1985 and 1996). I must, before leaving this topic, apologise for the apparent egocentricity that this style forces upon the writer; my teachers always deplored the use of the first person (especially the singular) in scientific reports but this style compels one to accept responsibility for making observations and proposing hypotheses and espousing theories—not a bad discipline really, even in the scientific world, but highly desirable in practical affairs of the kind that have ethical implications. In the rule-based methods, responsibility plays much the same role as truth plays in the fact-based methods.

The act of uttering a technically well-formed sign enables the making of a propositional act, by adding meaning, which leads, in turn, to the possibility of an illocutionary speech act when an agent adds an intention to the sign. For example, a pirate's parrot makes a squawk; the English-speaking community ensures that its members interpret the parrot's utterance as meaning 'He's a silly old fool.' and Captain Blood nods in the direction of the 'He' intended, thus signalling his wish to assert this sentence about him. If his intention succeeds, you will change your attitude towards the person referred to. These happenings we investigate as the *pragmatic* aspects of the signs. These illocutionary acts, when deliberately addressed (a commonly overlooked additional speech act) to a listener, lead to the recipient performing a perlocutionary act by making a change of attitude towards the subject of the message. Chains of illocutions and perlocutions form conversations between people, and conversations lead to social effects. (For the application of these ideas to information systems see Lehtinen and Lyytinen, 1986.)

The social effects of the conversations determine the value of the information exchanged. By studying information without concern for the *social level* of semiotic properties we prevent ourselves from investigating its value. Our discipline needs this perspective thus raising the question of how to deal with the social level precisely enough for our purposes: classical social theories depend too much on intellectual hand-waving and use no formal tools. We can introduce far more precision into our treatment of the social level by using the notions of norms and attitudes, as explained below. Meanwhile, consider the analogy between kinetic and potential energy, on the one hand, and signs and attitudes on the other. Physics describes light (kinetic energy) and accounts for some of its phenomenona by describing its absorbtion by electrons orbiting the nuclei of atoms (potential energy) before re-emission as light. Similarly, information has its social effects by altering human dispositions to act (their norms and attitudes) which then, at some later time, leads to people producing other information. Our evaluative norms also determine the value of information both directly and through its effects, and society determines those norms.

10.5   The Semiotic Framework

To summarise the above, let me put it into what I call the Semiotic Framework, in Figure 10.1. Notice that signs on every level depend for the correct formation of signs on the levels below and leave open a range of choices for using the signs on the level above. To a great extent, we can study the properties on each level independently of the other levels—a valuable way of decomposing complex problems into more manageable components. The Semiotic Framework serves as a basic checklist for every (I do mean every) information system problem: if the system does not function correctly on every level, it will fail to deliver value, so always check that your analysis has covered the whole of the Semiotic Framework (see Liu, 1993).

Many of our key concepts such as information, meaning and so on have quite different meanings on each of the semiotic levels. I tried to illustrate this in a few cases: information as numbers of physical tokens, entropy as the empiric measure, logical precision on the syntactic level; other measures based on subjective probabilities, semantic structure and social impact could lead to many other exact measures. Cause and effect provide physical meaning; encodings supply empiric meanings and translations syntactic meanings; semantics deals with the core meaning of meaning, the real-world signification of signs; pragmatic meaning corresponds to intention and social meaning to attitudes. You might try to find precise definitions for other information-related concepts such as relevance, error, ambiguity and so on. The muddled thinking that characterises so much work in information systems

stems, in my opinion, from the failure to distinguish these quite different sets of sign-properties resulting in the kinds of hand-waving definitions cited above.

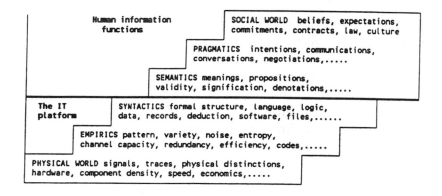

FIGURE 10.1 *The semiotic framework*

10.6   Organisations as Information Systems: The Norm as a Second Primitive Concept

Organisational semiotics links two primitive concepts—the sign and the norm—as closely as chicken and egg. Whenever we find people behaving in an organised way, they tend to behave with certain regularities which we call norms. Every norm has this structure:

IF condition THEN subject attitude consequent

Signs provide the knowledge about a *condition* which, if met, should lead the *subject* of that norm (some agent) to adopt an attitude towards some *consequent* (a sign for a proposition or a reference to something). The attitude represents variously a disposition:

1. to believe	e.g.	know, expect, imagine, . . .
2. to value	e.g.	like, deplore, hope for, . . .
3. to act	e.g.	be obliged to, be permitted to, be forbidden to, . . .
4. to perceive	e.g.	acknowledge, deem, recognise, . . .

Examples of each of these will help:

1. IF one throws an object up THEN one expects that it will fall down.
2. IF a person spits in public THEN everyone deplores that behaviour.
3. IF one accepts a present THEN one is obliged to say 'Thank you.'
4. IF a work is published in a signatory state THEN such states recognise a copyright in that work.

When a norm applies and the agent reacts as it says, then the consequence sooner or later leads to other signs, either directly, as in the third case, or because one observes the action in the first case, or because people act on the basis of the value judgement or the percept in the second and fourth cases. Without norms, at least those of our culture, we would have no signs and without signs the norms that constitute our social reality would not function or come into existence—chicken and egg, indeed!

Just as we now understand the structure and properties of matter by knowing its molecular structure, so we shall begin to understand the structure and functioning of organisations by finding out about their norm structures. We can represent norms precisely and doing so leads to the definition of information requirements as their logical consequence. In this manner, we have built systems of high quality at a lower than usual cost and to a higher quality than possible using standards methods, but also with the need for only a tenth of the usual documentation (Liu *et al.,* 1994). So organisational semiotics can deliver practical results.

In addition, norms fall into discrete and precise classes depending on the kinds of conditions, agents, attitudes and consequents involved, thus allowing us to characterise organisations with a broad brush but, nevertheless, with more precision than customary in classical organisational theory. For example, even the single classification introduced above into cognitive, behavioural, evaluative and perceptual norms characterises some of the differences between types of organisations. Thus, bureaucracies in government and financial services exists by virtue of their behavioural norms, with little need for any special cognitive, evaluative or perceptual norms beyond those of the general population; on the other hand, as one moves over the spectrum of manufacturing firms from routine mass production to innovative high-tech, one finds that they depend on increasing proportions of cognitive norms, and where a firm tries to move from a routine to an innovative style, it must substitute for the old behavioural norms, the cognitive norms of technical knowledge; professional organisations such as hospitals and universities exist largely to deliver the benefits of cognitive norms within a powerful framework of evaluative norms monitored by outside professional institutions. Given the numerous other precise taxonomies, we can use the mix of norms in an organisation to characterise it with some precision in ways that help us to select policies, for example, on how to introduce change in general or new technologies, in particular.

In the fashionable world of knowledge management, a problem that seems to exercise many minds today, how to define 'knowledge', finds a simple and thorough resolution using the concept of norms. I can find no other kinds of knowledge than we express either in norms or attitudes. The norms cover all the knowledge of a universal kind: how the parts of the world fit together and function (cognitive), how to act in different circumstances (behavioural), how to distinguish the good from the bad and right from wrong (evaluative), and what we find in our physical and social worlds (perceptual norms). Knowledge of a particular kind consists of attitudes to particular things and comprises our beliefs, obligations, value-judgements and actual perceptions. I find people offering to advise companies on knowledge management who cannot provide a clear definition of this precious resource. Unfortunately the gurus who play too great a role in our emerging discipline of information systems use terms such as 'knowledge' more for rhetorical effect than to denote anything precisely.

10.7   A Hard View of Soft Systems

Organisational semiotics contributes to our repertoire of methods for solving those so-called 'soft' problems, the ill-defined problems that require practical rather than theoretical solutions which we even find difficult to put into words. Currently we have to adopt either the narrowly technical view of information systems with its objectivist philosophy, impatience with human problems and eagerness to push each new technology into the organisation, or we can use one of the various methods for analysing ill-structured problems which, though helpful, cannot deliver a precise requirements specification dictating what technology we should pull into the organisation to meet its needs. We correctly continue to talk of an organisation in which we have automated some tasks as an organisation. The dual concept applies: every technical system can only function in the long term as part of an organisation, because people manage it, must monitor its performance, make repairs, deal with standby facilities, decide when to run it or not, and so on; and hence every machine should be regarded as no more than the automated part of a larger organisation. Organisational semiotics can begin, not only to fill the ground between the poles of the technical and the social, but to show that we can subsume the technical within the social.

On the basis of the norm-sign analysis outlined above my colleagues and I have evolved methods (Stamper, 1994) for requirements engineering. We have subjected them to some years of testing on such a wide range of problems that they have proved their effectiveness and adaptability. They comprise three main parts: problem articulation, semantic analysis and norm analysis. Semantic analysis deals with the identification of the signs people use to deal with the problem and how they relate those signs to actions; norm analysis identifies how to specify the solution in terms of the norms to follow; problem articulation starts from a vague or soft problem and finds the words and other signs, as well as exploring the cultural and physical constraints within which to frame the norms. This kind of soft systems method, while supporting lateral thinking during the analysis process, also delivers comparatively precise results which lead, if so desired, to technical solutions.

PAM, problem articulation methods (Stamper, 1994; Kolkman, 1993), consist of semiotic analysis as a diagnostic tool, stakeholder analysis to find the actors and their relationships, valuation framing to examine the subcultures involved, collateral analysis which relates the problem to the socio-technical infrastructure, contention manager to deal with conflicts among those involved, organisational morphology to structure the norms within a unit system, and unit system analysis to fill in the details of the components of the solution. Each technique provides the user with structured support on how to proceed at any point but support of such universality that it does not prejudice the outcome.

To illustrate PAM, I shall explain the core idea behind Organisational Morphology because it shows how to use the norm-sign idea and it also illustrates the universality which we have aimed at in formulating the various PAM techniques and the need to test them against as diverse a range of problems as possible. Start from this fundamental observation: every physical or organisational human artifact we can use without any explicit norms once we have had enough practice, and often we have evolved them without ever making an explicit design. Should we want to make an explicit design, we can minimally specify how to perform the substantive tasks which I define as all those except norms about communicating between the subjects or about controlling that they obey their norms. If we give a complex task to a small team they can do it in this kind of informal fashion where we can safely assume that everyone knows or can easily find out all the information relevant to their norms, and that everyone will act according to the relevant norms and everyone knows of this mutual openness and trust and can safely act on it. Then, when the task grows too large for the intimate team, we can introduce norms about explicitly communicating some few things that the relevant team members would not otherwise easily learn about; and we can also lay down norms to provide rewards and sanctions to induce conformity to the substantive norms where we suspect laxity or opportunism might cause the system to fail. These refinements apply recursively to produce norms about messages, messages about messages, controls over message passing, control over controls and messages about controls, . . . messages about the control of messages about control of controls. . . (as an example of the last consider: after one month making a request (message) to check (control) that the report (message) about auditing (control) the application of the expense limit rules (control). I leave my readers the easy task of constructing more illustrations on these lines.

This morphology of norms applies to *every* kind of organisation or technical device, hence it has the desired universality and it also leads us to discover the necessary signs and norms. Moreover, as it make no assumption about how to implement the norms, we can either build them into an automated system or we can, through training, introduce many into the informal culture. Most information systems methods (wrongly called methodologies) lead the organisations using them to increase the levels of formality and automation whereas MEASUR can just as easily help one to reduce bureaucracy and focus technical solutions on the most relevant tasks by showing where to adjust the culture for a better result.

10.8   The Diversity of Organisational Semiotics

I have introduced organisational semiotics by telling you about the MEASUR methods which my colleagues and I have created. But I do not want you to assume that no other approach to the subject exists. On the contrary, this new way of thinking about organisations has diversity as its most exciting feature. The information systems researcher should look at the work of the authors cited here and those cited by them, but especially useful should be the bibliography in Andersen *et al.,* 1996, resulting from the Informatics and Semiotics Workshop at Schloss Dagstuhl. There they will find several totally different approaches derived from two quite different kinds of functional linguistics, from cybernetics, from speech act theory, from semantics, from psychology, from the philosophy of ethics and law, and so on. Organisational semiotics draws on many established subjects and in doing so draws their relevant aspects together into a structure of greater rigour than we have so far devised for our emerging discipline of information systems.

Anyone interested in this subject should access the working papers on *http://www.uow.edu.au/commerce/buss/sysco.html* and contribute their own work.

References

Ades, Y., 1994, System quality using MEASUR: a comparison of two systems, *EMIR working paper*, University of Twente, Enschede.

Andersen, P.B., 1990, A theory of computer semiotics, in *Semiotic Approaches to Construction and Assessment of Computer Systems*, Cambridge University Press, Cambridge.

Andersen, P.B., Nadin, M. and Nake, F., 1996, *Informatics and Semiotics,* IBFI-Schloss Dagstuhl, Universität Saarlandes, Saarbrüken, Germany

Bar-Hillel, Y., 1964, *Language and Information: Selected Essays on their Theory And Application,* Addison-Wesley, Reading Mass.

Borland, D., 1974, The language of e-prime in *Coping with Increasing Complexity*, D. Washburn and D. Smith, eds., Gordon Breach, New York and London.

Borland, K.L.R. 1974, Coping with semantic problems in system development, in *Coping with Increasing Complexity*, D. Washburn and D. Smith, eds., Gordon Breach, New York and London.

Carnap, R. and Bar-Hillel, Y., 1953, Semantic information, *British Journal for the Philosophy of Science*, 4:147-157.

Hirschheim, R., Klein H.K. and Lyytinen K., 1995, *Information Systems Development and Data Modelling: Conceptual and Philosophical Foundations*, The University Press, Cambridge.

Kolkman, M., 1993, *Problem articulation methodology*, PhD Thesis, University of Twente, Enschede.

Lehtinen, E. and Lyytinen, K., 1986, An action based model of information systems, *Information Systems*, 13(4):299-318.

Locke, J., 1700, *Essay on human understanding*, Dover, New York, (1959).

Liu, K., 1993, *Semiotics applied to information systems development*, PhD Thesis, University of Twente, Enschede.

Liu, K., Yasser A. and Stamper, R., 1994, Simplicity, uniformity and quality - the role of semantic analysis in systems development, in *Managing Quality Systems*, Ross *et al.* eds., Computational Mechanics Publications, Southampton.

Nauta, D., 1972, *The Meaning of Information*, Mouton, The Hague.

Peirce, C.S., 1931-35, *Collected Papers, 6 Vols.* C. Hartshorne and P. Weiss, eds., Harvard University Press, Cambridge, Mass.

Saussure, F. de, 1949, *Cours de Linguistique Général*, Paris

Shannon C. and Weaver, W., 1949, *The Mathematical Theory of Communication*, University of Illinois Press, Urbana.

Stamper, R., 1973, *Information in Business and Administrative Systems*, Batsford, London and Wiley, New York. (2nd edition Basil Blackwell, Oxford, forthcoming).

Stamper, R., 1984, Collateral systems, eneral sub-systems, systems metrics, and assessment schedule for the comparison of requirements analysis methods, in *Criteria for Comparing Systems Requirements*, D. Law and R.K. Stamper, eds., GMD Bonn and NCC Manchester.

Stamper, R.K., 1994, Social norms in requirements analysis - an outline of MEASUR, in *Requirements Engineering: Technical and Social Aspects*, M. Jirotka and J. Goguen, eds., Academic Press, New York, 107-139.

Stamper, R.K., 1996, Signs, information, norms and systems, in *Signs at Work*, B. Holmqvist and P.B. Andersen eds., De Gruyter, Berlin.

Tarski, A. 1935, Concept of truth in formalized languages, in *Logic, Semantics and Mathematics*, A. Tarski ed., Oxford University Press, Oxford, 152-278.

PART 3: PRACTICE AND EDUCATION

Paul McGolpin and **John Ward** differentiate between data processing, management information systems and strategic information systems (SIS). They point out that strategic information systems emerged in the 1970s and 1980s and although there are similarities with data processing and management information systems it is the impact from business and organisations that seem to differentiate them. Strategic information systems are used to change how businesses conduct their business and to help an organisational management to gain competitive advantage. McGolpin and Ward describe their research, which set out to investigate the reasons for success and failure in SIS. The research provides a framework for understanding the issues affecting success and it attempts to determine the degree of success. Their research investigates the implementation of SIS and provides some valuable lessons about the role of the Chief Executive Officer in the enterprise, and about the contextual environment in defining the success and for the planning method and planning approach adopted. The authors describe a tool for the analysis and examination of complex models (NETMAP) which they suggest provides the researcher with a greater flexibility in analysing the research data. The chapter provides the reader with some useful insights into organisational IS practice and is a contribution to IS research.

Brent Work's chapter begins by raising the question whether an information systems curriculum is really necessary. Work points out that an official curriculum invariably means standardisation and narrowing of perspectives, and may even eliminate some stimulating ideas and perhaps marginalise the people who generate them. Work raises the Kuhnian argument that a standard curriculum guides the process of homogenisation that eventually results in the lack of communication between disciplines. The answer to the question why the IS community seems to want an official curriculum is, Work proposes, to ensure quality. Moreover, an agreed discipline, he continues, is crucial for an academic career. Work makes the contention that without standards there is no discipline and without discipline an academic cannot progress. However, the real situation is that IS is still a shared interest spread across a variety of departments which, Work suggests, is because IS as a subject has yet to coalesce as a discipline. He concludes that if we wish to stake our claim among other academic communities we must continue to seek consensus on the curriculum as one means of strengthening our sense of identity. He argues that the creation of IS as a discipline is not the ultimate aim but it is because of the distinctive view of technology which the IS community seems to have. Work argues for a revival of a liberal education in which the interconnectedness of all areas of learning is prime rather than a concentration upon interdisciplinary which re-enforces the artificiality of the modern dimensions of educational models. The chapter is controversial and because it is it raises many issues about a IS education which should be considered before we plunge headlong into short-term curriculum design.

Chapter 11

FACTORS INFLUENCING THE SUCCESS OF STRATEGIC INFORMATION SYSTEMS

Paul McGolpin and John Ward

11.1 Introduction

A number of writers (e.g. Galliers and Somogyi, 1987; Wiseman, 1985; and Ward and Griffiths. 1996) have described the evolution of technology-based information systems (IS/IT) in terms of three eras or stages. The first two, probably best described as the 'Data Processing Era' and the 'Management Information Systems Era', had been recognised earlier by Nolan (1979) but the third era—the 'Strategic Information Systems Era' was considered to have emerged in the late 1970s and early 1980s.

Most authors agree that what initiated each era was a new purpose or objective for investment in IS/IT. The essence of the Data Processing (DP) era, which commenced in earnest in the 1960s was the use of technology to improve operational efficiency by automating information based processes. This implies not changing what is done, but how it is done. The Management Information Systems (MIS) era emerged during the 1970s and new investments were made with the objective of increasing management effectiveness by satisfying their information needs. While both are aimed at improving the overall performance of the organisation and hence its competitiveness this would be achieved indirectly by improving operational *efficiency* and management *effectiveness*. Of course both of these are still important objectives of IS/IT applications and as the technology evolves there is ever more scope to deliver benefits from DP and MIS investments, i.e. the eras are ongoing.

The argument for the emergence of the SIS era was based on evidence, from a number of well-documented examples, that some organisations were using IS/IT to change how they conducted their business with the direct intent of gaining a competitive advantage. Examples of such achievements by American Airlines, American Hospital Supplies and Thomson's Holidays and others are well known. While some recent researchers (e.g. Kettinger *et al.*, 1995) have questioned the degree to which these systems delivered sustained advantages, there is no doubt that initially at least they had significant impact on the nature of competition in each industry.

As Wiseman (1985) points out, strategic information systems are often not intrinsically different from other DP and MIS applications, it is their impact on the business and organisation that distinguishes them. Synthesising the views of a number of authors, including most recently Neumann (1994), a suitable definition of Strategic Information Systems was arrived at for the purposes of the research described in this chapter:

> Strategic Information Systems are applications of IT which have a significant impact on the organisation's competitive strategy by changing the nature and/or conduct of its business.

This definition reflects both a particular intent and a recognition that the application will not merely improve current business practices but will change them. While every organisation in the 1990s could almost certainly identify SIS opportunities that satisfy this definition, it does not mean that SIS is an entirely recent phenomenon. In the book by Caminer *et al.* (1996) describing the history of one of the earliest computers—LEO (Lyons Electronic Office)—the application of new computer technology to the Lyons Teashops Distribution system bore most of the hallmarks of a strategic information system—in 1954!

The research described here is based on a detailed study of eleven more recent examples of SIS, and examines the possible reasons for the relative success or failure of each. It builds on the work of previous researchers who identified many of the potential causes. The approach taken here is more holistic than previous work in terms of its consideration of the whole application life cycle and the range of process and contextual factors included to fit the definition of Strategic Information Systems above.

11.2   An Overview of the Research

11.2.1 Research Objectives

There is little research that explicitly addresses the specific factors affecting success with strategic information systems. There is also little research that examines the issues by considering the full range of factors across the complete application life cycle. The lack of an holistic approach to the analysis of the factors appears to be an important gap in the existing body of knowledge.

This research, therefore, took a holistic perspective in the examination of organisations' practical experiences with strategic information systems. It took into account the traditional literature on the subject and also the newer aspects that are now appearing: benefit management and the context issues. The key objectives of the research were:

1. to develop a framework for understanding the issues affecting the degree of success with strategic information systems;
2. to identify those particular factors that determine the degree of success with strategic information systems.

The specific questions, underpinning the research objectives, focus on the factors that explain the degree of success. However, the research was intended to provide a greater understanding of the underlying patterns and relationships across the application life cycle. It also examined the particular influence of the context within which strategic systems are identified and implemented, compared with the more traditional life cycle aspects, such as planning, evaluation and implementation factors.

The essential questions that the research aimed to answer were:

1. Is it possible to identify the main factors that explain the degree of success with strategic information systems and if so what are they?
2. To what extent are contextual factors important in explaining the degree of success with strategic information systems?
3. Are any combinations of factors, across the life cycle, particularly significant in explaining the degree of success with strategic information systems?

11.2.2 Research Models

In order to address these questions two basic research models were used to structure the approach. The first is a basic life cycle process model of an application which is relevant to all types of IS development. It consists of four phases—planning, evaluation, implementation and benefit realisation as shown in Figure 11.1.

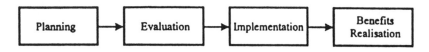

FIGURE 11.1 *Application process life cycle model*

The first three of these phases are recognised in most systems development methodologies and in the literature. They can be defined as:

1. *Planning*—the approach taken to IS/IT planning within which the need or opportunity for investing in a Strategic Information System is identified.
2. *Evaluation*—the way in which the investment is justified and the basis on which a decision is made to proceed to implementation.
3. *Implementation*—the means by which the organisation delivers the technical and business components of the application to match the requirements.
4. *Benefit Realisation*—is perhaps less well understood as part of the life cycle model, but its importance has emerged recently in the literature and was confirmed by early field work in this research. While benefits can only in practice be realised on completion of implementation, activities, which are perhaps best described as Benefit Management Processes (Ward and Griffiths, 1996) need to be instigated earlier in the life cycle if all the potential benefits are to be identified and realised.

Given the definition of SIS in terms of strategic impact and business change a process model is insufficient to explain the various dimensions from which factors affecting success arise. A well established structure defined by Pettigrew and Whipp (1991) to understand the complexity of strategic change was used to develop a more comprehensive view of the issues and possible interactions.

Figure 11.2 illustrates Pettigrew and Whipp's model for the implementation of corporate strategies. They examined a number of UK based organisations and reviewed their competitive performance in relation to their ability to adapt to major changes in their business environment. The framework describes the main forces which impact overall organisational success in major change initiated strategies. They argue that there are three essential forces impacting the nature of strategic change for organisations. These are defined as *context, content* and *process.*

Process is defined as a set of phases involved in identifying and implementing business strategy. *Content* is comprised of the set of choices and assessments which have been made by management and lead to goals and objectives. *Context* is the social, political and organisational environment within which strategy is identified and implemented.

The basic argument is that the ability of an organisation to compete relies on two key qualities:

1. The capacity of the firm to identify and understand the competitive forces in play and how they change over time, linked to
2. The competence of the firm to mobilise and manage the resources necessary for the chosen competitive response to be successful.

If these are the general tenets by which organisations are to be successful in the 1990s then the same argument and logic could be applied to the implementation of strategic information systems. The model can therefore be usefully applied to the identification and implementation of strategic information systems, and provide a framework upon which to base the research. Applying the model to the SIS environment, the following statements can be made:

1. *Content*—can be considered as the range of IS/IT-based opportunities and choices made by the organisation in order to deliver their corporate strategies. In terms of this research,

content refers to the strategic information systems being examined.

2. *Process*—can be interpreted as the main processes an organisation adopts in order to identify and implement a strategic information system, i.e. as the four phase process model described above.

3. *Context*—refers to the organisational, social and political issues within which the strategic information systems are identified and implemented.

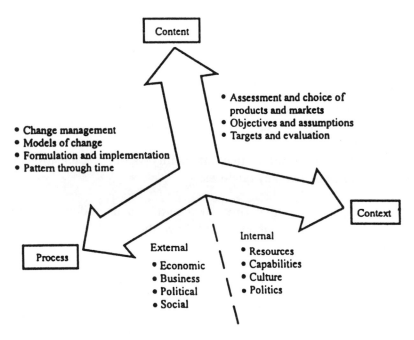

FIGURE 11.2 *Understanding strategic change: three essential dimensions*

A model that incorporates many of the essential characteristics of strategic information systems is provided by Venkatraman (1994). The model (see Figure 11.3) identifies five types of application. The application types increase in terms of the amount of business change required in order to deliver the expected benefits, from applications which primarily focus on the automation and integration of well-defined business processes (levels 1 and 2) to applications which enable major business changes to be implemented and which can change the scope and nature of the business (levels 3, 4 and 5).

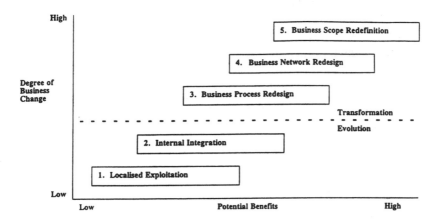

FIGURE 11.3 *The relationship between the benefits of IS investments and the degree of business change needed to realise them* (Venkatramen, 1994, with permission of the Sloan Management Review)

The essential point of the model is that applications types 3, 4 and 5 require significant changes in the business processes of the organisation and can have a significant strategic impact. In this way the model provides a useful method for classifying strategic information systems into three types:

- *Level three*: Business process redesign. This level involves the reconfiguration of the business using IS/IT as a central lever. The business process itself is redesigned to exploit available IS/IT capabilities. Level 3 applications provide major opportunities for organisations willing to rethink the core characteristics of their main business processes. There may be high costs and risks, and IS/IT may be a small part of the overall business solution.

- *Level four*: Business network redesign applications are concerned with redesigning the nature of the exchanges between participants in a business network. The concept is similar to level 3 but with the difference that level 4 applies externally, between organisations. In this context the word network means not just an electronic network, but also an organisation's business relationships with its customers and suppliers.
- *Level five*: Business scope redefinition applications of IS/IT are concerned with using IS/IT to extend or enlarge the scope of a business by allowing the organisation to enter new markets and/or developing new products or services.

Each of the case study applications selected for study satisfied the criteria defined by one or more of levels 3, 4 or 5. In combination these three models were used as a basis for constructing the research approach and analysing previous literature.

11.2.3 Definition of 'Success'

Given the objectives of the research it is obviously crucial to define explicitly what is meant by 'the degree of success'! The measure of success defined for this work was based on obtaining an agreed senior management view of the success, based on their perceptions and documented evidence of *the extent to which the expected benefits were realised.* 'Expected benefits' means those benefits which were used to justify the investment.

Earl (1993), in examining senior management views of success with specific IS/IT planning approaches, categorised perceptions into four categories: high success, success, moderate success and unsuccess. These categories were adopted in this research and are defined in terms of the degree of benefits delivered:

1. *High success:* The senior management view is that the strategic information system delivered more than the expected benefits.

2. *Success:* The senior management view is that the strategic information system delivered the expected benefits.
3. *Moderate success:* The senior management view is that some benefits were delivered but this fell short of the full set of expected benefits.
4. *Unsuccess:* The senior management view is that the majority of the expected benefits were not delivered, or no benefits were delivered.

By requiring an organisation to define their perception of success in terms of the degree of the delivery of the expected benefits, and also by requiring the organisation to reach an agreed view of the degree of success, this approach addresses a number of criticisms in the literature.

1. It overcomes the criticisms of the usual surrogate measures of success which tend to be based on technical factors, the extent to which a system is used, or user satisfaction with the system.
2. It is related to benefit delivery and hence to business impact, due to the nature of the benefits from strategic information systems.
3. It is based on the agreed perceptions of the senior management who are the main stakeholders in the strategic success of an organisation.

11.2.4 Research Approach

The research was carried out between 1993 and 1995 and involved five stages: (in practice stages 1-2 were conducted in parallel).

1. An analysis of previous research and associated literature to elicit factors which are deemed to affect the degree of success in information systems investments, across any of the stages of the application life cycle.
2. Some initial field work in 11 organisations (not the same organisations involved later in the case studies) to verify how readily the factors could be recognised in real situations and develop a comprehensive and structured approach to identifying the presence/absence of a factor and data describing the factor. Another objective of the phase was to determine whether any

other apparently relevant factors existed, in addition to those identified by previous research.

3. An initial survey was carried out using a simple questionnaire to identify companies who had recently implemented SIS in the various categories defined by Venkatraman (1994). From, the respondents to the survey 11 potential case studies for more detailed analysis were identified.

4. In each of the case study companies three senior executives were interviewed using a structured question set to identify how successful the application was and to elicit information about the factors identified. Project documentation was also studied to obtain more information and match against interviewees responses. The case notes were written up and sent to the interviewees to confirm they were accurate.

5. The data was analysed quantitatively, using conventional statistical techniques and qualitatively, using pattern matching software (NETMAP), to determine whether/which factors could be demonstrated to be significant across the range of degrees of success.

Given that nearly 50 factors were identified, each of which could have a range of values/attributes, both numerical and descriptive and 11 case studies were involved, there is no space in this chapter to describe the factor attribute analysis in detail.

The discussion below provides more depth about each stage and identifies the key findings throughout the stages, and discusses in detail all aspects of the factors which were shown to be significant.

11.3 The Search

The objective of the first two stages of the work—literature analysis and initial field work—was to develop a set of factors which might prove significant in determining the relative success of SIS. There proved to be a wealth of literature, much of it based on empirical work, about each of the first three stages of the application life cycle—planning, evaluation and implementation. Much of the previous work refers to IS in general, but more recently some was of specific relevance to what are defined here as *strategic* IS.

TABLE 11.1: *Planning factor definitions, suggested options*

FACTOR	SUGGESTED OPTIONS	FACTOR DEFINITION
1. Emphasis/ Objective	• Solving a business problem • Solving a technology problem • IS/IT business alignment • Investment prioritisation • Resource allocation	*The main reason for undertaking the planning process*
2. Scope	• Organisation wide • Divisional • Business unit • Departmental	*The level in the organisation at which the planning process took place*
3. Initiator	• Chief executive • Divisional director • IS/IT director—IS/IT function • Departmental manager	*The individual or part of the organisation responsible for beginning the planning process*
4. Detail	• A business problem • Technology problem • Applications/package selection • List of candidate projects	*The degree of integration between the IS/IT plan and the business plans*
5. Techniques	• Strategic analysis • Technology-based planning • External consultants • Tailored approaches • None	*The tools / models / frameworks which were used in order to identify the SIS*
6. Method	• Cross-functional teams • Business plan reviews • IS/IT teams	*The main approach to developing the IS/IT strategic plan*
7/8. Involvement	• High • Medium • Low	*The degree to which the business and the IS/IT function were involved in the planning process*
9. Champion	• Yes • No	*The existence of a senior management representative who acted as the champion of the planning process*
10. Output	• A defined business project • A defined technology project • Prioritised IS/IT investment • A list of candidate opportunities	*The main deliverable of the planning process*
11. Normal Approach	• Organisational • Business led *(as per* • Method driven *Earl 1993)* • Administrative • Technology led	*Which of the five classifications of planning method is the norm in the organisation*
12. This Approach	• Organisational • Business led • Method driven • Administrative • Technology led	*Which of the five classifications of planning method was adopted for the planning approach which led to the identification of the SIS*

Most of the previous research focused on one of the stages, and almost none considered the overall application life cycle—confirming the potential value of this work. It is impossible here to review the relevant literature and the analysis/synthesis which led to the derivation of the factors listed in Tables 11.1 to 11.3. However, some of the key literature is referred to in the context of the conclusions drawn from this work. During the field work, with companies known to have experience implementing SIS, these factors were examined in terms of their relevance to that experience.

With regard to the benefit realisation stage there was little previous research. However, in the field work issues associated with benefit realisation were identified by the participants as probably more important than many of the others. When asked to identify the top issues from the literature they felt affected success the top three were:

1. Benefit Management (i.e. a Benefit Realisation issue)
2. IS/IT Credibility (a Contextual issue)
3. Over emphasis on Financial Justification (an Evaluation issue)

From a closer examination of the first of these, three particular aspects of Benefit Management emerged as appearing to be particularly critical in many organisations

a)   Scoping the benefits
b)   Managing delivery
c)   Convincing top Management

Running concurrently with this work, another programme, sponsored by a consortium of large companies, was researching the topic of 'IT Benefit Management'. That work was developing and evaluating new techniques, processes and practices to improve the identification, validation, measurement and delivery of business benefits from all types of IS investments. The results from that research, based on an assessment of benefit management effectiveness in 10 major projects, were used to develop a set of factors and associated attributes relevant to benefit realisation. (see Table 11.4).

TABLE 11.2: *Evaluation factor definitions, suggested options*

FACTOR	SUGGESTED OPTIONS	FACTOR DEFINITION
13. Emphasis	• Purely financial • Purely strategic • Strategic and financial • Financial and some strategic	*The degree to which the focus of evaluation was on 'hard' benefits and 'strategic' benefits*
14. Range	• Financial • Financial/strategic • Strategic/financial • Strategic	*The range of benefits included in the evaluation and justification process.*
15. Detail	• Low • Medium • High	*To what level of detail were the benefits examined using a well understood evaluation approach*
16. Level	• Senior executive • Business unit • IS/IT function • Other	*The level in the organisation at which evaluation and justification took place*
17. Owner	• Senior executive • Business unit • IS/IT function • Other (e.g. finance/audit)	*The individual or part of the organisation responsible for the evaluation and justification process*
18. Stage	• Planning • Evaluation • Implementation • Continuously	*The stage in the life cycle at which evaluation and justification took place*
19. Techniques	• None • Payback • C.B.A. • D.C.F. • R.O.I. • Other	*The techniques which were employed in the evaluation and justification process*
20. Intangibles	• Fully measured • Listed • Ignored	*How any intangible benefits were dealt with*
21/22 Involvement	• High • Medium • Low	*The extent to which the business and (22) IS/IT functions were involved in the process*
23. Normal Approach	• Yes • No	*Was the usual approach to evaluating and justifying investments employed for the SIS*

TABLE 11.3: *Implementation factor definitions, suggested options*

FACTOR	SUGGESTED OPTIONS	FACTOR DEFINITION
24. Organisation	• Investment programme • Traditional IS/IT project	*Was the project organised along traditional IS/IT project lines or was consideration given to the delivery of the business change aspects of the overall solution*
25. IS/IT Role	• Ownership of the implement-ation • IS/IT project manager • Responsible for the technical component • Functional advice • No involvement	*The specific role of the IS/IT function in the implementation of the SIS*
26. Business Role	• Ownership • Business project manager • Specify requirements • No involvement	*The specific role of the business in the implementation of the SIS*
27. Senior Executive Role	• Highly involved • No involvement • Passive involvement	*The specific role of the senior executive management in the implementation of the SIS*
28. Owner	• The business • The IS/IT function	*The part of the organisation given specific accountability and responsibility for the implementation of the SIS*
29. Approach	• Iterative methods • Traditional methods • In-house bespoke • External bespoke	*The method was taken to the delivery of the technical solution for the SIS*
30. Tools	• Prototyping • Rapid application development • Traditional development tools • None	*The tools and techniques employed by the project team to deliver the technical solution*
31. Normal Approach	• Yes • No	*Was the normal approach to delivering information systems taken for this SIS*
32. Change Process	• Yes • No	*The existence of a well under-stood change process as part of the overall implementation approach*

The elicitation of *contextual* factors affecting SIS success was potentially an impossible task, in that there may well be many contextual issues without the IS literature which could indirectly affect the success of SIS. Given that some 200 items of literature were analysed, it was felt that the only realistic method was to identify from *that* literature factors which were more general, (i.e. could affect any or all of the life cycle stages) rather than being relevant to a single stage alone. The resulting contextual factors are listed in Table 11.5.

TABLE 11.4: *Benefit management factor definitions, suggested options*

FACTOR	SUGGESTED OPTIONS	FACTOR DEFINITION
33. Process	• Not detailed • Detailed	*The existence within the organisation of an approach for managing the delivery business benefits and was this employed on the SIS project*
34. Benefit Plan	• None • A benefit plan	*The existence of a detailed plan for the delivery of the business benefits part of the project*
35. Identification Stage	• Planning • Evaluation • Implementation • Post-implementation • Continuously • None	*The point in the life cycle where the benefits from the SIS were identified*
36. Commitment	• Senior management level • Middle management level • No evidence	*Was there a clear commitment to the achievement of the benefits and at what level was accountability and responsibility given*
37. Reviews	• Continuously • At the end of the project • Never	*Were reviews of benefit delivery carried out?*
38. Change Plans	• Yes • No	*Benefits linked to changes in the business process*
39.Continuation	• Yes • No	*At the end of the project was there a process for identifying potential future benefits from the SIS*

The columns *Suggested Options* in each of Tables 11.1-11.5 were derived from a combination of the literature and possible attributes and values identified in the initial field work. Figure 11.4 shows how these factors align to the basic research models.

TABLE 11.5: *Context factor definitions, suggested options*

FACTOR	SUGGESTED OPTIONS	FACTOR DEFINITION
40. IS/IT Perception	• Strategic • Not strategic	*The perception of the potential of IS/IT within the business*
41. Senior IS/IT Manager	• A manager • Head of department • Director • On the board	*What level in the organisation was the most senior IS/IT manager*
42. IS/IT Organisation	• Central planned • Free market • Scarce resource • Leading edge • Necessary evil • Monopoly	*What 'mandate' did the IS/IT organisation operate under within the organisation*
43. Planning Change	• Yes • No	*Has the planning approach changed?*
44. Evaluation Change	• Yes • No	*Has the evaluation approach changed?*
45. Implementation Change	• Yes • No	*Has the implementation approach changed?*
46. Organisational Change Method	• Yes • No	*The existence of a well understood and implemented change management methodology within the organisation*
47. Strategic Benefits	• Willing to invest • Not willing to invest	*To what extent was the organisation willing to invest in strategic benefits*
48. Organisation Driver	• CEO • Divisional director • Business unit manager • IS/IT manager	*Who in the organisation was the main driver behind the change?*

11.3.1 The Case Studies

From an initial postal questionnaire sent to 240 major companies (excluding the 11 used in the earlier field work), 40 responses were obtained from organisations who had recently implemented SIS as defined for the purposes of this research. The aim was to find cases representing the spectrum of degrees of success and from a range of different types of industry. Eventually 11 organisations, which overall satisfied the requirements, allowed access for detailed analysis. Initially these 11 were thought to be evenly spread across the levels of success defined earlier, but later it became clear that some were in fact less successful than originally claimed. In total the systems represented an investment of over £200 million. The costs varied from under £10 million in several projects to nearly £100 million in one case.

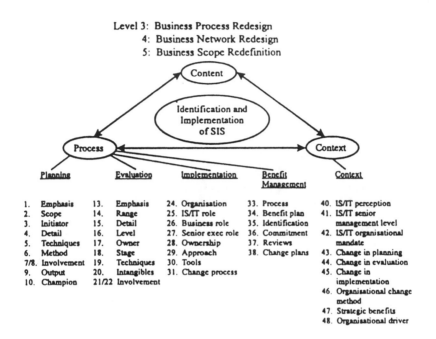

Level 3: Business Process Redesign
      4: Business Network Redesign
      5: Business Scope Redefinition

1.	Emphasis	13.	Emphasis	24. Organisation	33. Process	40. IS/IT perception
2.	Scope	14.	Range	25. IS/IT role	34. Benefit plan	41. IS/IT senior
3.	Initiator	15.	Detail	26. Business role	35. Identification	management level
4.	Detail	16.	Level	27. Senior exec role	36. Commitment	42. IS/IT organisational
5.	Techniques	17.	Owner	28. Ownership	37. Reviews	mandate
6.	Method	18.	Stage	29. Approach	38. Change plans	43. Change in planning
7/8.	Involvement	19.	Techniques	30. Tools		44. Change in evaluation
9.	Output	20.	Intangibles	31. Change process		45. Change in
10.	Champion	21/22	Involvement			implementation
						46. Organisational change
						method
						47. Strategic benefits
						48. Organisational driver

FIGURE 11.4 *Detailed research model*

It would be inappropriate to provide details of the organisations and the particular systems here, but Table 11.6 describes the type of business, a basic description of the strategic nature of the application and the agreed consensus view of the degree of success of the system. In all cases, the applications addressed a specific competitive/strategic issue (or more than one) and the nature of changes required to the business could be aligned to one or more of the three transformation categories described earlier.

In all case studies available supporting documentation was reviewed to confirm the accuracy of the interview answers given, as far as possible. Multiple sources of evidence were provided by interviewing at least three senior managers in each organisation. The following profile was developed as a guide for identifying the most appropriate senior managers to participate in each case study:

TABLE 11.6 *Case studies—overview*

No	ORGANISATION	APPLICATION PURPOSE	SUCCESS RATING
1.	**Information Services**	*To build direct systems links to customers and facilitate faster new product introduction*	Moderate success
2.	**Retailer**	*To provide its own credit card to customers and gain valuable customer information*	Success
3.	**Energy Distribution**	*To develop direct system links to major customers and provide new value added services*	High success
4.	**Industrial Products Manufacturer**	*To provide improved, integrated services to its industrial customers across Europe*	High success
5.	**FMCG Manufacturer**	*To improve the effectiveness of product promotion and the speed of new products throughout the branch network*	Moderate success
6.	**Financial Services**	*To enable more rapid development and introduction of new products throughout the branch network*	Unsuccess
7.	**Financial Services**	*To develop a new business segment in collaboration with its agents*	Unsuccess
8.	**Healthcare Manufacturer**	*To implement new logistics and supplier management systems across Europe*	Success
9.	**Energy Supply**	*To decentralise management accountability for profit/loss to individual business units*	Unsuccess
10.	**Engineering**	*To radically restructure the design processes to be able to open up new international markets*	Unsuccess
11.	**Speciality Goods Manufacturer**	*To improve customer service to respond to more demanding delivery requirements and reduce untenable stock levels*	Unsuccess

- The senior business manager whose functional area was most impacted by the strategic information system *(Profile 1)*.
- The senior IS/IT manager in the organisation involved with the strategic information system *(Profile 2)*.
- A senior manager not directly affected by the investment *(Profile 3)*.

The interview questions were designed to address each of the variables in as precise a manner as possible, providing either a choice of options or allowing the interviewee to answer in his or her own words. Each individual was interviewed separately in order to gain their own answers to the questions. Any major areas of divergence in the answers given were identified after the interviews. On each area of divergence the interviewees were then required to meet in order to reach a consensus answer for the organisation. This agreed view was then communicated in writing to the researcher.

In order to ensure validity of interpretation the interview notes were given to a sample of senior managers within the researcher's organisation. Each manager was asked to examine the descriptions of the factors and to classify them according to the attributes for each variable, provided by the options developed in the derivation of the research variables. The results were compared with the researcher's own interpretations. Where there were any differences the researcher took the view of the validator, unless there was an obvious lack of understanding shown.

11.3.2 Analysis of Results

The results were analysed in two ways. First conventional quantitative analysis was performed on the data using a set of statistical techniques. This revealed a number of simple correlations which clearly distinguished factors relevant to *High Success* and *Unsuccess*. However, it could not with any reliability determine differences between the other levels, nor identify related combinations of factors across the life cycle. To elicit a more detailed understanding a qualitative analysis tool (NETMAP) was used. NETMAP is a set of computer programs which identify and analyse formal and informal networks among data—both quantitative and qualitative in nature. It also produces a graphical, easy to interpret representation of the clusters identified. Its emphasis is on the analysis of patterns and relationships across large volumes of data.

It is a proven research tool which appeared to be ideal for this analysis. It did enable the data to be analysed in a wide variety of dimensions and combinations and enabled the more detailed and complex research questions to be answered. The result was unique sets of clusters of factors relating to each success rating.

Once more there is not space here to give the detailed data from the case studies nor the detailed results of the analysis. These run to some 90 pages of data, 40 tables and 28 cluster diagrams! Only the significant results from these extended analyses are considered below.

11.4 The Findings

Based on extensive statistical analysis a set of factor attributes which most significantly correlated to the higher degrees of success were identified.

The most significant was a contextual factor (No. 46—Table 11.5): *Organisational Change Method*, i.e., the existence of a well-understood change management 'methodology' in the organisation, not specific to the implementation of IS/IT projects.

Following that were a whole set of factors concerning the role of the senior executive(s) in the project—Nos. 3, 16, 27, 36 and 48, i.e., factors from all life stages: *Initiation of the Planning Process*, the *Level at which Evaluation* took place, a high degree of *Involvement in Implementation*, senior management accountability/responsibility for *benefit achievement*, and the CEO being the key *Organisational Driver* behind the need for change. While in some ways this is not surprising, the finding suggests that senior executive involvement throughout the application life cycle is critical. It is not sufficient for senior executive involvement in just the planning and evaluation stages, as has been demonstrated from previous research.

Other factors of lesser but distinguishable significance were:

No. 13:   evaluation emphasis on 'strategic' rather than financial benefits (see Table 11.2);

Nos. 23/44: the project was evaluated in a different manner from normal IS/IT investments (Tables 11.2 and

11.5); i.e., the more successful SIS projects received 'special treatment' in comparison to normal IS investments.

Nos. 33/35: in the most successful projects the emphasis on delivery of the business benefits was evident in the existence of a defined, communicated *benefit management process* and the clear *identification* of benefits expected *in the planning stage* (see Table 11.4).

However, apart from these factors the quantitative analysis was not able to identify other factors and was never considered to be able to distinguish combinations of factors.

The use of the NETMAP software was intended to and proved able to meet this requirement. The data was 'run through' four times:

a) in total;
b) excluding contextual factors in order to identify their significance or otherwise;
c) excluding the benefit realisation factors to test whether explicit attention throughout the life cycle to factors, which recent research suggested were important in achieving the realisation of the intended benefits, not only affected but influenced the perception of success;
d) in pairs of life cycle stages to identify which if any combinations of stages were most critical to success.

The cluster analysis compared the attributes of all factors and provided a significance index which described the degree to which, for any particular factor, the attributes were commonly present in one cluster and commonly absent in the other. The higher the index, the more exclusive was the attribute found in only one cluster. Obviously for many factors there was little if any distinct pattern to the attribute occurrence, however as described below a small number of factors in each analysis had distinctly different characteristics across the four degrees of success.

Analysis (a) and (b) above revealed different sets of distinct clusters as shown in Figures 11.5 and 11.6.

The first analysis (a) was able to distinguish sets of factor attributes which clearly differentiated *High Success* projects from all others and also *Success* projects from *Unsuccess*. These factors and attributes are described below.

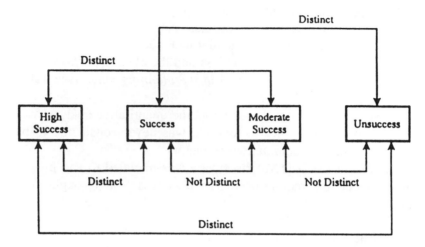

FIGURE 11.5 *Cluster relationship mapping (including context)*

When contextual factors were removed (analysis b)) a different pattern emerged (as in Figure 11.6).
- it was no longer possible to distinguish *High Success* from anything other than unsuccess;
- it was now possible to distinguish *Moderate Success* from *Unsuccess*.

This implies that contextual factors are important determinants of achieving *High Success*, and that contextual factors are not important determinants of *Unsuccess*. Process factors are more important in the latter case.

In analysis (c), when the Benefit Realisation stage was removed, it was possible to distinguish between *Moderate Success* and higher levels of success, suggesting that active benefit management is essential to achieving *Success* or *High Success*. However, it could perhaps be argued that attention paid to benefit realisation may only enable knowledge of whether or not it achieved the expected benefits!

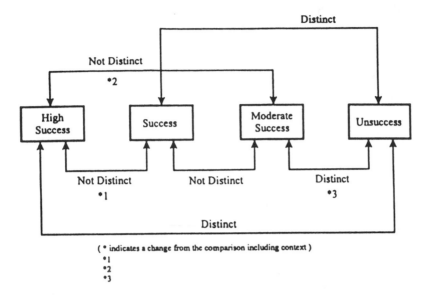

FIGURE 11.6 *Cluster relationship mapping (excluding context)*

When pairs of stages in the life cycle were compared (and each compared with contextual factors) a few distinct clusters were revealed. These were:

1. *Planning and Evaluation*—clear differences were identified between the combination of approaches to planning and evaluation in Success and High Success cases, compared with the others.
2. *Planning and Implementation*—in this analysis the Unsuccess case studies formed a discrete cluster, showing that both of these process stages if inappropriately managed lead to Unsuccess.
3. *Planning and Benefits Management* produced the same result as 1. above.
4. *Benefits Management and Context* again produced a similar distinction as in 1. above.

None of the other pairings produced significantly differentiated groupings. This analysis reinforced the findings described earlier.

The qualitative analysis identified the same factors/attributes as the quantitative analysis but in addition provided a more detailed explanation of the likely causes of the different degrees of success. Combining the results of the four analyses the key factors/attributes which appear to explain the degrees of success are as follows.

1. *Planning: Output (No. 10—Table 11.1)*—in the Success and High Success the output of planning was seen as a *defined business project* not merely an IS/IT project.
2. *Evaluation: Involvement (No. 21/22—Table 11. 2)*—the Moderate Success, Success and High Success cases had considerable involvement from business management in the justification process whereas in the Unsuccess group, justification was mainly the responsibility of IS/IT Management.
3. *Benefit Realisation: Benefit Plan (34—Table 11. 4)*—the Moderate and Unsuccess projects had no form of benefit plan, i.e. identifying non IS/IT activities required to deliver the business changes and consequent benefits.
4. *Context: Strategic Benefits (47—Table 11.5)*—the High Success cases were distinguished from the others by the willingness of management to invest based on 'strategic' as opposed to measurable, quantified, financial benefits.

In addition to 4. above, which distinguished High Success from all other ratings, two contextual factors distinguished High Success from Success.

1. The senior manager directly responsible for IS/IT was a board member (No. 41—Table 11.5).
2. The approach adopted to planning the particular application differed from that normally in use for IS/IT project planning (No. 43—Table 11.5).

Two further implementation factors were clearly different between *Moderate Success and Unsuccess*:
1. *IS/IT Role (No. 25—Table 11.3)*—in Unsuccess projects the project was 'owned' by IS/IT and project managed by them.
2. *Business Role (No. 26—Table 11.3)*—in moderate success projects 'ownership' was clearly identified with the business who appointed a Business Project Manager.

TABLE 11.7 *Characteristic planning factor attributes*

Planning Factors	High Success and Success Group	Moderate and Unsuccess Group
Emphasis/Objective	Corporate strategy/competition	-
Scope	Enterprise wide	Business Unit
Initiator	CEO	IS/IT
Detail	Package solution	Technology solution
Techniques	Tailored	-
Method	Cross-function	-
Business Involvement	High	Low
IS/IT Involvement	High	High
Champion	Yes	No
Output	Business project	IS/IT project
Normal Approach	Administrative	Administrative
This Approach	Organisational	Administrative/business led

TABLE 11.8 *Characteristic evaluation factor attributes*

Evaluation Factors	High Success and Success Group	Moderate and Unsuccess Group
Emphasis	-	Financial
Range	Strategic/financial	Financial
Detail	Detailed	Not detailed
Level	Senior management	Middle management
Owner	Business	IS/IT
Stage	Planning/evaluation	Evaluation
Techniques	Strategic analysis	Payback/ROI
Intangibles	Quantified	Not quantified
Business Involvement	High	Medium
IS/IT Involvement	High/medium	High
Normal Approach	No	Yes

While these were the factor/attribute combinations that the analysis revealed as the most significant in defining the degrees of success, other patterns were identified which were more frequently present in one cluster than another. By synthesising the results from all the analyses (both quantitative and qualitative) and assessing the results in two major groupings—High Success and Success versus Moderate Success and Unsuccess, Tables 11.7—11.10 describe the factor attributes that were characteristically present in each group.Obviously some case studies showed a range of attributes in both groupings, especially the Success and Moderate Success ones.

TABLE 11.9 *Characteristic implementation factor attributes*

Implementation Factors	High Success and Success Group	Moderate and Unsuccess Group
Organisation	Investment programme	IS/IT project
IS/IT Role	Functional advice/deliver technology	IS/IT ownership/project manager
Business Role	High involved, ownership/project manager	Resources/requirements
Senior Eecutive Role	Actively involved, goals in plan	Not involved
Owner	Business	IS/IT function
Approach	Iterative	Bespoke/turnkey
Tools	Prototype	Traditional
Normal Approach	Not followed	Followed
Change Method	Yes	No

TABLE 11.10 *Characteristic benefit management factor attributes*

Benefit Management Factors	High Success and Success Group	Moderate and Unsuccess Group
Process	Detailed	None
Benefit Plans	Benefit plans	None
Identification Stage	Planning/evaluation	Evaluation
Commitment	Senior executive	None
Reviews	Post-implementation/continuous	None
Change Plans	Detailed	None
Continuation	Yes	No

Table 11.11 describes the characteristic contextual attributes of the High Success case studies versus *all* other cases.

TABLE 11.11 *Characteristic context factor attributes*

Context Factors	High Success Group	All Other Groups
IS/IT Perception	Strategic	(Varied)
Senior IS/IT Manager	On the board	Not on the board
IS/IT Organisation Mandate	Monopoly to central planning	Monopoly or free market or scarce resource
Planning Change	Yes—outside normal planning approach (business led/organisational)	Inside normal approach (administrative/business led)
Evaluation Change	New process	No
Implementation Change	No	(Varied)
Organisational Change Method	Exists	No
Strategic Benefits	Willing to invest	Not willing to invest
Organisation Driver	CEO (change programme)	Not CEO in most cases

Finally to examine how well the various factor attribute combinations in each case study combine to describe the reasons for the relative success a 'score' was calculated for each phase of each case and in total. The basis for the score is as follows: how the particular attribute matches the most common attribute at each level of success (taking the highest degree of success where attributes are not differentiated). The scores used were

High Success	=	+2
Success	=	+1
Moderate Success	=	-1
Unsuccess	=	-2

Table 11.12 summarises the results.

While most of the scores align, as they should, to the earlier results, the analysis shows up a couple of apparent anomalies:

TABLE 11.12 *Case study success scores*

Case Study	Success Rating	Phases
1	MS Total = +6	Planning Evaluation Implementation Benefit Management Context
2	S (+22)	Planning Evaluation Implementation Benefit Management Context
3	HS (+39)	Planning Evaluation Implementation Benefit Management Context
4	HS (+36)	Planning Evaluation Implementation Benefit Management Context
5	MS (-32)	Planning Evaluation Implementation Benefit Management Context
6	US (-32)	Planning Evaluation Implementation Benefit Management Context
7	US (-33)	Planning Evaluation Implementation Benefit Management Context
8	S (+4)	Planning Evaluation Implementation Benefit Management Context
9	US (-25)	Planning Evaluation Implementation Benefit Management Context
10	US (-40)	Planning Evaluation Implementation Benefit Management Context
11	US (-36)	Planning Evaluation Implementation Benefit Management Context

TABLE 11.2 (*continued*)

Common Significant Factors				Overall Score
5	2	1	1	+9
2	1	4	1	-2
3	3	2	0	+7
1	0	1	2	-3
1	0	3	2	-5
3	2	3	0	+5
1	3	4	1	-1
3	3	2	0	+7
5	1	0	0	+11
1	0	2	0	0
5	2	0	0	+12
3	2	2	0	+6
3	3	2	0	+7
5	1	0	0	+11
2	0	1	0	+3
5	2	3	0	+9
3	2	2	0	+6
3	3	3	0	+6
5	0	1	0	+9
3	1	1	0	+6
0	0	3	3	-9
0	3	4	3	-7
1	1	2	1	-1
0	0	1	4	-9
0	0	2	2	-6
0	0	0	4	-8
0	3	3	3	-6
1	1	1	3	-4
0	0	1	4	-9
0	0	1	2	-5
0	0	2	1	-4
0	2	1	4	-7
1	1	1	5	-8
0	0	1	4	-9
0	1	2	2	-5
2	2	2	0	+4
0	4	3	2	-3
1	1	3	0	0
4	1	0	0	+9
0	0	2	2	-6
0	0	2	1	-4
0	3	2	3	-5
1	1	3	1	-2
0	0	1	4	-9
0	1	2	2	-5
0	0	1	4	-9
0	2	1	4	-7
1	1	0	5	-7
0	0	1	4	-9
0	0	2	3	-8
0	0	2	1	-4
0	2	2	4	-8
1	1	0	5	-7
0	0	1	4	-9
0	0	2	3	-8

1. Case Study No. 1 has a score more aligned to Success than Moderate Success (ie. it is positive).
2. Case Study No. 5 has a very negative score more aligned to Unsuccess than Moderate Success.

Within the detailed analysis reasons were found for these anomalies.

1. While Case Study 1 shows many characteristics of Success and even High Success, and the project was implemented as required technically, the strategic benefits used to justify the system never materialised. Lower order operational benefits (cost savings) were delivered but no action was taken to actively pursue the strategic benefits claimed, if they were ever really feasible.
2. It was understood in Case Study 5 that it would require significant changes in working practices across organisational functions to achieve the full range of benefits. These change issues were never addressed at any stage of the project life cycle and hence the system only delivered some local efficiency/cost reduction benefits—but was not a complete 'unsuccess'—none of the intended 'strategic' benefits were delivered, so perhaps within the strict definition of SIS it did not succeed at all.

While the research only analysed 11 case studies, which were not a balanced sample across the spectrum of success ratings, it was possible to identify factors which had different attributes, to varying degrees of significance, at the four defined levels of success. It was also possible to identify combinations of factors across the life cycle stages which offer at least a partial explanation for the varying degrees of success. The detailed findings are indicative rather than conclusive given the size of the sample, but patterns emerged which provide some new insights about the causes of success or otherwise in SIS. In terms of the original research questions -

1. it is possible to identify factors which appear significant in explaining the degree of success with SIS.

2. contextual factors are important determinants in achieving the highest degrees of success.
3. there are combinations of factors across the life cycle that are apparently important in explaining the degree of success.

11.5 Conclusions

11.5.1 Applicability of the Research Framework

It can be concluded that the research framework is able to explain the fundamental reasons for the degree of success with strategic information systems. In particular it can be shown that the key differentiators between the levels of success are:

High Success and Success:

Contextual factors, especially those related to the change methodology and the role of the senior executive across the life cycle are most important in explaining the difference between High Success and Success. It also appears that the approach to evaluation, particularly an emphasis on defining strategic benefits early in the life cycle, is important in explaining the difference between High Success and Success.

The contextual environment defining the High Success organisations is one in which there is a high acceptance and awareness at senior levels of the potential strategic impact of IS/IT. The organisation has a clearly expressed and communicated vision of what the business needs to accomplish in order to achieve its goals and these goals are translated into the requirements for SIS.

There is a change oriented, strategic initiative within the organisation driven by the CEO, and IS/IT is perceived to be a key enabler in delivering the initiative. The change issues are well understood and actively planned in parallel with the IS/IT projects. The senior IT manager is a Director and probably a board member and involved in the strategic management process of the organisation. IS/IT planning takes place within the context of the organisational change initiative and is therefore likely to be outside the normal IS/IT planning process.

The contextual environment defining the 'success' organisations is one in which the business is driven by strong Line of Business

Directors who have devolved responsibility for IS/IT decision making. However, they tend to rely on a close working relationship with a strong senior IS/IT manager who influences and assists the business throughout the life cycle. The IS/IT manager is the catalyst for encouraging the business to take a more strategic perspective towards the identification and implementation of their IS/IT investments. However, this increased strategic perspective is taken within the normal approach to planning for IS/IT.

Success and Moderate Success:

Benefit management factors combined with planning factors are important in explaining the difference between Success and Moderate Success.

The main factors identified were the existence of a detailed benefit management process and a benefit plan, the latter being seen as an important aspect of planning overall.

The 'Success' projects had a well-developed understanding of the need to actively manage the identification, measurement and delivery of the benefits. They had implemented a 'methodology' to address those issues and develop a 'business benefit plan'. While the issues were recognised in the moderate success cases, the organisations had no method or plan to manage the benefits.

Unsuccess and Moderate Success:

Planning and implementation factors are most important in explaining the difference between Moderate Success and Unsuccess.

The difference between these two success ratings was due mainly to planning and implementation. Implementation was slightly more important than planning. The analysis identified the role of the senior executive, the role of IS/IT and the role of the business as the important implementation factors. It can be concluded that it is the organisational and people implementation issues rather than the particular development approaches, tools or techniques which are important in explaining the difference between Unsuccess and Moderate Success.

The significant planning factors (other than those related to the life cycle role of the senior executive) were planning method and planning approach. It can therefore be concluded that these factors are also important in explaining the difference between Unsuccess and Moderate Success.

The research model appears to provide a framework which can be applied to organisations in the process of identifying and implementing strategic information systems. It is possible to propose a set of general themes which organisations should address as they aim to improve the degree of success with strategic information systems. These points are summarised in Figure 11.7.

1. Organisations which perceive their degree of success as *Unsuccess* can initially improve their position by addressing their Planning and Implementation processes.
2. Organisations which consider themselves as *Moderately Successful* can improve their success by developing a comprehensive approach to Benefit Management which is initiated during the Planning phase.
3. Those organisations who have achieved some degree of *Success* and want to continue to improve should address the following contextual and evaluation factors:
     • initiation by a senior executive of SIS, as integral to achieving business changes;
     • the organisational change method;
     • strategic benefits—be more willing to invest without financial justification (ie. evaluation emphasis).

The research does not suggest that organisations perceived as Unsuccessful can become Highly Successful through merely addressing the factors above. The suggestion is that organisations must evolve through a process which involves improving planning and implementation in any IS/IT project, then become adept at managing successfully the delivery of the business based benefits and then as their experience and maturity develops address the issues of adopting a change management based approach where IS/IT is only part of the overall solution. While the research does not explicitly show this 'experience effect', it is strongly implied in the results.

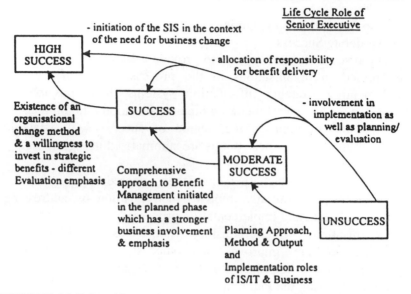

FIGURE 11.7 *Significant factors increasing the degree of success in the strategic information system—summary*

It should therefore be possible to predict with some certainty the likely success of a strategic information system by an analysis, early in the project, of these significant factors, particularly those factors relating to planning, benefit management and context. It can be seen from the analysis that while all the phases are significant, planning, benefit management and context are the most significant in determining levels of relative success. The multiple regression analysis provided results which were closely associated with the case study actual degree of success. This shows that the model could perhaps be used to predict the likely success of a strategic information systems project.

11.5.2 Conclusions with Respect to Previous Research/Literature

A considerable volume of literature, both empirical and otherwise, was analysed to develop the initial list of factors and attributes (see Tables 11.1—11.5). It is worth reflecting how the results of this research relate to the conclusions from previous work. In general that literature can be structured according to the research model used here.

Planning

There is considerable literature providing evidence about the importance of planning in the overall approach for success with strategic information systems (e.g. Flynn and Goleneiwska, 1993; Earl, 1989, 1993, Galliers, Merali and Spearing, 1994; Neiderman *et al.,* 1991). This research confirms this view, however it particularly concludes that planning alone is not a determinant of success. Planning combined with benefit management is the combination which best defines the differences between success and unsuccess. This research also suggests that poor planning often leads to unsuccess, i.e. if an organisation adopts an inappropriate planning approach the chances of failure are high, regardless of how other phases are carried out.

The most common success factor determined by previous work is argued to be the involvement and support of the senior management (e.g. Flynn and Goleneiwksa, 1993; Wilson, 1989; Lederer and Sethi, 1988; Lederer and Mendelow, 1988; Earl, 1993). This research strongly supports this view. Whereas the previous literature tends to focus on the importance of the role in the planning phase, this research concludes that the role of the senior executive is a life cycle issue, impacting all the phases in the research model. This research has provided support for previous work by Earl (1993) on planning—his planning classification is valuable in assessing the nature and effectiveness of different planning approaches in relation to the outcome of SIS projects.

Evaluation

In the literature a common argument is that an over emphasis on return on investment measures (ROI) is inappropriate for the evaluation and justification of the types of benefits involved in strategic information systems (e.g. Cooke and Parrish, 1992; Farbey, Land and Targett, 1993; Willcocks and Lester, 1994; Symons, 1994). The overall view from the literature was that financial techniques should be used in conjunction with other multi criteria techniques in order to provide a thorough evaluation (e.g. Farbey *et al,.* 1993; Ward, 1990; Parker, Trainor and Benson, 1990; Peters, 1989). It was found, that the High Success and Success organisations tended to employ a wider range of evaluation techniques than the Moderate Success and Unsuccess organisations. High Success and Success cases used both financial and strategic evaluation techniques. Moderate Success and Unsuccess cases employed predominantly financial based evaluation techniques. This finding lends support for the view that organisations should use a wider range of evaluation tools.

The literature also argues that the use of evaluation techniques in organisations is still predominantly financial based and that evaluation approaches have not kept pace with the strategic content of the investments they are supposed to evaluate (e.g. Ballantine *et al.*, 1993; Willcocks and Lester, 1994). This research suggests that organisations are adopting more formal evaluation and justification approaches and these approaches are mainly based on the use of financial based techniques. The more successful organisations do appear to be attempting to analyse strategic benefits in a fairly unsophisticated way. The overall evaluation approach appears not to have developed very far.

Implementation

Most previous literature argues that successful implementations should have clearly defined roles for the main participants: senior management, business management, IS/IT management. The research analysis clearly identifies the importance of the active involvement of the senior management in the implementation process. The business role and IS/IT role are also identified as significant independent variables.

Three surveys were identified in the literature which explicitly dealt with the implementation issues involved with strategic information systems: Wilson (1989), Crescenzi (1988) and Pagoda Associates (1994). The main implementation issues identified in these surveys can be summarised as:

- resourcing difficulties;
- a senior executive acting as the champion;
- a cross-functional team-based structure with effective business and IS/IT partnership at senior levels;
- the nature of the business;
- traditional methodologies no longer appropriate;
- a lack of change management skills.

Of these general issues this research identified the role of the senior manager as critical to success. In the analysis of the context factors, the existence of a change management methodology was also identified as significant.

Under the planning heading the need for cooperative working between business and IS/IT staff was identified as was the balanced roles of the two groups in implementation. This work also agrees, given the importance of change and benefit management processes that traditional methodologies are not sufficient.

Benefit realisation

The literature argues that few organisations have adopted well managed approaches to the delivery of business benefits (Crescenzi, 1989; Willcocks and Lester, 1994; Peters, 1990; Ward and Griffiths, 1996). In the survey by Ward and Griffiths, only 10% of organisations had a benefit management methodology. This research also found that a minority of the case study organisations had a coherent, structured approach to managing the delivery of the business benefits. The existence of a benefit management process initiated early in the life cycle was found to be significant in achieving success.

The research clearly shows that benefit management is a critical aspect of the life cycle model, and therefore warrants detailed research in order to develop models and approaches which can be adopted in organisations.

Context

The level of involvement and commitment, while addressed within other phases of the research, was defined as a contextual issue. As discussed above, an aggregated factor relating to the involvement of senior management across all phases of the research model was identified in the research and confirms the literature view that this is an important factor in the success of strategic information systems.

The literature on contextual issues argues that in order to achieve success with strategic information systems organisations should recognise that business change is an important aspect of the achievement of benefits. Particularly the organisation should have an approach to organisational change (Prager and Overholt, 1994;

Benjamin and Levinson, 1993; Pagoda Associates, 1994; McKersie and Walton, 1991). This research identifies the existence of a change methodology within the organisation as significant in the success of strategic information systems. This factor occurred as significant in both the quantitative analysis (highest correlation coefficient) and the qualitative analysis.

11.6   Other Conclusions

The research introduced an innovative tool (NETMAP) for the analysis and examination of complex models involving large numbers of variables, in this instance for the analysis of case study data. The findings from the use of the qualitative tool compare favourably with the findings from the more quantitative analysis.

The qualitative analysis approach has been shown to overcome the limitations, often expressed, of the use of traditional statistical techniques. It provided a greater flexibility in analysing the research data and ultimately provided more insight and depth in analysing the patterns and relationships across the life cycle model. This would not have been feasible using traditional techniques.

The research methodology combined the use of both survey and case study approaches. The initial survey was able to establish/confirm the importance of benefit management and context issues in the research model. The case study approach was adopted to examine the research model in detail and in a real-world environment. Much of the research in the field of IS/IT tends to rely on the use of one particular method. This work has confirmed the merits of the multiple methodology approach, especially where the research is exploratory in nature.

This work, however, has its limitations and the results are indicative not conclusive. It has perhaps added some new insights and developed a framework and approach which could be the basis for further work, covering a wider range of more explicitly defined factors, especially general business contextual factors, in a larger sample of business situations.

References

Ballantine, J.A., Galliers, R.D. and Stray, S.J., 1993, Information systems/technology investment decisions: the use of capital investment appraisal techniques in organisations, *Proceedings of the International Conference on IT Evaluation*, Henley, July 1993.

Benjamin, R.I. and Levinson, E., 1993, A framework for managing IT enabled change, *Sloan Management Review*, Summer.

Caminer, D., Aris, J., Herman, P., and Land, F., 1996, *User-Driven Innovation - the World's First Business Computer*, McGraw-Hill, London.

Cooke, D.P. and Parrish, E.B., 1992, Justifying technology: not measuring up, *CIO*, 18 June.

Crescenzi, A.D., 1988, The dark side of strategic IS implementation, *Information Strategy - The Executives Journal*, 5(1).

Earl, M.J., 1989, *Management Strategies for Information Technology*, Prentice Hall.

Earl, M.J., 1993, Approaches to strategic information systems planning: experience in 21 UK organisations, *MIS Quarterly*, 17(1).

Farbey, B., Land, F. and Targett, D., 1993, *How to Assess your IT Investment: a Study of Methods and Practice*, Butterworth Heinemann.

Flynn, D.J. and Goleniewska, E., 1993, A survey of the use of strategic information systems planning approaches in UK organisations, *Journal of Strategic Information Systems*, 2(4), December.

Galliers, R.D., Merali, Y. and Spearing, L., 1994, Coping with information technology - how British executives perceive the key information systems management issues in the 1990s, *Journal of Information Technology*, 9(3), September.

Galliers, R.D. and Somogyi, S.K., 1987, From data processing to strategic information systems - an historical perspective, in *Towards Strategic Information Systems*, 5-25, Abacus Press.

Kettinger, W.J., Grover, V. and Segars, A.H., 1995, Do strategic systems really pay off?, *Information Systems Management*, Winter.

Lederer, A.L. and Mendelow, A.L., 1988, Convincing top management of the potential of information systems, *MIS Quarterly*, 12(4), December.

Lederer, A.L. and Sethi, V., 1988, The implementation of strategic information systems planning methodologies, *MIS Quarterly*, 12(3), September.

McKersie, R.B. and Walton, R.E., 1991, Organisational change, in *The Corporation of the 1990s*, Scott Morton, ed., Oxford University Press.

Neumann, S., 1994, *Strategic Information Systems: Competition through Information Technologies*, MacMillan College Publishing Inc.

Niedermann, F., Brancheau, J.C. and Wetherbe, J.C., 1991, Information management issues for the 1990s, *MIS Quarterly*, 15(4), December.

Nolan, R.L., 1979, Managing the crises in data processing, *Harvard Business Review*, March/April.

Pagoda Associates, 1994, - *Understanding Why Systems Fail to Deliver a Recipe for Successful Investment in IT Projects*.

Parker, N.M., Trainor, H.E. and Benson, R.J., 1989, *Information Economics*, Prentice-Hall.

Parsons, G.L., 1983, Fitting information systems technology to the corporate needs: the linking strategy, *Harvard Business School, Teaching Notes*, (9-183-176), June.

Peters, G., 1989, Evaluating your computer investment strategy, *Journal of Information Technology*, 3(3), September.

Peters, G., 1990, Beyond strategy: benefits identification and management of specific IT investment, *Journal of Information Technology*, 6(4), December.

Pettigrew, A. and Whipp, R., 1991, *Managing Change for Competitive Success*, Blackwell Business, Oxford.

Prager, P.P.and Overholt, M.H., 1994, How to create a changed organisation, *Information Systems Management*, Summer.

Symons, V., 1994, Evaluation of information systems: towards multiple perspectives, in *Information Management*, L. Willcocks, ed., Chapman and Hall, 252-268.

Venkatraman, N., 1994, IT enabled business transformation: from automation to business scope redefinition, *Sloan Management Review*, 35(2), Winter.

Ward, J.M. and Griffiths, P., 1996, *Strategic Planning for Information Systems*, (Chapter 1) John Wiley and Sons.

Ward, J.M., Taylor, P. and Bond, P., 1996, Identification and realisation of IS/IT benefits: an empirical study of current practice', *European Journal of Information Systems*, 4(4), February.

Ward, J.M., 1990, A portfolio approach to evaluating information systems investments and setting priorities', *Journal of Information Technology*, 6(4), December.

Willcocks, L. and Lester, S., 1994, Information systems investments: evaluations at the feasibility stage of projects, *Technovation*, 11(5).

Wilson, T.D., 1989, The implementation of information systems strategies in UK companies: aims and barriers to success, *International Journal of Information Management*, 9(4).

Wiseman, C., 1985, *Strategy and Computers*, Dow Jones-Irwin.

Chapter 12

SOME REFLECTIONS ON INFORMATION SYSTEMS CURRICULA

Brent Work

12.1 Is an Official Information Systems Curriculum Really Necessary?

Sitting here looking at the blank page in front of me, I regret that I ever agreed to write a chapter about information systems curricula. To be completely truthful, I am not particularly keen on official curricula. Any such programme is a means to standardization. It narrows the perspective of the field. It eliminates some interesting people and some dangerous ideas. It impedes the possibility for innovation. It is a vehicle in which the mediocre can run down the exceptional in order to achieve uniformity. In his book *Against Method* Feyerabend writes: 'given any rule, however 'fundamental' or 'necessary' for science, there are always circumstances when it is advisable not only to ignore the rule, but to adopt its opposite.' (Feyerabend, 1978, p.23). Recommended curricula are similar. They imply a fixed view of information systems that cannot be correct in every circumstance.

Why does the IS community need an official curriculum? Of course, the usual answer is to ensure quality. Standardisation produces a consistency in the teaching of any subject. This uniformity may even serve as a basis for accrediting courses. Any programmes that do not cover a substantial amount of the material prescribed in the official curriculum or that do not relate this material in the recommended way risk failing the test. They may not be accepted as belonging within the discipline. Standards then reduce the variability in the structure and the content of academic courses. A discipline disowns programmes that fall outside the acceptable range. However, the process of accreditation does not actually guarantee excellence; it only rules out extremes. Poor and outstanding programmes alike may fall foul of official curricula. So strong is the power of standards, even guidelines may restrict the diversity of courses.

At the risk of being branded a cynic, I would suggest that official curricula, especially when used as the basis of accreditation, have another, more practical, advantage for a discipline. Kuhn makes this clear when he writes:

> [T]hey [members of a discipline] have undergone similar educations and professional initiations; in the process they have absorbed the same technical literature and drawn many of the same lessons from it. Usually the boundaries of that standard literature mark the limits of a scientific subject matter, and each community ordinarily has a subject matter of its own.... As a result, the members of a scientific community see themselves and are seen by others as the men uniquely responsible for the pursuit of a set of shared goals, including the training of their successors (Kuhn, 1970, p.177).

In this passage Kuhn suggests that a standard curriculum guides a process of homogenisation. It defines a means by which the young are infused with the ideas, experiences, myths, opinions, and goals of a discipline. It describes an initiation rite for a specialist community and serves as a way of excluding those whose views the community finds unacceptable.

Of course, modern academia is nothing more than an agglomeration of specialisms. Each claims its own area of expertise and each is self-defining. Consequently, physicists and sociologists cannot communicate. Historians and engineers have no mutual understanding. No two disciplines have common views or knowledge since they have no shared process of indoctrination. The only thing that unites them is their common dependence on the mechanisms of their communities—techniques, methods, texts, and curricula. It is the existence of these disciplinary artifacts that qualifies a field as a legitimate academic subject. Without them a discipline clings precariously to the edge of the academic precipice. Its practitioners can only worry for their tenure, promotion, funding, and opportunity to publish.

If, as Kuhn implies, an agreed curriculum provides the central underpinning of a discipline, then it is crucial for an academic's career. If there is no standard, then there is no discipline. If an academic is not affiliated with a discipline, then prospects are tenuous. Of course, this is precisely the problem of information systems. It is still struggling to be recognised by academia.

As early as 1980 Keen argued that information systems was simply 'a convenient umbrella for a hybrid, applied field that was more easily defined in terms of the MBA curriculum than research.' (Keen, 1980, p.9). Four years later McFarlan wrote:

> ...[T]he IS field is still struggling to define, clearly articulate, and execute a meaningful research tradition.... [D]ifferent institutions hold widely varying notions about a suitable IS research strategy, and there is a significant lack of consensus within the field about what direction research should take in the next decade (McFarlan, 1984, p.2).

At the 1989 ICIS, McLean in a session entitled 'MIS: Academic Discipline or Temporary Phenomena' observed '[a]n argument is raging throughout academia and industry to determine whether or not there is an enduring need to maintain information systems (IS) as a separate, distinct academic and professional discipline' (McLean, 1989, p.398).

The history of recommended curricula demonstrates the uncertain definition of information systems as a discipline better than these quotations. In November 1995 four professional bodies offered a new guideline for IS curricula (Couger et al., 1995). The new curriculum was not an isolated event, but arose from a long-running consideration of the deficiencies of traditional computer science degrees. The Association for Computing Machinery (ACM) has recommended guidelines for IS curricula three times previously (Ashenhurst, 1972; Couger, 1973; Nunamaker et al., 1982). The Data Processing Management Association (DPMA) first announced a model IS curriculum in 1981 (Adams and Athey, 1981) and then made two major updates to it (CIS'86, 1986; DPMA, 1991). In the UK the tradition of IS curricula is just as well established, even if somewhat less regular (Buckingham et al., 1987). Other academics have provided an ideal for information systems education in countries further afield, such as Australia (Hudson, 1992) and Hong Kong (Ng Tye et al., 1995). The formidable list of proposals clearly indicates both the perceived importance and the lack of consensus concerning a standard IS curriculum.

Yet, despite all of these efforts to define information systems as an academic discipline, the situation remains unchanged. For example, the UK Academy for Information systems (UKAIS) is a body which represents almost 450 information systems academics in Britain. Some of its members teach in departments of information systems, but more are in departments of computer science or in schools of management. There are even small numbers located in science policy groups, sociology departments, and research institutes. In the British government's recent research assessment exercise, the UKAIS argued that information systems should constitute a distinct unit of assessment, in other words a separate discipline. Despite these protestations, the Higher Educational Funding Councils of the British Government refused the request and indicated that information systems research should be reported under library science. In the future government funding for information systems research will, therefore, be tied to that of university libraries.

The failure of information systems teachers and researchers to find a home within academia indicates clearly that our subject has not yet coalesced as a discipline. Because a standard curriculum is a necessary condition to recognition by other, already established, disciplines, it is important for every IS academic's career. Any discussion about what we teach is also an attempt to define who we are and what we do. Our ambivalence on IS curricula betrays the schizophrenic nature of our field. Therefore, if we are to stake our claim to a place among other academic communities, we must continue to seek consensus on curricula because a standard will strengthen our sense of identify as a community. This is a matter of self-interest.

12.2 What is the Distinctive View of Information Systems?

However, I want to argue that uniformity of instruction and self-interest of the instructors are neither the only nor the best reasons for developing an official curriculum. I believe that the creation of an information systems discipline is not the ultimate aim. I feel that the goal which we within the IS community share has an audience far beyond our community. This is because information systems rests on a simple, but distinctive, view of technology. This attitude is central to the study of information systems and it is the real benefit of the subject.

12.2.1 A Means Rather Than an End

Certainly, information systems is a practical discipline. It is like law, medicine, and architecture rather than history, philosophy, or physics. IS as an academic field concentrates on the development of computer systems, primarily software, which collect, store, manipulate, and distribute the information required by any organisation. This narrows the technological focus of the subject quite precisely to specific types of software: programming languages, database management software, general purpose operating systems, and the like (Glass, 1992). Yet, it is not this technological emphasis which defines information systems as an area of study. Instead, I wish to contend that at the heart of an IS discipline is the belief that technology is not an end in itself, that new technologies assume economic, social, political and cultural value only within the context of organisational and managerial innovation.

This view is in sharp contrast to the assumptions of subjects such as electronic engineering and computer science. Electronic engineers have concentrated on applying recent, phenomenal developments in electronics in order to create new computing and communications hardware. Computer scientists have interested themselves in the creation of large suites of software, such as compilers, file access methods, and graphics editors which control the hardware made possible by engineers. Yet, neither academic community has any particular interest in how these inventions are used. In truth it is in their own interests for both electronic engineers and computer scientists to see hardware and software as ends in themselves. We might pardon them for believing that the more technology which they create, the better. Yet, there are no studies, of which I know, that link the quantity of technology directly to either economic or social benefit.

On the contrary, it is generally acknowledged that computing systems often fail to live up to expectations. For instance, not only is it rare that information technology makes a perceptible impact on a company's profitability, it hardly even works as desired. There are studies which confirm these opinions reaching from the 1970s (Lucas, 1979) to as recently as 1995 (Willcocks and Griffith, 1995). Investigators have consistently found the causes of failure to be primarily human, not technical: poor management; inadequate training of users; ignorance of the need to revise processes and procedures; organisational politics. The report on the collapse of the London Ambulance Systems serves as a tragic illustration of these symptoms (South West Thames Regional Health Authority, 1993). We all know of other examples. Unfortunately, the misconception that technology, particularly information technology, is an end, rather than a means to an end, permeates government, business, education, and the mind of the public. As long as this is so, we shall see the story of the London Ambulance System repeated again and again.

12.2.2 The Abstraction of Work and its Consequences

The view that information technology itself is not the objective, but that it helps us to fulfil our desires is simple and obvious. However, the implications of this premise are profound and not altogether manifest.

Some technologies, such as the space shuttle and genetic engineering, allow us to realise things which we were unable to do previously. Other technologies enable us to achieve familiar outcomes in new ways. For example, the cinema serves a human need not dissimilar to that supplied by theatre. Nevertheless, cinema has proved to be a visual medium, while the theatre has always been an aural experience. Cinema thus requires a different approach to acting, directing, and writing than the theatre, if a similar effect is to be achieved. Few technologies can serve as direct replacements for earlier technologies. Word processors require different strategies for correcting mistakes or for placing footnotes at the bottom of a page than typewriters do. In other words, new technologies require innovation in process, technique, tactics, and methods, if their benefits are to be realised. This implies a change in means. In some cases they even allow for the satisfaction of new desires. This implies a change in ends.

Consequently, innovation is essential if the potential of technology is to be realised.

Information technology is a particularly interesting illustration of this principle. Zuboff gives us a most precise account of what alterations are needed when IT is thoroughly and consistently employed (Zuboff, 1988). From carefully observing the automation of factories and offices, she infers that IT is bringing about a transformation in working practices. IT makes it feasible to collect and manipulate details of organisations' operations never before conceivable. If this information is used imaginatively, it may have an enormous beneficial impact. However, in order to exploit the information, its analysis must become a major emphasis of operation. This shifts the focus of tasks from physical labour to symbolic manipulation. Workers observe and act directly upon reality less and less. Now, they effect their actions upon symbols on a screen. IT becomes an intermediary between workers and physical objects.

This abstraction of work requires action-centred skills to be replaced by more intellective ones. Reich claims that this requires a work force of 'symbolic analysts' (Reich, 1993). Zuboff explains that action-centred skills are implicit. Since they depend only on the ability to perform a particular physical action, they need not be articulated. Communication among those performing action-centred tasks can, therefore, be minimal since these workers have a shared context. On the other hand, Zuboff argues that:

> Without a context in which meanings can be assumed, people have to articulate their own rendering of meaning and communicate it to others. Indeed, the very activity of constructing meaning often necessitates a pooling of intellective skill in order to achieve the most compelling interpretation of the text.... Pooling intellective know-how... depends in large measure upon language—not as minimalist vehicle in the consolidation of face-to-face interaction, but as precise vehicle for conveying explicit reasoning, often in the absence of action. (Zuboff, 1988, p.196)

Hence, symbolic manipulation depends on the ability to interpret, to use language precisely in order to explain, and to collaborate in reaching a conclusion.

Womack, Jones and Roos amplify Zuboff's views in their much discussed book *The Machine That Changed the World*. They argue that the mass production system has given way to lean production in many industries, particularly automobile manufacturing. They claim that lean production is characterised by two organisational features:

> It transfers the maximum number of tasks and responsibilities to those workers actually adding value to the car on the line, and it has in place a system for detecting defects that quickly traces every problem, once discovered, to its ultimate cause.
>
> This, in turn, means teamwork among line workers and a simple but comprehensive information display system that makes it possible for everyone in the plant to respond quickly to problems and to understand the plant's overall situation. (Womack *et al.*, 1990, p.99).

In this way Womack *et al.* tie teams directly to IT. In fact they insist that teamwork is at the heart of lean production. Shared responsibility requires shared information, but it also depends on shared skills. Every team member must be able to assume any role whether as an operator or as a decision maker. Each worker must possess a formidable range of abilities. These include not only technical skills such as welding, materials-ordering, and the use of IT, but also social and intellectual abilities such as fitting into a team and problem solving. Under these circumstances, specialists are a luxury.

The implications of the line of research represented by Zuboff, Womack *et al.*, and others suggest then that the content, structure, and organisation of work must be altered radically if all of the benefits of IT are to be realised. In particular workers will have to share tasks and responsibilities. In order to do this they will need a range of capabilities rather than a single specialism. They will also need intellect rather than physical dexterity.

12.2.3 The Evidence of IT's Impact

There is little evidence though that organisations have learned the lessons of these studies. In practice the know-how required of the lean factory worker is probably not so extensive as Womack *et al.*

suggest, because their products have simple designs and much of the needed expertise resides in their machinery. Head writes that:

> ...the 'integrated worker' employed by Japanese industrial corporations need have few recognizable skills at all, as I found during my own visits to the European plants of Nissan and Honda. I asked personnel managers at both plants what importance they gave to the educational and vocational qualifications of most of their prospective shop floor employees. In both cases the answer was 'very little' (Head, 1996, p.48).

Despite their glorification of teams Womack *et al.* conclude that one of the greatest advantages of lean production is an increased reliance on less-skilled and lower-paid workers (Womack *et al.*,1990,p.260). This is because specialists demand higher pay to offset their investment in training.

Business process redesign has had the same effect on clerical workers. As Head notes of a BPR exercise at IBM Credit:

> Reengineering teams descended on these clerical assembly lines and swept them away. They installed in their place employees using software that could accomplish the tasks hitherto carried out by the specialists. Except for a few exceptional cases, which are still handled by a team of specialists, the functions once divided among the various departments have now become the responsibility of a single employee who is called the 'deal structurer' (Head, 1996,p.49).

This portrait reminds me of the recently privatised utility which showed me the results of its latest redesigned process. Not a single task had been deleted or added. The sequence of the steps remained unchanged. No concurrency of activities had been introduced. The proposed redesign consisted entirely of replacing people with expert systems for those operations which dealt copiously with data. This constituted a major rethinking of the company's employment policy without reconsidering the process at all.

One merchant bank in the City of London offers a similar vision of the future. Its economics department determines a new investment strategy weekly. These strategies require that the money managed by the bank be moved from one set of stock exchanges to another within a matter of hours. This virtually requires the design of new processes every seven days. This is no trivial matter since the bank consists of a network of brokerages and dealers around the world: some are subsidiaries of the bank; others agents for the bank. Each has made its own IS provisions. Some have their own systems in-house; some have their systems maintained by facilities management companies. There are no standards for hardware, communications, systems software, or programming languages. Therefore, integration into a single infrastructure is financially, intellectually, and politically impossible. The merchant bank has resolved this problem by hiring bright young graduates. They have good degrees in a variety of disciplines. The bank gives them all substantial IT training. Then the graduates use their technical and business knowledge to piece together data from all around the world to accomplish each weekly strategy. The pressure is high and their careers are short-lived, but they are little more than information-age clerks.

Rather than requiring a highly educated work force, these ruthlessly rationalised offices depend on a few information workers who have a basic knowledge of the business, the ability to be polite to customers and to management, and of course, IT skills. The need for more generalised skills by the work force arises from the simplification of organisational design and the embedding of expertise in software, not from the need to use information more imaginatively.

Zuboff foreshadows this outcome in her later chapters. Some of the automation which she observed in the 1980s may have led operators and clerks to innovate. However, by 1995 those who articulated their conceptual understanding have found their models petrified in software. Their expertise has become a commodity and, consequently, its economic value has been minimized. Meanwhile, the decreasing cost of collecting and manipulating data has made it economical to monitor workers' performances closely rather than to trust their dedication. To paraphrase one manager whom Zuboff interviewed: a few people are now working for smart machines rather than a number of smart people working around a machine.

12.2.4   The Revolt of Managers

Why has information technology led to the devaluation and the increased control of labour? Zuboff argues that the contradiction lies in the relationship between knowledge and authority. She observes that:

> The objective integration of the production process created by the new information and control systems creates jobs that take an integrated view of operations, and such jobs are intrinsically more responsible. The message underlying the emerging job structure is that being exposed to data implies that a person sees, comprehends, and is appropriately responsive.... The assumption here, only occasionally made explicit, is that such a newly visible data becomes the responsibility of those who see it (Zuboff, 1988, p.297).

Thus, if organisations are to use information effectively, they must assign each decision to the person best able to make it. In many instances this will be a worker, not a manager. As a result, workers should have access to all information which they need to do their jobs. They need to become adept at interpreting the information available to them and they should learn to make informed decisions. They must also assume responsibility for their own judgements. Zuboff argues that this is the primary reason why today's work force needs a more general education.

Clearly, reducing the need for supervision is a direct threat to managers. Zuboff suggests that modern managers derive their authority from the notion that they have access to information and have been trained to make the most effective use of it. Workers have physical, not intellectual skills. Therefore, workers cannot be trusted to make appropriate use of information. Instead the new information which arises from automation is best used to reduce the need for workers. Any other view would undermine the position of management. This argument leads to the deskilling, if not the displacement, of labour.

However, Zuboff does not see the alternative to authoritarian rule to be the demise of management altogether. No, information workers need formidable capabilities in order to make decisions in information-rich environments. To develop these talents managers must become 'drivers of learning' rather than 'drivers of labour'.

Managers who can nurture organisational capabilities will need very different knowledge and skills.

Hence, Zuboff argues that it is management which is responsible for the deskilling and the reduction of the work force. As long as managers continue to insist on their exclusive right to authority, the move towards cheap, generally trained personnel will continue. Yet, if Zuboff is correct, organisations cannot achieve radically improved levels of productivity and quality until their managers abandon the notion that workers cannot be trusted. The economic implications of ignoring this lesson may be dire. Thus, making the 'informating' potential of IS apparent to managers is of critical importance.

12.2.5 Democracy in the Information Society

It is difficult to miss the political implications of this argument. If the greatest benefits of IT arise when businesses delegate authority, then political decision making should be distributed when information is easily available throughout a society. This implies a truly democratic society. However, if loss of control endangers the status of managers, it must also call into question the authority of politicians. Therefore, we could expect IT to be used by governments to increase control over their citizens in the same manner that businesses appear to be using IT to increase the monitoring of their workers. Yet, history suggests that the consequences of extreme social control can be disastrous.

Therefore, I believe that the IS community has both an important economic and a social message to convey. IT can make us a richer and more democratic society, but may have quite different effects if used as a means of control. Which of the two outcomes follow will not be determined by chance or by the internal logic of the technology. Human beings will decide and will be solely responsible.

We must, therefore, establish ourselves as a reputable discipline if this lesson is to be taught. If the process of developing curriculum guidelines offers a means of defining our discipline, then it is a worthwhile activity. If we must establish an official curriculum in order to gain acceptance of the premise that human beings are responsible for the judicious use of IT, then we must standardise. However, we must never forget that this is in the public interest first of all and in our own self-interest secondly.

12.3   The Liberal Nature of Information Systems

Up to this point I have argued that it is important that information systems should take its place as a legitimate academic discipline and that in order to do this it needs to establish guidelines for a curriculum. Yet, what should the basis of that curriculum be? The simplest answer is that the practicality of information systems is its foremost characteristic. So, I hastily surveyed the literature and I found 15 papers published in major journals in the last 15 years in which academics had asked practitioners to enumerate what a good IS professional knows. There is much uniformity in the responses to this question, but the results seem puzzling.

12.3.1 A Discipline of Generalism

I think that a recent survey sponsored by the Boston chapter of the Society of Information Management (SIM) fairly summarises the previous literature (Lee *et al.*, 1995). It categorises the knowledge needed by IS professionals into four areas: technology, technology management, business, and interpersonal management. A multivariate analysis of the relative importance of these four areas indicates that interpersonal management was regarded as the most crucial area by both IS consultants and IS managers. Both groups ranked technological know-how as the least valuable.

Of course, one could criticise aspects of this and similar studies. Yet, it firmly indicates that IS practitioners feel that interpersonal skills are at the heart of relevance for an IS education. To be exact they suggest that a good IS professional is distinguished by his ability to be persuasive, to achieve goals, to work amicably with others, and to listen. There is little about this programme which is unique to an IS curriculum. These 'skills' are a feature of general education. In fact they are still found among graduates of good secondary schools.

Likewise, business knowledge hardly differentiates an IS education. Management schools do provide this material. The same is true of technical management, for example at many universities engineering departments teach project management. Although the tone of these courses may be inappropriate for IS professionals, the difference hardly characterises IS as a unique discipline.

It is only the technology which might distinguish IS programmes from any others. Yet, the SIM study ranks technological knowledge at the bottom of the list. Most other studies of industrial requirements agree. For example, a similar study by Ng Tye, Poon, and Burn of 96 graduates working in the computing industry in Hong Kong produced comparable results (Ng Tye *et al.*, 1995). It indicates, for instance, that of the ten skills which graduates find most relevant, only two are 'technical'. They are the structured design of programmes and of data. I have taught both of these since 1977, so they can hardly be state-of-the-art. Of the other skills cited, seven are interpersonal.

These findings pose two fundamental problems for information systems teachers. First, why is there so little material unique to IS in these proposed curricula? Disciplines thrive by staking out unique intellectual territory, not by invading others. Secondly, why is interpersonal management the most emphasised feature? Are there any medical courses in which 'bedside manner' takes precedence over the pathology of diseases?

I can only surmise from this literature that practitioners regard information systems as essentially interdisciplinary. The most distinctive aspect of IS is not a single subject, but the relationship among several. They must regard Information System as integrative in nature. This is why the curriculum which they propose is general, not specialised. Of course, this answer poses more problems than it resolves. How can there be a generalist discipline? In fact why should practitioners view themselves as generalists rather than specialist technologists? How can this characterization of IS as not being confined to a single field and of the IS practitioner as not practising a specialist profession be in their self-interest?

The contradiction is further apparent in the emphasis on interpersonal management. As we have seen, an organisation's ability to communicate, to collaborate, and to share responsibility influence its success in employing IT. While specialism may promote a shared context within a community, disciplines retard conversation with non-members. Viewing IS as a profession and as a legitimate academic subject, therefore, impedes its effectiveness.

If we as scholars and practitioners cannot convey our ideas to industry and to society at large, we cannot hope to see information technology used sensibly. Yet, in order to gain a place in academia must we cloister ourselves? How can there be a generalist discipline? This is the major dilemma of information systems.

12.3.2 The Utility of a Liberal Education

I believe that the answer to this dilemma needs to be remembered, not discovered. I feel that the idea of a liberal education provides the forgotten clues needed to resolve this apparent contradiction.

One of the most formidable advocates of liberal education was John Henry Newman. In his inaugural lecture upon becoming the rector of the Catholic University of Ireland he laid out his view of a liberal education. Cardinal Newman believed a university was a place for the teaching of universal knowledge. He wished not to restrict the range of subjects to be taught, for he felt that knowledge was seamless, indivisible. So, he sought to broaden the curriculum.

> Thus is created a pure and clear atmosphere of thought, which the student also breathes, though in his own case he only pursues a few sciences out of the multitude. He profits by an intellectual tradition, which is independent of particular teachers, which guides him in his choice of subjects, and duly interprets for him those which he chooses. He apprehends the great outlines of knowledge, the principles on which it rests, the scale of its parts, its lights and its shades, its great points and its little.... Hence it is that his education is called 'Liberal'. A habit of mind is formed which lasts through life, of which the attributes are freedom, equitableness, calmness, moderation and wisdom.... This then I would assign as the special fruit of the education furnished at a university (Newman, 1969, p.365).

Nevertheless, the word 'liberal' strikes a chill in many hearts today because of its political and economic connotations. A liberal education is thought to be fit only for a man of leisure, a gentleman, in other words a man of no utility. However, those who attribute this view to Newman are misinterpreting his writings. Newman actually felt that a liberal education had a distinctive utility. As he wrote:

> ...he [the liberally educated man] has come to it [his discipline], as it were, from a height, he has taken a survey of all knowledge, he is kept from extravagance by the very rivalry of other studies, he has gained from them a special illumination and largeness of mind and freedom and self-possession, and he treats his own in consequence with a philosophy and a resource, which belongs not to the study itself, but to his liberal education (Newman, 1969, p.382).

For Newman then those who are liberally educated may deploy their specialist learning within a full knowledge of its context and its limitations. This acts as an antidote to the dangers of specialization so vividly described by Ortega y Gasset in *The Revolt of the Masses*:

> He [the specialist] is not learned, for he is formally ignorant of all that does not enter into his speciality; but neither is he ignorant because he is 'a scientist,' and 'knows' very well his own tiny portion of the universe. We shall have to say that he is a learned ignoramus, which is a very serious matter, as it implies that he is a person who is ignorant, not in a fashion of the ignorant man, but with all the petulance of one who is learned in his own special line (Ortega y Gasset, 1957, p.112).

In short a liberal education has the greatest relevance in that it insists that specialised knowledge be restricted to its own sphere. Liberal education does this by providing a context for specialisation which offers a shared vocabulary and shared ideals for all educated people.

In fact liberal education is practical in a more obvious way, because it was just this educational reform which introduced science and technology into English higher education. The institution which best represented the ideal was London's University College which opened in October 1836. In order to earn a Bachelor of Art, evidence of a knowledge of natural philosophy, classics, biology, logic, and ethics was required. However, mathematics played a central role in the curriculum since it supplied the language for rigourous thinking. Then, having attained a pass degree, students might sit for honours in one of the aforementioned subjects or in chemistry or physiology. There was also professional education in law, medicine, and engineering. This was a curriculum radically different from those found at the Oxbridge colleges of the day. It is a curriculum radically different from that found at University College today.

Some associate liberal education with the arts and the humanities only. They feel that it is antithetical to scientific disciplines. This is clearly untrue. A liberal education stresses the interconnectedness of all areas of learning rather than their separateness. It is specialisation which increasingly encourages antipathy between academic subjects and fragments the fabric of scholarship.

12.3.3 The Elitism of Liberal Education

Critics of liberal education more frequently attack its elitism though than its lack of utility. They would say that it is a programme for the education of the man who is in possession of an independent fortune. This idea is simply not true. The Royal Charter which established University College announced that the King '... deems it to be the duty of his royal office to hold forth to all classes and denominations of his faithful subjects, without any distinction whatsoever, an encouragement for pursuing a regular and liberal course of education.'

The mechanics institutes which were founded in many provincial cities in the decade before University College probably manifest the spirit of liberal education even better. As Donald Cardwell suggests in his book *The Organisation of Science in England* these institutes had four objectives:

> [F]irstly, the injection of science into the workshops of the country with consequent economic benefits.... Secondly, the wider diffusion of science and rationality would, it was hoped, banish superstition and ignorance. Thirdly, the movement was expected to hasten the progress of industry by increasing the numbers of those able to pursue it; and lastly, in accordance with the views of Adam Smith they hoped that science and education would offset the degrading effects of the industrial division of labour (Cardwell, 1972, pp.42-43).

Clearly, this original interpretation of liberal education stresses both economic and social improvement. It is not only utilitarian, but democratic, in its thrust.

> To me, as an American, these aims recall the Jeffersonian vision of '... a community of intelligent, resourceful, responsible, and self-governing citizens' (Lasch, 1995, p.76).

Critical to the realization of Jefferson's ideal is self-reliance, the ability to exercise one's own judgement. This depends on two things. First, a citizen needs economic independence. For Jefferson this arises from the ownership of land, because a man who holds his own acreage can provide for himself. Hence, he has no employer to instruct him. Secondly, a citizen needs intellectual independence. A working man must be 'intelligent' and 'resourceful', if he is to make the best use of his capabilities, but more importantly, he must be open to reasoned argument, if he is to assume his civic 'responsibilities'. It is education, a liberal education, which prepares him for the political discourse which is the lifeblood of democracies.

Both mechanics institutes and the Jeffersonian tradition provided noble aspirations and so, both failed. In Britain illiteracy, unbalanced syllabi, the lack of economic incentives, and the absence of state support led the working class to abandon the institutes (Cardwell, 1979, pp.71-72). Instead the middle class appropriated mechanics institutes. Thus, liberal education became tinged with elitism.

In the USA the notion of liberal education as a means to a truly democratic society had more practical support from the government. In 1862 the Lincoln administration passed the Homestead Act which provided 160 acres of agricultural land to any settler who would occupy and improve it. This legislation offered Americans economic independence. Two years later the Morrill Land Grant Act offered free land to states in order to found colleges for the populace. This legislation offered Americans intellectual independence. However, both reforms depended on the view that the USA was an agrarian society. As the frontier closed and as industrialisation surged ahead, the idea of liberal education gave way to the notion that education was the key to social advancement.

12.3.4 The Renewal of Liberal Education

Liberal education then is broad, not narrow. Rather than being in direct opposition to specialist disciplines, its true role is to delimit them. This is one of its chief benefits. It does this by encouraging reflectiveness. The intellectual frame of mind which results may serve as the basis for an individual's self-reliance and for a democratic society. This seems to me an apt description of what an education in information systems should accomplish. I, therefore, want to suggest that we need to revive the ideals of liberal education, but today, it needs to adopt a form in which information systems plays the central role, just as mathematics did in an earlier time.

Clearly, viewing information systems as a set of liberal arts rather than as a specialist discipline resolves the dichotomy between generalism and specialism which lies at the heart of the subject's ambiguity. An IS professional must draw on a variety of fields, some theoretical, some applied, if he is to practice successfully. In order to do this he must not simply be familiar with these subjects, he must also understand their limitations and their relationships to one another. Specialist education does not sufficiently value this type of learning.

Knowledge is necessary, but not sufficient, to ensure the successful practice of information systems. This depends on understanding that technology is a means to an end. This is the lesson that IS professionals must teach to their audience. We must teach this lesson to our students who are future IS professionals. It is a difficult lesson to teach though because specialisation demands that we create our own vocabulary and our own view of the world. Consequently, we have no shared language, experience, or understanding. It is little wonder that IS professionals feel that they need to communicate and to cooperate with their clients better. It is less often said, but equally true, that their clients need to articulate their needs and to listen more closely as well. A liberal education would provide IS professionals, information workers, and managers with a common ground upon which meaningful discourse could take place.

Of course, the most important aspect of a shared education is not the knowledge which it conveys but the intellectual practice which it develops. As Newman argued, liberal education's utility arises from the habits of the mind which it instils. These habits are similar to the intellective skills which Zuboff, Reich, and Womack *et al.* claim are crucial in organisations which use information technology intensively. Liberal education, therefore, is the best known method for developing those talents needed by IS professionals and by information workers.

As I argued earlier, in an agrarian age a liberal education *should* have provided intellectual independence, just as the ownership of land *should* have brought economic independence. These two capabilities—one mental, the other financial—were prerequisites to democracy. This vision failed though because education became a means of social advancement rather than a means to democratisation. However, the chance which was lost at the outset of the 19th Century may be regained in the 21st. In a post-industrial world a liberal education offers not just intellectual, but economic independence. The intellective skills of which Zuboff writes should form the modern worker's financial capability. They are his claim to employment. They remain with him and can be extended by him. They cannot be taken away by employers or by governments.

12.4 A New Structure for Liberal Education

In the previous section I made some brash claims. I proposed that rather than being a single discipline, information systems should be considered as a set of liberal arts. I suggested that a liberal education founded on these subjects develop the intellective capabilities needed not just by IS professionals, but by information workers and by citizens in a society heavily dependent on information technology. Moreover, such a programme would provide a shared education which would encourage better communication and cooperation among workers, professionals, and managers.

These claims may be appealing, but they are only philosophical speculations. They are difficult to judge without knowing something about the structure and the content of the proposal. Naturally, this is not easy to provide. Thinking through the implications of this suggestion at the level of a curriculum requires a mastery of the material that few, if any have. It must certainly be the task of a group, not an individual. Moreover, the first attempt, regardless of whom is involved, cannot be totally successful. It will need practice, experimentation, patience and time. I, therefore, intend only to offer a sketch of this new form of liberal education.

12.4.1 The Three Layers of Liberal Education

Liberal education was not itself a 19th Century invention. It dates from late Roman times and was the foundation of university teaching throughout the Middle Ages. In medieval universities, such as Oxford and Paris, scholars began by learning the seven liberal arts. These consisted of the *trivium*—grammar, logic (which was sometimes known as dialectic) and rhetoric—and the *quadrivium*—arithmetic, geometry, music and astronomy. A thorough grounding in these arts was a prerequisite to the study of any profession—law, theology, or medicine (Knowles, 1962). This subject matter suggests that a liberal education was chiefly a means of gaining proficiency in literacy and numeracy.

In the 19th Century men like Newman revived the notion of liberal education. However, they realised that knowledge could no longer be categorised into only seven arts as defined 1500 years earlier. Instead they argued that students needed to sample a diversity of arts and sciences in order to prepare themselves for advanced studies. Central to their programme of study was mathematics which was the language of physical science and which systematised the principles of rigourous discourse.

I would suggest that information systems has to address three specific questions:

- What role does information have in organizing?
- What are the benefits and liabilities of using new electronic technologies to collect, store, manipulate, and distribute information?
- How can these benefits be realised?

I want to propose that these three problems form a tripartite structure for the study of information systems somewhat analogous to the *trivium*, the *quadrivium,* and the professional levels of the medieval liberal education.

12.4.2 Learning to Practice Information Systems

The last question is the most practical of the three. It corresponds to the final level of a liberal education—the study of a profession. Certainly, understanding how to employ generic hardware and software to build and to maintain information systems is an important aspect of this question. This is still the technological problem which confronts information systems practitioners. It is the aspect of information systems which forms the basis of a specialism and the area upon which most curricula focus.

Recommended curricula such as that recently proposed by the ACM, AIS, DPMA, and ICIS cover this territory adequately. A knowledge of hardware, software, development techniques, and technology management is necessary. However, placing the practice of information systems in the same relation to its foundational subjects as professions such as medicine and law have to the liberal arts makes the practical nature of IS clear. While theory underpins medicine and the law, practitioners can only learn to apply this knowledge from experience. Therefore, IS professionals may learn about practice in the classroom, but they cannot practice there. This they can only do on the job. This implies a very different notion of professional education for IS students than we have today. Yet, adopting this approach would align this aspect of IS education much more closely with other types of professional education.

12.4.3 Learning the Reference Disciplines

Before practising information systems a trainee needs to have a great deal of theoretical knowledge. Anyone who has tried to build an information system knows that the major impediments to realising its benefits are human, organisational, and political. Clearly, any competent practitioner must have a knowledge of the theoretical underpinning of his discipline. It is the second of the three questions which I posed earlier that determines the scope of this knowledge.

This creates a significant problem for information systems practitioners because in most applied subjects there is a consistency in approach between the theoretical principles upon which the subject depends and their application. For instance, general practitioners usually view patients as biochemical systems and thus, find the application of biochemical theories straightforward. It is, therefore, difficult for them to deal with psychological illnesses which cannot necessarily be reduced to chemical malfunctions of the brain. In short there is a dominant science or reference discipline on which most professions depend.

I have already argued that information systems is different. That is why it depends on a set of liberal disciplines rather than a single reference discipline. The IS practitioner deals with organisations in general—businesses, charities, government agencies, markets, even societies. Since one finds organisation in almost all types of phenomena, almost every discipline treats it in some way. Therefore, there are economic, social, political, and cultural explanations of organisations. In information systems we have a broad spectrum of ideas to draw upon as the basis for our practice.

This embarrassment of intellectual riches ought to enhance information systems, but unfortunately, it more often retards it. I think that there are three reasons for this. First, there is no consensus regarding whether organisations are social, economic, political, cultural, or even some other form of phenomenon. Of course, the answer to this dilemma is that organisations are none of these. These are simply ways of studying a set of common phenomena. Morgan in his book *Images of Organisation* (Morgan, 1986), for instance, describes eight major metaphors for understanding organisations. Each offers only one perspective which is derived from a particular reference discipline— engineering, biology, cybernetics, cultural anthropology, etc. In reality organisations and the process of organizing are both more complex than any of these views admit. Each image is only partial. Clearly, information systems must have a less restrictive view of organisations, if it is to serve its generalizing mission. It must seek to synthesise these many analogies or learn to employ each in a complementary fashion, as physics has learned to deal with particles and waves.

Secondly, the failure to admit to this multiplicity means that there is little basis for discussion between those who espouse different reference disciplines as fundamental. In order to be credible a theoretician must be a follower of some school. Setting out one's ideological stall at the outset of every paper or presentation is a ritual that all IS academics learn quickly. Kuhn would suggest that in order to become a discipline, information systems theoreticians need a unifying paradigm. Since I have argued that IS is that rare thing a general discipline, maybe what is required is an agreed way of dealing with multiple views.

Thirdly, most of the theories concerning organisations come from the human, or as Simon refers to them the artificial (Simon, 1981), rather than the natural sciences. This seems obvious since we wish to create information systems for businesses, markets, and societies—man-made artefacts. This causes a clash with IS practitioners who depend almost entirely on the engineering analogy—organisations as machines. The conflicting ideologies supported by practitioners and theoreticians mean that it is particularly difficult to attach theoretical foundations for pragmatically developed methods (regardless of how useful the methods may be). Likewise, it means that it is not easy to deduce techniques which are rigorous enough for practitioners from available theories. This situation clearly arises today because we do not understand the appropriate relationship between the theoretical and the practical levels of an IS education.

12.4.4 Towards a New Science of Organisation

Up to this point my proposed model for a revision to liberal education is straightforward. I suggest replacing the traditional liberal arts with the so-called reference disciplines of information systems. I grant that the argument over what these reference disciplines are would be interesting and probably heated, but I shall pass over this issue. Once students have acquired an understanding of the benefits and liabilities of information technologies by studying these reference disciplines, they may begin to learn the practice of information systems under the guidance of senior professionals, as in other professions. Nothing in this programme seems too shocking. However, I wish to argue that there is a more fundamental layer of knowledge which requires another level of education. This is the knowledge needed to answer the first of the three questions—what role does information have in organizing? I think this material must play the role which mathematics did in the 19th Century notion of liberal education.

I suggested above that the reference disciplines offered complementary views of the set of phenomena which are central to the study of information systems. It is not yet clear what these phenomena are. It seems to me that in order to treat the reference disciplines as complementary one needs to have a deeper understanding of the nature of these phenomena.

The best developed approach to this problem considers these phenomena as systems. The systems method arose from the world of military planning and is often associated with the Rand Corporation. Forrester's *Industrial Dynamics* (Forrester, 1961) is the most widely known treatment of this approach. Some would argue that this tradition has played too influential a role in the development of information systems. However, Checkland's application of these concepts to soft systems is probably more helpful for the practice of information systems (Checkland, 1981).

Systems are not, however, the only available ontology. Recently, the advocates of the twin ideas of complexity and chaos have made much progress in describing these underlying phenomena. The study of these concepts have received treatment as mathematical constructs (Gleick, 1988), as entropy (Prigogine and Stengers, 1985) and as 'information' (Shannon, 1938). The fledgling cognitive science represents a third approach to the definition of phenomena which underly the reference disciplines of information systems (Gardner, 1985).

I have proposed elsewhere that representing organisations as networks of cooperative agents offers the foundation for a science of organisation (Work, 1994). The cooperating agent analogy is an ascendant concept within IT. The rage for object-oriented languages is well known. The shift from sequential to parallel computer architectures dominates both hardware and system software research. The latest network products all have client/server architectures. Neural networks have become the central concern of the AI community. Another emerging area of research is the creation of groupware in order to make computer supported cooperative work (CSCW) more feasible. All of these approaches depend on the analogy of cooperating agents.

But IT is not the only field in which cooperating agents have been used as an explanatory device. In economics both agency theory (Ross, 1973) and transaction cost economics (Williamson, 1975) espouse the view that exchange is the primary economic activity, not production. Both views consider economic contracts as a means of establishing a single goal among agents. Agency theory assumes opportunism among agents; transaction cost economics argues that organisations are a means of combating opportunism, uncertainty, and information asymmetries. The sociologists Pfeffer and Salancik have argued that an organisation's behaviour is a response to its environment which consists of agents who may provide resources. Since some of these resources are necessary for survival, an organisation must satisfy the expectations of certain interest groups (Pfeffer and Salancik, 1978). This resource dependency perspective suggests that an organisation's success depends on its interpretation of its environment. Social psychologists have long held a similar perspective. Role theory, for example, asserts that misunderstanding arises in exchanges because of the different expectations of participants (Katz and Kahn, 1978). Searle offers similar evidence of the presence of the ontology of cooperative agents within linguistics (Searle, 1969). In his book *Speech Acts* he argues that language is both a vehicle for interpretation and for commitment to some shared activity.

I certainly do not claim to have produced the necessary theory or to have established a research tradition for the cooperative agent view. My discussion of the foundations of these economic, sociological, social psychological, and linguistic theories has been terse. Dealing with just one of these in such a short space would be impossible. I have mentioned them only in order to indicate that the use of collaborating agents as an ontology for organizing is not new. It has an established intellectual pedigree.

Obviously, this final layer of knowledge is difficult to define because it does not yet exist. It forms the structure of a long-term research project rather than a curriculum. It is probably utopian. I offer it only as a distant goal. Even if we did have this knowledge or technique as the basis for curricular discussions, it would be difficult to convert into practice. The divide between practitioners and academics will not be healed soon.

12.4.5 A Better Means of Preparing IS Professionals

The benefits of an educational programme such as I have sketched are several. First, students can only learn to create information systems by building them, not by reading about them. Like other professions, IS professionals should learn their trade from practitioners. While the classroom is a fine place to learn the concepts upon which methods, techniques, and tools rest, it is not an appropriate means of learning about the cut and thrust of systems development. Moreover, this form of education would undermine the arbitrary distinction between academic and professional which exists within the IS community. Teachers must practice and the best practitioners must teach. This is the nature of any applied subject.

Secondly, by undertaking a liberal before a professional education, students will avoid the narrowness of the specialist. They will come to their subject as Newman claimed 'from a height'. This will allow them to understand the relationships between various reference disciplines and the limitations of their own profession. This is particularly important in technological subjects because it is to easy when focusing on technology to view it as an end in itself.

Thirdly, the chief aim of a liberal education is to develop students' abilities to abstract and to analyse. These faculties remind me of Schon's notion of a 'reflective practitioner' (Schon, 1983). This view posits that life is complex and constantly changing. Therefore, we should not impose old solutions onto new problems. Instead, we should think of life as an inquiry. One in which we should be prepared to listen to others' ideas and to be critical of our own. This requires us to be open and reflective. Schon argues that instilling this reflectiveness within a student forms the bedrock of professional education. Clearly, abstraction and analysis, persuasion and argument are the tools of reflection. Technical knowledge is the grist. Without it there is nothing to generalise or to criticise; there is nothing to write or to discuss. Technique, facts, and theories then are merely the surface structure of any professional education. Schon intends his proposal for radically new techniques for professional education as a means to encourage reflectiveness in his students. Yet, a critic might suggest that the need for more reflective practitioners may arise from the dissociation of liberal and professional education.

12.4.6 A Shared Point of View

Of course, I have attempted to show that it is not only the IS professional who needs to be reflective. Zuboff, Reich, and Womack *et al.* all describe the new information worker as being in need of a wide range of social and intellective skills. In fact I have argued that a reflective habit of mind provides the modern worker with both financial and intellectual capabilities. These are the talents which he needs in order to be self-reliant and to participate in a true democracy. A liberal education designed to answer the first two of these fundamental questions of information systems would provide both the worker and the citizen with these faculties. Moreover, if workers, managers, and IS professionals shared the same educational formation, they would have a common vocabulary, similar attitudes, and a shared point of view. This would be in sharp contrast to the obstacles which now separate them.

Information technology offers new and better ways to achieve our desires. It requires from us more intellect, wider knowledge, greater cooperation, and increased trust. These things should have a significant impact on the nature of our work and on the way we organise and manage it. They should also affect our system of education, not by replacing lecturers with multimedia instructional material via the Internet, but by reconsidering what the purpose of education is. Specialisation is antithetical to many of these ideas. Its key feature is that of fragmentation while information technology's is that of sharing.

I believe that one key to the future can be found in the past; this is liberal education. Paradoxically, I think in order to plead this case to our academic colleagues, we must make a stronger argument for information systems as a discipline even though its nature is general.

References

Adams, R. and Athey, T.H., eds., 1981, *DPMA model curriculum for undergraduate computer information systems education*, DPMA Educational Foundation Committee on Curriculum Development, Park Ridge, Ill.

Ashenhurst, R., 1972, Curriculum recommendations for graduate professional programs in information systems, *Communications of ACM*, 15:364-398.

Buckingham, R.A., Hirschheim, R.A., Land, F.F., and Tully, C.J., 1987, Information systems curriculum: a basis for course design, in *Information Systems Education. Recommendations and Implementation*, R.A. Buckingham, R.A. Hirschheim, F.F. Land, and C.J. Tully, eds., Cambridge University Press, Cambridge, 14-133.

Cardwell, D.S.L., 1972, *The Organisation of Science in England*, Revised Edition, Heinemann, London.

Checkland, P., 1981, *Systems Thinking, Systems Practice*, John Wiley, Chichester.

CIS'86, 1986, *The DPMA model curriculum for undergraduate computer information systems*, Data Processing Management Association, Park Ridge, Ill.

Couger, J., 1973, Curriculum recommendations for undergraduate programs in information systems, *Communications of ACM*, 16: 727-749.

Couger, J., Davis, G.B., Dologite, D.G., Feinstein, D.L., Gorgone, J., Jenkins, M.A., Kaspar, G.M., Little, J., Longenecker, H.E., and Valacich, J., 1995, IS'95: Guidelines for undergraduate IS curriculum, *MIS Quarterly*. 19(3): 341-359.

DPMA, 1991, *Information systems: The DPMA curriculum for a four year undergraduate degree*, Data Processing Management Association, Park Ridge, Ill.

Feyerabend, P., 1978, *Against Method. Outline of an Anarchistic Theory of Knowledge*, Verso, London.

Forrester, J., 1961, *Industrial Dynamics*, MIT Press, Cambridge, Mass.

Gardner, H., 1985, *The Mind's New Science. A History of the Cognitive Revolution*, Basic Books, New York.

Glass, R.L., 1992, A comparative analysis of the topic areas of computer science, software engineering, and information systems, *Journal of Systems Software*, 19:277-289.

Gleick, J., 1988, *Chaos: Making a New Science*, Heinemann, Oxford.

Head, S., 1996, The new, ruthless economy, *The New York Review of Books*, 29 February:47-52.

Hudson, H.R., 1992, *Report of the Discipline Review of Computing Studies and Information Sciences Education*, Australian Publishing Services, Canberra.

Katz, D. and Kahn, R.L., 1978, *The Social Psychology of Organisations*, second edition, John Wiley, New York.

Keen, P.G.W., 1980, MIS research: reference disciplines and a cumulative tradition, *Proceedings of the First ICIS*, Philadelphia, 9-18.

Knowles, D., 1962, *The Evolution of Medieval Thought*, Vintage Books, New York.

Kuhn, T., 1970, *The Structure of Scientific Revolutions*, second edition. The University of Chicago Press, Chicago.

Lasch, C., 1995, *The Revolt of the Elites and The Betrayal of Democracy*, W.W. Norton, London.

Lee, D.M.S., Trauth, E.M., and Farwell, D., 1995, Critical skills and knowledge requirements of IS professionals: a joint academic/industry investigation, *MIS Quarterly*, 19(3): 313-340.

Lucas, H.C., 1979, *Why Information Systems Fail*, Prentice Hall, Englewood Cliffs, N.J.

McFarlan, F.W., 1984, Introduction, in *The Information Systems Research Challenge*, F.W. McFarlan, ed., Harvard Business School, Cambridge, Mass.

McLean, E.R., 1989, Synopsis for panel on MIS: academic discipline or temporary phenomena, *Proceedings of the Tenth ICIS*, J. DeGross, J. Henderson, and B.R. Konsynski, eds. Boston, Ma.

Morgan, G., 1986, *Images of Organisation*, Sage Publications, Beverly Hills, Ca.

Newman, J., 1969, The idea of a university, in *The Great Ideas Today 1969*, R.M. Hutchins and M.J. Adler, eds., Encyclopædia Britannica, Chicago.

Ng Tye, E.N., Poon, R.S. and Burn, J., 1995, Information systems skills: achieving alignment between the curriculum and the needs of the IS professional in the future, *Data Base*, 26(4): 47-61.

Nunamaker, J., Couger, J., and Davis, G.B., 1982, Information systems curriculum recommendations for the 80s: undergraduate and graduate programs, a report of the ACM Curriculum Committee on Information Systems, *Communications of ACM*, 25:781-805.

Ortega y Gasset, J., 1957, *The Revolt of the Masses*, W. W. Norton, New York.

Pfeffer, J. and Salancik, G.R., 1978, *The External Control of Organisations. A Resource Dependence Perspective*, Harper and Row, New York.

Prigogine, I. and Stengers, I.,1985, *Order Out of Chaos. Man's New Dialogue with Nature*, Flamingo, London.

Reich, R.B., 1993, *The Work of Nations*, Simon and Schuster, London.

Ross, S., 1973, The economic theory of agency: the principal's problem, *American Economic Review*, 63:134-139.

Schon, D., 1983, *The Reflective Practitioner: How Professionals Think in Action*, Temple Smith, London.

Searle, J., 1969, *Speech Acts*, Cambridge University Press, Cambridge.

Shannon, C.E., 1938, A symbolic analysis of relay and switching circuits, *Transactions of the American Institute of Electrical Engineers*, 57:1-11.

Simon, H.A., 1991, *The Sciences of the Artificial*, second edition, The MIT Press, Cambridge, Mass.

South West Thames Regional Health Authority, 1993, *Report of the inquiry into the London ambulance service*, London.

Williamson, O.E., 1975, *Markets and Hierarchies. Analysis and Antitrust Implications*, The Free Press, New York.

Willcocks, L. and Griffith, C., 1995, *Are Major IT Projects Worth the Risk?* Oxford Institute of Management, Templeton College, University of Oxford, Oxford.

Womack, J., Jones, D.T., and Roos, D., 1990, *The Machine That Changed the World: The Story of Lean Production*, Maxwell MacMillan International, New York.

Work, B., 1994, An emerging paradigm for information systems, *Proceedings of Sixth ISTIP Conference*, Sunningdale Park, 9-13.

Zuboff, S., 1988, *In the Age of the Smart Machine. The Future of Work and Power*, Heinemann Professional, Oxford.

PART 4: CONCLUSIONS: THE FUTURE?

This book began by considering the emergence of IS as a discipline distinct from say, computer science, and continued by exploring different views of its nature at the moment. In our introduction we mentioned that one reason for the importance of IS as a discipline was its potential ability to control the, possibly undesirable, effects of rapid technological development. This hinted at the dark side of technology. The final chapter of the book, a personal view by **Ian Angell**, portrays one possible future for mankind in stark and unrelenting fashion. Whether this future will come about we do not know, but its very plausibility attests to the importance of choices and decisions made at this point in time.

The chapter should perhaps have a health warning: *Reading this chapter may seriously damage your complacency*!

Chapter 13

WELCOME TO THE 'BRAVE NEW WORLD'

Ian O. Angell

13.1 Introduction

Having read thus far in this book, you will have been exposed to a
wide range of information systems issues, each of which will affect
the future, to a greater or lesser extent. These chapters have tended
to look *inwards*, at the subject of information systems itself. This
final chapter, however, will take a step backwards and look *out*
from that research to make specific (sometimes uncomfortable,
often contradictory) predictions about the impact such systems will
have on the broader socio-economic environment, an environment
that will confront everyone involved with the analysis, design and
management of information systems. To do this I will address four
specific issues: (a) why the business world, and society in general,
seems to be increasingly uncertain; (b) why the integrity of
information systems is crucial for coping this uncertainty; (c) why
IS security is such an important component of that integrity; and (d)
what form the management of information systems will take.

Welcome to the future. Welcome to a world as different from
today, as today is from the pre-industrial age. Welcome to the
'Brave New World'. But why new? New, because a new order is
being forced upon an unsuspecting world by advances in
telecommunications and mobile computing. Companies are
mobilising and globalising. New technology is turning everything
on its head, plunging our world into turmoil. It is driving us
towards the verge of a new revolution, an Information Revolution,
that is taking us out of the Machine Age, into .... who knows what –
into that *Brave New World* (Huxley, 1932).

But why brave? Brave, because this is not a world for the timid.
This is a world where the socio-economic certainties of the
twentieth century are collapsing – where everything is changing,

and I really'do mean everything: politics, economics, business – society as a whole. And I really do mean change; not the nice tidy change that management gurus sell you in their 'change management seminars'; not a nice tidy transition, but a severe and total dislocation with the past.

From the tone of that latter sentence the reader will realise that the perspective chosen by the author of this article is unashamedly unconventional (and it must be said unscientific). For you, the reader, to understand fully what follows, it is important that you understand where I am coming from. According to the Burrell and Morgan (Burrell and Morgan, 1979) categorisation, I am a Radical Humanist, and it shows. Burrell and Morgan claim that societal research, and hence researchers, can be classified within a two by two matrix. One dimension claims researchers are either objective or subjective. The other contrasts a view of society in terms of integration and cohesion, against one in which society is in a continual state of conflict and crisis. Burrell and Morgan claim that the matrix delivers four quite distinct and mutually exclusive paradigms: Functionalist, Interpretivist, Radical Structuralist and Radical Humanist. Indeed most IS researchers, including many of the authors of this book, are quite clearly Functionalists although Interpretivism is creeping into IS research (Ciborra, 1994; Walsham, 1993). Consequently, before continuing it is useful to digress here and consider the two most relevant categories for this chapter, by contrasting my views of the predominant norm, Functionalism, and my own Radical Humanism. For, if you disagree with the analysis being presented, ask yourself is that analysis wrong or is it that you simply cannot relate to a highly subjective interpretation of a world full of conflict.

13.1.1 The Functionalist Paradigm

Functionalism is the conventional mode of thinking in the modern world (objective/stable). Functionalists claim there is a science of society, just as physics is a science of nature. This is Mr. Spock's claim that rational observers come to the same conclusions because there is an objective reality and logic inherent in each situation. Functionalists say that social reality is governed by immutable laws of causality. These can be discovered through the scientific method, based on unbiased observation, supported by empirical evidence, and then used to advantage to explain and build cohesive and stable structures in society: the fundamental tenets of social engineering. Such a normative approach dehumanises the situation, just like the Star Trek hero, with his insistence that there are such things as right answers, which can be prescribed through logic.

13.1.2 The Radical Humanist Paradigm

Radical Humanists (subjective/conflict) see functionalism as a slave mentality. They argue that there is a vicious circle of cognitive tyranny in technology that has crushed humanity down to a *One-Dimensional Man* (Marcuse, 1991) - humanity is now subservient to the technological structures of its own making. Radical Humanists believe change comes through vision and ideas, not by manipulating the algorithms of an assumed inevitable causality, but through power. They claim our understanding of the world is created, not discovered. Gains come from investing in human potential within conflict and not from an obsession with discovering *de facto* universal truths in society. Their goal is emancipation from the cognitive domination of the 'powers that be' within the status quo, every status quo, particularly overturning the currently dominant mind-set of 'scientism', with its tendency to alienate human consciousness.

Each paradigm contradicts the views of the other three: Functionalism being diametrically opposite to Radical Humanism. Arguments between proponents of different paradigms will not be easily resolved because they are not arguing about points of fact. They are arguing from different perspectives, about different things; the words they use have different meanings. Scientific method means different things to different paradigms. Functionalists find it convincing. But as for me, a Radical Humanist, I find its imposition thoroughly offensive.

13.2   The Madness of the Age

How dare the snake-oil salesmen of this trivial delusion claim to have ring-fenced human society with method! To give method and function their due, they are fine for managing a production line of widgets. This is the world where Functionalism was born; here the insights of Deming, Juran and Crosby, De Marco and Yourdon, SSADM and BPR make perfect sense. But how dare charlatans (Crosby (1989) has written that Juran thinks him a charlatan) generalise these ideas (valid in their own particular domain) and promote them as a science (no a pseudo-science!) that is capable of dealing with all the complexity and uncertainty exploding in human society today, an explosion caused in the main by new technology – particularly now with frenzied companies automating, downsising, delayering and outsourcing, with business entering cyberspace, exporting jobs and goods to and from the ends of the earth.

Surely deep down, we must all realise there is a perverse nature to the uncertainty we face. Yet still you can hear the optimism of tidy minds out there saying: functionalism is wonderful! But you know what Oscar Wilde said: 'the basis of optimism is sheer terror.' I always warn everyone involved with information systems to be very wary when they go looking to business schools and universities for answers. For we academics are part of an education system that actively promotes these methods, 'sanctifying so many lies', rather than studying them in a balanced way. Madness!

But 'Madness is something rare in individuals – but in groups, parties, peoples, ages it is the rule' (Nietzsche). And the madness of our particular age is an obsessive compulsive neurosis. A madness that believes, that through applying the methods of science and technology to every aspect of the human condition – why I call it a pseudo-science – the world will become tidy, organised, 'the way it ought to be'.

The basic problem is that this pseudo-scientific ideology has mixed up cause and effect. The dominant belief is that with 'proper control procedures' we can impose order. But control doesn't create order, quite the contrary; it is order that tolerates control. Then and only then can control impose structure and stability; but don't confuse order with structure and stability, don't confuse cause with effect. It is essential to recognise order as being transitory; controls are allowed to work, and then they fail; consequently the certainty of structure collapses. Uncertainty precedes a new order, and new control.

13.2.1 Uncertainty

It is ludicrous to think we can control uncertainty. Yet this is the goal of so-called management science. When faced with profound uncertainty, companies attempt to impose these excessively tidy methods on their world, when they haven't the slightest idea of what they mean by uncertainty. For uncertainty does not conform to a neat computational logic, it is a foreboding, where the surprise of imminent change is outside of our control.

What do I mean by that word? This I can explain best by telling a story: I was once at a commercial conference entitled 'Managing Uncertainty', where the technology session consisted of myself and a statistician. He talked for 45 minutes on distributions, expectations, functions, formulae and curves. You can imagine that the business audience found it inspiring stuff! Within five minutes eyes began to glaze over. After ten minutes he had an audience of one – me: I was on the stage, I had to listen.

When it was my turn, I walked over to the podium, and just stood there .... and stood there .... and stood there. For a whole minute I just stood there. I fidgeted uneasily, and shot frantic and terrified glances at the audience. At first there was silence, then a few murmurs, then a growing rumble of concern. I hammered home my point, by calmly stating: 'now that is uncertainty, it has nothing to do with statistics'. The world of business is not about production lines, it's about power. It's about devious individuals like me, and anyone involved with the management of information systems and who depends on statistics and methods won't have the slightest idea where we're coming from. Functionalist methods are not going to help them fend us off.

Joseph Weizenbaum (Weizenbaum, 1976) tells a highly relevant story. *A policeman sees a drunk scrambling around on his hands and knees, under the street lamp."I'm looking for my keys, I lost them over there", the drunk says, pointing into the darkness. "So why look here?" asks the policeman. "Because this is where the light is!"* The particular light of Functionalism is not capable of illuminating the really important management problems as we enter the Information Age. We have to ask whether the IS community is looking in the wrong place? Are we solving yesterday's problems? For us and the drunk alike, the lamp-post of Functionalism is more for support than for illumination.

13.2.2 The nature of work

Of course managers are going to need support. For with the Information Revolution comes the breakdown of the institutions of the present. The idea of a job, born with the Machine Age, is changing beyond all recognition as we enter the Information Age. Despite all the bleating, companies have realised that they can no longer afford to carry a large inventory of 'people product' of varying value and quality. It is no accident that most companies are presently instigating major *downsizing*, *delayering* and *outsourcing* programmes. Middle management too is under threat. Under the euphemistic banner of Business Process Re-engineering (Champy, 1995), companies are making redundant a quarter of managers. Technology first hit the workers, then middle management; I predict senior management is next for pruning! The motto for everyone is 'add value or perish!' There is no room for sentimentality in this Brave New World.

Of course, out-of-touch politicians, both the knaves and the naive, incant the abracadabra words 'training in New Technology' and 'jobs through growth' in order to conjure up new jobs for the huge number of soon-to-be-unemployed - if only it was that simple. When will these politicians ever learn *that technology is the problem, not the solution*. Today, productivity is delivered by a technology needing only a few machine minders. Growth is created from the intellect of knowledge workers (Drucker, 1992), not from the labour of low grade service and production workers, nor from the purring of fat cats.

13.2.3 The 'Nature of the Firm'

Furthermore, not only has the nature of work changed with new technology, so has the 'Nature of the Firm' (Coase, 1991). In order to consider the firm of the future, we have to ask the more fundamental question: 'why do firms exist at all?' Why should entrepreneurs and workers choose to group together in a firm, rather than buy and sell each other's services on the open market?

Ronald Coase claimed that the deciding factor is transaction costs: that is the costs incurred by buyers and sellers in the development of their commercial contracts. Coase claimed that each firm is formed when it is cheaper for a collection of business units to organise themselves into a group rather than to buy contracts from the marketplace. But, and it is a big but, each firm will stop growing at that point where the goods and services they need can be purchased more cheaply in the market. This idea is dynamite for the Information Age and it explains much of the turmoil we feel today. For now 'spot markets' are forming in cyberspace.

Information technology has changed fundamentally the nature of transactions, and hence their costs. Some costs are becoming very much cheaper, with others more expensive; although it must be admitted that at present it is not clear which are which. And not just the costs are changing. Earlier I happily used the word 'organise' as though there is only one way to organise: information technology has shown the lie to that too.

The transnational enterprise is a clear demonstration of how tomorrow's firm has decentralised and distributed itself around the globe: how it has become the *virtual enterprise* – project based and networked around global information systems. Its control procedures are totally different, as are the internal and external transaction costs it incurs. Is it even organised in the sense that we understand firms today? Whatever the answer, it is clear that the coefficients in Coase's equilibrium formulae will have to change. The structure of yesterday's company was an answer to the question 'what is a viable company?' against the judgements of the transaction costs from the Machine Age. But the answers delivered in the Information Age will be radically different. The dominant monolithic fir.n, the juggernaut of the factory metaphor, that won the battles of natural selection during the Machine Age, is finding itself totally outmanoeuvred by new organisational forms emerging in the Information Age; worse it is facing meltdown.

It is clear from Coase's theory that the large number of job losses reported across the Western world is not the result of some temporary downturn in the economic cycle, but is instead the result of structural change. It is no good waiting for the upturn when new service work will be created. For fundamental changes in the natures of work and the firm are taking place. The changes are as profound as when agricultural workers left the land for the cities, and the whole fabric of society mutated.

Telecommuting is the first step of workers leaving the cities for cyberspace. Telecommunications and international transport, not to mention the instantaneous 'distance no object' electronic delivery of 'information products', means that the transaction costs of production in the global marketplace have become very much lower. Arguably this has dropped to a point where billions of new workers have now entered into the marketplace. This is sending shock waves through western workforces previously protected by national interests, but which are now incapable of fending off foreign incursions. On the other hand the need to impose standards that satisfy widely differing markets, and the vastly increased requirement for security for what are now a firm's highly decentralised and hence vulnerable business units, have had the effect of raising transaction costs.

13.2.4 Cohesion or Collapse?

Fundamental to Coase's theory is the idea that it is property rights rather than goods that are being traded. What is at issue is how these rights and the transaction of property rights are costed and protected; and how conflicts over such resources can be resolved. He emphasises that firms will only succeed in a society which stresses the importance of property rights, rules and laws, and a judicial system, so that individual entrepreneurs can be helped to help themselves.

The real power of Coase's work is that it is not just about firms, rather all types of social groupings that exist in an economic environment arbitrated by costs. He includes any self-organising social grouping: companies, enterprises, 'clubs', countries; a particular society or the society at large. Coase is clear that the nation-state too is an economic institution, a national firm, that will also have to be judged against changing circumstances. So his theories not only describe the rise and fall of corporations, but also explain the economic well-being or otherwise of states.

Obviously, my description of Coase's highly sophisticated theory is vastly oversimplified. But I want to get over to you its importance as an explanation for why firms, why states exist, and why they die.

Coase does have his critics, who claim that his point of breakdown for the firm is too rigid. Robert Puttnam (Puttnam, 1993) and Douglas North (North, 1990) have been prominent in arguing that market mechanisms in themselves cannot define the break point between cohesion and collapse. For each economic entity is an investment mix of social and financial capital, a weave of mutually agreed formal and informal contracts and rituals. It does not exist solely in the one-dimensional universe of economic viability; explanations must look beyond fiscal and monetary policies.

That having been said, it is well to remember that competition is a harsh task-master, and any company, and country that strays too far from the tough discipline of the economic dimension will be rapidly and severely punished.

13.2.5 Hotspots

But social as well as economic rewards come from collaboration and cooperation, and group members value them both. The balance sheet is not a simple question of financial profit and loss; as long as there are sufficient profits in the wider grouping, and someone is willing to cross-subsidise and pay the difference for the sake of the group, then transaction costs can be written off. But there must be sufficient profits to pay for it. And there's the rub. Inefficient companies, and countries, are rapidly using up their fat stocks of goodwill.

In the past, the reality was that some group members were happy to pay more (or receive less), just to be part of group.The question we ask is 'how much more or less?' and 'for how much longer?' For there is a perceived value of being part of an economic entity. The consequent formalised trust and mutual interest that membership of a group implies, the very glue that holds a group together, has the effect of actually reducing internal transaction costs. When participants trust one another, costly checks and balances are not needed, and individual members are willing to lower their expectations (their price); all of which increases the efficient use of resources.

The opposite of course is true for degenerate groupings: in Western societies for example, structural unemployment, particularly among uneducated young males who are being thrown onto the margins of society, is highly disruptive, and thus increases transaction costs. Society becomes less pleasant, less safe, and those who foot the bill feel less inclined to continue doing so.

Trust in a society is always very finely balanced, and it can so easily be upset. Another fact of life is that formal and impersonal (bureaucratic) arrangements always involve greater transaction costs than the informal and personal. For informality is a statement of trust within a group, formality is a statement of control. The trick is to have an organisation with enough internal trust so that it can be left to be self-organising in face of external threats: and this requires effective security procedures.

The economic performance of a firm, of a country depends on a balance between social capital and investment in both physical infrastructure and individual intellectual capital, against an ever changing background of economic forces. It does not depend on some homogeneous labour force that acts as a source of physical power. Michael Porter (Porter, 1990) claims that it is the social clusters within networks of firms that creates the self-generating feedback of growth: *hotspots*. Neither natural nor the human resources in themselves can explain the wealth of rich countries. It is their internal arrangements, their institutions, their policies, their history.

13.2.6 The Knowledge Worker

However, both Coase and North agree that in the Information Age the continuous innovation of the knowledge worker is key to success. But there are clever people everywhere, so why is prosperity so unevenly distributed? Why, if two companies, in two countries have the same economic endowment, technology and skills, do their productivities differ (Olsen, 1996)? What separates success from failure is the way the group sets about ruling itself, the type of rules it makes, and the way it treats and protects the creators of wealth.

Rampant individualism can never be the answer in the long term; as always individuals must group together if they are to be effective economically. However, as the arbiter of success undergoes change, so does the nature and effectiveness of those groups. Mark Casson (Casson, 1990) argues that the mutuality of interests of the workforce, suppliers and financiers is important, as is their trust in the integrity of their relationships. This is particularly true with information goods, where assets lie in human talent, which has the inconvenient habit of walking away from all conditions it dislikes. For there are always tensions, which if the culture doesn't have the mechanisms to dissipate the stress, will undermine everything. By the same token, an individual cannot expect just to fit in anywhere. It requires that host institutions must be welcoming – the individual must be wanted. The new rootlessness of economic mercenaries in aggressive market economies, mercenaries who are looking out for welcoming institutions that are in tune with their own aspirations, has the power to destabilise the wealth of any unsupportive community. Successful communities are those that are sociable, welcoming, attractive and secure to the mobile rich, and at the same time economically viable.

The economic forces that drive growth are the same as they ever were; and they are still out there. Neoclassical economic theory would have us believe that the growth of an economy depends on the relationship between capital and labour, which can be explained mathematically, by a so-called 'production function'. However, these two inputs have failed to explain variations in output satisfactorily, and so economists have added a third parameter: technical progress. In his popular explanations of this situation, Patrick Minford describes two schools of thought on such progress (Minford, 1993). The first, typified by Robert Solow (Solow, 1988) saw technical progress as fairly stable, as was labour, leaving the investment and accumulation of capital as the means of controlling growth.

The second, 'new growth theory', exemplified by Robert Lucas (Lucas and Sargent, 1981) and Paul Romer (Romer, 1986), saw wide variations in technical progress, mirroring variations in human skills and knowledge. The joy of the latter theory is that it proposes 'increasing returns' – now winners can win even more. Not that it denies the law of 'diminishing returns', where income from increased production and sales rises slower than costs. Both phenomena coexist and are complementary; diminishing returns may dominate a rational marketplace of stable products, but in the white heat of technological innovation such 'fundamental laws' throw little light on the irrational behaviour in an economy where the sky's the limit. In this new world, firms do not merely react to market signals and accept their judgements, aggressive firms set their own prices, they broker and define their own value.

Romer considers such technical progress as two separate issues: human capital (an educated and skilled workforce) and ideas (ownership and development potential of same). The key to growth is the availability of knowledge workers who can profit from a hoard of old ideas and the abundance of new ones, thereby accelerating the acquisition of new knowledge workers and ideas.

Suddenly labour and intellect are no longer treated under one heading; no longer are individuals seen as standardised units. Suddenly talent, entrepreneurship, innovation, the great dividers of humanity, are accepted as factors of economic success. And these are in short supply, and hence are in great demand. Egalitarianism goes out the window in this 'dog eat dog' world. Growth is no longer dependent on physical capital and labour. The principal source of future wealth is both the quality of technological knowledge available in a society, and the way that knowledge is growing. Endogenous growth (growth from within) is now the buzz-word that even blind-sided politicians are using.

What is more, innovation does not just happen simply because of scientific discovery and technological research; these deliver mere possibilities. Such knowledge cannot be banked like capital or stored like a commodity, to be used anywhere. There are no plans for innovation, only the initiation of the process of discovery. Innovation requires an economic stimulus/catalyst. It happens when science and technology are applied as inventions in a dynamic economic hotspot of innovation, investment and profit. Innovative firms cluster in hotspots, the very concentration acting as a magnet for established innovators and a spur for new enterprise, witness the development of Silicon Valley or Singapore.

Spectacular growth comes from these self-perpetuating hotspots, which thrive on their own energy. This energy drives a rapid, almost uncontrolled diffusion of technological techniques and knowledge. The hotspot itself drives the engine of endogenous growth by delivering innovation, but only within a network of trust relationships and an institutional environment that both mobilises intellectual talent and promotes and finances entrepreneurial activity by delivering the right incentives.

13.3 Why Information Systems Security is so Important

So, what has all this got to do with the management of information systems? The thesis of this article is that the organisation of the future will be the virtual enterprise, organised around an information system, and whose size will be optimised around the new transaction costs. It further claims that the biggest transaction cost of this virtual enterprise is the security of the firm's information systems. Why security? Clyde Barrow, of Bonnie and Clyde fame, had the answer. When asked 'why do you rob banks?', he answered 'because that's where the money is'.

Information systems are where the money is, because that's where the business is. The information system is the firm, nothing else is permanent among the agglomeration of transitory projects. If the integrity of that system is corrupted, then the organisation is finished: the projects will network with other systems, other virtual enterprises. Hence the information system the organisation of the future: its only permanent element, and IS security is crucial!

This scenario is reinforced by rising levels of unemployment. Work will become increasingly casual or part-time among service workers. The disposable income for most of society will be drastically reduced. Societies are stratifying; new elites are appearing. The rich are getting richer, and the poor poorer.

The future is about inequality; and at the very bottom of the heap western societies are already witnessing the emergence of a rapidly expanding underclass (Herrnstein and Murray, 1994). The streets of London are again littered with beggars. The self-glamorising 'New Age travellers' cannot disguise the fact they are just a bunch of nomadic losers, whose survival depends on handouts from the tax-payer. The tax-payer will increasingly demand restrictions on the mobility of travellers in return for their charity. Is the new Criminal Justice Act in the UK just the first step to the re-invention of the Poor Laws?

In the transition we can expect massive civil unrest and disorder. The 'soon-to-have-nots' have nothing to lose and will riot. This is what happened in France in the winter of 1995, when workers and students took to the streets against Alain Juppe's government (Smith, 1995) in defence of their cradle-to-grave health and welfare systems.

13.3.1 The Age of Rage

The lights are going out for wide sectors of society, and for whole categories of employment. We are entering a new Dark Age: an age of hopelessness, an age of resentment, an Age of Rage. Dissent is fermenting, and in their pent-up anger, normally law-abiding citizens are being sucked into the culture of protest and crime. There will be many more like Alan Teale (Gartland, 1993), who in the late 1970s was secretary of the Lloyd's Insurance Brokers Association. But in 1981 he was passed over for the top job at the newly formed British Insurance Brokers Association. Bitter, he embarked on a career in mail fraud, money laundering and other financial crimes in the USA, the Caribbean, Belgium and Ireland.

Whole sections of society that previously felt their future secure, can see it slipping away from them to be replaced by economic exploitation and 'unfairness'. Soaring unemployment levels among white collar workers make them furious at losing their 'jobs for life'. A middle-class rage is delivering well-educated and articulate recruits into the clutches of experienced agitators and criminals. The police authorities are becoming increasingly concerned at the skill base in these groups and the resources available to them. And all of this is happening at a time when the vast majority of the population has very little to complain about. But what happens when the level of unemployment becomes a social disaster?

There are already anarchists on the Net; electronic copies of bomb-making manuals such as 'The Anarchist's Cookbook'. Lenin called the radio 'a newspaper without paper and without frontiers'; what would he have made of the Net? What will a new Lenin do with the Net? Anarchists communicate via electronic bulletin boards, with their files booby-trapped with viruses that attack the computers of those whose attention is unwelcome. They are spreading sedition by circulating information on how to infiltrate various 'class enemy' organisations: the police, government departments and particularly transnational companies.

It is all too easy to dismiss this anarchic phenomenon as just the fantasising of social inadequates. But some of the Walter Mittys out there are becoming serious sociopaths. Anarchists plan to rob banks, break into credit card systems; they are using email to organise mass international shoplifting sprees. Urban terrorists will bomb economic targets. Encrypted pages show how to manufacture incendiary devices, bombs and chemical weapons. Grudge terror, whether the grudge is real or imagined, is a reality. The unabomber (Gladstone, 1996) and the attacks on Barclays Bank (Bennetto, 1996) are just two cases in point.

A more focused form of rage is also now appearing in the unemployed: 'redundancy rage'. Newly redundant workers attack senior management and ex-colleagues in the workplace, on the street and in their homes. There have been rumours that a certain Los Angeles company has had five senior executives murdered in the past two years. In 1989 a highly depressed Joseph Wesbecker shot 20 ex-colleagues at the Standard Gravure works (Cornwell, 1996). The question of whether or not he was under the influence of Prozac is irrelevant. Whether on Prozac, narcotics, alcohol, or just good old fashioned hate, there are many out there who think it is open season on the employed and their employers.

Information systems managers are going to have to deal with disgruntled losers who organise attacks against their telecommunications and computer infrastructure, their personnel and their business in general. Attacks will hit the Net and come via the Net. Those with a grudge know that no company can survive in the global economy without the integrity of its information system intact. Criminals also know this; since the days of Mayer Lansky (Naylor, 1987), organised crime has been an avid user and abuser of international telecommunications. In fact it is arguable that through his money-laundering exploits in the 'thirties, Mayer Lansky was the mid-wife of the Information Age.

Even greater care must be taken with the security of computer hardware, documents and disks. Ex-employees with in-depth knowledge of a company's systems are an obvious target for the attention of criminals and anarchists. For a new type of scavenger is abroad, one who scours the garbage heaps of discarded people and IT material for the slightest scrap of information tradeable to opportunistic white-collar criminals. These are not middle-class amateur opportunists, and their crimes are not victimless; we are all their victims. Organised crime is infiltrating every legitimate business.

And as the underclass increases there will be an explosion in the 'black economy', in essence an alternative economy. Involvement in organised crime will be the only option open to the losers who are surplus to requirements in the legitimate economy. Barry Rider (Rider 1993) estimated that in 1990 the Yakuza made a profit of £5.56 billion, eight times that of Toyota. 98% of companies listed on the Japanese stock market make large payments to organised crime for 'research' and other services.

With so many people dependent on crime for their livelihood, real-world crime will find its counterpart in Cyberspace: computer and telecommunication variants of protection rackets, blackmail, murder, kidnapping, smuggling, counterfeiting, fraud, threatening behaviour, vandalism ('fax graffiti') and pornography will inevitably appear. It is clear that the 21st century criminal is no street hoodlum (Moore, 1994). He will be well educated and sophisticated, wielding state-of-the-art technology and weaponry. And attacks will come, not from a lone bandit, but from the most ruthless form of organised crime. Such are the adversaries of computer security in the new millennium.

It is no use looking to the police for help with this. Security is the job of the IS manager. The main role for police will be the maintenance of civil order. Governments are 'control freaks', they will never give up pushing the population around. But because of the lack of revenue, other police duties, such as solving crime, which today we to take for granted, will increasingly be outsourced by politicians to private agencies.

13.4 A Strategy for Success?

So what does all this uncertainty, unemployment and unrest mean for business? The purchasing power of every traditional customer base will polarise. As the rich get richer, and the poor get poorer, companies will have to produce completely new products for totally new markets, requiring a complete rethink of their operational procedures and strategies. But this is not a time for despair, quite the opposite. It is in such times that new empires are made: and today that means new business empires. It is a time of great opportunity for the few. Information technology has astounding implications for anyone who can grasp its potential. But it will take clever strategies to succeed; strategies based on totally new paradigms that can deliver a vision that 'is the art of seeing things invisible' (Jonathan Swift). What is more, 'the difficulty lies not in [just] creating new ideas but in escaping from old ones'

(John Maynard Keynes). Unfortunately it is all too common for businessmen to react to uncertainty by saying 'I don't want vague visions of the future; I want specific answers to my business problems, and I want them now'. But there are no right answers in times of uncertainty – the business world is far too volatile for that. A strategy is needed – and that does not mean choosing a once and forever answer.

It is clear that telecommunications and information systems are now the very core of today's enterprises. Therefore, strategy across all business sectors must involve a commitment to using mobile multi-media technology, to educating the whole company in its potential, application and dangers. The problem is that IT is expensive and painful – but not as expensive and painful as the alternative, bankruptcy. It is a fact of life that all businesses will be forced to change their technological installations over and over again. If businesspeople think that the choices they make today will last their company into the next century, then they must think again. They must think back – the decisions they made five years ago are most likely to be problems today. Welcome to the real-world.

But don't think that outsourcing of the IS function is the answer! By all means outsource billing and payroll systems. But networks and databases are now the core of the virtual enterprise. Its very existence depends on their integrity! Now it is clear that companies who outsource open themselves up to the inevitability of 'consultancy creep'.

13.4.1 A New Paradigm for Management: Alchemy not Science?

The myth of 'being in control', the myth of functionality, so readily demonstrated in numerous failed high profile applications of information technology, illustrates the related folly of believing in rigidly proactive 'scientific' management. The only logical approach is to initiate plans, but to be flexible enough to react quickly to whatever risks or opportunities appear; and so maintain the initiative. A blinkered faith in planning, and using the past as a mirror to the future, is likely to lose the initiative by constraining the understanding, insight and lateral thinking of quality employees. 'Perfection in planning is a symptom of decay' :

Parkinson's Second Law (Parkinson, 1986). Companies must come to grips with both the importance and the limitations of IT.

How can those involved in all aspects of information systems management ensure that companies act strategically? In the past, business problems were treated 'scientifically' (by functionalists), predominantly as technical tasks, without adequate strategic understanding of the socio-economic context within which the computerised systems are embedded. But the future will be uncertain, it will be different. Only one thing is certain, the backward looking methods of science and statistics that map yesterday onto tomorrow are not going to help.Maintaining the integrity of highly diverse and decentralised systems will be a management nightmare. Everywhere, outmoded business systems and processes are failing, which is why trendy ideas like Business Process Re-engineering are proving so seductive. But whole new management processes, not merely re-engineered ones, are called for. The accountant's view of the company is no longer appropriate since assets are now intellectual not physical.

The idea of 'equilibrium' that underlies so much of the 'scientism' of modern economics and management theory has been shown to be a myth, merely a comforter for those lost in the post-modern world. As George Soros (Soros, 1994) so eloquently put it, there is no such thing as a state of equilibrium, only the question of where we are in the perpetual movement between 'near-equilibrium' and 'far from equilibrium'. And today we are FAR from equilibrium. It will take very special people to succeed in this dynamic environment. Soros calls such people today's alchemists. They are pragmatists, who do not promote false theories of scientific and technological truth, but who base their actions on their vision, and what they believe to be 'procedurally successful' (Soros, 1994).

For alchemists know that a good technology platform, although necessary, is not sufficient for success. What makes the real strategic difference is the management of the quality and integrity of a company's knowledge workers. The symbolic analysts who succeed in this dynamic environment treat technology as only one element in a socio-technical system – an information system. However, in its present form, the management of information systems will not cope with the increased pressures placed on it. A new style information systems manager is needed: the alchemist.

Alchemists are strategic brokers; they use their information systems to broker the identification and solution of business problems (Reich, 1991), and deliver organisational procedures and technological applications that can succeed in the midst of social, political and economic upheaval.

So the study of information systems is not just about identifying and solving problems in which the functionalist approach can be marginally justified. It is about brokerage, coping with the complexities that emerge out of consequences of applying technology. This will need charismatic leadership, not blindly following the dictates of some inert set of strategic matrices laid down by yesterday's business schools. Paradoxically, information systems is more about people than technology, about the self-organising systems that are created in the choices and actions of people, about their consequences and not good intentions. To cope the subject of IS must bring in ideas from a broad range of social sciences: anthropology, philosophy, law, economics, politics etc; theology even.

How do I see the discipline of IS evolving? In the short to medium term I see it more of an indiscipline. I deliberately leave readers, not with answers, but with even more questions. I leave them in a totally different world, a world in transition, a world where there are no stabilities, no certainties, a world calling for perpetual experimentation. And in that world the future is created not discovered, created through the application of information systems. Information systems practitioners must impose their will on this future; they must therefore be alchemists not scientists. Consequently against this Brave New World' the alchemical stance of Radical Humanism makes far more sense than does that of Functionalism. Are you an alchemist? Can you accept responsibility for the future? Do you have the vision to win?

> How many goodly creatures are there here!
> How bounteous mankind is! O brave new world,
> That has such people in't
> (*The Tempest*, William Shakespeare)

But there are so many ungoodly beasts out there too, all tooled up with the latest IT equipment. Are you brave enough to win against these monsters (mobsters)?. Are you brave enough for this Brave New World?

References

Bennetto, J., 1996, FBI joins hunt for Barclays Grudge Bomber, *Independent*, 12/4/96:3.

Burrell, G. and Morgan, G., 1979, *Sociological Paradigms and Organisational Analysis*, Heinemann, London.

Casson, M., 1990, *Enterprise and Competitiveness*, Clarendon Press, Oxford.

Champy, J., 1995, *Reengineering Management*, Nicholas Brierley Publishing, London.

Ciborra, C., 1994, The grassroots of IT and strategy, in *Strategic Information Systems: A European Perspective*, C. Ciborra and T. Jelassi, eds., Wiley, Chichester.

Coase, R.H., 1991, The nature of the firm, in *The Nature of the Firm: Origins, Evolution and Development*, O.E.Williamson and S.G.Winter, eds., Oxford University Press, Oxford.

Cornwell, J., 1996, *Harm: Mind, Medicine and Murder on Trial*, Viking, New York.

Crosby, P.B., 1989, *Let's Talk Quality*, McGraw-Hill, New York.

Drucker, P., 1992, *Post Capitalist Society*, Butterworth, London.

Gartland, P., 1993, Scalped by a pin-striped Cherokee, *Times*, 26/10/93.

Gladstone, M., 1996, Unabomber suspect ordered to California, *Los Angeles Times*, 22/6/96:16.

Herrnstein, R. and Murray, C., 1994, *The Bell Curve*, Free Press, New York.

Huxley, A., 1932, *Brave New World*, Chatto and Windus, London.

Lucas, R.E. and Sargent, T.J., 1981, *Rational Expectations and Econonometric Practice*, Allen and Unwin, New York.

Marcuse, H., 1991, *One-Dimensional Man*, Routledge, London.

Minford, P., 1993, Economic view - unlocking the secret of capitalist growth, *Daily Telegraph*, 6/9/93:20.

Moore, R.H. Jr, 1994, Wiseguys: smarter criminals and smarter crime in the 21st century, *Futurist*, 28(5):33-37.

Naylor, R.T., 1987, *Hot Money and the Politics of Debt*, Unwin Hyman, London.

North, D., 1990, *Institutions, Institutional Change and Economic Performance*, Cambridge University Press, Cambridge.

Olsen, M., 1996, Big bills left on the sidewalk: why some nations are rich and others poor, *Journal of Economic Perspectives*, Spring.

Parkinson, C. Northcote, 1986, *Parkinson's Law*, Penguin, London.

Porter, M.E., 1990, *The Competitive Advantage of Nations*, Macmillan, London.

Puttnam, R.D., 1993, *Making Democracy Work*, Princeton University Press, Princeton.

Reich, R.B., 1991, *The Work of Nations*, Vintage, New York.

Rider, B., 1993, The financial world at risk: dangers of organised crime, money laundering and corruption, *Managerial Auditing Journal*, 8(7):3-14.

Romer, P., 1986, Increasing returns and long-run growth, *Journal of Political Economy*, 94(5).

Smith, A.D., 1995, France battles for welfare, *Guardian*, 20/11/95.

Solow, R.M., 1988, *Growth Theory: an explanation,* 2nd edition, Oxford University Press, New York.

Soros, G., 1994, *The Alchemy of Finance*, Wiley, New York.

Walsham, G., 1993, *Interpreting Information Systems in Organisations*, Wiley, Chichester.

Weizenbaum, J., 1976, *Computer Power and Human Reason: From Judgement to Calculation*, Freeman and Co., San Francisco.

INDEX